The Valley of
Cross Purposes

The Valley of Cross Purposes

Charles Nordhoff and American
Journalism, 1860–1890

Carol J. Frost, PhD

To order additional copies of this book, contact:

Xlibris

1-888-795-4274

www.Xlibris.com

Orders@Xlibris.com

750497

thevalleyofcrosspurposes.com

CONTENTS

Carol Jean Frost, PhD

Oct 8, 1959 - Dec 4, 2016

FOREWORD

In 1989, Carol Frost began preparations for her doctoral degree in American Civilization at Brown University. She wanted to write a biography about an important, but currently not well known, public figure. Her faculty advisor, John L. Thomas, suggested Charles Nordhoff; and with that, the primary work of Carol Frost's life was launched. Over the ensuing years, she wrote the biography you have before you, the biography of a man who ran away from home at thirteen, who endured and was forged by a brutal nine years at sea as a common sailor, and who went on to become the nineteenth century's most significant and influential journalist.

Providing a time-machine-view into Nordhoff's personal life and the tectonic events of the 1800s, the story Carol uncovered is both compelling and deeply relevant to society today. Told with sensitivity, insight, and style, Carol brings Nordhoff, his life, and the issues of his time, into vivid relief. In May of 1993 Carol's efforts earned her a PhD in American Civilization and set the stage for a planned publication. But that would take much longer than she imagined.

In August of 1989 Carol wrote her first letter to me, Charles Nordhoff's great-grandson. We embarked on a long, if intermittent, correspondence, and in the late 1990s, she visited with my wife and me at our home. Over the years her letters told of severe illnesses and a constant battle to maintain her health and finances at levels that would allow her to write. With despair, I read what was to be her final, handwritten, barely legible letter dated March 11, 2014. In it, she told of how she was now struggling for her life with a rare and often deadly infection from a bite from her beloved cat. When the Post Office returned my next three letters to different addresses marked "not deliverable," I worried that she had died before her book could be published.

A web-search, however, led to Carol's sister who sent me her nursing home address, and I traveled there to visit with them both. I found Carol understanding and responsive, but able to speak only very little. Earlier, and despite the downtime imposed by her poor health, Carol had managed to present samples of her thesis to several important university presses. From their readers high praise was always received, yet a contract remained elusive.

At our nursing home meeting, I accepted the responsibility from Carol to do the job she was no longer able to do: publishing her book. She thanked me, my son Michael, and her sister Kathleen for taking on this effort. We have also had the good fortune of guidance and encouragement from Jacqueline Jones, Chair of the History Department at the University of Texas, Austin.

In pursing publication, we started with Carol's May 1993 thesis. We also had a variety of later notes and revisions, carefully organized and scanned by Kathleen. After a slow start, and hoping to have a book to show Carol before she died, we elected to self-publish. We were not successful in our hope: she died on December 4, 2016 before final publication. Happily, Kathleen had been able to show her a copy of the book's cover in her final weeks, eliciting a warm, if silent, smile.

Among the many dramatic stories captured in her thesis is the story of Nordhoff's strenuous fight against the rich U.S. sugar and pineapple growers' effort to annex Hawaii, and his escape from the physical violence threatened him by the annexationists. Her thesis, however, was published before a dramatic turn in this story when, in November 1993, President Clinton signed An Act of Congress formally apologizing to the Hawaiian people for the unjust annexation of their homeland one hundred years earlier. While Nordhoff would never know of the apology, and it did not return the islands to the Hawaiian people, the apology alone resoundingly vindicates Nordhoff for his principled and risky opposition. In order to capture the full sweep of this century-long epic, Chapters 11, 12, and the Epilogue of this book are from Carol's 1999 revisions, which include discussion of the apology. All other sections are directly from her thesis.

It is a testament to Carol's extraordinary persistence and skill that this improbable book exists at all. Her research revealed that one of the reasons so little was known about Nordhoff is because he worked assiduously to deflect attention from himself and his accomplishments, including having his papers destroyed. Nordhoff was indeed a giant of his time and Carol tells of the remarkable, $5,000 per year pension, given to him by James Gordon Bennett, Jr., publisher of the populist, liberal *New York Herald*. The gift reflects the great regard Bennett had for Nordhoff as Editor and Manager of the Herald during his highly successful final ten years of employment.

Further evidence of Bennett's appreciation of Nordhoff is found in a story told to me as a teenager by the older generations of my family. They told of a giant, five-and-a-half-foot-tall by ten-foot-wide mirror in a gilt frame installed as a surprise in the Nordhoff's Hudson Palisades house by Mr. Bennett, a mirror of exceptional size for the time. As I think about it now, in light of the man Carol has so vividly revealed for us, I wonder if Bennett gave this mirror to Nordhoff, his admired friend and employee, and had it installed in his Palisades home thinking it would be hard for Nordhoff to hide this accolade under a bushel.

We hope you will enjoy getting to know the remarkable man that was Charles Nordhoff and reading the careful, captivating, and lucid writing and insights about him to which Carol Frost devoted the majority of her life. Her work is more than just a compelling history: Nordhoff's principled attention to the emerging, highly-influential role of journalism in public life, and the democratic, civic-minded principles to which he hewed, are just as relevant in our time as they were in his. Perhaps even more so.

February 2017   Walter N. Morrison, with Michael C. Morrison

INTRODUCTION

One March day in the year 1900, Charles Nordhoff stood before a small gathering of the Tuesday Club in San Diego, California, to deliver an address titled "Reminiscences of Some Editors I Have Known." At seventy years of age, his face bore the marks of the years: behind his wire-rimmed spectacles, he had prominent laugh lines, but the set of his mouth and his demeanor in general betrayed the determination that had characterized his life. His vision dimmed by cataracts, he spoke from notes written in a large hand. Without preamble, he began with Fletcher Harper, the first in his pantheon of editors; and as he continued, his audience was left to place him within the story he told. This would have been easy enough for them to do, for he had been one of the most prominent and controversial journalists of his day.

"Garrulity is the vice of old age," Nordhoff would say to friends in his later years, but his "Reminiscences," if slightly garrulous, were pointed in intent.[1] He spoke, briefly but with considerable warmth, of Fletcher Harper, who had hired him to work for the Harpers' publishing house in 1856 when he was an unknown twenty-five-year-old. Of his next employer, William Cullen Bryant and the New York *Evening Post*, he had less to say, although he praised Bryant's partner, Parke Godwin, for his greater broad-mindedness. These were just preliminaries to the real heart of his speech. For the most part, he wanted to describe his working relationship with James Gordon Bennett, Jr., publisher of the New York *Herald*, who, he told the audience, had been "viciously misunderstood, misrepresented, and calumniated," but in his opinion a truly great "statesman-journalist."[2]

Nordhoff was a modest man, with a keen sense of privacy, and he had never spoken publicly about his career before the Tuesday Club address. Characteristically, he was selective, revealing only what he wanted the audience to know, and he mentioned his own role only minimally. The editors were, after all, his subject; and like the good journalist that he was, he stuck to the story.

[1.] CN to Daniel Coit Gilman, April 6, 1900, Gilman Papers, Eisenhower Library, Johns Hopkins University.

[2.] CN, *Reminiscences of Some Editors I Have Known* (San Diego: 1900), 14.

Yet Nordhoff had been eminent in his own right, perhaps the preeminent journalist of his time, and an account of his own career would have revealed more about journalism during the previous forty years than any discreet rendering of the work of prominent editors like Bryant and Harper could. Journalism had been transformed in the three and a half decades since the Civil War, from a small-scale highly personalized enterprise into a quasi profession, dominated by highly capitalized big businesses; and the impact of this transformation had left journalists uncertain and quarrelsome about their own role in society. One thing had not changed: journalism was still openly politicized, and newspapers generally bore clear ideological identities. But people were talking, more and more, of the need for a neutral nonpartisan press. It was an idea that Nordhoff held in utter contempt.

To Charles Nordhoff, journalism was meaningless without political engagement. "The *Evening Post*, while I managed it …," he once informed a fellow journalist, "was not a newspaper. I can't take any interest in the tons of rubbish which enterprising people call news."[3] The *Evening Post* was, in fact a newspaper—but it eschewed coverage of events unless it could interpret their larger significance; and reports of unexceptional crimes, fires, or trivial happenings did not appear in its pages. "News" being beside the point for Nordhoff, his own career was one of active social involvement. As the editor of the influential *Evening Post*, and later, as a Washington "Special Correspondent" for the *Herald*—the most highly paid Washington journalist of his time—he had used his access to politicians to forward the causes he believed in. He wrote for newspapers with an eye to educating the public in what he referred to as "sound doctrine," and he paid a high price for his efforts, as his ideas of "sound doctrine" did not always accord well with those of the contemporary guardians of reputation. His story has long been obscured, but it is a telling one.

Nordhoff's career is emblematic of the highly politicized nature of late nineteenth-century journalism and the intriguing role that journalists played in shaping national politics. As an outspoken social critic, Nordhoff left a mixed legacy. His work for the *Herald* dispels the conventional wisdom that the *Herald*—and other mass-circulation newspapers—were apolitical sex-and-crime scandal sheets. His books, several of which remain in print today, are too often considered out of the context of his life. Without fuller knowledge of their interconnections, Nordhoff's writings, depending on which of them one focuses on, can lead one to judge Nordhoff to have been either strikingly progressive or blind to injustice.

In this seeming inconsistency lies the central lesson of Nordhoff's life. Like many Americans of his time, he was, in fact, not so much inconsistent as

---

[3].   CN to Samuel Bowles, January 6, 1876. Bowles Papers, Yale University Library.

disoriented, confused by a world in which the rules he had lived by as a young man no longer made sense. The lurches and lags in Americans' adjustment to the growth of industrial capitalism, or what has been called the "incorporation of America," can be explained as the difficulties of a generation seeing its world, and its understanding of that world, transformed beyond recognition.

Politically committed as he was, Nordhoff's attempts to make sense of Gilded Age America brought him into the center of numerous controversies. He did not mention, that March day at the turn of the century, those controversies, not even when they would have illuminated the characters of the famed editors who were the subjects of his talk. Omitted was any mention of the scandalous way in which he had been forced to resign from the New York *Evening Post* for refusing to acquiesce in the corruption of its editorial policy in the days of Boss Tweed. He left out the stories of how he was accused of everything from treason to insanity during the controversy over Hawaiian annexation in 1893, how he was threatened with death while in Honolulu reporting on the political situation there, and how his relationship with James Blount, the government official who ultimately recommended that Hawaiian annexation be refused, was investigated by Congress.

He failed to mention the story of how he had been assaulted and nearly killed during the draft riots of 1863, how he had championed the equality of newly freed slaves that same year, how he had become so vocal an advocate of the rights of the working class after the war that *Nation* editor E. L. Godkin called him a "red"—and this despite the fact that barely a year before, Godkin had wanted Nordhoff to join him in founding *The Nation*. His arguments with Andrew Johnson over Reconstruction policy went unremarked. That the Republican Party had found him dangerous enough to engage in a smear campaign against him in the 1870s would not have surprised his listeners, although he had been a standard bearer for the Republican Party during the first years of its existence. But this controversy, too, he left unnoticed. Nor did he mention his role as a *Herald* correspondent in Washington in any detail—not his decision to print letters in 1881 incriminating the former Secretary of State, James G. Blaine, in an international scandal, inspiring the powerful Blaine's lasting enmity; not the years of raging against a "capitalist, monopolist" Senate; nor did he speak of his role in making the New York *Herald* the bête noire of Gilded Age tycoon and all-purpose villain Jay Gould.

He did not speak of the cosmopolitan circle of friends with whom he had surrounded himself, from litterateurs and reformers to scientists and U.S. Presidents. His list of friends and colleagues reads like a *Who's Who* of late nineteenth-century American culture and politics: Hamilton Fish, Charles Sumner, James Russell Lowell, George William Curtis, Henry Adams, Charles Eliot Norton, Carl Schurz, John Cleveland Cady, Samuel Langley, James Bryce,

Simon Newcomb, George Kennan, Sr., George Bancroft, Daniel Coit Gilman, Henry George—the list goes on and on.

He didn't speak of his several books: not *The Communistic Societies of the United States*, an enduring social document and, for him, the cause of some private agony; not his early books about life as a sailor, which historian Alan Nevins claimed had been read by "hundreds of thousands"; not his civics textbook, which went through ten editions in the United States, as well as translations for use in Mexico and Argentina. And although San Diegans regarded Nordhoff's *California: For Health, Pleasure, and Residence* as instrumental in the speedy development of Southern California in the 1870s and '80s, and would claim in 1901 that the region's prosperity was "largely due to him," he did not speak of that book at all.[4]

Perhaps Nordhoff's reticence concerning the more colorful aspects of his career can explain the manner in which his fame so swiftly dissipated after his death in 1901. His distaste for seeing himself mentioned in newspaper reports was widely known, and he refused to cooperate when other journalists, regarding him as a celebrity, tried to profile him in feature articles. It seems likely that he destroyed his papers, or had them destroyed, out of fear of future biographers.

This fear stemmed as much from diffidence as from a desire to keep his personal life private. After the widow of one of his contemporaries had published a compilation of the late journalist's work—preserving writing that Nordhoff knew was dashed off in haste, on deadline, whether the fires of inspiration burned or not, and for ephemeral purposes—he viewed it as a cautionary example. It "showed me that none of us ought to have our newspaper writings collected," he wrote. "...As for me, I don't want any book about me when I am gone."[5]

It is true enough that Nordhoff made mistakes, sometimes grievous ones, and that with a century's hindsight, we can see those mistakes all too clearly. But he placed himself at the center of epochal events and did what he could to affect those events. He may have feared the harsh judgments of posterity, but near oblivion, rather than condemnation, has been Nordhoff's fate. While controversy makes for colorful history, it helps to be on the winning side, and Nordhoff alienated the guardians of good taste and conservative values too often for him to be remembered kindly in their writings—or to have his existence acknowledged at all.

---

4.   Kevin Starr, *Inventing the Dream: California Through the Progressive Era* (New York: Oxford University Press, 1985), 26.

5.   CN to Samuel Bowles, June 27, 1877. Bowles Papers, Yale University Library.

Barely four months after his death in 1901, the publishers of the New York *Evening Post*, where he had played a central role for ten years, held a commemorative dinner in honor of the newspaper's centennial—and did not mention Nordhoff in their chronology of past editors, or comment in their speeches on his leadership. Only a lower-level employee who had worked under Nordhoff as a young man dared to speak of Nordhoff's courage, his kindness, his intelligence. The rest were silent.

Such silence from employees of the *Evening Post*, a newspaper that had treated Nordhoff badly and with a striking neglect of editorial integrity, is not surprising. Just as important, however, may have been the fact that Nordhoff left the eminently "respectable" New York *Evening Post*—beloved, in 1900, of the friends of business and strike-breaking—for the "odious" New York *Herald*, a paper of much vaster circulation and more populist politics. In attempting to bolster the reputation of his last employer, James Gordon Bennett, Jr., in his final public appearance, Nordhoff may have recognized the fate that was in store for himself.

The reputation of the *Herald* as a less "objective" or "serious" newspaper than the *New York Times* or *Tribune*—determinations first made by people who cannot be said to have been disinterested in their political attitudes—has relegated the late-nineteenth-century *Herald* to its own kind of oblivion: often mentioned but seldom consulted by historians, possibly for the simple reason that few American libraries have regarded its purchase as a worthwhile investment. Working for Bennett and the *New York Herald*, and allying himself with their populist politics, may well have cost Nordhoff the modest share of historical attention that his less-interesting contemporaries, working for more conservative journals, easily received. The rich diversity of public opinion, as demonstrated by various mainstream newspapers, deserves renewed attention, and Nordhoff's role in that contentious world reveals the clarity with which some dissenters could make themselves heard through the popular media.

The story of the strivings of a man like Nordhoff—generously motivated, perceptive and intelligent, and dedicated to democratic principles—can illuminate America's mistakes and triumphs in its entry into the modern age. Providing economic justice while retaining liberty in the new corporate order, keeping a country united as it recovered from a civil war and its population grew ever more diverse, finding a way to serve his country through the horse-trading medium of politics without sacrificing his principles, these dilemmas plagued Nordhoff's conscience and absorbed his energies throughout his entire life, for he had grown up in a different world. Nordhoff, as he once wistfully remarked, "did his damnedest."

CHAPTER 1

A Dog for Everyone to Kick At

"It was on a bright July morning that we entered New York Bay," a twenty-five-year-old Charles Nordhoff recalled, writing of the end of his days as a sailor in 1853, "... and I stepped ashore, after an absence of over two years from the United States, with three suits of seaman's clothing in my chest and an English sixpence in my pocket, the result of those two years of hard work, exposure and deprivation."[1] Not just two, but fully nine years of work as a common sailor had convinced the young man that if he wanted more from life than insecurity, poverty, and mistreatment, he had to come ashore and make a new life for himself. "A glimpse of common sense penetrated for a moment the thick mist of romance with which I had always sought to surround the life I had chosen, as I stood on the wharf," he recalled, "and I remembered with what a light heart I had ... sailed from that same pier." At the age of twenty-four, his heart was no longer light. As a sailor, he had seen the doors of opportunity slammed shut before him, and he was afraid it might be too late for him to ever again pry them open. He was, however, determined to try; and in writing of his life as a sailor, he took the first step away from it.

In 1844, at the age of fourteen, Charles Nordhoff wanted to see the world, and so he ran away from his Ohio home to become a sailor. He was an orphan, apprenticed by then to a printer, the ward of a German Methodist bishop. His father had died when the boy was nine years old, four years after bringing the child to America from Prussia. Karl Nordhoff did not bring his wife with him, and young Charles never saw his mother again.[2]

---

1.   CN, *Whaling and Fishing* (NY: Dodd, Mead & Co., 1895, rep. of 1855 edition), 345.

2.   Memoir of Sarah Whitall Nordhoff, transcription in possession of Franklin Nordhoff of Torrance, California; *Appletons' Cyclopedia of American Biography*, 1883; and CN, *Man-of-War Life* (Annapolis: Naval Institute Press, 1985, reprint of the 1855

A skinny, sickly bookworm of a boy, Charles avidly read the popular sea fiction of James Fenimore Cooper and Frederick Marryat, his imagination captured by the exotic scenes and adventures, which, they promised, the seafaring life held for anyone lucky enough to undertake it. Convinced that his life in the print shop was destroying his health, Charles took the twenty-five dollars he had managed to save, "two clean shirts and a pair of socks," and caught a steamer headed east, ending up in Baltimore.[3] When no shipmaster would hire him there, he caught the packet for Philadelphia. He soon realized that he had almost no money left to support himself during a long and uncertain search for a ship, and he decided, with characteristic prudence, to take a job as a "printer's devil" with a Philadelphia newspaper. There he bided his time, looking always for a chance to go to sea.

The chance soon arose. In the spring of 1845, the USS *Columbus* was about to embark upon a round-the-world voyage. By now, Charles had learned that he would need a reference to receive any consideration at all for a shipboard job, and so he obtained a note from the editor of his newspaper and went to an official of the Philadelphia navy yard, one Commodore Jesse Elliott. When Elliott tersely refused him, he silently remained before the Commodore until at last Elliott decided to try to talk sense to the boy.

"Look here, my lad," Nordhoff remembered him saying, "take my advice: get this crazy notion out of your head ... If you go to sea, you will be nothing all your life but a vagabond, drunken sailor—a dog for everyone to kick at." Smart and stubborn, young Charles was not so easily deterred. He waited a few days before accosting Elliott again, laying before him paper and pen to write the necessary recommendation, putting on his "most beseeching look." Elliott gave in at this entreaty, and the boy ran off to enlist. After receiving a cheap set of sailor's clothing from a navy contractor, he boarded ship without telling his friends goodbye, afraid of further interference with his plans.[4]

So Nordhoff's nine years at sea began, happily enough to start with, but soon to bring a series of experiences that left him disillusioned with the romantic vision of life at sea, with the fairness of American society to the members of its lower orders and with the vaunted opportunity of all Americans to rise from humble positions. From the outset, Nordhoff perceived that the navy's rules and regulations could be (and often were) skewed to favor the unscrupulous and punish the naive, and he soon learned that with no money and no status, he was often at others' mercy.

---

edition, edited by John B. Hattendorf), 1, 11–12. Hattendorf (p. xv) calls *Man-of-War Life* "a minor masterpiece."
[3.] CN, *Man-of-War Life*, 12.
[4.] CN, *Man-of-War Life*, 21–23.

As he was to manifest in all his later work—whether writing of newly freed slaves in South Carolina, of Hawaiians or Californians or communitarians—Nordhoff's perspective as he first surveyed his shipmates was anthropological. He studied the sailors, acquiring through the process a deep respect for their resilience, generosity, and humanity. During the nineteenth century, it would have been hard to find more despised free workers than sailors, who were regarded by polite society much as Commodore Elliott had warned Nordhoff: as vagabonds, drunkards, the true mudsill of society.[5] And Nordhoff, coming as he did from a polite middle-class milieu, was exposed to a side of life he had not thought possible in America: a life of hard work that earned no respect, of striving that opened no opportunity, of victimization regarded as evidence of the victim's character flaws. If he had read Richard Henry Dana's *Two Years Before the Mast* (which had become a best seller by the early 1840s) as well as the romances of Cooper and Marryat, his ideas of the sailor's life would have been given a realistic edge, for Dana too had been appalled, in his brief sabbatical away from Harvard, with what hardworking men could be subjected to. But Dana was twenty years old when he undertook his sea voyage, able to regard his surroundings with the superiority of a Boston Brahmin well aware of the temporary nature of his captivity. Nordhoff, too young to easily discard a dream or admit defeat, felt he had burned his bridges behind him, and he meant to make a life for himself at sea. His growing awareness of what that life would involve, therefore, struck deeply at all his hopes and aspirations. Had he trapped himself forever?

Nearly a decade later, the memory of the treatment meted out to sailors remained vivid to Nordhoff; and he decided to explain their plight to the public in three books, written in rapid succession in 1854 and '55—*Man-of-War Life*, *The Merchant Vessel*, and *Whaling and Fishing*. A keen observer, Nordhoff united realistic depictions of forecastle life with criticism of the system. As his first effort at journalism, the 1855 narratives already displayed the reformist impulse that characterized all his later work—a reformism that was predicated on clear, graphic depictions of conditions and communities as he perceived them. When he engaged in moralizing, almost always it sprang from the purported facts of a given case—a method that would be used by later generations as "muckraking" and investigative journalism.

In *Man-of-War Life*'s treatment of flogging in the navy, for example, Nordhoff combined matter-of-fact description with an outraged and even bitter denunciation of the practice he had just described so coolly. In one episode, certain crew members, having gotten "gloriously fuddled" on smuggled-aboard

---

5.   Margaret Creighton, *Dog-Watch and Liberty Days: Seafaring Life in the Nineteenth Century* (Salem: Peabody Museum, 1982).

alcohol at one port of call, found punishment reserved for their first Saturday back in open sea. Unaware of what it portended, Nordhoff noted "an unusual stillness, all laughing and singing hushed," until all hands were summoned to "witness punishment." "The dread reality burst upon my mind," Nordhoff remembered. "They were going to flog the poor fellows in the brig," and the rest were to be forced to watch "the barbarous display." And so the ritual began.

> "Thomas Brown," calls the captain, gruffly. The man steps forward in silence. "You were drunk, sir. Master-at-arms, strip him."

> ...The master-at-arms having helped the poor fellow off with his shirt..., the quarter masters are ordered to "seize him up." He is walked forward, on to the grating, to which his feet are securely fashioned by lashings, his wrists being in like manner lashed to the hammock-rail, above his head.

After a "few moments of dread silence," the boatswain's mate, holding a cat-o'-nine-tails, was ordered to "do your duty." Nordhoff would not soften the ensuing events, but recorded the scene meticulously:

> [The mate] advances, and, poised on his right foot, swinging the cats over his back, takes deliberate aim at the human back spread before him. *Thug*, sounds the cat. "*One*," solemnly announces the master-at-arms. The victim does not move. Thug—two. Now the flesh on his back quivers and creeps, the injured muscles contract, and the stripes assume a bright red tinge. Thug—three. The stripes turn a dark purple, and the grating shakes convulsively with the reluctant start wrung from the strong man in agony. Thug—four. Blood—Oh! God, I could look no more, but burying my face in my hands, turned from the sickening scene. But still the dull *thug* resounded in my ears, followed toward the last by a low moan, until twelve was reached, when the boatswain's mate was stopped, the poor fellow taken down, his shirt flung over his bleeding back, and another victim called forth.[6]

Twenty sailors were flogged that Saturday, though Nordhoff could not bear to watch. "Many more times was I compelled to hear the sharp whistle of the

---

6.   CN, *Man-of-War Life*, 121–2.

cat..., and the dull sound of the blow as it met the quivering flesh," he added, "but never more did I *see* a man flogged." By the time his account was published, flogging in the U.S. Navy had been abolished some five years;[7] but with all his humanitarian impulses still outraged, he added a bitter condemnation of the "editors and legislators who sit in their cozy arm-chairs, ... and talk wisely about the necessity of flogging for sailors." If they could even once see or feel the impact of their policy "and experience within their own breasts the feeling of dark humiliation which falls upon the soul at seeing the manhood thus being scourged out of a fellow-creature," they would soon change their position. "Let them see once the *down* look of the poor victim of a barbarous tyranny, and they will not say 'it does not hurt a sailor.'"[8] And if the powerful could not personally witness the human degradation they sanctioned, Nordhoff was determined to make them see it through his own writing.

Freedom of speech was severely restricted on board the ship, all protestations chargeable as mutinous. "You are allowed to *think* what you please," the sailors would say, "but you must not think aloud," and so they maintained "an ominous silence" about flogging.[9] In writing such an account of the punishments exacted aboard ship, Nordhoff, like many other writers of the 1840s and '50s, hoped to speak out for his silenced fellow sailors; and in pillorying complacent editors alongside legislators as the perpetrators of an inhuman practice, he clearly recognized the editor's job as a significant force, for good or ill. As he composed *Man-of-War Life*, the question of a vocation loomed large in his mind, and he was groping toward an answer.

By the end of the three-year voyage of the *Columbus*, Nordhoff had had his fill of the navy. On a ship of 780 men, work, leisure, and life were all strictly regimented and routinized in a hierarchical arrangement that left nobody unaware of his status. Nordhoff learned that his station was at gun no. 36, his hammock was no. 639, his ID no. 574, and his mess no. 26. Such bureaucracy bore little resemblance to his boyhood dreams of adventure at sea, and it proved emblematic of the voyage and military life as a whole. He described the titles, duties, and rankings of all the men aboard ship as if in a Linnaean classification of species.[10]

The sailors relieved their boredom on watch by telling tales that delighted young Charles. They also teased him mercilessly about his scrawny build, and

---

7. Hennig Cohen, introduction to Herman Melville's *White Jacket* (New York: Holt, Rinehart, and Winston, 1967), xxvi. See also Margaret Creighton, *Dogwatch and Liberty Days: Seafaring Life in the Nineteenth Century* (Salem: Peabody Museum, 1982).

8. CN, *Man-of-War Life*, 122.

9. CN, *Man-of-War Life*, 123.

10. CN, *Man-of-War Life*, 43–64.

during his first weeks at sea, he alternated between elation and tears. But by playing by the unwritten rules of the sailor community, and accepting his low status within it, Nordhoff managed to win the older men over.[11] Among the boys themselves, there was a code of honor that prohibited one from reporting the misdemeanors of another. In self-defense, the smaller and weaker of the group learned to band together against the "tyranny" of the stronger boys.[12] Life aboard ship was providing the young Nordhoff with a thorough education in human relations, and even in power politics.

In addition to the outrage of flogging, he held many other grievances against the navy. The matter of shore leave still rankled, years later, as he recounted how much he had anticipated exploring their first port of call, Rio de Janeiro. Nordhoff fell irredeemably in love with the tropics during his sailing years, and he described the day that the *Columbus* first entered Rio as unique to the tropics, with "that peculiar softly-lit bright haze ..., not hiding, but only tempering the fierce splendor of an almost vertical sun, and infusing all nature ... with a mellow, lazy tranquility." The beneficence of the climate seemed to affect the very temperament of the crew, as "every harsh or discordant noise was hushed; the violence of the most uproarious was tempered or stilled." But the lyrical mood of the moment faded as the crew realized that they were not to be allowed off the ship or even to view the harbor unencumbered: "strict orders were issued, that no one should show his head above the hammock rail." Nordhoff had been ready to climb up into the spars to get a panoramic view of the harbor, but found himself thwarted,

> reduced, in common with seven hundred other anxious souls, to the miserable shift of taking a peep at our surroundings through a port-hole, by which process we were able to gain about as much information concerning the town and harbor, as one would be likely to get of the general appearance of a room, by examining it through the keyhole of the door.[13]

He had joined the navy to see the world, he remarked wryly, "not bargaining, however, for so *distant* a view"; and if opportunity had presented itself, he would have deserted ship right then and there.[14] Gratuitous reminders to the men of their inferior status occurred constantly. The crew was not only denied an unobstructed view of the harbor, but they were also not told on what day they

---

11.   CN, *Man-of-War Life*, 67–68.

12.   CN, *Man-of-War Life*, 74.

13.   CN, *Man-of-War Life*, 104–5.

14.   CN, *Man-of-War Life*, 114.

would once again set sail or what their next destination would be. The rigid hierarchy that reserved fresh food for officers while the sailors ate dried beef and worm-eaten hardtack had its effect on the rationing of knowledge as well: sailors were kept ignorant for no reason, Nordhoff wrote, except that "the crew have no *business* to know."[15] Moreover, the division of labor among the workforce kept an inexperienced sailor like himself from learning much "sailorship," reinforcing the emptiness of the days.[16]

Many months later, on the return voyage from Asia, the *Columbus* made a stop in Valparaiso, Chile. It was December of 1846, a year and a half since the *Columbus* first set sail; and the entire crew was given, for the first time, a few days' "liberty" on shore. As a boy, Nordhoff had already been allowed shore, but never in the places he truly yearned to see, and his frustration mounted as the months passed. While other sailors, finally freed from regimentation, spent their leave drinking, fighting, and whoring, Nordhoff later wrote, he went off with another teenager to see the sights. He returned to the ship "fully satisfied with our so-long desired 'liberty.' Satisfied," he went on, with some vehemence, "... that Valparaiso was a humbug, that "liberty" was a humbug, and that a man-of-war, considered as a standpoint, whence to see somewhat of the world, is the most egregious humbug of all."[17] And though he discreetly omitted the fact from his book, he tried to jump ship. For this attempted desertion, he was given twelve lashes.[18]

Criminal behavior, and disregard for law, was utterly foreign to Nordhoff's nature, and he must have been pushed beyond the breaking point by the time they had reached Valparaiso. Though he didn't admit in his book to attempted desertion, clearly his emotions were stirred by the memory of the stop in Valparaiso, and he interrupted his narrative at this point with a plea for understanding. "Here was a ship which had gone quite around the world," he wrote,

> ... had visited various ports in the Brazils, the East Indies, China, and the Sandwich Islands, and now, when nearly two years from home, the crew was for the first time allowed to set foot on shore. Having passed by ... the places which we

---

15. CN, *Man-of-War Life*, 117.
16. CN, *Man-of-War Life*, 193.
17. CN, *Man-of-War Life*, 210.
18. John B. Hattendorf, introduction to CN, *Man-of-War Life* (Annapolis: Naval Institute Press, 1985), xvii. Hattendorf cites the record of Nordhoff's punishment as U.S. Naval Academy MS35, "Record of Punishments, USS *Columbus*, 14 May 1845–26 February 1848," Nimitz Library, U.S. Naval Academy.

were most anxious to examine closely, all hands were at last permitted to set foot on a foreign shore, and saw—what?

Valparaiso was poor recompense for the long wait and provided little outlet for the pent-up energy, mental and physical, of the crew—or so it seemed to Nordhoff:

> First, I saw a lot of drunken sailors. Next, a number of … fellows, … whose principle duty … was to keep said sailors within proper bounds. Thirdly, I had seen a few trees, a little grass, a number of grog-shops and ten-pin alleys, the cathedral, the calaboose, and the plaza. And fourthly, I had seen, aye, and felt too, an innumerable host of fleas. Were not these sights rather dearly paid for by a two years' cruise at sea, deprived of every comfort, outside the pale of all civilized society, living on stinking beef and pork, and worse than stinking water? Truly, I had "paid too dear for my whistle."[19]

His mood coloring all his memories, Nordhoff added a dark comment on the history of Valparaiso's harbor, where an American ship had been destroyed by the British during the War of 1812. "I had stood where once the entire people of a city were congregated, as in a vast circus, witnesses to two companies of Christian, civilized men killing and maiming each other, one calm summer afternoon, on the broad area of the lower bay."[20] There were times like this— many of them, in his coming years as a journalist—when Nordhoff's faith in human goodness utterly failed him. There was too much evidence against it, in his judgment, and at times the bleak awareness overwhelmed him. Deeply religious himself, Nordhoff found religious hypocrisy—Christians slaughtering Christians, or, as he would later write, pious landlords earning money by maintaining slums—a particularly outrageous vice.

As he cataloged the rigid hierarchy of shipboard life, Nordhoff described conditions vividly, almost with a grim satisfaction in shocking his readers. The food the sailors ate was one more appalling indication of their status. With an almost inhuman, meticulous detachment, Nordhoff described the ship's biscuit stores, which had become infested with weevils. The weevils were "little gray bugs, looking on a minute inspection, somewhat like a miniature elephant," and they hopped about like fleas. "It was necessary to split a biscuit in halves before eating it, to shake these little fellows out—although this trouble was

---

19.   CN, *Man-of-War Life*, 211.
20.   CN, *Man-of-War Life*, 211.

not always taken." The weevils presented less of a problem than an infestation of worms in the bread, he added; "(it is no use to shrink from the tale, 'tis the plain truth,) and these disgusting animals ate out the inside of the biscuits, leaving nothing for us ... but a thin and tasteless crust. Yet this bread we were compelled to eat—for there was none other."[21] It was not easy on them, he wrote, but "what will not custom and hunger do." Morality had nothing to do with it, or taste. If sailors drank reeking water, and if they ate meals such as the one at which Nordhoff saw a biscuit "literally *crawl off the mess cloth*," they were only doing what anyone, placed in their circumstances, would have had to do.[22] And he had only mentioned the stomach-turning details, he added virtuously, "to show how sailors do fare sometimes, and not infrequently."

Even death demonstrated the stark distinctions in treatment accorded the officers and the crew members. While sailors were simply sewn up into their hammocks and tipped overboard from the moving vessel, one young officer's death (from the unheroic cause of delirium tremens) was memorialized by halting the ship and holding a full service to which all the sailors were summoned. The loss of a shipmate, though unmarked by ceremony, nevertheless deeply grieved the sailors, for their community was a peculiarly close-knit and interdependent one. In fact, it was this community of shipboard life which, Nordhoff believed, produced such strong and virtuous characters among the sailors. Interdependence brought out "all the better qualities" of individuals. Unlike Emersonian individualism, Nordhoff's view of the individual could not be separated from the people and conditions that surrounded it.[23]

Almost always Nordhoff explained behavior in terms of environment and necessity, and this extended from the sailors' consumption of rotting and infested food to, later, the behavior of other social groups, such as newly freed slaves who continued to congregate at night after years of having been forbidden to do so during the day. The generosity of his universalism was limited, but young Nordhoff knew from personal experience that people were not wholly free to choose their lives or determine their actions. However, he lapsed into racist thinking when the *Columbus* sailed into Chinese waters. His sympathy failed him utterly when considering Asians, whose culture and habits were so very different from his own; and while he appreciated the exoticism of their Chinese pilot's appearance, he studied him much as one would study an interesting specimen of animal life. When at last several of the ship's boys were allowed ashore in China, they blithely invaded one of the homes nearby, poring

---

21. CN, *Man-of-War Life*, 154–5.
22. CN, *Man-of-War Life*, 155.
23. CN, *Man-of-War Life*, 158.

over the implements and furnishings with no thoughts as to their unwanted incursions on the Chinese inhabitants' privacy.[24]

Virulent racial and cultural stereotyping were common at midcentury among white Americans, and Nordhoff was less offensive about it than some. Still, the Japanese seemed to him "a far better developed race … than we had met with since leaving the United States"; they lacked the "sly look of mean cunning" of the Chinese, nor did they exhibit the "lassitude" common to East Asians. Nordhoff, as usual, made an effort to discover the local people's habits, diet, manners, dress, and commonalities of appearance. The *Columbus*'s mission in Japan was to attempt to persuade the Japanese emperor to open trade with the United States, but this failing, they were requested to leave. "The authorities evidently desired to wipe out every trace of the visit of the barbarians," Nordhoff noted without comment. The Japanese supplied the Americans with water and provisions, "the only service … asked in return," being "to *stay away*." When the wind failed on their scheduled day of departure, hundreds of small Japanese boats gathered and towed the huge man-of-war out to sea.[25]

His reaction to the Hawaiian Islanders was typical: the natives and their land were "primitive," but "susceptible of great improvement," and he applauded the work of New England missionaries in forwarding civilization there. The fact that the Hawaiian women were modestly clad in muumuus was evidence of the missionaries' influence. But Nordhoff knew that not all westerners affected Hawaii in such a beneficent way, and he reprovingly noted that the missionaries' work was being undercut by the "irregular conduct" of American sailors. Vaguely referring to them as men who "disgrace the name of Christianity by their actions," he blamed them for introducing "new vices" to the natives and encouraging old ones. The Hawaiians were being corrupted and infected (literally) by contact with licentious whites. To Nordhoff, not all white people could claim the rank of the civilized.

As he gained in experience, Nordhoff revelled in adopting the superficial marks of the sailor as well. He later regarded this phase of his career with the relentless scrutiny that he would often turn upon himself as well as others, a mocking and distancing of his former illusions. "In my pride of heart, at the glorious eminence to which I had arrived," he wrote from a distance of many years, "I *patched* my trousers, and rubbed tar on my frocks, that he that ran might read me a sailor. In short, I made a laughing-stock of myself."[26]

The journalist was being formed during these years, as Nordhoff's habits of observation and investigation sharpened. One of his most pointed criticisms of

---

[24].   CN, *Man-of-War Life*, 159–175.

[25].   CN, *Man-of-War Life*, 179–189.

[26].   CN, *Man-of-War Life*, 193.

the navy was that its military rigidity kept the sailors ignorant and foreshortened their vision, the precise opposite of the effect travel ought to have upon people. Writing of the ill-fated "liberty" at Valparaiso, he queried,

> What did Tom Starboard or Jack Halyard learn, pray, of the general customs and manners of the people of Chili [*sic*], during their three days' visit to the shore? They experienced the presence of a mounted police; they had informed themselves of the localities of the various grog-shops; they had perhaps made the acquaintance of sundry other persons and places—not to be mentioned to ears polite; and the sum total of their real information concerning the country consisted in this, that the people speak ... Spanish, and that their houses are infested with ... fleas. And it will be so. While you belong to the ship, you will see nothing.[27]

Nordhoff, while he belonged to the ship, saw quite a bit—all of it shipboard, however, and most of it confirming his belief that the sailors' restricted lives kept them from developing their god-given skills or even from behaving as responsible adults. They were not allowed to be responsible for anything, Nordhoff declared, and the habits of mindless routine and blind obedience permeated all their actions.

One sailor aboard the *Columbus*, he learned, had journeyed across Mexico from Acapulco to Vera Cruz. "I gave him no peace until he had imparted to me the whole story of his adventure," Nordhoff wrote. But the fellow's mind was simply benumbed. All that Nordhoff could learn from him of Mexico and Mexicans was "that the women were pretty, the men ugly, the people generally hospitable but poor, the liquor bad and the country unhealthy." And what had Nordhoff hoped to learn from his informant?

> What the country produced; how the people lived; what handicafts were practiced among them, and to what degree of perfection they were carried; what were the prevailing species of woods; in what differed the vegetation or the general face of the country from that at home—[this sailor], in his long and tedious journey of many hundreds of miles, on foot, had never thought of noting....Yet, ... this man was intelligent enough; but he had lost, in the monotony of sea life, those

---

[27]   CN, *Man-of-War Life*, 211.

powers of comparison and observation, without which one
need not go traveling.[28]

This formula—examining a region's production, crafts, flora and fauna,
and people's ways of life—was one which Nordhoff was to use again and again
in his own writings, most notably in his books on California and intentional
communities. His writing could be, in fact, literally exhaustive in its detail; but
Nordhoff, even at the age of twenty-five, believed that it was the complex fabric
of existence that made a culture comprehensible, and it was this he hoped to
glean from his companions' stories. The unvarying dullness of the sailors'
lives, the utter lack of change or challenges, struck Nordhoff as the great all-
encompassing evil of naval life, for it destroyed the men's spirit and intelligence.

And while his silent observations of the sailors' community partially
alleviated the boredom of life on the *Columbus*, there were times when Nordhoff's
own imagination grew exhausted. Stationed outside of Monterey, a nearly
uninhabited and undeveloped port of call, he recalled that there had been

> no bumboats, no foreign people to look at, no strange vessels
> coming in or going out, nothing to see, or to do, or to think
> about. ...I had read through already ... every accessible book
> on the ship.... I had matched myself at backgammon, against
> every player of note on board, and had become tired of
> continually beating certain ones, and being beaten by others.
> I had spun a [top], until disgust at the infantile amusement
> took possession of me.[29]

In desperation for something with which to amuse himself, he had his arms
"covered" with tattoos. (One can only imagine how this amply tattooed ex-
sailor impressed William Cullen Bryant and the other lofty literati with whom
he would later work.) "But, alas!" he wrote, "... when there was no longer left
any room on my arms, for additional Neptunes, ships, and whales," he reread
some "old acquaintances among the books." It was with great cheers from the
crew that the *Columbus* departed Monterey. Nordhoff had found California in
1848 undeveloped and uninteresting, and he saw the coast recede "with an
inward vow ... never to return hither."[30] He must have laughed at this youthful
certitude in later decades: he was to be acclaimed as the man to whom Southern

---

28. CN, *Man-of-War Life*, 212–213.

29. CN, *Man-of-War Life*, 227.

30. CN, *Man-of-War Life*, 228.

California owed its late-century booming prosperity, and after years of longing to do so, he spent his retirement years happily living near San Diego.

They sailed around Cape Horn and headed home with feelings of "hopeful suspense," regulations relaxed and the workload lessened for all the sailors. While his mates talked about returning home to hearth and kin, Nordhoff had other ideas. "I had started out to see the world," as he later described his reasoning, "-- and had failed in accomplishing my desire; and I would try again. I would sail in merchant vessels, ... and when I had seen all I wanted, *then* would go home."[31] Upon reaching Norfolk in March of 1848, the crew began to strip the ship in preparation for their discharge, and a bittersweet feeling of leave-taking swept over them all. "I felt—I must confess it," Nordhoff wrote, "as though I were about to depart from my home." His melancholy dissipated the moment he left the ship, exhilarated at being "*free* at last." Writing in 1855, Nordhoff took naturally to the rhetoric of antislavery as he described his liberation. "I was once more my own master, and ... I half involuntarily straightened myself, and threw back my shoulders, as though to fling off the long-borne yoke," he wrote. "I felt as though no consideration in the world could induce me to ship in the Navy again. I had had a surfeit of bondage."[32]

Not quite eighteen years old when he was discharged from the navy, and moderately well-trained as a sailor, Charles Nordhoff immediately accompanied two friends on a schooner to Boston. To sleep in a real bed instead of a hammock, and to take part in a prayer service at the sailors' home where he boarded, brought a pang of homesickness, and "my heart was full, at the thought of the loved ones at home." But he was too proud, and too stubborn, to act on these feelings. "Could I go home?" he asked. "What had I to tell, what had I to show, after my long absence? NO! I was determined to see a little more of the world before I showed my face there."[33] He accordingly went to the shipping office by the wharves and signed a contract to sail to Liverpool via New Orleans.

In contrast to the 780-member crew of the *Columbus*, the crew of the little barque on which Nordhoff made his first trip as a merchant sailor included only nine other men. The work was harder than in the navy, he found, but less regimented, the men coordinating their movements by keeping time with chanties; the crew members assessed one another favorably. Although Nordhoff's hands were blistered and his muscles ached after his first day at work, he found it preferable to the easier but duller routine of navy life. In the military, there was no freedom of speech and no responsibility for one's self:

---

[31]. CN, *Man-of-War Life*, 251.

[32]. CN, *Man-of-War Life*, 255.

[33]. CN, *The Merchant Vessel* (NY: Dodd, Mead & Co., 1895 rep. of 1855 edition), 14.

the naval sailor "eats, drinks, sleeps, and works only at the beck and call of his superior," Nordhoff noted. And it was utterly mindless, necessarily so:

> Instant, unhesitating, unthinking obedience to the order that is given—that is the one great rule, which is imposed upon the mind of the sailor, until—he rushes carelessly but consciously, in the face of death, or on to certain destruction.... Now it is true, ... that this kind of discipline is necessary on board a ship, ...where a great number of *bodies* are placed under command of one mind--but what kind of *men* does it make of these bodies? Plainly, it takes away all the more valuable part of the individual, his mind; or rather, it accustoms him to lay it aside as useless, and depend upon another for that which God has given to all.[34]

In later years, Nordhoff blamed militarism for many evils: taxes, unemployment, global depression. His insistence on the importance of the individual in creating his own life was platitudinous, but it also expressed a deep-felt respect for democracy over "expertise." All too often, he would insist, taking responsibility away from the ignorant (through voting restrictions, for example) was a sure means of keeping them ignorant. His antimilitarism was of a piece with his general philosophy.

In the merchant service, however, it seemed to Nordhoff that individual initiative flourished. The basic tenets of the free-labor ideology informed his perceptions: the merchant sailor did his duty without the threat of the lash hanging over him. "No one who has not experienced both states can imagine the degradation of the one, or the honest elevation of the other," Nordhoff commented. The work was hard, but the worker knew both his duty and his rights; there was a solidarity among the crew that sprang from this understanding of their rights, which enabled them to "present a front as of one man" to any officer attempting to trespass on those rights.[35] When the crew was given leeway to do its work in its own way, the results were invariably good. Of one Australian crew, Nordhoff remarked, "they themselves made the rules by which their officers were forced to abide ... And the crew, with a kind of feeling of honor, ... abstained scrupulously from taking any undue advantage of the power which they felt themselves possessed of."[36] There were, however, limits to this power.

---

[34] CN, *Merchant Vessel*, 25.
[35] CN, *Merchant Vessel*, 26.
[36] CN, *Merchant Vessel*, 188.

Just as in the navy, collusion between unscrupulous captains and merchants onshore kept up a system by which the sailors were cheated. The captains would turn their crew's pay over to the tailors, which they held as a credit against which the sailors were, in essence, forced to purchase clothing. The captain received kickbacks from the tailors for his cooperation. Nordhoff anticipated the reaction of his middle-class readership to this collusion and tried to counter it.

> "Well, but," says the landsman, "I would take neither clothes nor money, rather than be cheated so bare-facedly." This is all very good, and resolutions to that effect are made by nearly every American ship's crew …, and broken as often as made.

The sailors needed some money, after all, and had little choice. "So that Jack … quietly walks up and allows himself to be made cabbage of in the most approved style." And for this, the sailor was called "a spendthrift, and a vagabond fellow," while the man who cheated him "on Sabbath morning points him out to his children as an object of disgust and contempt."[37]

Throughout his career, Nordhoff continually pointed out the collusion of the ostensibly "respectable" in the oppressions and degradations of the people they despised. Slumlords, for example, merited an inner circle of hell. The well-to-do shared complicity in societal ills, and he excoriated those who condoned the status quo while condemning its victims. It was a dynamic he knew all too well, having lived on the receiving end of the bad bargains perpetrated on the poor.

Their return voyage in the autumn of 1848 came at the height of the Irish potato famine, and their cargo included iron, crockery, and Irish immigrants. Nordhoff wrote sympathetically, if stereotypically, of the Irish: they were "a tolerably rough-looking set," but possessed "that thorough-going Irish characteristic of being ready to lend a helping hand wherever there was work going on."[38] When the Irishmen offered to haul anchor in return for hearing the chanty man sing, the chanty man responded with a casual cruelty, telling Charles that he would "set all the men and women crying" and regaling them with a "sad and plaintive tune" that went, in part:

> We're going away from friends and home,
> 　　*Chorus*—Oh sailors where are you bound to,
> We're going away to hunt for gold,
> 　　*Chorus*—Across the briny ocean.

37.　CN, *Merchant Vessel*, 67–8.
38.　CN, *Merchant Vessel*, 69.

Father and mother say good-by,
    Chorus—Sailors where are you bound to,
Oh sisters, brothers, don't you cry
    Chorus—Across the briny ocean.[39]

The immigrants, forced to leave behind their own homes and families, responded as predicted. They had been "laughing and talking," but before two stanzas had been sung, all were dabbing away tears. Nordhoff was sorry for them, if uncomprehending. "It was rather cruel sport, I thought," he wrote, "yet I would scarcely have believed that they would have been so easily affected." The rest of the sailors began a "more cheerful tune, to win Paddy back to his usual bright spirits."

Nordhoff's mixed feelings toward the Irish, jammed as they were in the ship's steerage, ranged from pity for their sufferings to near ridicule of their almost total ignorance of America. Steerage was "a crowded and miserably dirty hole," as he described it, "the stench ... enough to make any one sick," with "no privacy at all," with "from six to ten persons ... in each [berth]"; the cooking facilities were so inadequate that many never "had a mouthful of warm victuals from day to day." One man, so poor that he could afford only his own passage, smuggled his wife aboard in a trunk. But Nordhoff simply did not understand the extremities of misery that had forced these people to abandon their homeland, and he wondered at their "implicit confidence" in immigrating to a country "without means or friends." His inability to understand the Irish was all the more striking in view of his efforts to rehabilitate the reputation of another despised group, the common sailors. By 1855, when he wrote *The Merchant Vessel*, the Irish-Americans were regarded by many as causing severe social problems for America; and with the Know-Nothing and Nativist movements at high tide, most commentary on the Irish was vicious in the extreme, making Nordhoff look supportive in comparison.

Nordhoff's mild incomprehension may not have furthered American sympathy for the Irish, but neither did it stoke the flames of xenophobia.[40] Similarly, he had positive things to say about the Chinese expatriates he encountered in Malaysia during another voyage, but couched them within the common American representation of Chinese as dull and indolent. They were, outside of China, "smart, thriving, and industrious people," in implicit contrast to the character he had perceived in the Chinese within their own borders.[41]

---

[39]   CN, *Merchant Vessel*, 70.

[40]   CN, *Merchant Vessel*, 71–73.

[41]   CN, *Merchant Vessel*, 204.

And yet if he was guilty of the racism common to his time, the young Nordhoff disdained certain species of national chauvinism and prided himself on his liberality. The crew of one of his ships, the *Ariadne*, was a diverse mixture of nationalities and races, with bigotry and national rivalries running rampant among them. "The English hated the Manillamen, as 'conniving fellows,'" Nordhoff noted sardonically,

> because these would not get drunk with them; while the Spaniard made friends of them because they spoke his language. The St. Helena man was ranged on Johnny Bull's side, while the Swede rather inclined to Yankeedom. The two Frenchmen assumed an air of the loftiest contempt for all our little cliques and parties....

With his by-now-habitual efforts to please his mates, Nordhoff regarded himself as above such petty behavior. "I had been so long a citizen of the world," he recalled proudly, "that it was not a matter of much difficulty to steer my course safely between all parties, and make friends of all." At first mistaken for a Briton, however, he "took care to proclaim myself an American," which, perhaps, he equated with world citizenship.[42]

After arriving in Philadelphia at the end of one voyage in December of 1848, Nordhoff considered the well-known miseries of a winter voyage across the North Atlantic and contemplated shipping next in an "Indiaman." His lifelong hatred of cold weather was already full-blown, but somewhat perversely, he agreed with a shipmate to sign up for another voyage to London, for "there was ... adventure in the voyage, some new experiences to make." His stubborn pride was involved as well: he decided that if other sailors could endure the "sufferings" of such a trip, so could he.[43]

The crossing was a nightmare. They departed on a bitterly cold day, the river choked with ice and gale-force winds whipping up waves that drenched the ship with icy spray. Throughout the monthlong passage, "not one of the crew had on a dry stitch of clothing," while their bunks were "half afloat, blankets were rung out every watch, and mattresses were mere moldy masses of wet and rotting straw." They were plagued by waves that destroyed boats, shredded sails, carried off water casks, and swept away every moveable object on deck. It was a hellish experience, the gale making it "impossible to draw a breath when looking to windward." They could make their way around ship only by clinging to life ropes while the spray covered their bodies with a "crust of salt."

---

[42].   CN, *Merchant Vessel*, 248–9.

[43].   CN, *Merchant Vessel*, 74.

Blinded by the spray, the sailors found their hands raw and bleeding, their feet numb and cold; the ship leaked, forcing them to constantly pump, and it was dangerously difficult to steer.[44]

So miserable was their existence that the sailors, according to Nordhoff, lost their will to live. Their labor at the pumps, he wrote,

> was performed not with the energy of persons working for something they would like to save. It was more as a matter of duty to the vessel and her owners. For so much had we suffered with wet and cold, that we had begun to look upon our now probable fate as, at any rate, a relief from misery too great to be borne much longer.[45]

Nightmarish occurrences mounted: hail that injured the crew, St. Elmo's Fire dancing on the yardarms, and an electrical storm that threw the captain and one crew-member into temporary states of catatonia. The final leg of the trip on the Thames was needlessly laborious for the worn-out and demoralized crew, for their captain refused to hire the customary tugboat to pull them up the river.

But they were powerless to escape. The sailors agreed to remain for the return trip to Philadelphia, for unemployed sailors populated the London wharves, and they weren't eager to join their ranks. Here, the insecurity of the sailor's life was fully borne home to Nordhoff, stripped of all romance and fancy when they encountered two unemployed sailors begging to be given the ship's discarded worm-eaten biscuit. He and his shipmates called the two strangers on board, fed them from their own supplies, and learned the fate that awaited any sailor unable to find a ship to work upon:

> They had been two months on shore, had sold every stitch of clothing they owned except [what] they had on—had even disposed of their shoes, and were walking the streets barefooted. They had been turned out of their boarding-houses, and had, for some weeks, slept on boxes and bales, in corners of the docks.... All this, too, in the month of November.[46]

---

44. CN, *Merchant Vessel*, 79–91.

45. CN, *Merchant Vessel*, 87.

46. CN, *Merchant Vessel*, 244.

Unable to see the ship made more seaworthy in an inspection system skewed to favor the word of captains, the sailors resigned themselves to another hard North Atlantic passage. Reflecting upon their inability to call upon the law for their relief, Nordhoff noted that many laws that were intended to protect sailors often wound up having the opposite effect, as minimums became standards.[47]

Not all merchant service was so punishing. Nordhoff's next trip, to Calcutta, was aboard a fine ship with kind officers and a capable crew, and he was kept busy with the relatively easy work of mending sail, a skill at which he had developed some facility. Aboard the *Akbar*, he found a feeling of brotherhood among the small crew, "a bond of unity" that fostered generosity in which "a complete community of goods prevails." Frequently, two men would become closely bound to one another in what was called "chummyship," an almost marital tie, and modern scholars have speculated on the degree to which homosexual practices may have flourished on long voyages.[48]

Continuing his study of the sailors' characters, Nordhoff observed that many were well-read, capable of "shrewd criticisms … which would not have done dishonor to some occupants of chairs professorial" while their wide travels gave their minds "an inquiring turn."[49] There was a quality of coldness, verging on the merciless, with which Nordhoff scrutinized others, probing them and drawing them out despite themselves ("I gave him no peace until he had imparted to me the whole story," as he wrote of one such encounter) while revealing little of his own thoughts. He could manipulate even dear friends in trying to satisfy his never-satisfied curiosity. One sailor, a brawny man named Jack Haley whom he remembered even fifty years later, was known for his soft heart. "I knew his weak side, and … felt sure of being able to coax him into a yarn," Nordhoff remarked.[50]

On another voyage, this time with Australian sailors, he noted their remarkable taciturnity; they seemed to take "special pride in saying but little." But their reserve did not deter him from his "persistent exercise of that Yankee faculty, asking questions."[51] One Australian sailor had been tattooed all over his body, sparking Nordhoff's curiosity, but only "after the most persistent and repeated questioning" did the sailor explain how his bodily ornamentation had come about when he had been captured by aborigines. Probably a painful memory, the episode was not one of which the man would willingly speak.

[47.]   CN, *Merchant Vessel*, 109, 150.

[48.]   See, for instance, Robert K. Martin, *Hero, Captain, Stranger* (Chapel Hill: University of North Carolina Press, 1986).

[49.]   CN, *Merchant Vessel*, 133.

[50.]   CN, *Man-of-War Life*, 93.

[51.]   CN, *Merchant Vessel*, 162–3.

"It was only by dint of the most persistent and adroit questioning," Nordhoff repeated proudly, "taking him when he was in his best humor, ... that I obtained his story." Again, the young man's ability to insinuate himself into others' good graces, even consciously manipulating them, was intrinsic to his art of drawing out revelations from the unwilling. "Here a little, there a little, I picked up all his experience," Nordhoff wrote with disarming candor, "and had I not, by the practice of various little arts, made myself a favorite with him, I should never have gotten any of it."[52]

With another reticent subject, the inquisitive Charley "left no means untried to obtain from him some information" about his previous life on an Australian ranch, "but found it difficult." He "struck the right key," he found, when he observed "a pleased sparkling in his eye" upon the man's hearing a quotation from Shakespeare. "This afforded me a little insight into his peculiarities," Nordhoff explained, "which I failed not to take advantage of. I talked *books* with him, and here I found his one vulnerable point," and the young Nordhoff "pestered him with questions" until he received the answers he sought.[53]

For his own part, he allowed that the Australians seemed to appreciate his own character as "somewhat of a silent person." Nordhoff, though warmly sympathetic at times, could also hold himself aloof, perhaps a strategy borne of caution that enabled him to accommodate the volatile tempers and circumstances with which he surrounded himself. Even at the height of his career, as the nation's best-paid Washington correspondent in the 1880s, his private gregariousness and striking sense of humor were unknown to those outside his circle, who regarded him as a bookish, "exclusive" Teuton.[54] He would draw other people out with ceaseless inquiries, and yet he always resisted having his own privacy invaded.

Nordhoff repeated many of the "yarns" told him by other sailors, some of them with pointed political implications to the United States of 1855. In one, a Spaniard had told of sailing on a slaver, commanded by a murderous captain under false colors. This captain cared little about life, according to the Spanish sailor, and made the voyage hard enough for the sailors before the mast. "But the hold, boys, oh, it was horrible," Nordhoff remembered him saying.

> The stench was enough to knock one down. And the constant moaning, and the pitiful looks of the poor wretches, as they reclined, one on the top of the other's legs, (so closely they were stowed) haunted me for many a day afterwards. ...Our

52.   CN, *Merchant Vessel*, 180.
53.   CN, *Merchant Vessel*, 215.
54.   See, for example, "National News Spinners," Brooklyn [NY] *Times*, January 22, 1887.

cargo had begun to die off, and now every morning watch we were obliged to go below, and unlinking the dead from the living, drag the emaciated corpses upon deck, and toss them over to leeward.[55]

Within his own experience, Nordhoff recalled the slave labor on the salt flats of Dutch-controlled Venezuela. "The Dutch are proverbially hard masters," he wrote. "I could scarcely believe that human beings could so badly use their fellow creatures…." The overseer "carried a long and heavy rawhide whip, which he applied with no sparing or light hand to the naked backs of women and men, if they did not trot off fast enough with their heavy burden." Furthermore, he noted, they were allowed only one meal per day, kept in a "state of semi-starvation … cruel in the extreme."

> The daily allowance of food to each working person is *one quart of unground corn*, and nothing else. This allowance I saw measured out to them myself, ere I could believe that any one would be so niggardly as to force working men and women to exist on such a mere pittance…. They are actually famished. Parties of them used to fight for the leavings of our cabin table, and fish-bones, potato peelings, slop of all kinds, were voraciously devoured by them. Poor souls, they lost no occasion to steal victuals that happened to be unwatched…. We often connived at their thefts, but our stingy captain was ever upon the watch to catch them in the act.[56]

He catalogued the slaves' other miseries: too few clothes, no shoes or sunhats, women forced to curtail nursing of their children to return to work. When later, as a writer for a prominent New York newspaper, he would hear similar stories from newly freed American slaves, Nordhoff did not doubt their veracity.

However preferable the merchant marine was to the navy, Nordhoff soon learned that it was similarly no life by which to see the world. The poverty of most sailors, the status-bound and insecure work, could not be easily overcome. It was not surprising, he wrote, that most sailors were eager to leave shore almost as soon as they arrived upon it. "Having no friends," he explained, "and debarred by his calling and his dress, if not by lack of education, from intercourse with any but those of his own class, a few days suffice to tire him of

---

55. CN, *Merchant Vessel*, 51–2, 56.

56. CN, *Merchant Vessel*, 280–284.

the stupid amusements into which he is dragged…."[57] Aside from the sailor's marginalized status, the thin margin of security with which he left one ship forced him almost immediately to sign on for work on another. The sailor "visits places of the greatest interest, but finds the circumstances which control him such as to deprive him of all the pleasures he had anticipated from his voyage." At one point, frustrated upon finding himself impelled to take a ship bound for Rio and Boston, where he did not wish to go, he wrote in retrospect that

> I was forced to confess to myself that the object I had had
> in view in coming to the East Indies had been very poorly
> fulfilled. I was bitterly disappointed when I thought that
> although I had been in Calcutta and Madras, I knew but
> little more of either place than if I had never seen them. That
> though I had made another voyage to China, I was but little
> wiser than before. That after all the hardship and trouble
> seen and suffered since I left the United States, … I was no
> more satisfied with the little I had seen than I was before I set
> out upon this voyage…. In truth I was learning by experience
> that of all travelers the sailor sees the least, and pays most
> dearly for it.[58]

Still, he could not give up. "With an obstinacy worthy, perhaps, a better cause," he continued, "I determined to make one more trial." He signed on for the passage to Rio on the *Ariadne*. Once in Rio, he could not even muster the strength to walk around the town in the evenings, kept busy all day as he was loading bags of coffee on board ship and frightened by rumors of Brazilian press-gangs roaming the wharves at night.[59] In an effort to counteract the popular image of the happy-go-lucky sailor, Nordhoff stressed the difficulties and disabilities that he and his shipmates were forced to endure. The work was severe, the responsibilities heavy, his pay barely enough to support him between voyages, and "he is no sooner on shore than he feels harassed by the necessity of hunting up a new ship."[60]

After returning to America, Nordhoff was relieved to find work on a ship heading for the tropics. It was, nevertheless, a trip custom-made to sour him forever on the merchant service; for the *Swain* was an ancient barely seaworthy vessel, its forecastle filled with a block of ice that engulfed the sailors' berths.

---

57. CN, *Merchant Vessel*, 184.

58. CN, *Merchant Vessel*, 247.

59. CN, *Merchant Vessel*, 254.

60. CN, *Merchant Vessel*, 259.

The ship was also undermanned, and it leaked. The captain failed to lay in sufficient provisions, and the crew was put on short rations that left them exhausted.[61]

Although sailors "dislike to go to law," Nordhoff commented, with a "dread of land-sharks," the crew of the *Swain* felt it their duty "to show this man, and others of his kind, that they could be held up to justice"; and back in the port of New Orleans, they took the captain to court. Once again, however, justice proved elusive and costly to the sailors, as the lawsuit lasted six weeks during which they could not earn their living while they remained on land. Finally, the captain was found guilty of "gross misconduct" and was ordered to pay fifty dollars to each member of the crew. It was small recompense, however. "We had been compelled to remain six weeks idle," Nordhoff noted, missing the good season for shipping in New Orleans, spending their earnings to pay their board, "and had now some difficulty in getting a ship. All to satisfy justice." As he sardonically concluded, the sailors had "many disrespectful remarks … concerning the blind Dame," and "departed the court-room, fully determined never again to appeal to her, but rather to take the law into our own hands."[62]

Finally fed up with the merchant service, Nordhoff made his next destination New Bedford, Massachusetts, the whaling capital of New England. He had considered signing on for a whaling cruise, and when he was repeatedly told that nobody would hire a seasoned sailor for such a long trip, it "had the effect of adding much strength to my at first but weakly entertained wish." Whether it indicated the love of a challenge or pure obstinacy, Nordhoff admitted that the "more insurmountable seemed the difficulties…, the more earnestly it took hold of my mind."[63]

By lying about his experience, Nordhoff was able to get a berth on a whaler that was about to set out for the Indian Ocean. Whaling masters preferred "green hands" because the typical whaling voyage lasted three years, and an experienced sailor would have the wherewithal and confidence to desert ship at any time, any place—while landlubbers would be less sure of being able to make their way in a strange country. Accordingly, Nordhoff found himself surrounded not by the usual seasoned sailors, whom he had learned to respect, but by a "motley crew" of incompetents. They included clerks, factory workers, farm boys, and other men inexperienced at sea, along with four Portuguese whalemen, "and the writer hereof, who wrote himself *seaman*."[64] Except for "one

---

61. CN, *Merchant Vessel*, 262–279.

62. CN, *Merchant Vessel*, 286–8.

63. CN, *Whaling and Fishing* (Dodd, Mead: 1895 edition, originally published in 1855), 21.

64. CN, *Whaling*, 47.

schoolboy, who knew everything, and was therefore unbearable," most of the crew was ill-educated and gullible. The neophytes promptly got seasick and kept to their berths for the first three days of the passage.

By the 1850s, whaling, and sea life in general, had been used by a variety of writers for literary and aesthetic effects—the circumscribed world of the shipboard community in counterpoise with the fathomless ocean, serving writers like Melville to frame meditations on life, brotherhood, the obligations of society, and the demands of coexistence in a world of differences.[65] Nordhoff, in contrast, constructed a world in *Whaling and Fishing* that depended on verisimilitude and an antiromantic stance to convey his own ideas of the good society. Already, his future career as a journalist was foretold in his books on the seafaring life: with a good eye for detail and an ear for the way people actually talked, he felt that "truth," well-portrayed, as he tried to do, was always more telling than fiction—for his purposes, at least. Firmly rooted in the here and now, he saw it as a duty to convey in his work the uglier aspects of a realm he had seen much romanticized. He believed that fiction had led him astray, for had not sea stories by Marryat and Cooper first planted in his mind the idea of going to sea?

And so he launched into description of his one cruise on a whaler with a cold eye. The green hands had to be taught to climb the rigging, to eat the usual bad food, to learn the names of various elements of the "tops," and even to develop their "sea legs." But the greatest shock to them was the effect of the rigid hierarchical arrangements of life on board ship—something to which Nordhoff had by then become inured. The inexperienced men had difficulty in adjusting to "the difference in rank, and consequent difference in physical comforts, which prevail on ship board." The officers had more and pleasanter living space; their food was better than that of the foremast hands. These neophytes could not grasp "how, under a republican flag," they could be prevented from even standing on the quarterdeck and being relegated to "the wretched hole forward of the windlass, as their appropriate 'sphere'-- all this," Nordhoff noted, "...the unsophisticated country man, brought up in the belief

---

[65]. Literary critics have written with considerable interest of the themes that may have reached their apotheosis in Melville's *Moby Dick* and *Billy Budd*, and informative works include: James Philbrick, *James Fenimore Cooper and the Development of Sea Fiction* (Cambridge: Harvard University Press, 1961); Bert Bender, *Sea-Brothers: The Tradition of American Sea Fiction from Moby-Dick to the Present* (Philadelphia: University of Pennsylvania, 1988); Robert K. Martin, *Hero, Captain, Stranger: Male Friendship, Social Critique, and Literary Form in the Novels of Herman Melville* (Chapel Hill: University of North Carolina Press, 1986).

that 'one man is as good as another,' can never properly understand, although he is obliged to submit."[66]

Nordhoff knew that shipboard life was undemocratic and even un-American, but his own realization of its unfairness was counterbalanced by his sense of its inevitability. He knew better than to expect "liberty" upon their reaching their first port in the Azores, though the new hands were angry enough to speak of deserting ship. "I had long since become hardened to such disappointments," Nordhoff wrote.

> ...I think the life of a man before the mast is calculated to make a stoic of any one. In no other condition that I know of, are all the hopes, aims and desires of one man placed so completely in the keeping of another—whose interests furthermore almost invariably clash with those of his subject. Nowhere else are the keenest desires so invariably doomed to disappointment—in no other situation is one obliged, for peace of mind's sake, to become so utterly apathetic. The fact is, sailors should be brutes—not men.[67]

As for his shipmates—they might have been men, but with the exception of the Portuguese—Nordhoff found them "dissipated," prone to "depravity and vice." The Portuguese were solid sailors, and they had a goal in life, which was to earn enough from whaling to at last settle down with their families in their homeland. To Nordhoff, they were "the only individuals ... with whom I could associate with any degree of pleasure."[68]

Although sailing was a hard life, Nordhoff had always derived sustenance from the close communities that developed on board ship. On the whaler, even this redemptive feature was missing. His companions earned his hearty contempt for their incompetence and affectation. "I, in virtue of being a *real, genuine tar,* despised these fellows from the bottom of my heart; and it must be owned," he added, "they hated me with a fervor which was only equaled by its powerlessness."[69] Even after many months of working together, the bond formed among the crew was weaker than most, and when two men died of malaria in Madagascar, their mates' grief was relatively short-lived. "Our crew were not seamen," Nordhoff judged; they lacked the "finer traits of character" of true

66. CN, *Whaling*, 53.
67. CN, *Whaling*, 59.
68. CN, *Whaling*, 60–61.
69. CN, *Whaling and Fishing*, 61, 63.

sailors. "They were selfish" and incapable of developing the strong affection for one another that merchant seamen often did.[70]

And the work itself, in preparation for reaching the whaling grounds, was "wearisome drudgery," largely maintenance work. Their first encounter with a small species of whale, the blackfish, proved a frustrating experience. Hours of rowing after the animals was exhausting work, and Nordhoff concluded that "although doubtless it is high sport to the black-fish, it is anything but fun" to the sailors engaged in chasing them. "[J]ust before we got within darting distance, ... the provoking fellows would toss their heads and disappear from view beneath the water," he explained. Then the sailors would "hear a puff immediately behind us, and lo! there they lay, at heads and points, like a lot of overgrown pickled herring." Whaling, to Nordhoff's jaded eyes, was turning out to be more ludicrous than romantic.[71]

A conversation with the captain seconded his opinion.

> "It's a wretched business," said the old man, seriously—"a wretched business. ...[A]s I grow old, my desire to stay at home with my family increases, and it seems like tearing one's heartstrings to depart on a cruise with the probability of being gone four long years. I have been five voyages," he continued...."In fifteen years of my whaling life, I have spent just seventeen months at home. I have never been present at a birth or death in my family."[72]

Nordhoff had just passed his twenty-first birthday. He was no longer an adolescent, and sailing had become more than a youthful fling. The captain's view, borne of long experience, depressed him. The captain's picture was "a sober, sad reality," Nordhoff admitted. "It was the review of a life ... of energies wasted, purposes defeated, and bright hopes withered" and brought Nordhoff a pang of homesickness. "In short," he went on, "I was getting 'blue,' blue as the azure sky overhead, but not near so cheerful."[73] In the absence of congenial companions and with nothing of interest to occupy his mind, he began to take a harder look at his chosen life than ever before, and he did not like what he saw. It troubled him.

When they reached the whale grounds near Madagascar, the crew members were not required to do any work at all other than to seek out whales. Although

---

[70]. CN, *Whaling*, 215–216.
[71]. CN, *Whaling*, 68.
[72]. CN, *Whaling*, 77.
[73]. CN, *Whaling*, 77–78.

at first they appreciated the freedom from drudgery, within a week, the sailors grew bored. Nordhoff was alarmed at the implications, as he remembered the "wandering, lackluster look" of old whalemen he had seen ashore. The whaleman's "mind has been gradually killed," he deduced, "by lack of use."[74] He kept his own mind occupied with observations of the local wildlife. Natural history was to be a lifelong interest of Nordhoff's; and as they searched for whales, he developed a keen appreciation of the antics of schools of porpoises, nautilus, and even fugitive whales. It was with relief, nevertheless, that he marked their first sighting of a sperm whale off the West African Coast. "All was life and bustle," he reported, as they prepared for a hunt, "and the stagnant pools of our blood were once more enlivened by a little excitement."[75]

The crew fanned out in boats to pursue the whales, Nordhoff serving as one of the oarsmen in the first mate's boat. One of their number managed to harpoon a whale, which sounded, reappeared, and fled. The boat, attached by the harpoon line to the whale, was dragged behind the injured animal; and for nearly eight hours, they continued to pursue it until finally the mate was able to lance its side. They were out of sight of the ship and all the other boats when the whale, in its agony, plunged headfirst beneath the waves,

> in the motion striking his flukes against the boat's bottom, and breaking two or three planks. No sooner had he felt [the boat], however, than turning..., he returned to the surface head foremost, open-mouthed, striking and thrusting with his long, slender jaw, as though it were a sword. One blow from this jaw stove in the whole bow of the boat, and she filled and turned over, almost before we could leap into the water.[76]

Clinging to their oars and the wreckage of the boat, the crew anxiously watched the whale's motions, fearing that it might swamp them all in its death throes. An hour later, another boat from their ship approached, which the whale also attacked before the creature got loose and fled for good.[77]

They did, eventually, succeed in killing their first whale, which was chained securely for the night; and Nordhoff looked forward to experiencing the next step in the process: "cutting in" the blubber.[78]

---

74. CN, *Whaling*, 95.
75. CN, *Whaling*, 95–100.
76. CN, *Whaling*, 108–9.
77. CN, *Whaling*, 110–111.
78. CN, *Whaling*, 113–122.

He described the process coolly. First the head was cut off, then the "blanket pieces" stripped from the carcass and hauled onto the ship, the jawbone severed and used for ivory, while sharks ("sea-lawyers") gathered about the bloody remains in the water. Once the whale was thus dismantled, fires in the tryworks were lit and the crew started chopping up the flesh. Given the task of cutting up blubber from the animal's head, Nordhoff was struck by its size. "This huge cube of nearly nine feet," he marveled, "was only a portion, perhaps a fair half of his *head*." He pondered, "as I slashed away at it, my puny strokes seeming like those of an ant nibbling at an apple," the enormous bulk the entire animal would have had. There was little time for such thoughts, for soon the "trying-out" began, the blubber being rendered into oil.[79]

It was an infernal scene. "The flames, darting high above the try-works, revealed the masts, rigging and decks, in an unearthly glare," as Nordhoff described it, "among which the men jumping or sliding about decks …, seemed like demons dancing about an incantation fire. But with this picture all the romance departs." Lest his readers fall into the same illusions as he had, he drew a vivid picture of the grimy, greasy business. "The smell of the burning cracklings is too horribly nauseous for description," he wrote. "It is as though all the ill odors in the world were gathered together." With oil sloshing over the deck, it became impossible to walk about, "and the safest mode of locomotion is sliding from place to place, on the seat of your pantaloons."[80]

Oil permeated everything: there was no escape from it. "Shirts and trowsers are dripping with the loathsome stuff. The pores of the skin seem to be filled with it. Feet, hands and hair, all are full. The biscuit you eat glistens with oil," he went on. "The knife with which you eat, leaves upon the morsel, which nearly chokes you as you reluctantly swallow it, plain traces of the abominable blubber," and "you are compelled to breathe in the fetid smoke of the scrap fires, until you feel as though filth had struck into your blood, and suffused every vein in your body."[81]

And yet it seemed to Nordhoff that greed overcame the others' natural revulsion. "It is horrible," he pronounced. "Yet old whalemen delight in it. The fetid smoke is incense to their nostrils. The filthy oil seems … a glorious representative of prospective dollars and delights." In contrast to Melville's lyrical depiction of whalemen grasping hands as they worked in the blubber, an emblem of brotherhood with the men joined together in an almost sexual ecstasy, Nordhoff recounted fishing out pieces of decaying meat from a barrel as the ultimate horror. Leaning into the cask, breathing in "the noisome stench,"

---

79. CN, *Whaling*, 125–128.
80. CN, *Whaling*, 128.
81. CN, *Whaling*, 128–9.

one had to "feel around with his hands, to grasp the slimy morsels which are not fit for the try-kettles." And still the lure of gold, rather than any human bond, seemed to Nordhoff to keep the others happy in their work. He worked alongside the captain in one cask, but after half an hour, he "was obliged to say that I could not stand it longer. I was deathly sick. 'That's nothing, Charley,' said [the captain], 'just fancy it's dollars you are groping among, and the matter will assume a very different odor.'" Nordhoff could not agree. "I thought that too high a price for dollars." Thus ended his first experience with stowing down whale oil.[82]

Another whale was caught and rendered, and then several monotonous weeks of inactivity followed, weeks of such crashing boredom that Nordhoff began to brood about the effect of such inactivity upon the human mind and spirit. He watched himself with alarm for any sign that he too was adopting "that absent, awkward habit" that he had noticed among old whalemen, and he decided that he could take no more. At their first port, "I would take my leave of whaling—not conceiving that I was bound to remain where I plainly saw that both mind and body would wilt away."[83]

There were always inquiries and investigations to be made, however, to a man of Nordhoff's insatiable curiosity. On one occasion, in attempting to "examine the internal economy of an ant's nest," he had to leap into the water to rid himself of a swarm of ants, but his interest in natural history continued unabated.[84] He once more took to quizzing his shipmates, this time for all they knew of whales, until they "sometimes declared me to be an arrant bore." If he had an anthropological bent, in looking into human societies, he similarly pieced together an ethnography of the sperm whale: their diets, their means of defending themselves, their physiology. He began to root for the whales. As they chased after one near Mauritius, he "could not help giving the wretched animal credit for great intelligence" in eluding their harpoons.[85] When they resorted to the stratagem of harpooning a female that would not abandon its calf, Nordhoff noted the mother's solicitousness toward its young. They felt, he remarked, "as though we were taking a dishonorable advantage" of the whale, but their scruples did not keep the crew from continually poking the calf with a lance to propel it and its mother toward the ship. They eventually killed the whale, but before they were able to cut its blubber in, it was eaten by sharks.[86]

---

82. CN, *Whaling*, 131.

83. CN, *Whaling*, 156–8.

84. CN, *Whaling*, 207–8.

85. CN, *Whaling*, 159–165.

86. CN, *Whaling*, 188–190.

Nordhoff was not the only dissatisfied man aboard the ship, but inexperienced sailors also had no alternative but to stay with the cruise, having no prospects of finding other work in a strange port. If the others were trapped, he was not, and he planned to jump ship in the Seychelles.[87] Nordhoff planned his own escape as carefully as any fugitive slave and with as much secrecy. A French ship's captain agreed to take him on, and he hired a local boatman to carry him out to the other ship under cover of darkness. They waited for nightfall in a hut near the shore. Before he could board the *Hercule*, a search party from the whaler was sent to look for Nordhoff there while he remained noiselessly in the canoe until the Americans completed their search. Then Nordhoff climbed aboard. "With a light heart I bounded to the masthead...," he recounted, "and in a very short time we were out of the harbor--and I was once more a free man." Here the parallel was made explicit: the "state of subjection in which men are kept on a whaleship," he stated, "...becomes nothing less than the most abject slavery."[88]

The next day, he acquainted himself with his new crew mates. They numbered fifteen and "were of all shades of black, from charcoal to dark brown," natives of Mauritius or the Seychelles, and less sailors than laborers and herdsmen. As soon as the captain learned that Nordhoff could sew, he set him to work mending sail, and Nordhoff had "a not uncomfortable place on board." But he was bemused by the crew's attitude toward him. "The only thing against me was my color," he wrote.

> To my misfortune I was the whitest man on board, and with the exception of the captain and chief mate, the only one who was purely white. This caused me to be looked down upon by my black friends, who, when I would commit any little extravagance, such as making myself a wooden spoon wherewith to eat my rice, ...or washing my hands and face at the close of a day's work, shrugged their shoulders in pitying contempt, and declared that nothing better was to be expected from a man of my color.

Certainly, in the racially charged 1850s, derogatory comments as to what one might expect of African-Americans were common among white Americans, and the condescension extended toward Nordhoff by the African crew members resonated with echoes of white Americans' racism. Despite his odd behavior, Nordhoff wrote, since he was hardworking and "always disposed to converse

---

87.   CN, *Whaling*, 170–173, 235–45.
88.   CN, *Whaling*, 247–50.

to the best of my ability, they voted me in the main a good fellow, much better than the common run of white folks." Because he had his own "opinion as to their merits," he added, "I could afford to be amused at their ideas of me." His meaning is ambiguous. Did he mean to suggest the folly of racist thinking? Or was this merely an amusing inversion of the natural order of things, quaint in the assumptions the natives expressed of white inferiority? He clearly felt himself superior to the black horse tenders of the *Hercule*, but whether he recognized this as racially based or not is questionable.[89]

As he often did, Nordhoff concealed his feelings when it was tactically expedient—almost to the verge of hypocrisy. "I had long ago learned the propriety in such cases, of laughing with the crowd," he remarked, "and practiced largely upon this theory now," but with "an occasional internal malediction on the stupidity of these fellows, who could so easily ignore all knowledge not possessed by them."[90]

The easygoing French captain promoted an "indolent, half-dreamy state" on board his ship; and Nordhoff, used to more demanding task-masters, "would have labored from eight till six, … but this was not suffered," and he relaxed. "I enjoyed the life exceedingly," he acknowledged, and contemplated making Mauritius his permanent home. When they reached the harbor of Port Louis, the unloading of the ship was postponed so that the returning natives might enjoy a day with their families. The reunions between crew members and their loved ones made Nordhoff realize how solitary, and lonely, he had become.[91]

"I alone had no friends to greet me, no one to rejoice in my return," he wrote; he reacted defensively and "began in the selfishness of my heart mentally to find fault with all about me, and more than half wished I had not come to Port Louis." His dark mood was soon interrupted. A young woman, whom he likened to the goddess of springtime, saw him sulking.

> As I sat apart, …feeling, and I dare say looking very dreary, a brown Hebe approached me, inquired, in broken English, "You got no friends, Jack?" "Not a friend," said I, in a gruff tone, as not thinking it desirable to have my loneliness commented upon by strangers. Watching me rather dubiously for a moment, she held out her hand, and said in a voice full of serious kindness, "Well, I be your friend, Jack."

---

89. CN, *Whaling*, 252.

90. CN, *Whaling*, 252.

91. CN, *Whaling*, 255.

His stubborn pride dissolved at this. "I did not put my arms around her neck and kiss her, as I should have done had I followed the impulse of my heart," he remembered. "But I thanked her deeply for all the sympathy." Angelique's brother, also named Charles, had been a member of the crew of the *Hercule*, but he had been lost at sea. She was "overjoyed" at befriending another Charles, "and in the simplicity of her heart at once pronounced our meeting Providential." Though there were doubtless prostitutes roaming the docks, in Nordhoff's account, Angelique offered only sisterly friendship; he later attended her wedding to another native of the island.[92]

Hired by the captain of the *Hercule* as a ferryman between his plantation and the town, Nordhoff settled into a peaceful, restful life on Mauritius, still observing, comparing, and judging his surroundings. Although the French, while they possessed the island earlier in the century, had made slaves of the Madagassy, under its current British rule, all the slaves had been freed. But all was not well. Indentured East Indians had taken over the hard work that the slaves had once performed, "poor people," Nordhoff pronounced, paid too little and "treated much worse than slaves." The result was a nightmare of social dislocation. The Indians would "become low spirited, and not unfrequently commit suicide." They would run away from the plantations, to be hunted down by policemen; any Indian seen on the streets was ordered to show papers documenting his right to be free, and if he could not, he would be imprisoned. "On the plantations the lash is freely used," Nordhoff continued, with a humanitarianism not unalloyed by racism, to "extort" labor from "these poorly paid, ill fed and naturally indolent people," and he likened their condition to slavery, with the added sin of hypocrisy, disguising the nature of such servitude as "apprenticeship".[93] Nordhoff believed he himself had been lured into something near slavery under false pretenses, and his sympathy for the indentured Indians was real enough, whatever his beliefs about their "natural indolence." All his life, he would veer between an egalitarian insistence that all people deserved equal opportunities and an uneasy suspicion that not all people could cope equally well with them. His travels as a young man early impressed him, however, with the evil that the powerful were capable of inflicting on the weak, and his usual response was to side with the underdog— for he had been in that role himself as a sailor, "a dog," as Commodore Elliott had warned him years before, "for everyone to kick at."

The British claimed "Malabar town" was a vice-ridden hellhole, but Nordhoff, firmly entrenched by now in his skepticism and in his need to investigate matters and make up his own mind, made several forays into the

92.   CN, *Whaling*, 258–9.
93.   CN, *Whaling*, 265–266.

area on his own. The community of the imported Indians was solid enough, testament to what these people might make of themselves given an equal chance, and he tried to take it on its own terms. "Here each family gathers about the door of its hut," as he recorded the scene,

> and listens to songs, or the music of the mandolin, the women talking, the men silently smoking.... Maidens dance upon the green sward, and little naked children play about the doors. All is a scene of quiet, peaceful enjoyment, which will convince anyone that, indolent as these people doubtless are, and intractable as they are said to be on the plantation, when left to themselves they are inoffensive, and have the elements of making of them good citizens.[94]

Nordhoff's repeated references to the "indolence" of the Africans and Asians betrayed the limitations of his cultural liberalism. Raised with the Protestant work ethic as a basic moral value, he tended to view with disapproval—if not envy—people who were not driven to work harder than their immediate needs required. He was, nevertheless, sympathetic to their basic humanity, however in need of reformation it seemed to be, and reserved an at least equivalent degree of contempt for those Europeans and Americans who would use them so badly and provide so little reward for the labor they exacted. As to the "elements of making them good citizens," which he believed them to possess, he probably viewed their stable families and (however minimal) ownership of property as hopeful signs of sound values, values that might mitigate an "indolence" that was possibly more cultural than inherent.

Still, he ranged the various races upon a hierarchical scale based upon the values of Protestant America. He contrasted the "orderliness" of the Indians with the Africans, whom he viewed as "exceedingly lazy, and much inclined to rowdyism and thieving," and the Chinese, "the most thrifty of the lower classes, ... frugal, not too honest, and exceedingly clannish." Furthermore, he noted without comment that the thriving Port Louis included "samples of almost every Asiatic, and many European and African nations." It was within this rich ethnic and racial mix that Nordhoff made his home for the next several months. "I was welcomed as though I was an old resident," he wrote, "and in a short time was established very comfortably, Angelique, who proved a dear good girl, providing as carefully for my wants as though I had been really her

---

CN, *Whaling*, 267.

brother." Race erected barriers against understanding for most people of the nineteenth century, but occasionally, Nordhoff managed to transcend them.[95]

Often the alienated observer, Nordhoff seems to have become engaged with his adopted community, his ironic edge muted. He once ferried Angelique and her friends to the cemetery on a Sunday morning, the girls "dressed in pure white, and each with an armload of flowers" while "low plaintive songs resounded from the boats across the still waters of the bay." He added, simply, that "the scene was very beautiful." Watching the young girls decorating graves, his imagination took flight. "As the maidens, in their white and flowing drapery, glided noiselessly yet cheerfully from grave to grave, doing kind offices to the resting places," they seemed to him "like a chorus of blest spirits come down to summon loved ones to their homes."[96]

Soberly, he noted that one grave—that of a sailor—was marked only by a rude wooden cross. The girls decorated this grave too with flowers, and perhaps projecting himself into the place of the dead sailor, Nordhoff considered that "in all his lonely seaman's life he had possibly never met with such kindness." Charles, now in his twenty-second year, became contemplative. "My life was now for some time happier than it had been for a long period past," he judged. "I was free: and the remembrance of my slavery on board the whaleship was yet sufficiently vivid … to make me appreciate very keenly the new liberty." He liked his work, which was easy and well-paying; he was surrounded by people who were, "if not very intelligent, …yet good, and well-meaning toward me." Angelique "bestowed upon me all the affection she had entertained for her deceased brother" and had even "prevailed upon her lover, who was captain of a little coasting schooner," to introduce him to other likely employers. He was, at last, safe, secure, and moderately comfortable.[97]

"But soon 'the demon of unrest' again stirred within me," he wrote. He liked Mauritius, but worried that his life there contained nothing "improving or elevating." And yet,

> eight years at sea had pretty effectually scotched any aspirations for a higher position which I once might have entertained. Life—the sailor's life, the only one of which I now had any well shaped idea—seemed at best but a troublesome and tiresome struggle. And so I brought myself to think the vegetative existence of a man upon an out of the way place like the Mauritius, at least better than a toilsome life in more

95. CN, *Whaling*, 261, 267–269.
96. CN, *Whaling*, 271.
97. CN, *Whaling*, 272–3.

civilized parts. Some indolence, some hopelessness, and a vehement desire for once to *enjoy* life, probably brought me to this conclusion.[98]

His ambition had been thwarted in his years before the mast, and he wrote scornfully of the romanticization of hard, thankless work. "It is all very well to theorize on the ennobling and elevating character of a perilous life," he remarked, but the sailor's life was "altogether too commonplace, too void of purpose," "its degradation … too great, its associations too wretched to leave the aspiring soul room for a better hope."[99]

Seeing no other way out, he began looking for another ship, resigned at least temporarily to his fate. Eventually, he wound up on a sleek clipper called the *Annie*, whose captain, he soon learned, deserved his reputation as a tyrant. Soon, mutiny was in the air.[100] After coming upon the other sailors plotting against the officers one afternoon, Nordhoff racked his brains for a way to prevent a scheme that promised to include murder along with lesser criminal acts. He decided to "hinder its farther progress, by showing up as clearly as I could its impracticability." This was a favorite gambit of his throughout his life: when trying to further some cause that carried, to him, great moral weight, he would argue for it on the basis of expediency. He had less faith in humanity's moral strength than in its instincts for self-preservation. Acting upon this logic, he questioned his shipmates about procuring food without the captain's credit, or what they might do about any pursuing ships, or how they could safely enter any port once the *Annie*'s fate was questioned. Calculations overcame heated tempers and thus ended "our pet conspiracy."[101]

Nordhoff's next voyage, again aboard a ship with cruel and irresponsible officers, took him to London, where he went straight to a sailors' boardinghouse and slept for twenty-two hours straight. "I was determined to return to the United States," he recalled, "and leave British vessels henceforth to British tars." He signed on to a ship bound for New York.[102]

Once again, however, an unscrupulous shipmaster embittered a voyage to Nordhoff, this time by telling him, on the day of embarkation, that he was no longer needed. Nordhoff had waited in London for three weeks for this berth, was out of money, and in desperate straits; so when the captain magnanimously offered to let him "work his passage," this he readily agreed to do. It soon

---

[98]. CN, *Whaling*, 273–74.

[99]. CN, *Whaling*, 274.

[100]. CN, *Whaling*, 286–294.

[101]. CN, *Whaling*, 295–298.

[102]. CN, *Whaling*, 333–9.

became apparent that Nordhoff and one other sailor who was also working his passage, far from being redundant, were needed to make up an adequate force on the ship, "so that by this operation, the captain was enabled to pocket the wages of two men during the passage home."[103]

And so it was that in 1853, Charles Nordhoff found himself upon the New York dock, hoping to start anew with little more than the clothes on his back. He considered the outcome of his foray into whaling with bitterness and regret, seeing "two years of my life to all appearance thrown away." Destitute and demoralized, he retreated to a boardinghouse whose owner extended him credit until, anxious for work, he accepted a place on a schooner bound for Massachusetts. Once the ship docked, Nordhoff remained on board as a caretaker, alone with himself and his books in the skipper's cabin. "I had ample time to take a cool review of the last few years of my life, and endeavor to plan out a future," he later wrote. He was twenty-three years old.

> I had, unconsciously almost, grown to man's estate. And I was now fully awakening to the fact, that in the life I was leading there was nought to elevate, everything to debase a man—that day by day, I was losing ground, and lessening my chances of ever returning to a better life. ...I was alarmed when I found how much ... I had grown into the peculiar ways of acting, and thinking even, of the genuine, irredeemable old sailor. "A change must be made," thought I. "But how?"[104]

As he contemplated the prospect of returning home to "the pitying smiles of former friends, who have ... distanced me in the race of life," his stubborn pride reasserted itself. He would not go home, not yet. Convinced that he would not soon be able to find employment on shore, he decided that he would first save up some money for the transition.

He began by working on the "coaster" between New York and Boston, but then decided that fishing was more to his liking and joined a fleet off Cape Cod, settling in at a boardinghouse in Harwich. Fishing, once the mackerel began to bite, left him with chapped and torn hands and an aching back; but initially he found it exciting, although undeniably a "business"; "sport it has ceased to be." After a few months, as autumn turned to winter, Nordhoff had saved about forty

---

[103.] CN, *Whaling*, 344.

[104.] CN, *Whaling*, 345–349. Oddly enough, he cites his age at this point as twenty-one, not twenty-three, but the chronology shows him to have been wrong, as does his chosen title for an omnibus version of his book, *Nine Years a Sailor*. Perhaps he felt so badly about misspent years that he wanted to deduct a few from the total.

dollars, and he left once more for New York to seek his fortune.[105] "It was not till this search for employment began," he wrote, "that I was made fully aware of how utterly useless a sailor is for aught, except the most severe physical toil, on shore." He worried that he had made himself "unfit" for any other life. "In New York I had no friends," he continued.

> Wherever I applied for employment, I was asked for references. Having none, it would next be asked, "What did you do last?" An acknowledgment that I had been a seaman was always productive of a speedy annihilation of my hopes. "I would like to take you," said the kindest man to whom I had occasion to apply, "but a sailor, you know, would never do for me. You would not remain a month in steady employment."[106]

Without friends or other connections in New York, Nordhoff soon abandoned that city for Philadelphia, where he had worked before sailing off on the *Columbus* so many years before. "What struggles were necessary before I was able, even here, with the assistance of friends, to gain a firm footing," he wrote, he would not describe at length; nor

> how I was on every hand met with suspicion and distrust; how no one could believe that I would remain steadily ashore; and how this very unbelief led me oft-times to think seriously of returning to my sea life--doubting myself, because others doubted me.

He finally procured work as a printer, but not before being deeply impressed with the bounds that were everywhere placed around him and by extension around all the sailors and all the common laborers, who might cherish hopes of improving their lives in America. After "a struggle through which I would not like again to pass," he concluded, "I at length proved to doubting friends that there is redemption for even a sailor."[107] Before many years had passed, his life would change dramatically, as he rose to the pinnacle of American journalism. No more would he be "a dog for everyone to kick at," but to the end of his days, he could not forget those years. He was then, and to himself would always be, a workingman.

[105.] CN, *Whaling*, 351–82.

[106.] CN, *Whaling*, 382–3.

[107.] CN, *Whaling*, 383.

CHAPTER 2

The Sphinx-Riddle of Life

"I think few men set out on their life-work, if it be any thing higher than mere selfish toil, with any clear ideas of what they are to do," Charles Nordhoff commented a few years after leaving the sea.[1] He had by then spent some time casting about in his own search for a vocation that might satisfy both his morals and his ambitions. It did not take him long to find his lifework. It lay in journalism, which, at least initially, proved to be a congenial and rewarding field.

Within seven years of leaving menial work at sea, Nordhoff had become a principal editor for one of the most influential newspapers in the country. He held this position at the New York *Evening Post* for ten years. It proved to be a prime vantage point from which to survey a nation at war with itself and to strengthen his already firmly held convictions concerning politics, democracy, and community, all of which were encompassed by the free-labor ideology of the early Republican Party. As an editor and occasional reporter, he was able to "preach," as he called it, on behalf of a wide variety of causes, most effectively when he was able to back his arguments in the detailed anthropological style that was to become a hallmark of his best writing. Journalism fulfilled its true mission, he was convinced, when the journalist, informed and engaged in the issues of the day, was not content merely to describe events, but to "breathe a soul of meaning" into them. At the *Evening Post* during the Civil War years, he sharpened his ability to do exactly that.

When Charles Nordhoff stepped ashore in New York in 1853, he was determined to put his life as a sailor behind him; and after some months fishing

---

[1.] Charles Nordhoff, "A Struggle for Life," *Cape Cod and All Along Shore: Stories* (Freeport: Books for Libraries Press, 1970), reprint of 1868 Harper's edition, 110. Although *Cape Cod* was published in 1868, the stories appeared in various periodicals at various times during the previous decade, and not all dates of original publication have been established.

off Cape Cod, he had saved enough money to move on at last. After his initial struggle to find work, he landed a job as a printer, making use of the skills he had learned as a teenager, and moved to the Midwest.[2]

He had no intention of remaining a printer all his life. Having no capital, Nordhoff soon made capital out of his experiences as a sailor, writing three books about them that were published in 1855. These books, he stated in the prefaces, were meant to deter other young men from being seduced as he had been by romanticized accounts of life at sea. Describing the exploitation he had suffered must have been a cathartic experience, but the books, critically as well as popularly successful, also proved to be an effective springboard to the headier literary circles of New York City.[3]

For a few years after the publication of the sailor books, Nordhoff lived and worked in Cincinnati, the home of his foster father and his future wife. A vital German-American community in Ohio supported various German-language newspapers and periodicals there, and Nordhoff may have found work with one of them, fluent as he was in his native tongue. He also published several

[2.]   Allan Nevins, *Evening Post* (NY: Boni & Liveright, 1922), mentions Nordhoff's printing job for the Philadelphia *Register*, and although his text is not footnoted, he evidently interviewed several of Nordhoff's contemporaries. "Charles Nordhoff," New York *Evening Post*, December 7, 1901, p. 25, states that Nordhoff worked for the Indianapolis *Sentinel*. Nordhoff himself, in *Reminiscences of Some Editors I Have Known* (San Diego: 1900), mentions his stint in the Middle West. In "Letters to Wage Workers," published in the New York *Herald* on July 14, 1895, he wrote that he had done "many other kinds of hard work, farming in the West among them."

[3.]   The three books, *Man-of-War Life, The Merchant Vessel*, and *Whaling and Fishing* were published simultaneously in Cincinnati by Moore, Wiltach, Keys & Company, and by the well-established Dodd, Mead & Company in New York. They were frequently reprinted and, according to Nevins in the *Evening Post* (p. 316), read by "hundreds of thousands." Eight editions of *Man-of-War Life*, five of *The Merchant Vessel*, and four of *Whaling and Fishing* appeared between 1855 and 1895. They also appeared in omnibus form, as *Nine Years a Sailor* and under other titles, four times in the United States and five times in Edinburgh before the turn of the century. In 1940 and 1941, abridged editions were published in New York and London (not surprisingly, while his eponymous grandson was at the height of his fame as a coauthor of the *Mutiny on the Bounty* trilogy). Blurbs from reviews were included as a preface to the 1874 omnibus, *Life on the Ocean* (London: MacDonald and Jane's, 1974 reprint) including reviews from the New York *Tribune*, *Harper's Monthly*, the Washington *Star*, the New York *Times*, the Louisville *Courier*, the Boston *Traveler*, and several Protestant denominational journals, most emphasizing the verisimilitude of description as well as the morals pointed by the tales.

essays in a nationally distributed magazine, *The Ladies' Repository*, edited by a Methodist minister with abolitionist leanings.[4]

Within a year of the publication of *Man-of-War Life*, Nordhoff signed a contract with Harper & Brothers for a "small book for children," *Stories of the Island World*, which presented conventional sketches of various tropical locales. Back in the pious milieu of Midwestern evangelical Christianity, Nordhoff had taken on a more judgmental tone toward other cultures than was apparent in the sailor trilogy: *Stories of the Island World* was essentially a paean to the Christian missionaries who attempted to convert "savages" and was a cliché-ridden work lacking the immediacy and heart of the earlier books. Nordhoff was always at his best as a reporter, a kind of early anthropologist, the strength of his arguments drawn from detailed, factual exposé; and although he was a perceptive and intelligent observer, he could lapse into conventional, almost mechanical literary devices and unexamined assumptions when writing of matters he did not know at first hand.[5]

In New York in 1856 to sign the contract for *Stories of the Island World*, Nordhoff met Fletcher Harper for the first time, the beginning of a lifelong association with the Harpers' publishing empire. Fletcher Harper has been credited with expanding the firm's book-publishing business, as well as creating *Harper's Monthly Magazine* and *Harper's Weekly*, two vastly different but equally successful periodicals. At the time of Nordhoff's visit, Harper was putting together a staff for the *Weekly*, and the young author appeared well-suited for an editorial slot at the firm. As Nordhoff remembered it, Harper had asked him why he was returning to Ohio. "I replied because I could find nothing to do in New York," Nordhoff answered, and Harper then and there offered him a position with "no specific duties." Nordhoff accepted. "The offer was too important to be refused," as he said. But with a certain prideful defensiveness, he told Harper that "if you don't like me ... you must agree to tell me so, and I'll leave at any time, and at a day's notice." It proved an unnecessary offer.[6]

[4.] See *The Ladies Repository*, volumes 15 through 17, for Nordhoff's articles. Information on the editor, Davis W. Clark, was supplied by the Cincinnati Historical Society. For information on the intellectual milieu Nordhoff found himself within, see Loyd D. Easton, "German Philosophy in Nineteenth Century Cincinnati—Stallo, Conway, Nast and Willich," *Bulletin of the Cincinnati Historical Society*, 20 #1 (January 1962): 15–28.

[5.] CN, *Stories of the Island World* (NY: Harper & Brothers, 1857). The contract is in the Harper & Brothers Papers, Columbia University Library, Contract Book #1:317, and is also characterized by Nordhoff in *Reminiscences of Some Editors I Have Known* (San Diego: 1901), 3.

[6.] CN, *Reminiscences*, 4. On Harper, see James Glen Stovall, "Fletcher Harper," *Dictionary of Literary Biography*, volume 79 (Detroit: Gale Research Inc., 1988),

Nordhoff moved to New York to begin his new job in early 1857 at the Harpers' huge establishment at Franklin Square. The Harpers publishing house was central to American commercial publishing, thanks in large part to Fletcher Harper's keen sense of popular taste and an unparalleled marketing and distribution network. The publisher was known to have been churning out ninety thousand volumes per week in 1853. The house employed notable litterateurs, including James Russell Lowell and George William Curtis, both of whom became early mentors to Nordhoff, who would remember both of them with gratitude forty years later despite very real political differences that had grown up between them in the intervening years.[7]

Placed in this enviable situation, Nordhoff felt, he later wrote, "as uncomfortable as a very young cat in a very strange garret." Fletcher and the other Harper brothers were kind employers, paternalistic toward their employees in days when there were few institutional buffers against misfortune, and Nordhoff delighted in Fletcher Harper's low-keyed good humor. "He was a most lovely character," he later recalled, "unpretentious, kind, considerate to all in his employ." But Nordhoff's job was ill-defined, and while he was anxious to please, he wasn't quite sure how to do so; his scanty education and working-class background undermined his confidence. His duties ranged from abstracting foreign-language newspapers to writing occasional light essays for the *Monthly* to reading incoming manuscripts, but his apparent competence did not allay his self-doubt. When one successful writer confided to Nordhoff his own background as an orphan, solely dependent on himself from an early age, the younger man wrote him a mournful letter of thanks for the "strengthening" history. "Sometimes the matter looks dark," he added. At the suggestion of an editor (probably Curtis), "whose kindness to a very depressed young man I have never forgotten," he began to "gut" books, providing reviews that were more summaries than critiques, and this not only provided good copy for the magazines, but also gave Nordhoff an education that more than made up for his lack of formal schooling. Still, he was acutely aware of his anomalous background and status, and even as he became more and more firmly established in the highest circles of politics and journalism, he would

---

174–180; Eugene Exman, *The House of Harper* (NY: Harper & Row, 1967) and *The Brothers Harper* (NY: Harper & Row, 1965); and J. Henry Harper, *The House of Harper* (NY.: Harper & Brothers, 1912).

7.   CN, *Reminiscences*, 4; CN to Charles Eliot Norton, January 26, 1893 and November 19, 1893, Norton Papers, Houghton Library, Harvard University.

forever remain the outsider who had clambered to an uncomfortable perch on the inside.[8]

When he had become certain that his job with the Harpers was secure, despite the deepening depression of 1857–8, Nordhoff returned to Cincinnati in August of 1857 to marry Eliza Letford. Lida, as he called her, was then eighteen years old, educated in the manner of the day at a women's college. Their first child, a son, was born the following summer and christened Charles Walter. Nordhoff loved children, once they were capable of some sort of conversation; he was affectionate and attentive to them and took them seriously, probably appreciating their unpretentiousness, one of the highest of virtues in his eyes. But with babies he had little to do or say, and as he wrote to his in-laws of Lida's safe emergence from the dangerous ordeal of childbirth, he could only report that the baby was, "everybody says, very lively" and that "his mother thinks he is the smartest & most wonderful child that ever was." He kept his own opinion, which with babies was usually one of bemusement, to himself.[9]

Lida was an active athletic woman; she went out sailing with Charles within a few weeks of Walter's birth. She seems to have been a good match for him; they shared a no-nonsense socially oriented piety and enjoyed stretching the boundaries of their world, travelling incessantly, riding horses together and apart in the wilds of New Jersey. One story, possibly apocryphal, holds that Lida saw the cliffs of the New Jersey Palisades from a friend's home in Yonkers and, curious to see what lay atop them, rowed a boat with some women friends across the Hudson to climb the 400-foot cliffside and survey the terrain atop it. She and Charles later made the Palisades town of Alpine their home.

In his few attempts at fiction, Nordhoff invariably made his heroines self-possessed; blue-eyed, brown-haired, outdoorsy, hardworking, and "in vulgar good health," suffused with a romanticized practicality. A typical heroine had "eyes which spoke a soul at peace with itself and with the outward world, a soul … fearing nothing, doubting nothing," patient with "the human weaknesses it met

---

8. CN, *Reminiscences*, 4; CN to Benson J. Lossing, September 20, 1858, Lossing Papers, Huntington Library.

9. CN to Sarah Anderson, June 4, 1858, and to Mary Letford, July 6, 1858, autograph collection, Vineland Historical and Antiquarian Society, Vineland, New Jersey. See also Hamilton County, Ohio marriage license, August 25, 1858, Hamilton County Courthouse. Scant information on Lida is mentioned in the *Dictionary of American Biography* entry for Nordhoff, volume 13, p. 548. "Capital Society Gossip," *The Daily Graphic*, March 12, 1877, mentions that Lida was a classmate of First Lady Lucy Hayes, who was educated at the Wesleyan Female College of Cincinnati. (On Lucy Hayes, see Emily Geer, *First Lady: The Life of Lucy Webb Hayes*. Kent: Kent State University Press, 1984).

with in daily life, as not perhaps altogether strange to itself."[10] A woman who seems to have known her own mind, Lida, of a more serene temperament than he, accompanied Charles everywhere, across continents and oceans. Her health grew fragile as the years went by, but in the early days, the only times she was kept from her normal activity were when she was recovering from childbirth or from horseback riding accidents of which there were more than a few. Charles's fictional imagination was limited, and it seems likely that he bore Lida in mind when he wrote that one heroine was "a girl with a smile like a June morning, but with a power of cool stare in her eyes."[11]

Happily married and ensconced in a little house in Flushing, Nordhoff continued to learn from the Harpers. He was particularly impressed with Fletcher Harper's "infallible instinct" for catering to a mass audience. When reading incoming manuscripts, Nordhoff was told to consider "whether we should publish it," which, the young man came to understand, meant "not precisely whether it had great literary merit, but whether it would be intelligible, interesting and useful to the average of American readers."[12] *Harper*'s editors were known to make it their lifetime roost, and Nordhoff could have remained as he was indefinitely, had not a gnawing suspicion that he was growing too comfortable with ultimately trivial work undermined his contentment. "The man who has a vocation he loves, and can afford to work at it," he wrote in one story at the time, "who has a wife he loves, ... who has youth, health, a good name, and a rising reputation in his profession: surely this man need ask no more of the gods?" He answered his own question unequivocally: such a man should "pray God to save his soul from the stagnation of utter content; from the fatal taint of a too-easy success."[13]

He began to write short stories, in a halting attempt at a truly literary career, and was able to get them published in the *Atlantic Monthly* as well as in *Harper*'s.[14] Several of the stories indicate his growing vocational dilemma, usually with talented young protagonists torn between ambition and duty, and often with resolutions brought about by dei ex machina that bore scant

---

10. CN, "Elkanah Brewster's Temptation," in *Cape Cod and All Along Shore*, 136–7.

11. See the correspondence between CN and Gordon L. Ford, in the Ford family papers at the New York Public Library, for general hints of Nordhoff's domestic life with Lida. The quote is from CN, "Maud Elbert's Love Match," in *Cape Cod and All Along Shore*, 219.

12. CN, *Reminiscences*, 5–6.

13. CN, "One Pair of Blue Eyes," in *Cape Cod and All Along Shore* (NY: Books for Libraries Press, 1970, reprint of 1868 edition), 161.

14. The stories were collected in *Cape Cod and All Along Shore*, but were individually published in the late 1850s and early 1860s, mostly in *Harper's Monthly*. The most successful, "Elkanah Brewster's Temptation," appeared in the *Atlantic* in 1859.

resemblance to any possible answer to Nordhoff's own troubles. He puzzled over what he termed "the sphinx-riddle of life," the solution of which might let him learn "what best he may do here for himself and the world." While he distrusted his own ambition, Nordhoff feared proving a mediocrity even more; and the doors of literary greatness, he suspected, were not opening up to him; one of his heroes, a neophyte painter, "painted many things fairly" while "he did yet put his very soul into none." His alter ego feared that unless he could find his own special vision, "he had, perhaps, better stop altogether"; and "bemired in his slough of despond," the character bears distinct resemblance to the "very depressed young man" Nordhoff represented himself to be as a young editor at Harper's.[15]

His uneasiness about his fitness for literary work was matched by a growing conviction that his slight literary efforts were not only unexceptional, but also a dereliction of duty in a nation that was falling to pieces. As sectional antagonism over the question of slavery mounted, Nordhoff found himself at odds with the Harpers, who were often accused by Northerners of being "Southern sympathizers." The *Weekly*, providing illustrated news and editorials to a national audience, circulated in the South as well as the North. Business commitments and profitable markets in the South dovetailed with the Harpers' Democratic political sympathies to convince them that the preservation of the Union had to transcend all other questions, even that of slavery. Their editorials counseled conciliation and compromise between the sections.

As the Harpers maintained a stubborn conservatism in the face of mounting sectional antagonism, Charles Nordhoff grew more radical. His first years back on dry American land saw a heightening political crisis, with continued resistance in the North to enforcement of the Fugitive Slave Act; passage of the Kansas-Nebraska Act, repealing the Missouri Compromise and reopening the question of slavery in northern territories, and subsequent terrorism in "Bleeding Kansas"; the *Dred Scott* decision, declaring that blacks could not be citizens of the United States and that territories could not legally exclude slavery from within their borders. By 1856, the Republican Party, dedicated to preventing the expansion of slavery, had attained national prominence; its presidential candidate, John C. Fremont, carried eleven of the sixteen free states. Political bitterness manifested itself even on the floor of the U.S. Senate, when a Southern Congressman caned Charles Sumner to unconsciousness.

Amid such growing hysteria, it would have been difficult for anyone to remain politically inert. Charles Nordhoff was no exception. During his years at sea, he had witnessed mistreatment of slaves in various countries and had heard horror stories from other sailors about life and death on slave ships. His own

---

[15.]   CN, "Elkanah Brewster's Temptation," in *Cape Cod*, 128–138.

experiences had demonstrated the corruption and exploitation made possible by arbitrary and unlimited authority. The major elements of free labor ideology, based in a producerist value system and predicated upon the necessity of open opportunity to secure the prosperous functioning of a righteous society, found justification in Nordhoff's experiences in the caste system of shipboard life. A confirmed egalitarian, religiously faithful to the morality of labor, Nordhoff was a natural recruit to the antislavery cause. By the late 1850s, the American dream seemed real enough to him: he had risen, by his own wits and hard work, to a far better station in life than that of a menial laborer. The danger apparently posed to America by the Slave Power seemed a terrible and all-too-real threat to the young *Harper's* editor. By 1860, Nordhoff had become an avid Republican.

The conciliatory course of the Harper brothers clashed with Nordhoff's growing politicization, and the innocuous articles he was writing for the *Monthly*—on such topics as "Follies of Fashion" and "The Capture of Elephants"—were no outlet for the intensity of his political convictions and his fervent need to act upon them. Fletcher Harper tried to explain to his protégé. "'I grew up under the Union and the Constitution,'" Nordhoff remembered Harper telling him, upon having learned that "with the zeal of a young and very positive anti-slavery man, I was grieved at his course." Harper insisted that the preservation of the Union was the paramount issue at hand, and he deplored abolitionist rhetoric that damned the Constitution as "a covenant with hell."[16]

Harper's conflation of abolitionism with the antislavery movement was a common mistake of the time. The Republicans believed that slavery, though permitted by the Constitution, was bound to wither away altogether, but only gradually. Hard work was the certain and only moral road to prosperity, and to live off the labor of others while keeping opportunities shut off from them was to endanger the very basis of American life. Nordhoff's belief in the reality of open opportunity was more tempered than that of many Republicans, but he did not question the inherent solidity or fairness of capitalism and free labor. He did see that if the Northern system was capable of using people unmercifully, due to what seemed to him failures of individual morality, the degradation of labor and closing down of opportunities for the common man in the South were structural, inextricably linked to the slave system itself.[17]

Republican politics and rhetoric were unavoidable in New York during Nordhoff's years with the Harpers. Newspapers such as Greeley's New York *Tribune* and Bryant's *Evening Post* tirelessly attacked the institution of slavery

---

[16].   CN, *Reminiscences*, 8.

[17].   On free soil ideology, see Eric Foner, *Free Soil, Free Labor, Free Men* (NY: Oxford University Press, 1970).

while Abraham Lincoln, as the Republican presidential candidate, spoke at Cooper Union in early 1860. Lincoln's legalistic and moderate antislavery views met with Nordhoff's approval. After Lincoln's election, as the Southern states began to secede during the winter of 1860–61, Nordhoff wrote his first overtly political work, a pamphlet titled *Secession is Rebellion!*, an outlet for the fervent antislavery vision that he could not express within the pages of *Harper's Weekly*. Despite its exclamatory title, the argument was closely reasoned, legalistic, its tone measured and calm. Nordhoff argued, with algorithmic logic, that the secession of the Southern states was neither necessary nor legal. He drew liberally upon the Constitution, citing it by chapter and verse. Much as he had once quashed talk of mutiny on shipboard by pointing out to the would-be mutineers the practical difficulties they were sure to encounter, he argued in *Secession* against disunion in pragmatic terms, addressing Southern arguments on their own ground. "Only Disunion can hasten the event of emancipation," he warned.[18]

Nevertheless, he maintained that the conflict over slavery was not at its core an issue of legality and practicality, but one of morality and hence (echoing William Seward) an "irrepressible" one. Northerners, he wrote, believed slavery to be "an anti-democratic evil—a great moral wrong," and the controversy a "conflict between right and wrong,—between God and the devil,—between knowledge and ignorance." The crisis continued to deepen, Lincoln was inaugurated, the South fired on Fort Sumter, and Nordhoff entered, once and for all, the world of politically charged journalism, to join the battle in the best way he knew. Writing, he realized, was not entertainment alone; it could be a power, an educating force. The sphinx-riddle of his life had been answered at last.[19]

Newspaper journalism in 1860 was overtly political. Most antebellum papers were subsidized by political parties, frankly partisan in their news coverage as well as their editorializing, and even the "independent" nonpartisan sheets had clear political sympathies. For a paper to avoid a politically consistent editorial stance was regarded as unprincipled; Greeley wrote that his *Tribune*, though begun with a subsidy from the New York Whigs, meant to avoid not only "servile partisanship" (in the sense of adherence to a strict party line), but also "gagged, mincing neutrality."[20]

The big New York dailies exemplified the brawling contentiousness of journalistic writing, with running editorial wars among the Republican *Tribune*, *Times*, and *Evening Post* and the Democratic *World* and *Herald*. There were

---

18.   CN, *Secession is Rebellion!* (New York: Baker and Godwin, Printers, 1860).
19.   CN, *Secession*, 17–18.
20.   Horace Greeley, *Recollections of a Busy Life* (New York: J.B. Ford, 1868), 137.

dozens of smaller newspapers published in New York as well, but these five dailies, most of them two-penny sheets, enjoyed substantial circulations and a national audience. All sold in the tens of thousands. The New York *Herald* was the most popular, with an unprecedented circulation admitted even by its adversaries to be at least 77,000. The daily newspapers provided a forum for scrappy political debate, impossible to ignore and attended to by politicians as well as the general public.[21]

Nordhoff's Republican pamphlet, which attained "a moderate share of attention" in predominantly Democratic New York, brought him in contact with the editors and proprietors of the *Evening Post*, Parke Godwin and William Cullen Bryant, who were then looking to replace two newly departed editors. They offered Nordhoff a position, which he accepted with alacrity. The *Evening Post*, with a circulation of 20,000, was widely respected as the paper of choice of a limited but influential audience of intellectuals, businessmen, and politicians.[22]

Even before he spent many weeks at the *Evening Post*, Nordhoff did recognize that daily journalism was riven by internal conflicts. In June 1861, just as he was beginning his newspaper career, Nordhoff published a short story in *Harper's Monthly* titled "What Is Best?"[23] A parable of journalistic virtue corrupted by the drive for high circulations, it told of the rise of one Stoffle MacGurdigan, a bright young man who goes into journalism at the urgings of an idealistic college professor, who assures him that the newspaper writer, no less than Martin Luther with his printing press, could change the world, as "with his little pellet of fact" he "blows to the winds the fine-spun theories of scheming politicians." "What a noble field for doing good!" exclaims MacGurdigan's naive fiancée when he declares his intention to pursue a "literary" career, "so many wrongs in the world yet to be put down by his brave and noble pen." And

---

21. Circulation figures for the *Herald* are given in Warren Francke, "James Gordon Bennett," *Dictionary of Literary Biography* volume 43 (NY: Gale, 1985), 41.

22. CN, *Reminiscences*, 9; Nevins, *Evening Post*, 267–8, 340–2. For the purposes of comparison, Nevins notes that the London *Times* had a circulation of slightly more than 50,000; the New York *Tribune* 55,000; and the New York *Herald* 77,000. Nevins also mentions encomia of the *Post* of William Jay, Charles Eliot Norton, W. H. Furness, and John Stuart Mill. Charles Dudley Warner in 1862 called it "the most fearless and rigidly honest paper in the country," "its ability … equal to its moral worth."

23. "What Is Best?" was included in an 1868 anthology of Nordhoff's short stories published by Harper & Brothers under the title of *Cape Cod and All Along Shore: Stories*, which was reprinted in 1970 by Books for Libraries Press (Freeport, New York). Page numbers in subsequent footnotes are those of this reprint edition, not the periodical in which the story originally appeared.

off he goes to the big city, soon to rise to the lofty status of Editor of a New York daily.

Discarding his faith, his morals, and his countrified fiancée, he quickly rises to the height of the profession. Invited to return to speak at his alma mater years later, he decides to set his old professor straight on the realities of journalism. "It is an error to suppose that a daily journal has a mission any more than any other commercial enterprise," he lectures the astonished Reverend Doctor. "One man sells cotton, and another man sells newspapers, and it is the business of each to ... gain the best profit he can from his investment." To do so, a successful editor had to court and win public favor, even if this meant publishing scandal and unsubstantiated rumor. "If I do not publish a certain statement some one else will," he explains, "and my readers go off to another paper." The public "does not care for principle. ... Let the news be exciting, and it cares not if it be also true. Let the article be slashing, and it matters little whom it slashes." Newspapers, in this scheme of things, never shaped public opinion; they could only lead it. "The man who has the loudest lungs in a crowd can lead it if he will," the editor continues, "but he can not lead it away from its purpose. He can only place himself skillfully at its head, and, knowing its aims, submit to be pushed on in advance." In short, "a newspaper is not a moral agent; it is a commercial speculation, whose only duty is success."[24]

The story is curiously ambivalent, for although Nordhoff holds up to a certain amount of ridicule the professor's vision of the press as the defender of liberty and righter of wrongs, it is abundantly clear that MacGurdigan is a man who has lost his soul. Nordhoff often mocked the lofty expression of ideals that he himself believed in deeply, seemingly anxious to prove that he had taken the world's measure and found it petty indeed. With the increasingly high capitalization costs of running a large daily newspaper, the conflict between the business of journalism and its public service obligations was already, in 1861, drawing a great deal of discussion; and Nordhoff's awareness of the traps lying in the path before him were not unfounded. Always, he tailored his arguments to their intended audiences—though he seldom tailored the point for which he argued. Where did one draw the line? The generally low opinion in which high-circulation newspapers were held by critics was based upon this very notion: that the drive for higher circulations would lead to "pandering," to journalism aimed at the lowest common denominator. In fact, Nordhoff would ultimately be confronted with the conflict between his editorial integrity and the profitability of the New York *Evening Post*—but the pressures were exerted from other quarters than he had warned of. He still had a great deal to learn

---

24.   CN, "What Is Best?" 56, 60, 90.

about the conduct of a "respectable" newspaper like the *Evening Post*—but some years would pass before the battle lines were clear.

The *Post* had a venerable history. Founded in 1801 as a Federalist organ published by Alexander Hamilton, it had turned to the Democratic Party during the Jacksonian era, when William Leggett and Bryant ran the paper on the principles of free speech for abolitionists, labor unionization, and antimonopoly. When the Democratic Party slid into the proslavery camp, Bryant, congenitally opposed to the Whigs for their protectionist-monopolist tendencies, threw his support behind the Free Soil Party in 1848—emblazoning the masthead of his paper with the slogan "Free Soil, Free Labor, Free Trade, and Free Speech"—and then six years later behind the Republicans. Bryant always maintained that the paper was "Democratic-Republican," or "Independent," adhering to egalitarian and democratic principles and supporting, at any given moment, the party that seemed to further those principles.[25]

Sixty-seven years old in 1861, William Cullen Bryant, the noted Transcendentalist poet and author of "Thanatopsis," controlled the *Evening Post*'s editorial voice. Although he had travelled considerably during the 1850s, delegating the management of the paper to subordinates, he became an active daily presence at the newspaper with the coming of the Civil War. A small man who, with his flowing white beard, resembled an Old Testament prophet, Bryant presented a sharp contrast to the business-minded, earth-bound Fletcher Harper. His biblically cadenced editorials thundered righteousness and soared to rhetorical heights seldom matched by his contemporaries. Bryant's calls for an uncompromising prosecution of the war seemed at times to threaten to burst into flames, even while he execrated the more spoils-minded Republicanism of an old nemesis, New York's William Seward. One editor remembered Democrat Samuel Tilden leaving the *Post*'s editorial rooms ashen-faced, shortly before the firing on Fort Sumter, warning Bryant that "if you have your way, civil war will divide this country, and you will see blood running like water in the streets of this city."[26]

---

[25]   For the *Evening Post*'s history, see Frank Luther Mott, *American Journalism* (NY: Macmillan, 1941), 184–6, 257–9, and 344–5; and Allan Nevins's detailed *The Evening Post: A Century of Journalism* (New York: Boni & Liveright, 1922). Nevins, before turning to history, had been a reporter for the *Post* and interviewed many "old-timers" at the paper.

[26]   John Bigelow, *Retrospections of an Active Life* (NY: Baker & Taylor, 1909), volume 1, p. 292. See also Margaret Clapp, *Forgotten First Citizen: John Bigelow* (Boston: Little, Brown, 1947), 140–141. On Bryant, see *The Letters of William Cullen Bryant, Volume IV: 1858-1864*, edited by William Cullen Bryant II and Thomas G. Voss (New York: Fordham University Press, 1984) for information on Bryant's relationship with Lincoln and Civil War politics in general; and Charles H. Brown, *William Cullen*

Bryant shared ownership of the *Evening Post* with his son-in-law, Parke Godwin, and his business manager, Isaac Henderson, who had risen in the ranks from a clerkship at the paper. Henderson was a shrewd businessman, little interested in the editorial side of the paper, and he had a reputation for being a sharp dealer. Bryant relied upon him to handle the newspaper's advertising accounts and other business affairs, and Henderson made the paper a highly profitable investment for all its owners.[27] Parke Godwin came from a more patrician background: Princeton-educated, he was a trained lawyer and a former editor of the journal of the American Fourierists as well as of *Putnam's Monthly Magazine.* With a reputation for both brilliance and indolence, he had a short-fused temper and, consequently, a rocky relationship with his father-in-law. Godwin shared editorial responsibilities with Bryant and Nordhoff until his departure from the paper at the end of the war.[28]

Bryant, Godwin, and Nordhoff, as coeditors of the *Evening Post*, shared a political dedication to moderate Republicanism. In personal terms, they were an odd trio. Bryant, in the opinions of many of his contemporaries, was cold and aloof, cordial to all with a dignity that kept people at arm's length. He wrote his meticulous editorials in a tiny hand at a desk cluttered high with books and papers, frugally reusing scraps of paper and old envelopes. He commanded, as one subordinate recalled, "respect rather than affection." Godwin was more gregarious, fond of society and an avid patron of the opera, with a temper that led him to leave the *Post* in anger more than once. Contemporaries charged him with squandering his talents, though his wide knowledge of history and economics served him well when he decided to work. His aggressive writing style was likened to the wielding of a rapier, a bludgeon, and even a triphammer, but he was known to write his editorials in bed at home and send them in to the office by messenger. His dislike of Henderson was well-known, punctuated by frequent explosions of temper, which Bryant simply ignored.[29]

Bryant (NY: Charles Scribner's Sons, 1971). See also Alan Nevins, *The New York Evening Post* (NY: 1922).

27. Information on Henderson is scanty, but his role at the *Evening Post* is well delineated in Nevins, *The Evening Post*; Brown, *William Cullen Bryant*; and Theodore Hornberger, *William Cullen Bryant and Isaac Henderson: New Evidence on a Strange Partnership* (New York: Haskell House, 1973).

28. On Parke Godwin, see *Dictionary of American Biography* VII: 351–2 (NY: 1936); Nevins, *Evening Post*, especially chapters 12 through 20; Brown, *Bryant*; and James Boylan, "William Cullen Bryant," *Dictionary of Literary Biography*, vol. 43, pp. 79–90.

29. John Ranken Towse on Bryant, "Staff Reminiscences—II," in *The Evening Post Hundredth Anniversary, November 16, 1801 - 1901* (New York: Evening Post Publishing Company, 1902), 101–2. George Cary Eggleston on Godwin, in Nevins, 435–6.

Into the fragile equilibrium of Bryant, Henderson, and Godwin walked Charles Nordhoff, thirty years old and ready to take on the world. He bore little resemblance to any of his compatriots, being neither dignified to the point of coldness as was Bryant, nor a smooth denizen of high society like Godwin. His tattooed arms were enough to mark the distinction between them. Walking still with a bit of a sailor's roll, he had an athletic physique, a brusque manner of speech, and "glittering" bespectacled eyes that missed nothing. The staff was most impressed with the force of Nordhoff's personality. "He was a quick-tempered, emphatic, but thoroughly just and kindly man," remembered one employee, "intolerant only of subterfuge or meanness," known for his simplicity, insight, honesty, and a sense of humor that "more than atoned for his occasional hastiness." Nordhoff tended to go at everything full tilt, all genial kindliness and sympathy or irascibility and impatience, growing indignant on others' behalf as readily as on his own. He could explode in rage at anyone he believed to equivocate, according to John Ranken Towse, an employee who remembered Nordhoff with admiration some forty years later. Towse recalled Nordhoff's "huge scorn for prevarication or double-dealing." If an underling made a mistake due to ignorance or carelessness, he might overlook it, "but anything in the nature of a shuffling excuse roused him to flaming ire," his personality being "impetuous and irascible, but naturally generous and tender-hearted." He had an intensity that was like the cool Bryant's inner moral fervor made manifest and directed nakedly at the world.[30]

If Nordhoff had learned anything during his years as a sailor, observing the myriad ways in which he and his fellow sailors were lied to and cheated, it was a keen faculty for detecting hypocrisy. He had a low tolerance for anything, however harmless, which breathed of deceit, pomposity, or affectation, and directed much of his mocking humor at the clichéd or conventionalized. He would write a note to a lawyer friend in typical prolix legalese upon learning that his friends "did design & intend & purpose, & had promised, agreed & covenanted" to visit the Nordhoff home,

> and he further testifies that he will do his best to make them happy, & would do more, if only his, the said Nordhoff's, wife, had not perversely, & with malice aforethought, regardless of said Nordhoff's comfort & happiness, ... abandoned his, the said Nordhoff's, bed & board, & gone incontinently to Vineland.

[30.] John Ranken Towse, quoted in Nevins, 319–20, and in "Staff Reminiscences," *Evening Post Hundredth Anniversary*, 101–2. It may have been an act of moral courage for Towse to speak so warmly of Nordhoff on the occasion of the *Evening Post's* centennial, as will be seen below.

"My hand & seal," he completed the document, drawing a furry and bright-eyed seal at the close. His humor could range from the gently satirical to caustic sarcasm, even with friends, whose subsequent wounded feelings always surprised him.[31]

His handwriting reflected the expansiveness of his temperament, using fat-nibbed pens and writing in a large scrawl, often fitting only a sentence or two on the *Post*'s half sheets of stationery, and sometimes in such a rush that correspondents despaired of deciphering his messages. At the *Post*, he was known to write furiously with a cigar clenched between his teeth, enveloping himself in clouds of smoke as he worked.[32] His duties during the war years included managing the *Post*'s small reportorial staff, commissioning articles from outside experts, editing wire service reports from battlefields, and writing articles and editorials as the occasion required. The *Evening Post* was not known for the comprehensiveness of its news coverage, but rather for its elegant and well-argued editorials, which could be quite lengthy. Bryant and Godwin wrote the lion's share of wartime editorials although Nordhoff could step into the breach when necessary.[33]

---

[31]   CN to Gordon L. Ford, June 8, 1868. This letter, evidently a joke the cataloguers did not comprehend, is split between two collections at the New York Public Library: the Gordon L. Ford/Ford Family Papers (undated page) and the Charles Nordhoff Papers (dated). The Nordhoff Papers are, in fact, simply a group extracted from the Ford Papers.

[32]   For instance, see James Parton to CN, December 18, 1866, James Parton Papers, Houghton Library, Harvard: "Neither Mrs. Parton, who is an excellent decipherer, nor I … can quite make out your last sentence." For the smoke, see Towse, "Staff," 101–2.

[33]   None of the *Evening Post*'s editorials for the period during which Nordhoff worked there are bylined. In making attributions of an editorial to Nordhoff, three factors were used. First, his style had become quite distinctive and markedly different from Bryant's or Godwin's, with certain characteristic rhetorical devices used again and again. ("Nor is this all" is one favorite when he was cataloguing the sins of some public agency or official, paragraph after paragraph.) These stylistic devices are carried over into Nordhoff's books. Second, and more reliably, there are periods during which it is known definitely that neither Godwin nor Bryant was working at the paper. After May of 1866, neither one was a sustained presence at the newspaper, leaving it largely in Nordhoff's hands until his departure in 1871: Godwin left in disgust with Henderson, and Bryant, devastated by the death of his wife, left the country for lengthy periods. When he was in the United States, he usually kept his distance from the paper, staying at his home on Long Island or in Cummington, Massachusetts, more interested in translating Homer than in the daily operations of the *Post*. Third, certain issues (particularly in the postwar years) are

The *Evening Post* maintained a staunch insistence on the justice and necessity of an unrelenting prosecution of the war that did not prevent it from being a fierce critic of laggard and incompetent Union generals. The demand for up-to-the-minute news from the battlefields accelerated the transformation of newspapers from small-scale opinion sheets to enormous highly capitalized news-gathering organizations, and most of the big New York dailies went into considerable debt to keep enough reporters on the field and enough telegraphically transmitted stories on the front page. The *Post* was an exception, however. As Nordhoff would later comment, it was never a "newspaper" in the new meaning of the term; it left the most enterprising "scoops" to competitors like the New York *Herald*. And as befit a journal that advocated a "pay-as-you-go" war, financed by taxes rather than by greenbacks, the *Evening Post* invested in a modest contingent of war correspondents, only a dozen or so being hired by Nordhoff during the four years' conflict.[34]

Like many Northern newspapers, the *Post* all too credulously reported a Union victory at the First Battle of Bull Run, but this was the fault of government censors as much as of overeager reporters. When the reporters realized that their initial optimistic reports were wrong, they could not correct them because the telegraph had been commandeered by the army and no negative reports were allowed through for several days. When the painful truth came out, the *Post* dutifully printed details of the generally disreputable behavior of Union troops, but again reversed itself within a few days and attributed stories of Union cowardice to inexperienced and unduly affrighted correspondents. The Union forces' retreat was necessary, it editorialized, "before numbers so overwhelming that it would have been madness to attempt keeping their ground." Throughout the war, most Northern newspapers exaggerated the size of Confederate forces; accurate numbers were, in fact, hard to come by. Nevertheless, the Bull Run treatment illustrated the difficulties and contradictions faced by journalists during the Civil War, attempting to maintain Northern morale without slipping into propaganda.[35]

The *Evening Post* was not such a booster of the Union war effort that it could not criticize what its editors saw as incompetence and "blundering" on the part of the commanding officers. In particular, the dilatoriness of General

known concerns of Nordhoff, either through his letters or his other writings. In a few cases, Nevins identifies certain articles as written by Nordhoff, and he states that he took care to do so only when he was absolutely certain of the attribution. When his determinations are in accord with the above factors, I've accepted them as valid.

34. Brown, *Bryant*, 440. Nevins, passim.
35. "Our Volunteers in the Battle of the Twenty-First," New York *Evening Post*, July 23, 1861. The editorial is probably by Bryant.

McClellan elicited scathing editorials from the *Post* writers, which in turn made the newspaper the target of critics who accused it of undermining the war effort. The paper was unstinting in its admiration of Grant's campaigns in the West, and several Union officers agreed to write lengthy signed accounts of their activities—accounts that tended to portray the Union armies in too-glowing terms, but which were, nevertheless, informative and dramatic accounts at a time when information was hard to come by. The task of reporting the war was not made easier by the activities of the Lincoln administration, which exerted various forms of censorship—through both the military and the State Department—and even arrested "Copperhead" newspaper editors who were seen as damaging Northern morale. "Under cover of 'Liberty of speech,' 'Liberty of the press,' and '*Habeas Corpus*,'" Lincoln stated in September of 1862, Confederate sympathizers "hoped to keep on foot amongst us a most efficient corps of spies, informers, suppliers, and aiders and abettors of thie cause."[36]

The *Evening Post* editorialized against military censorship as having the effect of fostering wild rumors and shaking the morale of Northern citizens unsure of the real fate of their army. It advised that reporters be given freer run of battlefields and that their reports be circulated without governmental interference: the public was capable of sifting truth from error. When military interference resulted in adulterated reports after the Battle of Fredericksburg, the *Post* ran an editorial stating that neither army officers "nor any one else has a right to convey the impression that we have gained a considerable success when in reality we have suffered a terrible defeat." Panics were the result of "imagination and fear," the editorial added, and the very effort to suppress the news led to gross exaggerations. Throughout the Civil War, Northern newspapers tried to navigate the thin terrain between propaganda and treason in their coverage of the war. To contemporaries, the *Evening Post*'s criticisms of the army verged on the latter while from a century's hindsight, it can be judged

---

[36]   See, for instance, "Mud and Discipline," New York *Evening Post*, February 19, 1862, and the Bobbett-Hooper cartoon in *Vanity Fair* of March 15, 1862, illustrating the reaction to the *Post*'s criticisms. Lincoln's infringements on freedom of the press are discussed in Mark E. Neely, *The Fate of Liberty: Abraham Lincoln and Civil Liberties* (New York: Oxford University Press, 1991) and Phillip Shaw Paludin, *A People's Contest: The Union and the Civil War, 1861-1865* (New York: Harper & Row, 1988, 1989), 239 ff. John F. Marszalek, in *Sherman's Other War*, provides a good synopsis of the various military strictures placed on the press. Lincoln is quoted in James McPherson's *Ordeal by Fire* (New York: Knopf, 1982), 295. J. Cutler Andrews's *The North Reports the Civil War* (Pittsburgh: University of Pittsburgh Press, 1955) is a heavily descriptive account of the difficulties under which Northern journalists operated.

that the paper sometimes veered off course in the other direction, turning to boosterism when it seemed the North might be weakening in its resolve.[37]

Nordhoff was never very interested in the military aspects of the war. His most vivid and sustained reporting during the war years concerned the social impact of Emancipation. Shortly after the Proclamation took effect on January 1, 1863, he travelled to the Union-occupied South Carolina Sea Islands to witness the transition of a community of former slaves to a system of free labor. Already, an influx of Northern educators, reformers, and government officials had made the Sea Island community a test case: if these freed slaves could continue to profitably farm cotton, they reasoned, then surely their transition to freedom would be a smooth one. Many of the former slaves had been inducted into the Union armies after considerable controversy; but the women, children, and less-fit men remained in their homes. The administrators of the occupying force determined the people's working conditions, and their insistence upon the continued farming of long-staple cotton, a notoriously unreliable crop, ran counter to the wishes of most of the community. Nevertheless, a trial of "free labor" was thus begun.[38]

Nordhoff took a steamboat loaded with munitions to Hilton Head Island in early March 1863. During his lengthy visit, he sent articles on conditions in the Sea Islands to the *Evening Post* for publication in a front-page series and collected material for a strikingly different article that was published later that year in *Harper's Monthly*.[39] The contrast between the article for *Harper's* and the newspaper reports demonstrates Nordhoff's ability to tailor his material to fit its targeted audience. The *Harper's* piece, aimed in large part at the families of white Union soldiers, excoriated the Confederates who had brought the country to war, portraying the enlisted men with sympathy and respect. No

---

[37.] "The Press and the Army," New York *Evening Post*, September 2, 1862; "The Censorship of the Telegraph," New York *Evening Post*, December 18, 1862.

[38.] The most detailed account of activities on the sea islands is Willie Lee Rose's *Rehearsal for Reconstruction: The Port Royal Experiment* (NY: Oxford, 1964). See also Joel Williamson, *After Slavery: The Negro in South Carolina During Reconstruction, 1861 - 1877* (Chapel Hill: University of North Carolina Press, 1965).

[39.] CN, "Two Weeks at Port Royal," *Harper's Monthly*, XXVII (June 1863): 110–18; CN, "The Freedmen of South Carolina," and "From Port Royal," in the New York *Evening Post*, March 26 and 31, 1863 and subsequent issues. Nordhoff's *Post* articles were gathered into a pamphlet, *The Freedmen of South Carolina* (New York: Charles T. Evans, 1863), possibly at his own expense. Citations below are to the pamphlet rather than the newspaper articles, which are for the most part identical, but it should be understood that his writings would have received a wider audience in the *Evening Post* than could be expected for the pamphlet.

African-Americans appeared in the piece. In contrast, the newspaper articles concerned the freed slaves almost exclusively: their characteristics, their living conditions, and their aptitude for life in freedom. The two pieces don't contradict each other so much as operate on complementary planes of concern.

Nordhoff had never been fond of the military. In tones only half humorous, he described for his *Harper*'s readers the "military despotism," which he found in control of the Sea Islands. Like Roman centurions, the generals enjoyed "endless power" over their troops and the inhabitants, which Nordhoff found disturbing, but he basked in the camaraderie of the foot soldiers and lesser officers. Hearing their accounts of battle scenes, Nordhoff realized that the reports he had read thus far were sadly lacking. It was no wonder, he wrote, "that Europeans speak of our conflict as commonplace," for those who had written about it were but "commonplace" themselves. He damned the mindless fact gathering of the reporters: they were "smart enough, perhaps, at hunting up 'news'"; but in their quest for "items," they were no better than truffle-hunting dogs—"they knew nothing, saw nothing, and smelt but one thing: their peculiar and abnormal training gave them only a nose for news." Their reports lacked the insight that might convey to readers the meaning of the war, its impact on the nation and on those who fought its battles.

> The incapables who are sent by enterprising newspapers to hang on to the camp … have neither time nor genius to perform a broader part. They are able to tell us … sometimes the general's plan before it is yet fully formed; they can write for us tedious columns of what we don't want to know; but as to giving us an idea of the war, of what qualities it has developed in American citizens, of what kind of men our soldiers are, how they bear their trials, what they think, what they talk of, what they aim to do, what they really do—scarcely one of them has done this.[40]

He had read only one account of the battle at Fort Sumter that had "the smoke of battle about it," which impressed upon him the bravery of the men thus engaged. In all the other reports, "you read only of smoke and clap-bang, and lay the paper down as wise as when you took it up." Accounts that imparted more of the drama and pathos of the war, of the braveries of sailors and soldiers, would, he thought, make the nation "prouder and heartier," better equipped to hold to its ideals.

[40.]   CN, "Two Weeks," 112.

He found no inspiration in the accounts of troop movements that dominated the newspapers, nor did he find that personally viewing the regiment en masse conveyed a whisper of the truth embodied in the soldiers themselves. Military formations were dehumanizing. "To see several thousand men drawn up under arms," moving as "one great machine," lined up by the thousand, "is surely a stirring sight," he admitted.

> But it did not move me greatly after all, for at that distance ... the men lose their individuality to you; they seem no longer so many thousand men, but a great many links in a great chain, so many parts of a great machine.

"You do not see the whites of their eyes," he continued; "you do not know whether they are hot or cool, whether they enjoy it or think it a bore, what they are thinking about at all under their blue caps." And if journalists insisted only on covering the movements of massed forces, they were neglecting the psychological impact of the war, played out as it would be in the minds of individuals.[41]

Nordhoff painted a pretty picture of the South Carolina springtime, with soft breezes, blue skies, and flowers everywhere, and "quiet nooks," which the war had not yet disturbed. But history tainted Beaufort for him, as he pondered the "fire-eating" secessionists who had made it their home. "Here, beneath these live-oaks, in this grove of tall and spreading pines, by these budding orange-trees," he ruminated in his best *Harper's Monthly* style, "... the Rhetts, the Barnwells, the Prescotts" planned "the ruin of their country." Because of them, many homes had been left without husbands and fathers —many, perhaps, among the readers of *Harper's*. "It is a pleasant spot, this Beaufort," he added in a grim coda, "but I hope whenever our soldiers leave it they will raze it to the ground, nor leave one stone standing on another of its foundations. The whole place is accursed."[42]

But if his *Harper's* article was meant to gratify the aggrieved sensibilities of the families that Union soldiers had been forced to leave behind, Nordhoff adopted a different voice in his columns for the *Evening Post*. Writing of the newly freed slaves and their Sea Island community, he was less histrionic and more coolly rational, and yet the articles resonate with optimism and a belief in the ultimate moral worth of the Union's war effort. Here, at last, was evidence of some meaning behind all the "smoke and clap-bang."

---

41.   CN, "Two Weeks," 118.

42.   CN, "Two Weeks," 112, 117.

With the very first column, he noted with approval the prominence of African-Americans among the Provost Marshal's troops and the evident industry with which many of them were learning to read and write. The primary concern of Northerners was whether the former slaves would work well as free men and women. Some whites were afraid that the blacks could not survive the competition of a free-market economy: that they were, variously, either too gentle and submissive or too benighted and degraded by their former condition to function without becoming dependent on the government as they had been dependent upon their masters, or, as Social Darwinists would have it, falling prey to the law of "survival of the fittest." People like Nordhoff, who believed not just in the morality but also in the efficiency and justice of the system of free labor, tended also to believe that education and training could make up for any disadvantages that slavery had conferred upon its victims. In America, the reasoning went that all persons could be elevated according to their innate capabilities.

As he surveyed the community, Nordhoff found hopeful signs everywhere that the transition from slavery to freedom would be an untroubled one. His faith in the power of education was nearly limitless, and his travels around the world had given him a less constricted view of the diversity of human culture than many of his contemporaries. Unlike many intellectuals of his day, he was reluctant to impute inherent disabilities to any race or class of people although he maintained that some cultures, through environmental forces, produced people of "higher" development or greater "civilization" than others. For the South Carolina freedmen, he had no such reservations. They were Christians, after all, born and raised in America. All that was required was that they be fully and legally included in American society. Nordhoff consciously wrote for an audience dubious of both the ex-slaves' capacities and their efforts, clearly attempting to mitigate prejudice. Typically, he would approach a stereotype as if he too had believed in it, only to undermine it with his fresh contradictory observations of the Sea Islanders.

In the opening paragraphs of his first *Evening Post* article, he described African-Americans industriously and capably working as sailors, stevedores, and soldiers. "By the time you have seen all this," he confided in the reader, "you begin to lose faith in the person who assured you that the negroes … are an idle, dissolute, worthless set of creatures, who are supported at an enormous expense by an abolition government, etc., etc."[43] Furthermore, the industry of men, women, and children alike justified their emancipation, for was it not better to put such energy at the service of the Union rather than the Confederacy?

[43.]   CN, *Freedmen*, 2.

In his praise for these hardworking women and children, Nordhoff appealed to the racial double standard that prevailed among his readers, for few Northerners thought that it was desirable for white women to work outside the home. Yet he noted that although the African-American women were "persevering in their industry," and earned as much as a similarly employed man, the black men shared their white brothers' unwillingness to grant women their due. He cited one conversation with a black manager:

> "De men's nearly all gone now, sir, and so de work don't go on; for, you see, de women don't work well when de men's gone." "But," said I, "Harry, the women *do* work. I see them on every hand, busy in the field." "Yes, sir, dey *work*," was his reply, "but dey don't work like men. After all, sir, one good-fornuffin man's worth two smart women any day."

Nordhoff noted that "ignorant men in the North" shared such opinions, but clearly gave his audience credit for more egalitarian views. He was never one to let an opportunity to score a point pass him by.

Although Nordhoff was not free of the taint of racism himself—he saw nothing wrong, for example, in the lower pay given to black men than to whites in the army—he was genuinely concerned for them, constantly recurring to their love of education and the energy with which they tried to better their lot. He had considerable empathy for the former slaves he surveyed, even as he recognized the gulf between them and the difficulties involved in breaching the distance. Only the children openly stared at him, crowding around while he toured their neighborhoods, while the adults, however curious about him they may have been, kept their own counsel. The people were "universally polite," the men touching their hats deferentially when they met Nordhoff in the road, the women curtsying before him. He understood that this deference would work against his gaining their confidence. Because of the tyranny under which they had lived, they would "most adroitly tell you precisely what you want to hear," he wrote. "To cross-examine such a creature is a task of the utmost delicate nature," and

> if you chance to put a leading question he will answer to its spirit as closely as the compass needle answers to the magnetic pole. Ask if the enemy had fifty thousand men, and he will be sure that they had at least that many; express your belief that

they had not five thousand, and he will laugh at the idea of
their having more than forty-five hundred.[44]

He did his best to elicit candid testimony from the former slaves, although
aware of his alien status among them. It was the stance of a participant-observer,
inside a situation and yet outside of it, that he had grown used to in his sailing
days and would resort to time and again throughout his career.

Most of the former slaves had remained in their old cabins, but some had
moved into their former masters' fine houses. "Doubtless," he wrote, "if it is true
that the laborer is worthy of his reward, they have a better right to these places
than the masters who fled from them"; and he faulted the army's division of land
among the people for being ungenerous, the plots too small to allow them real
independence. He surveyed the people's living conditions for signs of material
improvement. Their homes were clean, if poorly lit and rudimentary, and he
noted approvingly that their "wants" were increasing. At first, he admitted,
the prospect looked bleak to his middle-class eyes, once more adopting the
position of the Philistine about to be enlightened. People accustomed to "a
certain amount of comfort and tidiness" might find it "extraordinary" that the
Sea Islanders could live in such grim surroundings. "In our minds this squalor
is linked with drunkenness and vicious improvidence," he admitted,

> and we unconsciously dislike those who live in this condition.
> Those were my emotions, I confess, when I first entered the
> cabins of the people here. Those astounding agglomerations
> of rags, this which seemed to me the most dreary discomfort,
> the gloom …; all this made my heart sink, at first, and I said to
> myself, "Oh! dear! oh! dear! what can be done with all this?"[45]

Anticipating the probable reaction of his readers to this description,
Nordhoff attempted to forestall it. Perhaps their uncomfortable homes were
the product of poverty and ignorance not of their own making, for "I found
that the rags were clean," the neighborhoods were safe, and "the whole affair
is not nearly so bad as it looks." Furthermore, he noted a certain slovenliness
in the planters' homes that suggested to him that the African-Americans had
no good examples to learn from, for "the whites themselves did not know
what comfort or neatness was." The richest houses, he noted, lacked "what we
include in the phrase 'modern conveniences'"; and he hastened to remind
the reader that as slaves, the blacks were "kept to a certain uniform, in dress

---

44.   CN, *Freedmen*, 25.
45.   CN, *Freedmen*, 18–19.

and other surroundings," marks of their servility, "just as were the Jews in the middle ages."

> I am making no excuses for the blacks in all this. They do not
> need it, for they display a disposition to make a better figure
> in the world, which proves that it is not they, but their masters,
> who are to blame if they make a poor show now.[46]

The living conditions he found in the Sea Islands were simply the usual consequence of oppression and had nothing to do with the character or aspirations of the people. He reflected upon the legacy of deprivation under slavery, which all their resourcefulness had not been able to counteract. "Insufficient nourishment and untimely work" had weakened their health, and the people were smart enough to understand the damage that had been done to them. "They understand very well, themselves, that they have not had a fair chance in this way," he continued. The women believed that now, under freedom, they could raise stronger children, freed from the "custom" of the planters of extorting fieldwork from pregnant women up to the day of their delivery and returning them to it within a few weeks thereafter. One woman told him that the children born since the flight of the slaveholders were "fat, dey's big and hearty." He quoted her with some care. The new babies, she said,

> "an't like dem in de old time. De chillen born in de old time,
> dey poor tings, dey lean, *lean* like buzzard .... For why," she
> continued, "dey used to make we work, *work*, WORK, so
> poor moder hab nuffin to gib her child—child starve 'fore it
> born—dat's what makes 'em lean, like buzzard."[47]

Nordhoff noted that the only "labor- or time-saving arrangement" he saw provided by the planters was the periodic planting of palmetto trees among the cotton fields, to provide shade for mothers to nurse their babies quickly between their hours in the fields, "and that," he remarked in disgust, "saved time and labor only for [the planters'] profit."

Nordhoff insisted that the ways of the freed slaves were explicable on the basis of environment and not race, and that to blame them for adapting themselves to the constraints of slavery was simply wrongheaded, however maladaptive or immoral their behavior might seem to more privileged souls. Lying, for example, was a characteristic of most oppressed peoples, who knew

---

[46].   CN, *Freedmen*, 19–20.

[47].   CN, *Freedmen*, 6.

that they had to manipulate their surroundings for their own protection. Nordhoff did his best to draw parallels between the freed slaves and the Irish, poor whites, and mainstream American evangelicals. The African-Americans' religious demonstrativeness, for instance, was not so different from that of any Midwestern camp meeting. He noted that the families were close-knit and loving, and "the marriage relation is, in general, held sacred," though, he delicately added, the women were not "eminently chaste." But this too was a legacy of slavery, for slave owners had not discouraged their female slaves from getting pregnant, married or not.

Even with highly charged issues such as illegitimacy, Nordhoff kept a detached anthropological perspective as he investigated the Sea Islanders' lives, carefully noting their appearance, dialect, diet, costume, and habits. He tried to render the voices of his subjects in dialect for the sake of verisimilitude rather than mockery, much as he had recorded the Scottish brogues of old shipmates, and he only regretted that "the tones of the voice are impossible to give." Their thick Gullah dialect frankly baffled him, but he conceded that it had its own internal logic, as did any system of linguistics. "They have a curious accent, something like that of a Frenchman speaking English poorly," he explained;

> but in addition, they have numerous contractions, inversions of form, and cant phrases, which make the unaccustomed listener's work more difficult. "I go shum," was a puzzle to me, … till I learned that "shum" is simply a contraction for "see him," and the whole phrase means generally, "I will go and see about it."

Though their language was interesting, Nordhoff declared it to be "a barrier to intercourse" with outsiders, which "gave me, unconsciously, sometimes the feeling that I was speaking with foreigners," a state of affairs of which he disapproved.[48] But he pronounced "Roll, Jordan, Roll" to have "a glorious swing," and he recorded the lyrics of some of the songs, just as he had habitually copied down sea chanties as a young man. He foresaw, in the changes sure to come with freedom, the end of the insular folk culture developed among the Islands' black population; and he hoped that more songs might be written down, words and melodies both, for they would "quickly disappear," though "eminently worth preserving." Some decades would pass before cultural anthropologists would follow suit.

Anxious to dispel the Southern planters' old tales of the dangerous propensities of their slaves, Nordhoff emphasized the former slaves' docility

---

[48]   CN, *Freedmen*, 8.

and imputed any criminal behavior they exhibited under slavery to the demoralizing effect of slavery itself. They were "so harmless, so kind, so ready to submit to all laws and to proper guidance, so averse from violence," he noted, that white schoolteachers everywhere moved about them "unguarded, unarmed and unharmed." He even quoted one Union officer's opinion that the African-Americans were "always cheerful, docile, and easily ruled."[49]

This imputed harmlessness of the ex-slaves, he hastened to add, did not imply any lack of courage or will or impugn their manhood; and he was careful to note the valorous activities of the black soldiers, the valiant deeds of Robert Smalls and others who fled slavery with wives and children, and their zealousness in helping to round up conscripts. And the picture that Nordhoff painted of the Sea Islanders did not, in its entirety, consistently make them out to be so tractable and childlike, and the newspaper columns seem to be the product of two contradictory impulses. Nordhoff did not want any Northerners to fear the freed slaves or to believe the scaremongering of Southern propagandists against them, and so he described them in vague terms as harmless and docile creatures posing no threat to the existing order. But his love of pinning down the telling detail, his respect for his subjects, and his constant need to cite concrete examples precluded a totally skewed portrait. He could not help including vivid descriptions of the demonstrated anger and rage that the former slaves felt, when any of them were candid enough to open up to him. The reporter, in these cases, somewhat undermined the propagandist, and it is in these passages that his writing springs to life.

"For a people living under a patriarchal system," he noted—by which he meant one of supposed benign paternalism—the freed slaves "display a singular dislike of the patriarchs." The men and women all held their former masters to be "mean," he remarked, and at the least hard taskmasters. Even when Nordhoff heard one late planter referred to as "good Mr. Fripps," he found that what the people meant ill-accorded with his own notions of goodness.

> "Dey's all mean alike," said one man .... "Come now, Sam," said the questioner. "There was good Mr. Fripps, he could not have been mean." "Yes, sah, he bad to his people same as any of 'em." "Why do you call him good Mr. Fripps, then?" "Oh!" said Sam, "dat no tell he good to we; call him 'good' 'cause he good Metodis' man—he sing and pray loud on Sundys."[50]

---

49. CN, *Freedmen*, 3, and David Hunter quoted in ibid., 27.

50. CN, *Freedmen*, 7. Nordhoff always enjoyed pointing out religious hypocrisy.

Although the former slaves never expressed "words of hatred" for their past masters, Nordhoff perceived in them a loathing too deep for words. Any suggestion that the slaveholders might return elicited an "expression of horror" from the people that "was painful to me," Nordhoff recalled, "and surely disgraceful to the runaway patriarchs." Even a suggestion that one planter be brought back to the Islands to be hanged caused a group of women to cry out in a chorus, "much excited and shriller than ever—'No, no, don't fetch him here, we no want to see him nebber again!'"

In a vivid example of his willingness to portray the freed slaves as less than submissive, Nordhoff recorded one encounter with an old woman in her sickbed. She spoke with satisfaction about her master having had to abandon his sumptuous home, bitterly dwelling upon the money expended on its luxurious outfitting. "She dwells much upon the fact that her master had paid much money for the house," Nordhoff wrote.

> I asked, "Where did your master get so much money?" At this the old woman rose in her bed—she was sick, and my friends were paying her a visit of kindness—and with some excitement exclaimed, "Whar he git he money? Whar he git he money? Is dat what you ask--whar he got he money? *I* show you, massa." Pushing up her sleeve, she showed a gaunt, skinny, black arm, and tapping it energetically with her forefinger, exclaimed, "You see dat, massa? Dat's whar he got he money—out of dat black skin he got he money."[51]

In the pages of the *Evening Post*, Nordhoff let the woman have her say.

In a neat balancing act, Nordhoff managed to convey both a strong condemnation of the effects of slavery upon the people and an optimistic assessment of their virtues and potential. His was the dream of a color-blind society, with no need to take account of racial difference. A product of Jacksonian America, Nordhoff loathed any sort of special privileges or disabilities enacted upon a people. Neither blacks, nor women, nor Native Americans would benefit from special protections under the law, which would only damage their characters; nor, he believed, ought they be debarred all the rights extended to white men. (By the same token, governmental assistance to business, in the form of protective tariffs, subsidies, or land grants, was equally pernicious.) In a hundred instances, he wrote, "it was brought home to me that these freedmen are men and women as we are, and that the problem of turning

---

51.   CN, *Freedmen*, 7–8.

them into useful members of society is divested of most, if not all, its difficulties the moment we make this the first principle ruling our plans."[52]

Too perceptive to ignore signs of trouble, however, Nordhoff acknowledged that such an egalitarian reception might not be forthcoming from white America, North or South. In one incident, he witnessed Robert Smalls, a former slave who had gained national renown when he managed to pilot a steamship carrying his family and loaded with Confederate munitions past Fort Sumter to the Union forces beyond, subjected to humiliating treatment as he waited to see a Union Admiral. A general saw Smalls approach, in Nordhoff's account.

> The General called to the officer of the deck and said to him: "Officer, this *boy* wants to see the Admiral; will you please let him know that the boy is waiting!" Then turning to Smalls, he cried out, in a sharp voice, "Here, *boy*, you can go aboard...."

Nordhoff was chagrined. "Now Smalls is *not* a boy; he is a man of, I should think, thirty years," he wrote, and he "blushed" for the General's bigotry, for he was sure that a white man who had performed Small's brave feat would be duly honored. "But because this gallant fellow happens to have a black skin," he wrote, the General "speaks to him in a way that seemed to me, unwillingly listening to him, contemptibly mean." Nordhoff did not know how Smalls reacted to the insult, "for I dared not look in the poor fellow's face."[53]

Again and again, Nordhoff held out the hope that bigotry might be conquered, as it had been conquered in the past, and reason prevail. He recurred to the parallel of anti-Semitism. "Like the blacks," he noted, German Jews

> were regarded as of a peculiar race; ...and anyone who has travelled through Germany knows that the prejudice which existed there, till within twenty years, was just as strong, as unreasoning, and apparently as unconquerable as that which prevails in this country against the blacks.

With an irony that can only be appreciated by a less-innocent world, Nordhoff continued in his attempt to vindicate his native land and to hold up for Americans the possibility of change and the dissolution of prejudice. Although Americans might be unaware of the virulence of German anti-Semitism, "any German who reads this will bear me out in the assertion that

---

[52]   CN, *Freedmen*, 16.

[53]   CN, *Freedmen*, 26–7. Willie Lee Rose's *Rehearsal for Reconstruction* summarizes Small's exploits on pp. 149–50.

the Jewish race was as bitterly despised and the Jew's rights as little regarded by the common people in that country thirty years ago as are the black skin and the rights of its possessor in the South to-day." Bigotry, needless to say, was to prove more intractable, and less subject to reason, than Nordhoff hoped. But in the springtime of 1863, his faith in human goodness and rationality was still largely unshaken.[54]

By 1863, Charles Nordhoff had come to regard responsible journalism as essential to democracy, for only education of the common people could assure wise public action. In a time of civil war, this responsibility bore down heavily upon him. He had not enlisted in the Union army, but he clearly believed that battles waged on the editorial page of the *Evening Post* were as essential to the war effort as those fought in the field.

As the conflict dragged on and casualties mounted, it became apparent that volunteers alone would not suffice for the duration of the war. Desertions were rampant, and the volunteers of 1861 were soon to be mustered out. The *Evening Post* had been among the first to call for a draft. In doing so, it opposed Democratic papers that more closely reflected the sentiments of working-class people, who believed that a draft would weigh most heavily on the poor.

There had never been strong support for the war among struggling Northern whites, who resented the higher taxes and rampant inflation brought on by the struggle and feared that freed slaves would flood the Northern labor market, depressing their wages and raising unemployment. Nevertheless, Congress passed a Conscription Act in early March 1863. It included a provision allowing any draftee to buy his way out of service for $300. This amounted to six months' wages for the average worker. Blacks, not regarded as citizens, were not eligible for the draft, and these aspects of the Act fostered considerable resentment among working-class whites. When the first draft lottery took place in mid-July, racial and class tensions exploded in New York with a force that stunned the nation.[55]

On Monday, July 13, rioting broke out in the city and continued for four days, in a total breakdown of civil order that prompted the Lincoln Administration to send in Union troops, fresh from their victory at Gettysburg, to restore order. Arson and looting were rampant, and well over one hundred people were killed before the end of the violence. Newspapers that had favored the draft were a

---

[54]. CN, *Freedmen*, 19. One can only be glad that Nordhoff didn't live to see the rise of Nazi Germany.

[55]. Iver Bernstein's *The New York City Draft Riots: Their Significance for American Society and Politics in the Age of the Civil War* (NY: Oxford, 1990) provides an insightful and detailed examination of the riots and their context. The estimate that $300 equaled six months' pay is in Paludan, *A People's Contest*, 190.

natural target for the angry rioters, as were the draft offices, African-American establishments, and the homes of prominent Republicans.

After it was all over, Nordhoff wrote a lengthy account of the ordeal, presenting the conflict in almost Manichean terms of good against evil, good being personified by the Republican police chief and evil by the "mob."[56] The working people with whom he usually felt such empathy could not, in Nordhoff's mind, have been capable of such criminal behavior, and he believed that "demagogues" had somehow conceived of and incited the uprising. If, in fact, the Northern working people were not behind the war effort, and would not willingly fight for the Union, then the struggle for freedom and democracy in the South would have a hollow ring.

Nordhoff loathed seeing his own name in a newspaper story. Although he never used the first person in his article on the draft riots, the point of view, inclusion of some incidents and exclusion of others, all betray Nordhoff's presence at the scenes he depicted. As a general principle, he never wrote vivid accounts of events that he had not himself seen although he often quoted other witnesses when pertinent, making clear attributions. Judging from the story he told in the *Evening Post*, his investigation of the riots placed him in considerable danger. He was in for a harrowing four days.

Accompanying the police chief on the morning of the thirteenth, Nordhoff seems to have been present when a crowd violently attacked and beat the chief, who was spirited away unconscious. "At this time a well-known member of the press," Nordhoff wrote, "...was suddenly assaulted by the cry, 'Here's a d--d abolitionist! Hang him!'" As he described, with curious indirection, the subsequent events, there is little doubt that Nordhoff was telling his own story:

> An ineffectual remonstrance, and then retreat, but the mob were too much for him. Hit by a paving stone on the back of his neck, by another in the face, robbed of his watch and purse in the *melee*, he didn't know when or how; losing sense and memory, he struggled along, finally caught up by some firemen and hurried into their engine house, where the strong door, promptly barricaded, kept the assailants at bay....

The events of the following hours are only vaguely alluded to in the narrative, suggesting that he was temporarily deterred from his investigations. But he picked up the thread of the story quickly enough, describing with

---

56. CN, "The Story of the 'Four Days:' The Mob and Its Leaders," New York *Evening Post*, July 23, 1863, 1. The entire story appeared on the huge front page of the *Post*, and so further citations have been omitted for subsequent quotations from the article.

approval the efforts of police and militia to restore order. Meanwhile, he made provisions for the defense of his family and Brooklyn home. As the houses of prominent Republicans became targets of the crowd's anger, several being looted and set afire, Nordhoff reputedly provided Lida, then twenty-four years old (and apparently no pale and fainting creature), with a "stock of bombs" that she "stood ready to use in case of need" while he stood guard at the *Evening Post*.[57]

Adhering to his belief that the people were not acting out of spontaneous rage, but were being directed by some demagogic intelligence, Nordhoff described the rioters' splitting into three groups, each bent on attacking its own significant target. There had to be someone directing the crowd, he insisted, for the rioters "were men themselves incapable of self-direction; men of the lowest order and most brutal passions." He took some care to exclude certain groups from his condemnation of the "mob": firemen (perhaps out of gratitude for their having rescued him) and the Irish as a class. "Although the rioters were Irishmen," he admitted, "they were mostly of the abandoned class."

Rushing past this insight, which might have better explained the explosion of violence, Nordhoff emphasized the innocence of most of the Irish community, including priests and the many Irish members of the police force. He acknowledged that the violence was a symptom of large problems, the Conscription Act only serving as a lightning rod for simmering discontent. But the underlying problem was not the difficult living and working conditions of the poor, but the ambitious scheming of powerful, wily politicians, bent on consolidating power at any cost. Somehow, he was sure, the Tammany Democrats were implicated in all this. Had not the rioters cheered wildly, not only for Jefferson Davis, but also for Tammany stalwarts Mayor Fernando Wood and Governor Horatio Seymour?

But what disturbed Nordhoff most of all was the "running hunt for negroes." He believed that "the old antipathy of the Irish to the negroes had been eagerly seized upon by the leaders," fomenting racial hatred for selfish ends. In fact, African-Americans were attacked with appalling viciousness, and Nordhoff had seen more of this than he could stomach. "An infernal impulse" had driven the crowd, as they burned down the Negro Orphan Asylum and threatened to kill the fleeing children. One black man, he wrote, "had been murdered, mutilated, hanged and burned … under circumstances of atrocity without example." He may have been referring to one of the particularly bloody lynchings described in court documents, in which rioters cut off the dead man's penis and danced

---

[57]. "Charles Nordhoff: Some Reminiscences of the Man Who Edited the Evening Post Through the Period of the Civil War," New York *Evening Post*, December 7, 1901, 25.

about with it; he decried the incident as "a blot upon our city, the foulest that ever befel it," and sure to incur God's wrathful judgment.

On Monday evening, the offices of the pro-draft New York *Tribune* were attacked. While other Republican newspapers had taken defensive measures against the impending riots, *Tribune* editor Horace Greeley had refused to do so, citing his faith in the goodness of the common man. A crowd (the "negro-hunting gang," Nordhoff called them, "the flushed assassins") burst into the *Tribune's* ground floor offices and set them afire. (The building was saved.) By contrast, the pro-war *Times* and *Evening Post* had braced themselves against attack. At the *Times*, reporter Augustus Maverick recalled, the owners "planted revolving cannon in their publication office, and provided great store of other death-dealing weapons with which to repel invasion."[58]

The upper floors of the *Evening Post* building had been converted to a hospital for wounded Union soldiers and presented an obvious target to the rioters. Nordhoff, shaken and furious after the ugly scenes he had witnessed, saw assault on the *Evening Post* as an attack on free speech and democracy itself and posted notices warning that he had attached hoses to the building's steam pipes and placed them so that any marauders could be sprayed with boiling water (a less lethal defense than that of the *Times*, at least). It was later remembered that he stayed at the *Post* building for days on end during the riots, "quietly smoking and writing while the mob howled outside." The *Post* did not interrupt publication that week and was left unmolested.[59]

In the aftermath of the riots, Nordhoff blamed the city government and the Democratic politicians who ran it for a dilatory and weak response to the disorder and wrote that "several hundred lives and half a million property" had been lost because the militia had not been armed with live ammunition in the early days of the uprising. (In his horror, he exaggerated the number killed, which is documented at one hundred five.) There was considerable debate among the newspapers as to the nature of the violence and the proper response to it. Democratically inclined papers, such as the *Herald* and the *World*, insisted that it was, in fact, a spontaneous popular uprising against an unjust law. Their opponents, the *Tribune*, *Times*, and *Evening Post*, refused to believe that the violence was anything but the product of a small criminal class bent on mischief. The latter also united in casting blame on Democratic politicians for encouraging anti-draft feelings and fueling racial and ethnic tensions.

---

[58] See Bernstein, 21 and passim; Glyndon Van Deusen, *Horace Greeley*, 298–300; Augustus Maverick, *Henry J. Raymond and the New York Times for Thirty Years* (Hartford: A.S. Hale & Co., 1870), 164–6.

[59] Nevins, *The Evening Post*, 300–309; "Charles Nordhoff," *Evening Post*, December 7, 1901, 25; Brown, *William Cullen Bryant*, 451–3.

Nordhoff closed his account of the riots with praise for the "disciplined and uniformed police," first instituted by Tammany mayor Fernando Wood, and added, "May every bad engineer be so 'hoist with his own petard.'"[60]

On the second day of the rioting, the *Herald* editorialized that "the people" of New York had taken to the streets in anger, and the riots themselves were a "popular" and righteous outburst, and the *World* echoed those sentiments: "Does any man wonder that poor men refuse to be forced into a war mismanaged almost into hopelessness, perverted almost into partisanship?" To this the Republican response was quick and certain. "The *World* describes the mob of infamous thieves, murderers and house-burners, who have been rioting ..., as 'the laboring population,'" an *Evening Post* editorial noted, while "the *Herald* speaks of them as 'the people.'" It protested that such rhetoric, in effect, was an effort to "persuade the country that the workingmen of this city, taken as a whole, are a law-defying set of miscreants, capable of the most atrocious and also of the meanest crimes known to the calendar." Ignoring the opposition's insistence on the justice of the rioters' anger, the editors of the *Post*, Nordhoff included, simply could not accept the idea of simmering popular rage. The rioters were not "the people." "They are the vile scum which gathers in all great assemblages of man," the *Post* insisted, "which preys upon the industrious classes, and which is of service only to demagogues." It ended with a call for the common people to enlist, as vindication of the charge leveled against them.[61]

In subsequent issues of the *Evening Post*, considerable space was devoted to stories on the "Colored Refugees of New York" driven from their homes by the lynch mobs. With the memory of the Sea Islanders and what he had learned from them of slavery still fresh in his mind, Nordhoff could not, in 1863, consider any mitigating factors in the crimes of the rioters.[62] Lynchings and attacks upon the defenseless could not be understood, let alone justified, no matter what the provocation. His insistence that the riots were directed by "demagogues" reflected not only the influence upon him of the elite circle that surrounded the *Evening Post*, but also a fundamental revulsion from disorder and a belief that there could be no real conflict between two just causes.

[60.] Maverick, 165; Van Deusen, 300; CN, "Four Days."

[61.] "Insults to the People," New York *Evening Post*, July 15, 1863; other editorials are quoted in Brown, 452; Nevins, 308–9; Maverick, 165–6.

[62.] For example, "The Colored Refugees of New York," New York *Evening Post*, July 18, 1863; and "The Black Refugees on Staten Island," New York *Evening Post*, July 21, 1863.

In later years, Nordhoff would come to regret his vehemence toward the rioters, as he repeatedly saw the uprising conjured up as justification for depriving New York's immigrant and working-class communities of the vote. A deeper understanding of the complexity of social problems, and the intractability of racism, awaited Nordhoff in the postwar years.

CHAPTER 3
Educating the Common People

At the New York *Evening Post* during the Civil War, Charles Nordhoff assisted editors William Cullen Bryant and Parke Godwin in bearing the standard for the Union; but with the surrender of the Confederacy in 1865, he soon found other causes for which to fight. Both Bryant and Godwin abandoned the *Evening Post* to Nordhoff during the late 1860s, and he seized upon his new autonomy to make the *Post* more conspicuously a voice for tolerance and liberalism, calling for equal rights for African-Americans, Native Americans, women, religious minorities, and immigrants. At the same time, he viewed with dismay a Republican Party that seemed to be abandoning its high-minded origins for a more culturally exclusive and, it seemed to him, antidemocratic emphasis upon the right of the privileged to control public affairs. Without the issue of slavery to serve as a political litmus test, Nordhoff often found himself at odds with his erstwhile allies and with his employers as well.

In 1864, when Abraham Lincoln was opposed for reelection by Democrat George McClellan, Charles Nordhoff realized that the pro-Lincoln editorials of the *Evening Post* were preaching to the converted, as the *Post*'s readership was assumed to be a staunchly Republican one. Accordingly, during the month before the general election, he began to print a separate newspaper, a Republican campaign sheet in the form of a four-page weekly titled *The Workingman*, which sold for a penny. Its first issue reached a circulation of 50,000—two and one-half times that of the *Post*—and was aimed at the immigrant and working-class communities of New York, the same people who had taken to the streets during the draft riots of 1863. Nordhoff tailored his arguments for Lincoln in every way possible to the interests of his intended audience. It was all to no avail. New York voted solidly for McClellan that fall.[1]

[1.] Both Allan Nevins, in the *Evening Post* (New York: Boni & Liveright, 1922), 313, and Charles Brown, in *William Cullen Bryant* (New York: Charles Scribner's Sons,

In another attempt to reach a broader audience, Nordhoff gathered his *Evening Post* editorials urging ratification of the Thirteenth Amendment, which would abolish slavery everywhere in the United States, and published them in a pamphlet that he had freely distributed. The title made his intentions clear. AMERICA FOR FREE WORKING MEN! it shouted, Mechanics, Farmers and Laborers READ! HOW SLAVERY INJURES THE WORKING MAN. THE SLAVE-LABOR SYSTEM THE FREE WORKINGMAN'S WORST ENEMY. He presented endorsements from pro-war Democrats in a foreword and sent a copy to President Lincoln, requesting his imprimatur as well. "I have treated the question from the white man's & not from the negroe's standpoint," he explained, because he believed that Emancipation could not succeed, regardless of the fate of the Constitutional Amendment, unless the common people developed a "hearty hatred" of slavery.[2]

Nordhoff used statistics to buttress his case, a favorite tactic he would resort to again and again. The pamphlet's argument was standard free-soil ideology, with an emphasis on the class inequities perpetuated by the slave system, and went at the topic from every conceivable angle: political, social, economic, and cultural. In sum, he argued, slavery resulted in a dissolution of the bonds of community and mutuality, the give-and-take between classes that was spiritual as well as economic, and to Nordhoff the necessary condition for a healthy society. The most obvious problem in American life was slavery, and its solution was equally obvious: immediate ratification of the Thirteenth Amendment.

Nordhoff's *America for Free Working Men* was the final salvo in his battle against slavery, and once the Thirteenth Amendment was well on its way toward ratification, he turned his attention elsewhere. For an entire generation, disputes between North and South had absorbed the nation's attention and all of its political energies, but now, with slavery dead at last, he knew other problems awaited solution. During the first years after the end of the war, Northern activists like Nordhoff engaged in a flurry of projects and plans, eager to extend their victory over the Confederacy and slavery to one over social problems of all kinds.[3]

1971), 466, mention the existence of the *Workingman* as a product of the *Evening Post*. Extremely rare, the only known extant copies of the paper are at the American Antiquarian Society, dated October 8 and 15, 1864. The *Workingman*'s style, tone, and content—including numerous anecdotes drawn from the sailor's life—are unmistakably Nordhoff's.

2. CN to "His Excellency The President of the United States," January 10, 1865, letter bound into the Library of Congress's copy of CN's *America for Free Working Men!* (New York: Harper & Brothers, 1865).

3. Morton Keller, *Affairs of State: Public Life in Late Nineteenth-Century America* (Cambridge: Harvard University Press, 1977) is a useful survey of political action during the postwar period.

One such project was the founding of a new weekly journal of opinion, *The Nation*, modeled on the British *Westminster Review* as a forum for informed political discussion. The journal was the brainchild of a group of highly educated, well-to-do, and reform-minded Republicans, including Frederick Law Olmsted, Charles Eliot Norton, and E. L. Godkin, who was to become its first editor. Funding was provided by a group of abolitionists who expected the new journal to be devoted to promoting the welfare of the freedmen, but within six months of its first issue, Godkin bought them out, freeing his editorial hand.[4]

Nordhoff, by 1865 well-known to Godkin and his circle through his zealous editorializing at the *Evening Post*, was approached by Norton to assist in editing the weekly, but he declined to take a position that he saw as primarily managerial rather than editorial. He didn't believe Godkin wanted or needed another editor, particularly one with an independent turn of mind. Moreover, there were other projects being proposed that interested him more.[5] In addition to his stated reasons for declining the position, Nordhoff had little sympathy for certain views of the autocratic Godkin, who combined his reformism with an emphasis on the right of the wellborn and highly educated to take charge of public affairs. Though this was an increasingly common pairing of attitudes during the Gilded Age, it was anathema to the more democratically inclined Nordhoff. According to Godkin's standards, Nordhoff himself would at one time have been relegated to the ranks of the voiceless and powerless. His instincts in declining to join Godkin at *The Nation* were sound: Godkin later praised the man he hired in Nordhoff's stead for his "willingness to obey lawful orders."[6]

At the *Evening Post*, meanwhile, the end of the war brought Nordhoff greater freedom. Parke Godwin left the paper after an argument with Bryant over Isaac Henderson's continued connection with the newspaper, for Henderson had been indicted in 1864 by a Federal grand jury on charges of accepting kickbacks as Navy Agent of New York. He came to trial in May 1865 and was

---

4.   On the *Nation*, see Thomas Bender, *New York Intellect: A History of Intellectual Life in New York City from 1750 to the Beginnings of Our Own Time* (Baltimore: Johns Hopkins University Press, 1987), 176–191; William M. Armstrong, *E. L. Godkin: A Biography* (Albany: SUNY Press, 1978), passim; John G. Sproat, *"The Best Men:" Liberal Reformers in the Gilded Age* (New York: Oxford University Press, 1968), passim; and Laura Wood Roper, *FLO: A Biography of Frederick Law Olmsted* (Baltimore: Johns Hopkins University Press, 1973), 291–8.

5.   CN to Charles Eliot Norton, May 4 [1865], Norton Papers, Houghton Library, Harvard University.

6.   E. L. Godkin to Charles Eliot Norton, May 6 [1865], Norton Papers, Houghton Library, Harvard University.

acquitted on a technicality that Godwin did not believe negated his guilt. Godwin could not understand his father-in-law's loyalty to Henderson—Bryant had even written to President Lincoln in an attempt to get the charges against Henderson dismissed—and was convinced that Henderson's connection with the paper was damaging its credibility as a force for reform. "We cannot brand a defaulter, condemn peculation, urge official economy, or get into any sort of contrariety with other journals without having the charges against H. ...flung in our faces," Godwin warned Bryant. Their position was untenable. "Not once, but two dozen times I have been shut up by a rejoinder of this sort," he added, and Nordhoff had endured the same treatment so often that he was threatening, "peremptorily and positively," to leave the paper if Henderson continued to be connected with it.[7] Bryant stood by Henderson, however, and shortly thereafter, Godwin left the *Evening Post* in disgust for what turned out to be a thirteen-year absence. Despite his threats, Nordhoff remained, possibly realizing that Godwin's departure would give him a greater share of the paper's editorial voice.[8]

In 1865, Bryant was still an active presence at the *Evening Post* and its guiding force; but by the following spring, the health of his wife, Frances, who had been ailing for some time, suddenly took a turn for the worse, and he devoted less and less time to journalism. By April of 1866, Mrs. Bryant's condition had so deteriorated that Bryant had the Nordhoff family stay near his home on Long Island. While Lida helped the Bryants, Nordhoff commuted to the city each day, reporting back to Bryant on activities at the *Evening Post*. Bryant "did not go to the office for two whole months," Nordhoff wrote to Godwin that summer. "But I went over to see him every evening; took his instructions, read him all

---

7. Parke Godwin to William Cullen Bryant, July 31, 1865, Bryant-Godwin Papers, NYPL. On the Henderson corruption trial, and Godwin's response to it, see Nevins, 427–9, and Theodore Hornberger, ed., *William Cullen Bryant and Isaac Henderson: New Evidence on a Strange Partnership* (New York: Haskell House, 1973), introduction.

8. During the summer of 1865, Bryant purchased his old family homestead in Great Barrington, Massachusetts, and went there to escape the New York summer. According to John Bigelow, Bryant's removal to Great Barrington that summer began a period of inattention to the *Evening Post*; Nevins says that Bryant wrote most of the lead editorials until 1866, but very few thereafter. See Boylan, "William Cullen Bryant," *Dictionary of Literary Biography*, volume 43, 88; Nevins, 341. Godwin's movements are shadowy, but according to Brown (*William Cullen Bryant*, 477), Godwin and his wife went to Europe early in the winter of 1865–66, and remained there at least until 1867; there are letters from Nordhoff to Godwin in Paris dating from 1869. In 1868, Godwin sold his share of the paper to Bryant and Henderson, severing his connection with the *Evening Post*.

the important articles before they were printed; and in that he has managed the paper as much as he could under the circumstances."[9]

Frances Bryant died in late July 1866. Losing his wife of forty-five years devastated Bryant, and after a retreat to his summer home, he left for Europe in mid-November for a yearlong visit.[10] The poet returned to America early in the Autumn of 1867, but he was never again an active presence at the newspaper, preferring to spend his time at home engaged in literary pursuits, halfheartedly translating The *Iliad*.[11]

Nordhoff had gradually taken over editorial control at the paper. With Bryant's departure for Europe, the inhibiting influence his proximity had had upon the younger editor vanished, and the character of the paper altered dramatically. Gone, for the most part, were the articles on "Rambles in New England" and "Gossip From Paris," replaced by prominent and lengthy columns on topics such as workers' cooperatives, universal suffrage, and public health, housing and clothing reform, accompanied on the editorial page by attacks upon privilege and defenses of the rights of labor, women, African-Americans, Native Americans, and immigrants, often with scrupulous documentation to back up the arguments. In all these efforts, there burned the zeal of the crusader. Nordhoff was waging war on America's failures to live up to its democratic ideals, and he was doing so with relish.

"There is no doubt," Charles Nordhoff wrote to Parke Godwin in the late 1860s, "that Democracy, Socialism, morals and Christianity are inseparably one."[12] By "socialism," Nordhoff emphatically did not mean Marxism or the abolition of private property, but rather a voluntary social consciousness and brotherhood, the fellowship demanded by Christianity. The highest development of an interdependent society could be summarized in one word: cooperation. During 1867, under Nordhoff's guidance, a flurry of front-page articles and editorials appeared in the *Evening Post*, explaining the moral and material advantages to be gained through cooperative efforts of all kinds: stores, housekeeping, housing, and worker-owned industries and shops.[13]

---

9.   CN to Parke Godwin, August 3, 1866. See also CN to Godwin, May 26, 1866. Bryant-Godwin Papers, NYPL.

10. See Bryant's letter to Henderson dated December 1, 1866, from Paris, in Hornberger, 9.

11. Brown, 476–90.

12. CN to Parke Godwin, February 16 [1869], Bryant-Godwin Papers, NYPL.

13. Eighteen sixty-seven articles and editorials in the *Evening Post* include the following: 3/18/67, "Co-operation: Another Letter from Mr. Ruskin"; 4/20/67, "Story of Vineland"; 4/25, "Co-Operation: A Better Remedy than Strikes"; 5/6, "Co-Operation in this City"; 5/10, "Something Better Than Strikes"; 5/25, "One Remedy

The basis of Nordhoff's interest in cooperative organizations was his concern with rising labor unrest. Although he endorsed the right of workers to strike, he doubted that strikes could substantially improve the lot of workers, and he championed the idea of cooperation as an alternative. Cooperatives, unlike strikes or restrictions on working hours, did not violate the laws of classical economics, in which Nordhoff had an unshakeable faith. The eight-hour movement, for example, was in fact "a demand for higher wages," and only the marketplace could determine whether that demand was reasonable. Strikes seldom did workers any good, he argued, when one calculated the wages lost and the union dues paid over time. Nordhoff was inveterately opposed to the "closed shop" and the idea that a union might prevent an employer from hiring non-union employees, for this seemed a fatal abridgment of liberty of contract. With an essentially negative view of liberty, one that connoted absence of coercion rather than any positive power, Nordhoff viewed strikes and unions as divisive. Adhering to the old-style Republican free-labor ideology, he insisted that in fact, labor and capital enjoyed a harmony of interests, if only rightly understood. Cooperatives had the great merit of making the laborer and the capitalist one and the same.[14]

One might dream of utopia, but Nordhoff was interested in the concrete incremental steps that might be taken on the way to a better world. In cooperatives, people could freely choose to combine their efforts—their time, money, labor—for more efficient and equitable ends. Why should every family pay high prices for their small sacks of flour when several together could purchase more cheaply at wholesale? Why should artisans sell their skill and labor to an employer, when they might own their own business by pooling their small savings? Why should every woman have to haul hundreds of pounds of water to and fro in washing clothing and linens, when the laundry of an entire

---

for High Prices"; 5/28, "Co-Operation in France"; 5/13, "The Cost of Living: Why Prices are so High; The Remedy: Cooperation"; 5/28, "Co-Operative Movements in Chicago"; 5/29, "Co-Operatives in Chicago"; 6/4, "Profitableness of Co-operative Societies"; 6/12, "Books on Industrial Co-operation"; 7/5, "Co-Operative Stores: How to Conduct Them"; 7/23, "Cooperation in the Southern States"; 9/17, "Co-Operative Stores"; 9/26, "A Cooperative Restaurant"; 10/8, "Cooperative Stores in England"; 11/1: "Progress of Cooperatives in N.Y."; 11/13, "Cooperative Stores." After Bryant's return, articles on cooperatives still appeared, but with less frequency and prominence.

14. [CN,] "The Master Masons and the Bricklayers," *EP*, August 18, 1868; [CN,] "Something Better Than Strikes," *EP*, May 10, 1867; [CN,] "Capital and Labor," *EP*, June 21, 1869; [CN,] "The Labor Question," *EP*, May 5, 1868; [CN] "Strikes and Strikers," *EP*, July 31, 1868.

community might be done at once with little more effort? Rather than attacking the low wages and long hours of the untrammeled industrial capitalism that kept so many people in poverty, Nordhoff focused, for the most part, on the excessively high cost of living that resulted from the profit-mongering of society's "non-producers," another legacy of the Jacksonian value system with which he had been raised. *Evening Post* articles denouncing "middlemen" demonstrated with statistics how these non-producers were "supported, fattened, enriched" at the expense of the "hard-working mechanic, the industrious laborer, the toiling clerk."[15] Cooperative buying at wholesale would eliminate such parasites.

Nordhoff also urged families of modest means to buy apartment houses together rather than live at the mercy of landlords while single laborers could profitably form workingmen's clubs, which would procure them housing and domestic services. Familiar with the work of Ruskin, he suggested that such associations be formed along occupational lines, much as medieval guilds had been. The "congenial society of those engaged in like work," he believed, "would ... make them, by the mutual interchange of ideas, more intelligent, interested and useful workmen."[16]

Emphasizing the "perfect feasibility" of such cooperatives, Nordhoff explained the nuts-and-bolts mechanics of organizing and maintaining cooperative establishments. Without clearheaded administration, the best-intentioned schemes were doomed to failure. His model cooperative would be orderly and well-managed, with rules printed up and distributed to all members, committees of admission to screen applicants and regularly stipulated terms of investment and profit-sharing.[17] His faith in the practicability of cooperative schemes was buoyed by the evidence of successful cooperative movements being initiated all across the country, which he was happy to publicize.[18]

Ultimately, cooperation in Nordhoff's eyes was not solely, or even primarily, an economic measure. It was rather "a scheme of social and moral as well as of fiscal regeneration," encouraging "harmony and good feeling" and bringing "order out of chaos." Industrial workers might be freed to make of themselves what they would; through cooperatives, they could maintain a

---

15. [CN,] "The Cost of Living. Why Prices are so High—The Remedy—Co-Operation," New York *Evening Post*, May 13, 1867, 1.

16. [CN,] "The Cost of Living," *EP*, May 13, 1867.

17. [CN,] "The Cost of Living," *EP*, May 13, 1867; [CN,] "The Chief Hindrance to Cooperation," *EP*, June 9, 1869.

18. [CN,] "Co-Operative Stores," *EP*, September 17, 1867; "Progress of Co-operation in New York," *EP*, November 1, 1867; "Cooperative Movements in New York," *EP* May 28, 1867; "Co-operation in Chicago," *EP*, May 29, 1867; "Profitableness of Co-operative Societies," *EP*, June 4, 1867.

decent standard of living despite the inexorable laws of classical economics and the greediness of individual businessmen. Interdependence was the true means to independence.[19]

There were those, Nordhoff conceded, who believed that such cooperatives were not needed in the United States and were doomed to failure because "it is said, every skillful and industrious mechanic" could expect to rise to the position of employer and capitalist. But times were changing, and the old free-labor formula might no longer apply. In the cities, "many thousands of skilful and industrious artisans" could be found "whose fate it appears to be, for lack of capital, to remain servants all their lives." Although he appreciated the changes that industrialization was bringing to America's social and economic structure, as yet Nordhoff failed to understand the qualitative difference between the troubles of his "skilful and industrious artisans" and those of the unskilled factory operatives who formed the greater part of the working-class population. But he did perceive that the dream of upward mobility was fast fading. Cooperatives could open up opportunities once more so that "thoughtful and determined" working people might, "through organization and co-operation, become their own employers."[20]

Cooperatives were one means of improving standards of living, but as Nordhoff surveyed New York, walking through the crowded tenement districts of Lower Manhattan each day on his way to work, he saw the necessity of the concerted public action that only government could provide. As he envisioned the city of the future, planning and systemization would replace chaos and incoherence, for the "extraordinary growth of the great cities" demanded no less. "City improvements ought to be made with foresight," he wrote in one editorial, "and with reference to some comprehensive plan of what New York is to be in coming centuries."[21]

Warning against "a plan made by speculation and executed by 'jobs,'" Nordhoff proposed the establishment of an urban planning board made up of "competent engineers," an idea seized upon with enthusiasm by the Progressives three decades later. The common need for adequate transportation, ventilation, drainage and sewage systems, building codes, and well-paved streets "would demand scientific investigation" by the board. Its decisions would be advisory only, he added, flexible enough to accommodate technological innovation.

The health and convenience of the average New Yorker suggested to Nordhoff that the city would be better off investing in numerous small parks,

---

19.   [CN,] "Co-Operation in the South," *EP*, January 7, 1868.

20.   [CN,] "One Remedy for High Prices," *EP*, May 25, 1867.

21.   CN to Parke Godwin, June 26, 1868, Bryant-Godwin Papers, NYPL; [CN,] "The New York of the Future," *EP*, April 2, 1868.

scattered throughout the city's neighborhoods, rather than in the single great Central Park. Such small parks should be made "attractive for those to need them most; ... not country visitors, gay youth, and the drivers of fine equipages only, but those who are suffering from the confinement of garrets and cellars, from the close air of shops and factories." Similarly, the lack of adequate public transportation betrayed a lack of concern for "the people of New York—not the rich people who can afford to keep a carriage" or those who didn't have to face a daily commute to work, "but the poor, the laborers, and mechanics, the industrious workingmen and women" who needed "steam communication through the island, to make their lives endurable."[22]

The lack of up-to-date public transportation meant not only that workers spent "a sixth part of their working day on street cars or omnibuses," but also that they had to live in crowded homes, jammed together in Lower Manhattan, "the most costly place of residence on the continent," Nordhoff wrote, "if not in the civilized world." Wholesale reconfiguration of the urban landscape was needed. Nordhoff described the city "as we hope it will be in the year 1900" in decidedly practical terms: a technological wonder, functioning efficiently and mechanistically in natural harmony. The warehouses, classified by commodity for the convenience of shippers, would be moved to refurbished docks, equipped with cranes for hauling freight easily and cheaply; a steam-operated elevated freight railroad would encircle the island; two more railroads would "carry passengers at a speed of thirty miles per hour" to upper Manhattan; and several bridges would connect the city to Long Island and New Jersey.

Such arrangements would not preclude growth, but encourage it, as "Central Park will be really as well as nominally central" and the suburbs and upper part of the island became inhabited. Manufacturers would relocate to the less expensive suburbs, while private rail companies profitably ran commuter trains in numerous directions out of the city. As a result, the city itself would retain its cultural and commercial importance, as "all the great enduring attractions of the city" moved to border Central Park and retailing establishments concentrated in grand promenades.[23]

Although government's role in the renovation of New York City was left vague in Nordhoff's vision, in one way, its responsibility was clear: housing codes, strictly enforced, would "prevent property owners from gaining fifty per cent in rent at the expense of the lives, health and characters of unfortunate tenants." He often attacked slumlords in the *Evening Post*, for he insisted that his readers should recognize the complicity of "respectable" members of society in the squalid living conditions of the despised immigrants. He threatened to

---

22. [CN,] "The Veto of the Arcade Bill," *EP*, May 16, 1870.
23. [CN,] "New York in 19–," *Evening Post*, March 20, 1867.

publicize the name of "the owner of one of the vilest fever nests in the city," but
the man pleaded that he knew nothing about the condition of his property "and
begged that his family might not be disgraced by the mention of his name in
connection with these dens, from which, yet, he drew a part of their support." In
fact, publicity could be a tool of last resort for the Board of Health, which might
publish in newspapers the names of owners of tenements "in which health
and decency are outraged," which would "frighten many careless and reckless
owners into doing their duty." The generation of reforming journalists who
would call themselves "muckrakers" would place a similar faith in the efficacy
of moral publicity.[24]

Nordhoff would not rely on publicity alone to reform these careless
slumlords, however, and insisted that a strengthened Board of Health should
have the authority and responsibility for enforcing decent housing standards
on recalcitrant property owners. A cholera epidemic had been only narrowly
averted in 1866 by stringent new regulations regarding sewage and drinking
water, and Nordhoff insisted that similar measures be enforced as a routine
matter. Always resistant to strong centralized government, Nordhoff viewed
local government as the strong arm of the people, rightly entrusted with
power. Housing codes exemplified "one of the chief duties of government," he
wrote, toward the people crowded into the cities "where they are so helpless in
themselves, except for the interference of lawful authority." If only for reasons
of self-preservation, the comfortable members of society needed to realize that
the poor needed help. "We hope that this good work" of housing inspection
"...may be the beginning of a new era," he wrote, one of "order, comfort, and
content" for "hitherto neglected citizens." He continued with a warning: "It is
hard to ask that those for whom the community does nothing shall be always ...
friends of good government and civil order, but a freeman whose home is
attractive and dear to him can hardly be made an enemy of society." In 1863,
Nordhoff had written that the answer to the draft riots was greater force, more
live ammunition for the authorities with which to restore law and order; but by
the late 1860s, he had developed a deeper understanding of the despair that
underlay such rioting and an appreciation of the depth of change required for
its alleviation.[25]

Out west, the end of the Civil War had heightened tensions between Native
Americans and a new flood of white migrants. The transcontinental railroad
was well on its way to completion, easing Easterners' access to the western
territories and, not incidentally, effectively destroying the natives' economies,
based as they were on the dwindling buffalo herds. Many of the military officers

---

24.   [CN,] "Tenement Houses," *Evening Post*, September 9, 1869.

25.   [CN,] "Tenement Houses," *Evening Post*, September 9, 1869.

who had gained recognition fighting for the Union, notably William Tecumseh Sherman and Philip Sheridan (the latter widely quoted as saying that "the only good Indian is a dead Indian"), had turned their skills to the prosecution of the "Indian Wars." The "Indian problem" attracted the attention of Eastern reformers, many of whom saw parallels between it and the difficulties facing the freed slaves. What was to be done with a population whose ways seemed incompatible with American cultural values and which stood squarely in the path of western development?

One thing was clear to Nordhoff: the use of military force against the Indians had to stop. He was appalled at the recurrent wanton violence of the U.S. Army, too often directed at Native American women and children, and the smug assurance of many white Americans that they had every right to eliminate the Western tribes. In one acerbic account, he summarized the lengthy history of European Native American contact as one of simple selfishness. "The 'Pilgrim Fathers' of New England, who were in the habit of requiring a theory to justify their practice," he scoffed, "are reported to have adopted these resolutions:

> Resolved, first, That the world belongs to the saints.
> Resolved, second, That we are the saints.[26]

As the violence against Native Americans reached new heights in the late 1860s, Nordhoff noted that the invading miners and squatters were "practical people, who have no notion of faith without works." Unleashing the sarcasm he reserved for the self-serving hypocrite, he proceeded to note that these whites, believing that "'there are no good Indians but dead Indians,'" were acting accordingly, in violation of the most fundamental tenets of the Christian faith. "Montana is a long way off," Nordhoff noted caustically, "and when an Indian lives two thousand miles away he is not our neighbor, and we can hardly be expected to love him as we do ourselves."[27]

But even on grounds of expediency, such a war made little sense, he pointed out, for the costs involved were astronomical, hardly worth the result. He could not forebear returning to the moral repugnancy of the idea, however: it was savagery to attack the Native Americans in a murderous, bloody overreaction. "Wild stories" of the Indians' strength and organization were patently idiotic pretexts for violence, the whites' actions blatantly inflammatory. Reports of scalpings and mutilations by whites and bounty hunters appalled him as "the culmination of all the dishonor and barbarity to which our national character

---

26. [CN,] "The Proposed Indian War," *EP*, May 31, 1867.
27. [CN,] "The Proposed Indian War," *Evening Post*, May 31, 1867.

has been subjected" in its dispossession of the Indians.[28] Nordhoff, who believed that the Indians would benefit from adopting white America's way of life, nevertheless always held that certain human rights were due all peoples, regardless of their cultures. It was the lack of respect for the natives' basic humanity that made him grieve for the national soul.

The January 1870 massacre of a group of Piegan (Blackfeet) Indians in Montana, in which 140 women and children and 33 men were shot by white soldiers, was to Nordhoff the most shocking of the darkening stains on the national honor.[29] He rebuked the commanding officer, who had claimed to be simply following orders. The Colonel should have told his superiors that he could not "shoot down defenseless women" or "commit ...wholesale infanticide" and resigned his commission rather than submit to such unlawful orders. That this same Colonel was instead commended by a superior for his "activity and energy" during the massacre made a mockery of true heroism. "Activity there was, without doubt," Nordhoff wrote; "the slaughter of so many helpless women and children in a few hours attests the expeditious means used to put them out of the way," but it required little *energy* for the troops to "slaughter the defenseless" Piegans. "Every crack of a rifle took a child's life," he went on, "or the life of a woman or a decrepit old man. There was no resistance; our men were perfectly safe, and had as good an opportunity of taking sure aim as if they were firing at so many squirrels or partridges."[30]

Although details of the Piegan massacre had at first been concealed, the news finally slipped out, spurring cries of outrage from government officials and the general public alike. Generals Sherman and Sheridan scoffed at the protests. Nordhoff viewed their callousness with scorn. "General Sheridan complains of being 'embarrassed by the apparent sympathy of members of Congress and humanitarians generally,'" he wrote, "that is to say sympathy with the sufferers in this slaughter." He found it appalling that Sheridan would "sneer at those who are tender of human life" or regard the "wholesale butchery of the helpless" with such equanimity.[31]

The Civil War, Nordhoff wrote, seemed to have "diminish[ed] the general respect for the sacredness of human life." If the government tolerated such atrocities as the butchery of the Piegans, it would only accelerate the moral decline of the country. Had the British government countenanced a similar

---

28.   [CN,] "The Proposed Indian War," *Evening Post*, May 31, 1867; [CN,] "Savage War Against the Savages," *Evening Post*, June 21, 1867.

29.   On the Piegan massacre, see Dee Brown, *Bury My Heart at Wounded Knee* (NY: Holt, Rinehart, & Winston, 1970), 177 ff.

30.   [CN,] "The Piegan Massacre," *Evening Post*, March 11, 1870.

31.   [CN,] "The Piegan Massacre," *Evening Post*, March 11, 1870.

slaughter of an Irish village or the Russians of insurgent Circassians "on any pretext of public policy," he asked, "would the civilized world ever cease to ring with the denunciations of the barbarity?" No distinction could be justified between brutality toward Irish or Russian people and that toward the Piegans. A lack of respect for human life indicated a society more backward than that which it sought to "civilize." Civilization was not an inherent attribute of white America, but depended on the morality of its actions. "A powerful government which among all the expedients for reducing to peace a savage tribe within its limits ..., can imagine none more effectual than shooting its women and children," he concluded grimly, "does not deserve to be called civilized."[32]

As the New York State Constitutional Convention approached in 1867, Nordhoff viewed it as an opportunity to extend American citizenship and equality under the law to all people, Native Americans as well as African-Americans.[33] The Europeans had always intended to "exterminate" the Indian tribes, Nordhoff wrote, either through "direct violence" or "deprivation and decay." The result of white interference was a bastardization of tribal government, the erection of an elaborate fiction that lingered to that day. The United States had "perpetuated the tribal state," Nordhoff judged, as a "quasi government, having few rights and many duties and responsibilities, and no powers or prerogatives," a "strangulated government." The tribes existed only in a vestigial state, with none of the benefits and all the liabilities of their aboriginal governments.

Nordhoff did not consider restoration of tribal sovereignty a remedy for their "strangulated" state, however. Instead, he regarded all efforts to inculcate in the Native Americans the values of an individualistic property-owning work ethic as the correct course of action for white America; for private property seemed to him, as to most of his contemporaries, a spur to the habits of thrift, industry, and deferred gratification that were the presumed moral bases of the expanding American economy. The problem with these vestigial tribes was that they unjustly deprived their members of the opportunity to join fully in the blessings of American citizenship. Tribal governments were "a drag on the progress of society," he complained, and the tribes had never helped to advance "morals, industry, public wealth, or any other improvement." Nordhoff was convinced that the Native Americans' culture had had a degrading influence upon its people and that the more quickly the Indians were assimilated to white

---

32. [CN,] "The Piegan Massacre," *Evening Post*, March 11, 1870.
33. See Henry E. Fitz, *The Movement for Indian Assimilation, 1860-1890* (Philadelphia: University of Pennsylvania Press, 1963), a useful book despite the author's seeming acceptance of the reformers' negative view of Native American culture, and Robert F. Berkhofer, *The White Man's Indian* (NY: Knopf, 1978).

America, the better off they would be. And how was such a transformation to take place? Not by trying to exert influence over "tribes or communities in the mass, but upon the will of individuals." Like all people, they needed to see that with change would come "the common benefits of civilized society."[34]

Native Americans, like freed slaves, would pose no problem to American society if only they were accorded the same rights and lived under the same constraints as European-Americans. If Indians seemed to lack the character necessary to civilized life, was that not to be expected? While Americans were taught to "invite and encourage every man to be a voter and a land holder, as the surest means of making him a man," Nordhoff pointed out, they "allow the Indian to be neither a landowner nor a voter, and then wonder that he remains an Indian." The inconsistency of such a position was all too reminiscent of blame placed upon slaves for their "slavishness." The parallel with emancipation was irresistible. If the U.S. government dealt with "white, black and yellow men as individuals," he asked, why did it treat red men "only in the aggregate?"[35] "Now that the nation has all of a sudden recognized the equal application of the laws of common sense to the negro, as the only means for his protection and advancement," he wrote on another occasion, still there seemed to be no inclination to do the same for the Indian.[36] Rather than ridding the United States of Indian tribes by violence or "strangulation," then Nordhoff prescribed assimilation. He advocated that the New York State Constitution be rewritten to provide an example of "treating the Indians upon the simple footing of their manhood" by making them citizens and forcing them to divide up their tribal lands into individual holdings, allowing for communal ownership of land, but only by groups incorporated under New York law. Such cooperation, which he urged upon white Americans, he believed should be controlled within a larger individualistic culture. The entirely communal society of Indian tribes, outside the recognizable strictures of Christianity, struck him as simply backward.[37]

Nordhoff was not alone in decrying the violence against the Native Americans. As early as the 1850s, humanitarian reformers had been pleading the Indians' cause (although in doing so they advocated solutions hardly less inimical to Native American cultures than military action). Those opposed to the policy of violent warfare against the Plains Indians almost universally called for the same measures: citizenship and division of lands into individual holdings, the transformation of the despised Indian man into a middle-class property-owning breadwinning family patriarch. By 1887, the idea had gained

---

34.   [CN,] "The Indian Question," *Evening Post*, July 19, 1867.

35.   [CN,] "The Indians," *Evening Post*, December 5, 1868.

36.   [CN,] "Indian Suffrage in Michigan," *Evening Post*, July 27, 1867.

37.   [CN,] "The Indian Question," *Evening Post*, July 19, 1867.

enough political support that a federal law, the Dawes Severalty Act, forced the distribution of tribal lands among the individual members—an act that proved disastrous, as speculators quickly stripped the Native Americans of their land. But this lay twenty years in the future when Nordhoff was making his plea. He and his allies sincerely believed that they had the Native Americans' best interests at heart, particularly when faced with increasing violence on the frontier. They could not envision American citizenship as compatible with communal landownership and did not value the Native cultures to which common lands were of central importance. Nordhoff was certain, however, of one thing: the killing had to stop.

Assimilation was Nordhoff's usual answer to the problems of a pluralistic society, based upon a universalist view of human nature. Most often, he proposed the granting of equal rights to all peoples as the surest road to incorporating newcomers, thereby making the common culture expansive enough to accommodate difference. In an age of rampant anti-Catholicism, Nordhoff had no doubt as to the superiority of Protestantism for inculcating the habits of independent thought that democracy required, but he disapproved of militant Protestantism. If (Protestant) America wanted a common American culture, then it had better avoid forcing on the minority Protestant measures.

The autumn of 1869 brought news from Cincinnati of a controversy over the use of the Bible in the public schools. Nordhoff, like many Eastern journalists, regarded the issue as having important implications for Americans everywhere in the face of a growing Catholic immigrant population. The Cincinnati School Board had voted in November to prohibit the reading of the Bible or the singing of hymns in its public schools, prompted by an effort to incorporate parochial schools into the public system. Although its citizens were predominantly of German background, within the German community alone, considerable religious diversity reigned; there were Lutheran, Methodist, and other Protestant denominations among the German-Americans, along with Jewish and Roman Catholic congregations. The School Board's move to eliminate Bible reading in the schools was unprecedented and attracted national attention.[38]

Nordhoff, who had close family ties to Cincinnati, had recently been disturbed by attempts of the Catholic clergy in New York to secure public support for their parochial schools.[39] From the Catholic viewpoint, the use of the King James Bible in public schools made those schools unfit for Catholic

---

[38]   Robert Michaelsen, "Common School, Common Religion? A Case Study in Church-State Relations, Cincinnati, 1869-70," *Church History*, 38 (1969): 201–217.

[39]   See, for example, Nordhoff's editorial, "Public and Sectarian Schools," *Evening Post*, October 19, 1869.

children to attend and justified a separate parochial school system. Nordhoff, suspicious of the Catholic clergy and seeing their demands as an unwarranted encroachment on civic powers, believed that the Cincinnati School Board had resolved the problem admirably. Their opponents, however, had obtained an injunction against the execution of the board's decision.[40]

"They have a revival, in Cincinnati, of an old dispute," Nordhoff told the readers of the *Evening Post* soon after the injunction was ordered. Explaining the situation, Nordhoff allowed that it was natural for the Protestant community to be aroused by the School Board's actions. "Nevertheless," he added, somewhat gingerly, they ought to "consider whether it may not be wise to concede this point, and abandon the use of the Bible in the public schools, when it is opposed by any considerable number of parents." Such a concession could be necessary for the survival of the common schools, he believed, nor did he doubt that the use of the Bible was used "by the enemies of our public free school system" to "excite prejudices" against the public schools themselves. But the importance of the free schools transcended all other questions. "Is it worth while to arouse this feeling" of prejudice, he asked, when it might threaten the common school system, "one of the glories of our land?" Schools, he insisted, were secular institutions, meant to inculcate American values and crucial in providing a common cultural bond between an immigrant population and native-born Americans.[41]

In fact, the Bible was not a necessary or even a good textbook, he noted; "serious objections" could be raised if it were even used to teach reading, because of the difficult and obscure language often used. The place for the Bible was the Sunday school although he hoped that an ecumenical use of the Bible might be agreed upon, for the differences between the Catholic and Protestant versions were few. Surely Protestants and Catholics could, "by conference in a kindly spirit," agree upon certain selections from the Scriptures.

---

[40] Nordhoff editorialized against any mixture of politics with religion and not solely because of his antipathy toward the Catholic Church. In one such editorial (January 30, 1871), he rebuked a group of Protestant ministers who had united in petitioning the President to install the man of their choice as NY Collector of Customs, asking "what right have [the ministers] to interfere, not as citizens, but distinctly as clergymen, in public affairs? ...Suppose thirty-six Roman Catholic priests, speaking as priests, demanded of the President [similarly]? What outcries should we not hear about 'priestly assumption and arrogance,' about 'dangerous interference of priests with political affairs,' about the 'perils of liberty' and so on."

[41] [CN,] "The Bible in the Schools," *Evening Post*, November 6, 1869.

That the Roman Catholic hierarchy disapproved of any indiscriminate Bible reading was, to Nordhoff, incomprehensible.[42]

A few days later, the *Evening Post* reported that New York's city government had released figures on appropriations to 28 Protestant and 25 Catholic schools. Nordhoff editorialized sternly against such use of public moneys, which should not be used "in the furtherance of sectarian or partisan objects"; if there were students being ill-served by the current public system, he declared, then that system should be repaired, not supplanted by private ones.[43] In Nordhoff's reasoning, any public support of private schools was opening the door to a flood of demands for governmental assistance for purposes that he believed ought to be kept strictly private. There were many worthy private charities that might seek governmental support, but "let not the legislature give a cent, on any pretext, to any such undertaking," Nordhoff advised, adhering to the tenets of orthodox laissez-faire liberalism.[44]

On the general question of church-state relations, Nordhoff made his position clear: government was a secular institution. "Those who believe that the civil government ought to establish religion, and that virtue, truth, and immortality must fall unless formally countenanced by rulers and laws, generally hold to despotism as a living ordinance," he wrote. He cited the problems of the English, with a population of growing diversity, many members of which were understandably reluctant to support a state church to which they did not belong. The answer was adherence to the principles of James Madison: government ought not to try to support all religions equally, but rather support none at all.[45]

Delving more deeply into the issue, Nordhoff studied the pronouncements of the Catholic hierarchy on schooling and found confirmation for his suspicions that the question was not "whether the Bible should be read in the schools, but whether our public schools shall continue to exist." The Catholics wanted their children educated by their Church, and Nordhoff argued vehemently against such a division of childhood education along sectarian lines. Universal education was necessary for free government, and an uneducated populace was the most severe threat facing liberty. It was not a Catholic-Protestant issue, but one of general principles: "the education of children cannot, in a free state, be safely confined to any religious sect or denomination."[46] Public schools were

---

42. [CN,] "The Bible in the Schools," *Evening Post*, November 6, 1869.

43. [CN,] "Public Money for Sectarian Uses," *Evening Post*, November 10, 1869. See also his editorial, "Public Money for Sectarian Schools," *Evening Post*, March 31, 1871.

44. [CN,] "A Hint to the Friends of Public Schools," *Evening Post*, November 12, 1869.

45. [CN,] "Church and State," *Evening Post*, November 20, 1869.

46. [CN,] "The Common Schools," *Evening Post*, January 2, 1870.

"political institutions," he insisted; neither Catholic nor Protestant, they were needed to train the "rising generation in such a manner that they shall become intelligent, thinking members of our society, able to understand the nature of our free government, able to inform themselves in regard to public measures and to judge of them wisely, able to comprehend and willing to practice the duties of a citizen."[47]

The Pope had condemned public schools in his 1864 "Syllabus of Errors." Worse still, to Nordhoff, the doctrine of Papal Infallibility had recently been accepted by the Catholic clergy, which indicated to him that the Church was an unholy despotism that discouraged free thought. Duty-bound to follow the Pope's lead, the American prelates were calling for a division of public schools into separate systems for Protestants and Catholics or, alternatively, for the elimination of public schools altogether. Nordhoff believed that either course of action would have disastrous consequences, dividing society into separate classes, "trained to look upon each other with mutual dislike, perhaps with hatred," he wrote. Parochial schools "would be schools of the intensest bigotry."[48] His suspicions were given some justification in the "Syllabus of Errors" (which dismayed progressive elements of the American Catholic hierarchy), and he enumerated specific provisions of the Syllabus that he believed would divide society into warring camps. Catholic children would be taught that non-Catholics were not Christians; that non-Catholics' parents were not married under God's law, making their children illegitimate; that Church and State ought to be united; that "toleration of other religious persuasions is a sin"; and that the Church "has the right to apply force, ... to persecute even to the death." This was not only theoretically repugnant to Nordhoff; it seemed to portend a grave threat to national survival, to "not only religious but civil liberty."[49]

---

47. [CN,] "The War Upon Free Schools," *Evening Post*, January 8, 1870.
48. [CN,] "The War Upon the Schools," *Evening Post*, January 8, 1869. Robert D. Cross notes that critics had long accused the Catholic Church of being "hostile to the spread of knowledge." The Catholic clergy disagreed among themselves on the value of education. One priest, during the 1880s, when the question of parochial schools flared into heated debate, claimed that "We do not plead for illiteracy, but we are unable to perceive any great ignominy or serious inconvenience to a State in the fact that some of its colliers and ploughmen and cowboys and dairymaids are not able to read the morning paper." More liberal Catholics maintained that "universal suffrage demands universal education." Robert D. Cross, *The Rise of Liberal Catholicism in the United States*, 131. Nordhoff, obviously, thought the ability to read the newspaper was crucial.
49. [CN,] "The War Upon the Schools," *Evening Post*, January 8, 1870.

Nordhoff insisted that not even all Catholic parents wished to have a separate school system; for many sent their children to the public schools, not wishing to have their children "reared," as Nordhoff put it, "like an alien tribe in the midst of the nation, among us but not of us." Americans had to be educated as Americans first, with religious differences tacitly acknowledged, but ignored as much as possible. "Our present system," he wrote,

> in which the youth of all religious denominations are trained
> up together in the common schools—in which they are taught
> to respect each other personally, to allow each other's rights,
> to treat each other with mutual forebearance, to act upon
> common principles, as persons having ... common interests—
> is the only system which can answer for a republic like ours.
> He who seeks to overthrow it, and to substitute a system
> calculated to train up the different religious communions in
> estrangement and animosity, is an enemy to our institutions,
> an enemy to civil and religious liberty, an enemy to the public
> peace and the national prosperity.[50]

Tolerance was the transcendent ideal of America, Nordhoff believed, and although some of its other ideals might have arisen from Protestant values, he hoped that tolerance on all sides might broaden those values to accommodate differences among its people. Unity amid diversity was yet possible.

Nordhoff was well aware of the opinions of his old friends in Cincinnati, many of whom disagreed with him vehemently on the necessity of the Bible to public schooling. He was glad to argue with them. Rutherford B. Hayes, who had just won reelection to the Ohio governorship, wrote to Nordhoff that "I take the Bible side, largely because this war on the good book is in disguise a war on all free schools."[51]

Nordhoff responded quickly. "My article on the Bible in the Schools, though as I thought fearfully mild, so shocked one of our advertisers that he ordered his advertisement out of the paper." It was not the last time Nordhoff would feel such pressure, but he laughed it off. "He is a liquor seller," he explained, "& his advertisement consisted of three lines. The Evg. Post will go on for a short while yet." In a more serious vein, he questioned Hayes's formulation of the school problem, or rather, his tactics. "I guess you are right to fight for the Bible," he conceded. "That is a sort of bulwark & the struggle you make there

---

50. [CN,] "The War Upon Free Schools," *Evening Post*, January 8, 1870.
51. Rutherford B. Hayes to CN, November 10, 1869, RBH Letterbook, RBH Library, Fremont, Ohio.

will keep the enemy the longer from the main line. But," he added, it was not good military strategy. They were going to have to fight the Pope on the school question at any rate. "Is it not possible that we may have the best chance for a victory, by letting the Bible go. Then he will have to show his hand, as a hater of the free schools." His argument convinced Hayes, who sent Nordhoff's articles to a mutual friend, a pious Methodist in Cincinnati. "His ground is the true one," Hayes wrote; "we must not let them push religion out of the schools, but we must avoid forcing it on anybody." How could such contradictory ends be brought about? Lamely, Hayes declined to get into specifics. "Well," he wrote, "it is easier to do the thing than to tell how to do it."[52]

Hayes misunderstood his friend's position. Nordhoff did, in fact, want to "push religion out of the schools," for he saw such a move as the only way to "avoid forcing it on anybody." He may have underestimated the degree to which the public schools were permeated with Protestant ideals, but he did not doubt the justice of eliminating overt manifestations of Protestantism. Hayes, a consummate politician, was loathe to offend either party in the dispute. Nordhoff had no such qualms. As he understood it, his job was not to please advertisers or anyone else, but to speak the truth as he saw it.

Many of Nordhoff's editorials referred the reader to minutely documented articles concerning the problem at hand, and it was not unusual for him to resort to statistics in the editorials themselves in order to drive home a point. Immigrant ships, for instance, were obscenely overcrowded, as illustrated by three steamers from Great Britain that had just arrived, carrying 1,181; 1,238; and 596 immigrants respectively, "a continual herding together of poor immigrants." "No steamship," the editorial declared, "can give proper accommodations to twelve hundred passengers, and Congress ought to take vigorous measures to stop the many abuses to which the poor creatures who are constantly crossing the Atlantic are subjected."[53] Similarly, an editorial on the shoddiness of government-subsidized railroad construction quoted from government reports at length, with figures on the grading, sharpness of curves, liability to flooding, and jerry-rigged construction of various sorts, and concluding with two figures: the estimated worth of the railroad ($39,996,000) and the corporation's liabilities, not including capital ($71,715,847), concluding, therefore, that thirty million dollars had been "divided among the projectors and promoters of the road." The acreage given

---

52. CN to Rutherford B. Hayes, November 20, 1869, RBH Library; RBH to Mrs. John Davis, January 12, 1870, Hayes Letterbook, RBH Library.

53. [CN,] "Over-Crowding Emigrant Ships," New York *Evening Post*, June 15, 1869.

to the railroads, and the profits they claimed thereby, were a favorite topic for statistical analysis in the *Evening Post*.[54]

Although nineteenth-century editorials have the reputation of providing invective rather than substance, it is clear from Nordhoff's work on the *Evening Post* that many of the formulae attributed to twentieth-century muckraking were already well in use in the 1860s: statistics, narrative descriptions of social evils, and naming public figures who might be held responsible. In one column, Nordhoff listed the names and net worth of the ten most wealthy New Yorkers and pointed out that they were not men known for their active concern in civic affairs. In another, he provided lists with dozens of names of the individuals who supported a (implicitly corrupt) bill from Tammany Hall; in a third, he cited the enormously inflated bills that the city was paying for feather dusters, ink, and other necessities. Police reports on the numbers of homeless people seeking shelter in the station houses—which showed an increase from 86,224 per year for most of the 1860s to 105,460 in 1868—were accompanied by comment on the "vile" conditions that destitute families were forced to endure in the shelters. In considering the condition of working women, Nordhoff laid out the bare economic facts: their average wages were between $7 and $9 per week; room and board cost them $3 to $6 per week; laundry costs were extra; the price of four or five dresses each year at $6 each had to be added; and shoes were costly and did not last long. Not surprisingly, most could not save enough to raise themselves out of poverty.

The philosophy proclaimed by the *Evening Post* under Nordhoff's stewardship was one that was echoed by Progressives thirty-five years later: "If speech is free, if opinions are to be freely spoken and written, … is not every wrong sure to be reformed, without violence? Is anything more needed than that the public conscience shall be awakened?"[55]

The proper education and rearing of children was, to Nordhoff, the basis of the good society, the repository of America's hopes. Accordingly, school reform played a large part in his reformist editorializing. New York's school system, he wrote, needed to be more closely overseen, "moved and regulated" by the government, and made mandatory for all children, even if that required

54. [CN,] "Building a Railroad Across the Continent," New York *Evening Post*, May 1, 1869; "The Great States Given Away," New York *Evening Post*, January 14, 1869.

55. [CN,] "The Duties of Property," New York *Evening Post*, April 24, 1868; [CN,] "City Reform," New York *Evening Post*, April 7, 1871; [CN,] "539 Dollars for Feather Dusters," New York *Evening Post*, September 4, 1867; [CN,] "Free Lodging Houses Needed," New York *Evening Post*, February 11, 1868; [CN,] "The Female Labor Question," New York *Evening Post*, January 2, 1868; [CN,] "Is Impatience a Virtue?", *Evening Post*, June 10, 1869.

a "vigorously coercive" law. Experience had shown that "ignorance increases crime," while education reduced it, and that "offenses against society are most numerous among the illiterate."[56] Furthermore, democratic government required that all citizens "shall possess the means of properly informing themselves on public affairs—the ability, namely, to read, write, and cipher."

To this end, Nordhoff advised, every town should be required to have a school; those that did not should be severely penalized with steep fines that would "make it cheaper to build the schoolhouse than to pay the fines." These schools would be open at least six months of the year at public expense and controlled by local school boards.[57] As for the curriculum, Nordhoff advocated abandoning rote memorization for experiments and firsthand observation, with a decided emphasis upon science and natural history as well as political economy, all taught by the Socratic method.[58]

But parents were still crucial to their children's education, and Nordhoff became concerned by the waifs on the streets of New York, children left without responsible parents to care for them. Statistics and quantifiable evidence demonstrated a high correlation between parental abandonment and criminal behavior, he discovered upon investigating reform schools. Half of the reform school inmates had parents who had been imprisoned, and one-third of the children had been arrested more than once. One-fourth were homeless, and "almost all were the children of neglect, or poverty, of ignorance, of the street and the dock—in a word, of evil surroundings and influences." This kind of "gross neglect" only added these children to the "criminal class" when they reached adulthood—and even before.[59]

Although well-run orphanages might reclaim some of these lost souls, Nordhoff preferred the long-established practice of placing such children in foster homes, with the understanding that they would work in return for their upkeep. In this way, the children would receive instruction, moral if not academic, from responsible adults. As always, Nordhoff saw assimilation into the general population, rather than marking people out as a special class, as the desired end. Such foster children tended to "'melt into the population,' and become simply members of society," he wrote, "with a fair and equal chance for a happy and useful life." The care of such foster children was the social responsibility of those who were able to undertake it.[60]

---

56.   [CN,] "The Free College of New York," *Evening Post*, September 10, 1869.

57.   [CN,] "What Our School System Needs," *Evening Post*, February 13, 1867.

58.   [CN,] "Our Public Schools," *Evening Post*, September 29, 1868.

59.   [CN,] "Juvenile Reformatories," *Evening Post*, June 5, 1869.

60.   [CN,] "Dependent Children," *Evening Post*, May 14, 1869.

In this, Nordhoff was in earnest. Shortly after writing his editorial in May 1869 on the need for foster care, he and Lida adopted a six-year-old boy, just weeks after the birth of their fourth child, a girl they named Elsie. The duties of public life were inseparable from those of private life, Nordhoff's editorials always maintained, and he tried very hard to practice what he preached.[61]

If the provision of equal rights and education could diminish the differences that marginalized Native Americans, Catholics, orphans, and African-Americans, it would serve the same purpose, Nordhoff believed, for women as well. In contrast to most of his contemporaries, who believed that women were essentially different from men, he insisted that many, if not all, of the differences between women and men in society could be attributed to training and custom. In every aspect of their lives, women faced socially imposed disabilities. It was time for their emancipation, no less than that of the slaves.

On the most basic level, Nordhoff objected to the different standards of health applied to women and men, which left women all too often sickly, careless of their own physical well-being. "Ill-health has been, in this country, an almost fashionable quality for women," he once wrote. "To be 'delicate' ... has been thought charming," but he believed that attitudes were changing so that poor health "is coming now to be thought what it is, a serious misfortune." Nordhoff already had two daughters when he wrote this editorial—Amy, born in 1862, and Evelyn, born in 1865—and he wanted to educate them to be free of the restrictions that he believed women too often imposed upon themselves. The Nordhoffs practiced what they preached, it seems: Charles and Lida evidently taught their daughters to entertain guests not by warbling a tune or playing the piano, as was common in mid-nineteenth-century America, but by turning somersaults before the fire.[62]

---

61. Laurence Nordhoff was, according to Charles's will, adopted. The adoption records of New Jersey are sealed in perpetuity so the exact circumstances of the adoption remain unclear, but the 1870 census includes a seven-year-old Laurence. In a letter of June 28, 1869, to his friend, Gordon L. Ford, Nordhoff wrote, "I have found a boy. He is to come up for inspection tomorrow; & I hope he will do." It seems likely that this refers to Laurence. Gordon L. Ford Papers, NYPL. The will is in the Bergen County Courthouse, Hackensack, New Jersey; the 1870 census record is among those for the town of Alpine, in Bergen County, New Jersey.

62. See an unidentified fragment from a magazine story, an instantly recognizable portrait of Nordhoff, although he is not named, as the reformist editor of "the best newspaper in New York," who takes a visitor doubtful of his statistics on starving seamstresses to his Palisades home for a family dinner.

Nordhoff could see no inherent difference between the sexes that would require special educational standards for women or girls. "The counsel which a sagacious man would give to a young man," he believed, "he might with equal fitness give to the young girl. Be honest; be industrious; be virtuous...." A wise father's instructions to his son would serve his daughter equally well. The "mischief" was that girls were not taught as boys were. "They are ... regarded as of essentially different natures." To him, the simple pieties that would ensure a successful life were not restricted by gender, any more than they were by race or class.[63]

The same rule applied to women's place in the workforce. Acknowledging the strenuousness of domestic labor for most women, Nordhoff emphasized the more public troubles of women trying to earn a wage outside the home. In the pages of the *Evening Post*, he often called for improved education opportunities for women at all levels, from simple vocational training to medical schools. To ensure their independence, he suggested, young women trained to use a sewing machine ought to be given the chance to move up the vocational ladder by learning dressmaking. "To teach a girl how to sew," he noted, "is as much as though you taught a boy how to dig with a spade," a form of productive labor that nevertheless "can never be highly remunerated, because it is always over-crowded."

For all his belief in the value of even the humblest labor, Nordhoff knew that skilled laborers (his "mechanics" and "artisans") had far greater chances of attaining middle-class status than the unskilled. The only hope for the laborer, of whatever sex, lay not in improving the lot of the unskilled, but in elevating them to skillfulness. He did not really understand that the preponderance of new jobs in the industrial workplace had no need of skill and that rationalization and deskilling of jobs were already standard elements of mass production.[64]

He believed that the better-educated female workers, reacting to societal strictures, were keeping themselves back—understandably so, because society did not reward them as it should. "The laws, as well as customs, ... discourage enterprise in women," he noted in one editorial. "No matter what a married woman makes by her own industry—it is not hers, but her husband's, in most of the states. Why should she exert herself?" The work ethic had failed for American women because of restrictive laws, prejudiced employers, and social pressure. "What can an educated woman do?" he asked. "She can teach—at half wages; she can work in a cotton or woollen mill, or at sewing," and in each case "she receives less wages than the man." This waste of ability was one that America could ill afford. Until it were "'respectable' for gentlewomen to labor

---

63.   [CN,] "Advice to Women," *Evening Post*, August 17, 1868.
64.   [CN,] "Women's Dress," *Evening Post*, January 28, 1869.

openly and regularly at some useful and profitable avocation," thousands of women would continue "fretting their lives away" over inconsequential duties or earning subsistence wages rather than improving themselves in the world. But "the limitation of choice takes the heart out of their efforts."[65]

Nordhoff believed that one occupation for which women were well-suited was medicine (betraying, perhaps, an inclination to think of women as natural caregivers), and he applauded women doctors' dedication in the face of professional barriers. As always, he did not advocate any special assistance, but only a fair chance. "These heroic women ask no favors," he wrote. "They seek only justice."

> Those who sneer at what are called "women's rights" forget that the only right demanded by an educated woman is the right to make use of the knowledge she has gained by hard study. ... A share in the daily struggle for bread is all that these women physicians expect, and to this they are entitled.[66]

Additionally, the social fiction that women ought not and need not work was patently false. "Could [women] compete in the open labor-market of the world?" he asked rhetorically. "Well, they have at any rate the right to do it," he answered himself; "they do it now, in this country, several millions of them, under very grievous disadvantages." If they were in fact the weaker sex, he reasoned—a supposition with which he did not agree—"so much the more reason for giving them the best chance—or at least an equal chance."[67]

Diverging from the ideology of "separate spheres" for men and women, Nordhoff was sympathetic to the early feminists and gave a fair amount of respectful publicity to their efforts. He tacitly acknowledged a reciprocal relationship between societal expectations and those of the individual, but he disliked what he saw as excuses based upon amorphous social forces. "As for 'custom,' the opinions of society," he wrote, "that barrier is weak the moment it is attacked. ... This is not to say that there is no injustice, but that 'custom' is not so strong as many imagine."[68] It was within the women's own power to change their unequal status, Nordhoff insisted. In his view, responsibility for the fate of any group rested, ultimately, on the decisions made by its individual members.

---

[65].   [CN,] "A Plea for Justice to Working Women," *Evening Post*, June 5, 1867.

[66].   [CN,] "The Women Doctors," *Evening Post*, March 3, 1867.

[67].   [CN,] "A Plea for Justice to Working Women," *Evening Post*, June 5, 1867.

[68].   [CN,] "A Plea for Justice to Working Women," *Evening Post*, June 5, 1867. He was alluding to Caroline Dall's *The College, the Market and the Court: or, Women's Relation to Education, Labor and Law* (NY: Lee & Shepard, 1867).

"When women rebel," he wrote, "when they insist upon doing whatever they can, they will be free."[69]

Nordhoff's calls for the extension of equal rights to Americans of all races, classes, and genders did not endear him to E. L. Godkin, the irascible editor of *The Nation* with whom Nordhoff had earlier refused to work. The two editors could be allies upon occasion, campaigning for the elimination of corrupt officials.[70] Despite their agreement on certain questions, Godkin and Nordhoff held opposing philosophies on the meaning of representative government, as was made obvious during the 1867 New York State Constitutional Convention. Suffrage qualifications and electoral rules were at the center of the debate, and a move was afoot to remove local control of New York City's municipal administration to state-run commissions. Republicans hoped thereby to prevent the locally powerful Tammany Democrats, certain of the votes of the hundreds of thousands of immigrants and workers jammed onto Manhattan Island, from using the city for their own benefit.

Such measures were part of the postwar platform of a coterie of liberal Republican reformers like Godkin, bent upon instituting government by the better-educated through Civil Service reform and removal of government from the local to the state level. The idea that centralized government and a depoliticized Civil Service might, in effect, undermine the ideal of self-government was not taken seriously by these reformers, for they considered the goals of ending graft and increasing governmental efficiency to be of primary importance.[71]

Although his opinion would later change when confronted by the chaos the patronage system could cause at the federal level, during the late 1860s, Nordhoff disapproved of civil service reform as well as government by commission. To make government service contingent upon certain questionable standards of competence, rather than at the discretion of elected officials, held serious implications for the survival of democratic government, for it would remove government workers from direct responsibility to the people. A civil service–run bureaucracy might make sense in class-bound England, but not for the United States, where "the people govern" education was widespread and official duties were few. The clear lines of responsibility so necessary to self-government would

---

69. [CN,] "A Plea For Justice to Working Women," *Evening Post*, June 5, 1867.

70. E. L. Godkin to Charles Eliot Norton, April 23, 1867, in William M. Armstrong, ed., *The Gilded Age Letters of E. L. Godkin* (Albany: SUNY Press, 1974); E. L. Godkin to Norton, August 1, 1867, in Armstrong, *Letters*.

71. On the reformers, see John G. Sproat, *"The Best Men": Liberal Reformers in the Gilded Age* (New York, Oxford, 1968) and James C. Mohr, *The Radical Republicans and Reform in New York During Reconstruction* (Ithaca: Cornell University Press, 1973).

be blurred, if not erased, by such an institution as the civil service. Tying the hands of those responsible for hiring and firing government workers would displace responsibility from visible officials to a faceless bureaucracy.[72]

During the Constitutional Convention of 1867, Republican governor Reuben Fenton oversaw a wholesale effort to wrest power away from Democratic New York City politicians. Reformers had mixed motives, ranging from the political expediency of effectually disfranchising the state's Democratic stronghold to more pure-minded concerns for honesty and the improvement of poorly run city services.[73] The New York Constitutional Convention that convened in 1867 provided an opportunity for such reformers to act.

While most Republican journals, like *The Nation*, supported the efforts to remove municipal government to Albany, Nordhoff and the *Evening Post*— more faithful to the newspaper's Free Soil Democratic roots than to postwar Republicanism—were vociferously opposed. Addressing the same educated audience, these journals were representative of the splintering of the fragile coalition upon which the Republican Party had been founded, as the search for a positive platform replaced its essentially negative purpose of halting the advance of slavery. Editorial war soon began.

"The *Nation* is apparently shocked at a discussion in the *Evening Post*," Charles Nordhoff wrote, "... of what we called 'Hostility to Popular Government.'" He had been editorializing against the displacement of city government to Albany, maintaining that such an action presumed "that the people here, if they were entrusted with the management of their local affairs, would mismanage them." Such a presumption had "no proper place in a grave argument," Nordhoff insisted, "for the people here have not had a trial." A basic principle was at stake. Even if the presumption of popular incompetence were valid, Nordhoff wrote, "we reply that the people have the right to mismanage their own affairs, and no class or set has a right to take them out of their hands." He could not have come up with a statement more calculated to rouse Godkin's ire if he had tried.[74]

The Nation had called Nordhoff's editorial "in reality an assertion of the superiority of the majority to the moral law," but in a lengthy rebuttal, Nordhoff insisted that "we were not discussing the ten commandments, but the question of government." Furthermore, he added, *The Nation* itself had once written eloquently that "*there is no government so likely to consult the general interest and act for it*" as government by majority. "That is precisely our belief," he added. Majority rule was "the safest, the wisest, the most beneficent. That it is not

72. [CN,] "The Reform of the Civil Service," *Evening Post*, February 13, 1867.
73. James C. Mohr, *The Radical Republicans and Reform in New York During Reconstruction* (Ithaca: Cornell University Press, 1973).
74. [CN,] "The Hostility to Popular Government," *Evening Post*, June 14, 1867.

perfect or without error is natural, for it is human." He continued to use Godkin's words against him:

> "We do not believe," adds the *Nation*, "in its supreme wisdom or holiness." Nor do we; but we repeat in the words of the *Nation*, "no other government is so likely to consult the general interest and act for it," and therefore, without being either supremely wise ... for supreme wisdom is the attribute of the Deity alone --or holy, which is beside the question, we hold that it is the best attainable form of government.[75]

If the *Nation* warned against assuring "the people" of their "exemption from moral responsibility," so did the *Evening Post*: "that the responsibility, moral, pecuniary, political and social, of governing New York city, ... shall be put upon the majority here, for we are convinced that thus only can the majority be trained and educated to sound views." Lest he be misunderstood, Nordhoff added that Godkin had missed a crucial part of his argument. "We wrote: The people have a right to mismanage their affairs, and no class or set has a right to take them out of their hands. *Let the people mismanage; they will suffer by it; suffering will teach them wisdom; and if they have the power in their own hands, they will quickly retrace their steps and institute reforms.*"[76]

But as the Constitutional Convention continued its deliberations throughout the summer of 1867, the New York Citizens' Association, made up of wealthy and highly educated New Yorkers (including Bryant's friend Peter Cooper), began to agitate for the kinds of constitutional changes that Godkin had long espoused. Upon learning of a petition that the Association had sent to the convention, Nordhoff penned a scathing editorial that did not conceal his fury. The Citizens' Association "have sent to the legislature a long plea for commissions," Nordhoff began, calmly enough, "and against what they call 'the unrestricted use of the ballot box,' which, they say, amongst other things, 'will pave the way to anarchy.'" First of all, the statement betrayed a willingness to foment xenophobia and ethnic hatred, inimical to the peace of an immigrant nation.

> It is not quite fair to try to frighten the Convention by threats of anarchy, nor is it ingenuous to offer as a reason why the city is "unfit to govern itself," that "this city is the grand entrepot into which Europe continually pours her thousands of depraved and criminal classes—they are here to-day, the

---

[75]. [CN,] "Hostility to Popular Government," June 14, 1867.

[76]. [CN,] "Hostility," *EP*, June 14, 1867.

useful tools of worthless politicians who stop at nothing that
will secure power."

Faced with such a blatant appeal to nativist prejudice, Nordhoff insisted
that the immigrants were entitled to American citizenship by the time they
were eligible to vote, which was after five years' residence in the country. (He
ignored the widespread practice of illegally registering newly arrived men.) As
it elaborated on its fear of "anarchy," the Association alluded to the draft riots,
a move that struck Nordhoff as indicative of their disregard for the common
weal. He had long since regretted his own thoughtless anger during the riots,
and perhaps that regret sharpened his attack upon the Citizens' Association.
Seething, he continued to quote the petition, only to damn its authors for their
hypocrisy:

> And when we are told that "the thousands and tens of
> thousands that came forth from lanes, alleys, cellars and
> slums, and from dark holes and corners, in July, 1863, not
> only still exist, but have largely increased their numbers"—it
> is proper to ask who owns the "cellars, slums, dark holes and
> corners" out of which these wretches crept? who makes twenty
> per cent per annum by renting vile fever nests, slums, cellars,
> and dark holes to the poor?[77]

It was clear to Nordhoff that the overcrowded substandard housing and
poor sanitary facilities in the tenement districts had threatened the city with
a cholera epidemic; in their selfishness, slumlords endangered lives as well as
morals. He felt closer to the poor than to the elites of the Citizens' Association,
never forgetting that he had barely escaped a life of poverty himself. "When
the rich and comfortable people of New York show some regard for the lives of
the poor," he continued vehemently,

> when "respectable" men and women cease to live in style on
> the rental of vile, dark, poisonous tenement houses; when
> public opinion here makes it more disgraceful to own a pig
> stye and rent it out for the accommodation of human beings,
> than to live in one; when there is some sort of Christian
> sympathy between man and man here; then it may be time to
> blame the poor, the wretched, the criminal, for what they are.

---

77.   [CN,] "The 'Unrestricted Use of the Ballot Box,'" *Evening Post*, September 20, 1867.

He returned to the point he had made in June, but with his contempt for the genteel reformers etched more deeply in acid. "We assert once more that the people have a right to govern," he insisted; "they have a right to misgovern if they choose; and no part of them has the right to step in with pretensions to finer morality or greater wisdom, and claim the right to govern the mass." He concluded the editorial on a calmer note, with his own prescription for reform: decentralized democracy, in the Jacksonian mode, structured with clear lines of responsibility. The centralizing force of the federal government during the Civil War was clearly spent; Nordhoff's revulsion from concentrated government was part of a general, and growing, disaffection with federal power. "Let the people misgovern," he concluded; "only keep the government near them."

It was too much for Godkin. He angrily tore out the editorial and sent it off to Charles Eliot Norton in Boston, followed by his own opinion. "I sent you a scrap of Nordhoff's stuff yesterday," he wrote. "It amazes me to read such immoral trash. An ignorant, unthinking 'Red' in charge of an influential newspaper is an unpleasant sight, and I am afraid that is what must be made of it." He wasn't sure which was more suspect, Nordhoff's political morality or his intelligence, and he continued to rage. "When he talks of 'the people having a right to misgovern,' he most probably does not know what he means, and this is perhaps the kindest construction we can put on his balderdash."[78]

Godkin didn't confine his scorn to a private letter. Another *Nation* editorial immediately appeared, attacking the *Evening Post*. The *Post* "rebukes the Citizens' Association and everybody else for claiming the right to instruct 'the people' on any subject," Godkin wrote.

> We hope ... the educated and intelligent and Christian minority of this city will not be deterred by talk of this sort from telling 'the people' what they think, from asserting that they are wiser, are more enlightened, do know better what ought to be done, than the crowd which votes for Fernando Wood for mayor.[79]

Nordhoff promptly retorted, in the *Post*'s editorial column. "The *Evening Post* has never rebuked any one for 'claiming the right to instruct the people,'" he began; "on the contrary, it has always ... insisted upon the right of free discussion by press and speech—the right of everybody to try to "instruct"

78. E. L. Godkin to Charles Eliot Norton, September 27, 1867, in Armstrong, ed., *The Gilded Age Letters of E. L. Godkin* (Albany: SUNY Press, 1974), 114.
79. Quoted in [CN,] "The Sacred Right of Misrepresentation," *Evening Post*, September 26, 1867.

everybody else, that is to say." The *Post* had never tried to "deter" anyone from speaking out. Such an idea struck close to the heart of what Nordhoff believed journalism was meant to do: serve as a public forum, the "marketplace of ideas," in which truth, made clear to all, might triumph over falsehood. To him, it seemed as if the *Nation*'s part in this collective endeavor had gone terribly awry. For a weekly paper, presumably written more carefully than the dailies, to so misrepresent the *Post*'s statements betrayed a disregard for truth that was shocking. Nordhoff always felt sadly limited in his writing by the pressure to meet a daily deadline, and to see the luxury of time put to so little good use angered him. For "there is not a daily journal in New York, except perhaps the *Tribune*" (he could not forebear taking a swipe at his old sparring partner, Greeley) "which so often and so grossly misrepresents" its opponents, "as the *Nation*, published weekly."[80] Both Godkin and Nordhoff, by Autumn of 1867, must have been relieved that Nordhoff had so declined to assist Godkin in founding the *Nation*. There could have been no congenial partnership between the two men, so opposed were they in ideals and so alike in the volatility of their tempers.

In Paris, where he was trying to ease his sorrow over the death of his wife, William Cullen Bryant read the *Evening Post* as edited by Charles Nordhoff with growing disapproval. By May of 1867, even before the controversy with Godkin over New York's governance erupted so visibly, he was moved to write a cautionary note to Nordhoff. Rather than keep his communication with Nordhoff a private matter, however, he inserted the paragraph into a letter to Isaac Henderson, the *Evening Post*'s business manager and co-proprietor.

In a mild if chilly manner, he began. "There are two emotions raised by wrong-doing in those who are not active sufferers—one is indignation, the other sorrow --" and he believed that sorrow "implies, I think, a more properly disciplined state of the feelings, though I would by no means withhold a just resentment from doing its part." He found Nordhoff's outbursts distasteful. "It seems to me that the Evening Post never expresses anything but indignation," he continued, "when perhaps redress could be more readily obtained, and the wrongdoer brought to see his fault more certainly, by dwelling on the other side of feeling."[81] To Nordhoff, sorrow was too passive a mood with which to face wrongdoing, and his exchanges with Godkin throughout the months following his receipt of Bryant's letter do not demonstrate a willingness—or perhaps even the ability—to mute his criticisms or soften his demands for

80. [CN,] "The Sacred Right of Misrepresentation," *Evening Post*, September 26, 1867.
81. William Cullen Bryant to Isaac Henderson, Paris, May 4, 1867, in Hornberger, op.cit., 27.

reform. Unlike Bryant, he did not view journalism as a genteel endeavor; and unlike Henderson, he did not regard it as primarily a money-making business. Journalism, to Nordhoff, was a crucial element of democracy, with the almost sacred mission of educating the common people. Trouble was on the horizon.

CHAPTER 4

Redefining the Republican Party

Despite Charles Nordhoff's philosophical opposition to centralized government, the reality of postwar America was that the federal government was more powerful than ever before; and accordingly, he began to involve himself more and more with national politics and politicians. A man with a keenly developed sense of privacy, Nordhoff so disliked public exposure that for him to run for elective office would have been unendurable. But like most important journalists of his day, he was easily able to establish close working relationships with a variety of federal officials. It was understood that in order to be well-informed, an editor had to cultivate his sources (with a coziness that would later be regarded as entailing a conflict of interest), and any editor unable to establish such contacts was at a distinct disadvantage.

Nordhoff was not simply interested in learning from his sources in a disinterested way. As an editor of some stature, he was able to take on a sub rosa role in public affairs as well as the obvious role of public opinion shaper. His access to officials at all levels of the government allowed him to engage in the behind-the-scenes bargaining and compromise that underlay most governmental action.

To a large extent, Nordhoff's deepening immersion in national politics was the inevitable result of the problem of Reconstruction: how far could or should the United States government go in forcing change on the recalcitrant South? And where did good Union policy end and Republican political opportunism begin? Like many of his colleagues in the North, Nordhoff only reluctantly supported federal intervention in the former Confederate states, and he adhered to a legalistic view of racial problems that led him to equate the granting of full civil rights to African-Americans with an end to the saliency of race as a national concern. With the passage of the Fifteenth Amendment, he believed questions of economics and class should replace those of race and civil rights.

Fully established as a nationally known journalist by the late '60s, Nordhoff enjoyed a degree of security of which he took full advantage. His editorials and his private correspondence, during those years, display an exhilaration tempered only occasionally by the awareness that at the *Evening Post*, he did not work with an entirely free hand. Bryant and Henderson, as the owners and publishers of the paper, could still rein him in when his editorializing trod upon the people and institutions in which they held an interest—or which held an interest in the *Post*. If anything, however, their efforts only strengthened his determination to use the editor's desk as a pulpit from which to "preach" the truth as he saw it. When, finally, it seemed as though his editorship might be stripped of that purpose, he could see no point in continuing on at the *Evening Post*.

Throughout the war, the *Evening Post* had been hawkish in defense of the Union, but the postwar issues of Reconstruction promised no obvious solution. At first, President Andrew Johnson's program for the South impressed the editors of the *Post* as a sound one. Announced in May 1865, barely a month after Lincoln's assassination, Johnson's plan called for extending a general amnesty (with attendant restoration of property rights and the vote) to former Confederates who were willing to swear loyalty to the Union. The wealthiest white Confederate leaders would be required to apply individually to the President for pardon. The former Confederate states might regain admission to the Union upon their acceptance of the abolition of slavery, repudiation of Confederate war debts, and the convening of constitutional conventions.

Bryant and Nordhoff hoped that such reasonable measures might be sufficient to enact peaceful social change and a restoration of the country as a united whole. The editors' chief disagreement with the president was over universal suffrage, which they believed was a necessary prerequisite to a just and lasting peace. A steadfast believer in white man's government, however, Johnson left the question of suffrage to the discretion of the individual states; and for the purposes of electing delegates to the constitutional conventions, prewar suffrage qualifications would apply. Delegates to the states' constitutional conventions therefore included no African-Americans, and the white delegates showed no interest in enfranchising the excluded blacks. Presidential reconstruction was based not upon the extension of rights to former slaves, but on the exclusion of the old planter aristocracy. Even this exclusion soon appeared to be strictly illusory.[1]

By the winter of 1865–66, it was clear that the results of Johnson's program were seriously at odds with the wishes of the majority of northern Republicans,

---

[1]   Eric Foner, *Reconstruction: America's Unfinished Revolution, 1863-1877* (New York: Harper & Row, 1988), 176–227.

for by his wholesale pardoning of even the wealthiest and most influential former Confederates and his mandated restoration of abandoned and confiscated lands to their former owners, he in effect reinstated the old Southern leadership. Furthermore, the states' new constitutions established a series of repressive laws, the so-called "Black Codes," which severely curtailed the civil liberties, freedom of movement, and of contract of former slaves. Many Northerners saw in this a restoration of quasi slavery, a repudiation of the free-labor principles for which the Civil War had been fought, while credible journalists reported a change in the Southern attitude, from defeated resignation to one of defiance. Even Republicans who cared little about extending the franchise to African-Americans were appalled at the apparent reinstitution of unfree labor.

When in February of 1866, the President vetoed the Freedman's Bureau bill, introduced by the moderate Lyman Trumbull and intended to provide modest temporary assistance to the former slaves, Johnson's action crystallized even the most moderate Republicans' opposition to his policies. Soon after, Johnson vetoed a Civil Rights bill, designed to ensure federal protection of blacks' civil rights. Congress responded by overriding the veto—the first time a presidential veto had ever been overridden. As tensions heightened, the *Evening Post* upheld the basic justice of Johnson's Reconstruction plan while decrying his lack of support for equal rights for African-Americans and warning of the dangers of the powerful centralized government that the Radicals seemed to favor.

During the summer of 1866, violence erupted in New Orleans when a constitutional convention called by Louisiana's Republican governor was forcibly dispersed by whites joined by the city's police force—seemingly with the approval, if not at the behest of Andrew Johnson himself—resulting in the deaths of thirty-seven (mostly black) Republicans and scores of injuries. Nordhoff, dismayed by the prospect of an open breach between the President and Congress that might prove disastrous, believed that Johnson had made a "grave blunder" in approving the breakup of the Louisiana convention; and many people viewed the riot as, at the very least, the product of Johnson's excessive leniency. Johnson's action was "impossible to justify," as he wrote to Parke Godwin, and contradicted his purported belief in local self-government. "The Democrats are no better than the Republicans," Nordhoff noted; "they swallow all their state rights, & support the New Orleans act!" Although the Louisiana convention was, in fact, of dubious legality, Nordhoff thought that Johnson had "cut the ground from under himself," leaving his "best friends ... grieved & outraged."[2]

---

2.   CN to Parke Godwin, 8/3/66, Bryant-Godwin Papers, NYPL.

But the lesson Nordhoff discerned in the New Orleans riot was not that Presidential reconstruction policies were placing Southern African-Americans in danger of violence and redoubled oppression, but rather that federal interference in local affairs would inevitably lead to trouble. He suspected that the Republican Party had an interest in "stirring up throughout the country a very deep prejudice agst. Johnson & distrust of his fidelity to liberty," though he allowed that Johnson himself was largely to blame. Nordhoff hoped the riot would "awaken" the public to "the danger" of federal enforcement of civil rights, for with "prejudice" against Johnson so intense, and "the centralizers ... so unscrupulous," he feared that regrettable precedents would be set. The *Evening Post* opposed the Fourteenth Amendment, which was intended to assure that civil rights would be enforced in all the states, through federal law, if necessary. Blinded to the basic question of ensuring equal rights to Southern blacks in fact as well as in law, Nordhoff saw the paramount danger to democracy in federal interference with the local popular will. It was a curious case of tunnel vision for one who had so firmly supported the suppression of the Southern rebellion, but it was an attitude far from atypical among moderate Republicans.

During the autumn campaign of 1866, however, Johnson succeeded in deepening the "prejudice" against himself in his "swing around the circle"—a far-flung series of stump speeches in which he tried to rally opposition to the ratification of the Fourteenth Amendment. In effect, Johnson made the election of 1866 a referendum on the amendment, which would guarantee that no state could abridge liberties ensured by the federal Constitution. But he was so blatantly racist, so abrasive, and so willing to traduce his opponents during his tour that he alarmed even moderate Republicans. By late October, Nordhoff saw Johnson as his own worst enemy. "The fact is," he wrote to Godwin, the president had made "a righteous policy so rancorous to the people" that argument for that policy "is no longer possible, nor has been useful for three months past." Now that public opinion seemed to favor adopting the Fourteenth Amendment, and since the goal was to restore constitutional government as quickly as possible, the *Evening Post* now urged ratification of that Amendment. Nordhoff could only hope that Johnson would mend his ways and "advise the South to change course." Despite the reversal of editorial policy, he insisted that the *Evening Post* would "give up *nothing* we maintained before" in resisting Congress's schemes of centralized government.[3]

In New York, the opinions of the *Evening Post*, which accorded so little with either doctrinaire Republicanism or the Democracy, had roused "a terrible storm of politics" around Nordhoff's editorship. "'What do you fellows of the *Evg. Post* want,' asked a man of me roughly, on the street—an old acquaintance,"

[3.]   CN to Parke Godwin, 10/24/66, Bryant-Godwin Papers, NYPL.

Nordhoff wrote to Godwin. "'We want the Constitution,' said I. 'Damn the Constitution, who cares for a bit of paper' was the retort as quick as lightning." Nordhoff relished a good argument, and the *Evening Post*'s wariness of the "centralizing" Congress assured him of the opposition of many reformist Republicans. Charles Eliot Norton, editor of the *North American Review*, "wrote me that he continued to read the *Evg. Post* 'notwithstanding he was forced to disagree with its opinions,'" he happily informed Godwin. "I immediately wrote him back, that I continued to read the *North American* 'notwithstanding' &c. These Boston men are as intolerant as ever," he concluded, "& would gladly hang us all."[4]

If the election of 1866 was a referendum on the Fourteenth Amendment, then the verdict was clear: Americans voted overwhelmingly for Republicans who backed the Amendment, giving them a two-thirds majority in Congress. (Of course, voters in unreconstructed Southern States were excluded, giving an air of consensus to a still-bitterly divisive issue.) Despite the politically ominous situation in which they were placed, the Southern legislatures unanimously refused to ratify the Amendment. Congress decided to take matters into its own hands.

By January, various proposals were being debated in Congress for a new Reconstruction Act in defiance of the president. Nordhoff and the *Evening Post* supported such efforts. The President had begun with a plan, Nordhoff explained in one editorial, "which in wiser hands than his, and with the addition of a rigid enforcement of the laws, would, we believe, have answered very well." Regretfully, he continued:

> It was a plan perfectly safe and judicious, if only the President had continued to show himself thoroughly in sympathy with universal liberty and equal rights ...; if he had carefully carried out his own platform, that "treason must be punished;" that "new men must be brought forward in the southern states;" that "the old leaders must be put aside." But when he abandoned those principles ..., and not only pardoned but himself reinstated in power ... the very leaders whom he had so often and so justly denounced as unworthy of trust, he made that policy at once impracticable and unsafe. That is his own fault.

It was absolutely necessary that African-Americans be granted the suffrage so that they might form a coalition with loyal Southern whites and support

---

4.   CN to Parke Godwin, 10/24/66, Bryant-Godwin Papers, NYPL.

a genuine reunion of the states. More basically, they deserved the vote "by the legal right they possess as a part of the population to take part in the reorganization of civil government."[5] When Johnson vetoed a bill granting black residents of the District of Columbia the suffrage, Nordhoff wrote a sharp editorial in response. Johnson had declared the African-Americans "unfit for the suffrage," he noted. "How does he know?" He spelled out his democratic creed, aimed at Northern Republicans as well as Southern Democrats, that he had "faith in the people—and 'the people' means all the people, not the few who, by some lucky chance, may have secured wealth, or education, or local prominence."[6]

There was no need for extreme measures against the President, however. With a two-thirds majority in Congress, the Republicans could easily override any of Johnson's vetoes and, therefore, he could not stand in the way of any measure that Congress approved, Nordhoff insisted. He was powerless against such a Republican majority. Impeachment might well be legal, Nordhoff admitted, but it would be unwise, "bound to excite to the extremest pitch partisan passions, already unduly and injuriously stirred." The country, which had been in "an almost incessant turmoil" since the end of the war, longed "for quiet and rest." As long as he could believe that events would take care of themselves, Nordhoff also hoped for quiet. It was with some shock that he would soon realize that reconciliation and justice could well be derailed by the President's bad faith.[7]

Throughout January and February 1867, various permutations of a new Reconstruction bill were debated and amended by Congress. By late February, the measure that seemed likely to pass was one that called for military rule of the Southern states, disenfranchisement of a substantial portion of the old Confederate leadership, and mandating ratification of the Fourteenth Amendment and granting suffrage to African-Americans as conditions for readmission to the Union. With the flurry of proposals and counterproposals, the situation was convoluted enough that Nordhoff traveled to Washington to investigate.

The *Evening Post* had been one of Johnson's staunchest defenders, and as its readership was considered highly influential, Johnson had an interest in regaining the *Post*'s support. At that time, in official Washington, there were no formal means of communicating with the press—the first press office would not be installed until the McKinley Administration, in the 1890s. Instead,

---

5.   [CN,] "What Next?" *Evening Post*, 1/5/67.

6.   [CN,] "The Veto of the District of Columbia Suffrage Bill," *Evening Post*, January 7, 1867.

7.   [CN,] "Congress and the President," *Evening Post*, January 23, 1867.

officials would often meet with journalists on an informal basis, decided more by political affiliation and personal contacts than any institutionalized basis. For their part, journalists became not only friends and allies of politicians, but frequently were their advisors or even employees as well, serving as Congressional and Executive branch clerks during the off-seasons when their newspaper incomes often ceased.[8]

Nordhoff, as editor of the *Evening Post*, was welcomed to the White House for several talks with Johnson, who was eager to explain himself and win back a powerful ally. These conversations were less "interviews" in the modern sense than political strategizing sessions. There were no quotations or explicit references in the *Evening Post* to any firsthand contact with the President, and indeed there is no evidence that Nordhoff intended to use his discussions as journalistic fodder, except in the most indirect way. He hoped, rather, to convince Johnson to take a less inflammatory course toward the legislature.

He failed. Somewhat wearily, he described two visits to the president in a letter to Bryant. Johnson had defended his own policy; Nordhoff had been blunt in response, telling the president that "he had defended that policy, until circumstances, among them chiefly his own course, made it impracticable," and that the paramount concern was to quickly reunite the states under constitutional government. Johnson's policy was "dead, could not be revived," and public-spirited men were therefore duty-bound to unite on some "practicable scheme."[9]

At the time, Nordhoff was also meeting frequently with various Congressmen. When Johnson told him that he objected to one of the bill's provisions concerning the division of authority between himself and General Grant, Nordhoff "agreed with him entirely, … and as I was so fortunate as to be thrown with" the responsible Senators, he convinced them to amend the bill "as the President desired." He arranged to see the President once more, prepared careful notes on the situation, and at the meeting read them to Johnson. "We then spoke together at some length," he wrote,

8. For information on Washington journalism, see F. B. Marbut, *News From the Capital* (Carbondale: Southern Illinois University Press, 1971); James E. Pollard, *The Presidents and the Press* (NY: Macmillan, 1947); Donald Ritchie, *Press Gallery: Congress and the Washington Correspondents* (Cambridge: Harvard University Press, 1991); and Vincent Howard, "The Two Congresses: A Study of the Changing Roles and Relationships of the National Legislature and the Washington Reporters…, 1860-1913," Ph.D. dissertation, University of Chicago, 1976.

9. CN to William Cullen Bryant, February 21, 1867. Bryant-Godwin Papers, NYPL.

& he grew much excited, & expressed the most bitter hatred of the measure in all its parts, declaring that it was nothing but anarchy & chaos, that the people of the South, poor, quiet, unoffending, harmless, were to be trodden underfoot "to protect niggers," that the [ex-Confederate] states were already in the Union, that in no part of the country were life & property so safe as in the Southern states, that whatever their local differences might be, that the military (U.S.) ought to be, and must be, under the strictest subordination to the local state governments, &c., & that all that was needed was for Congress to admit loyal representatives.

Nordhoff tried to make this most impolitic of Presidents see political reason. "I answered him that Congress would not" admit Southern representatives, he explained to Bryant,

that the next Congress would be even more extreme than this, that while he & the Southern leaders delayed the storm gathered strength, that the present bill was harsher than the [Fourteenth] Amendment, & the next would be worse than this; that his refusal to sign it would merely give strength to [Radical Thaddeus] Stevens, & play into his hands, while it could cripple the sensible republicans, that if he signed it the Southern leaders would give it up, & accept it, & all our troubles would be ended, & that as a man desiring the speediest possible reconstruction, I thought it my duty to support the bill, & urge him to sign it.[10]

Johnson, seeing an ally slip away, tried to persuade Nordhoff of the sufficiency of his own program, and he accused Northern journalists of blowing out of proportion stories of Southern violence. "He spoke again of the peaceful condition of the South," Nordhoff recalled.

I said the Southern state governments did not protect life & property, & gave him some instances; he retorted that in the morning papers he had read of a rape committed on a girl of twelve, in New York, "and no press is made abt. that, but if it happened in the South, & the girl was black, what an outcry there would have been." I said "Yes, unless the criminal had

<hr>

10. CN to William Cullen Bryant, February 21, 1867. Bryant-Godwin Papers, NYPL.

been promptly arrested & surely punished;" he replied—"It's
all damned prejudice."

At this juncture, Nordhoff rose to leave, Johnson "assuring" him "three
times that he would be glad to see me at all times." But Nordhoff had taken
Johnson's measure, concluded that their principles were opposed beyond
reconciliation, and doubted that reasoned discussion would be to any further
avail. "The impression he makes upon me is that he is a pig-headed man," he
wrote,

> with only one idea, & that is bitter opposition to universal
> suffrage, & a determination to secure the political ascendancy
> of the old Southern leaders. He said to me "it is in the nature
> of things that they must rule the South"—I replied "very well,
> let them take their chance then, with the rest." Every time
> I spoke of universal suffrage, he stopped short, & changed
> the subject. At last I said, "in New York it is proposed to
> disfranchise the Irish & Germans, who are as ignorant as the
> blacks." He said this would be very wrong. But said I, how can
> we oppose that, except on the general principle of universal
> suffrage? Then he was silent again.[11]

Nordhoff also encountered several of Johnson's "intimates," who, he said,
filled Johnson's ears with "the most nonsensical & vile Copperhead sentiment."
This Washington sojourn and face-to-face confrontation with Andrew
Johnson were decisive in radicalizing Nordhoff's views on Reconstruction. As
long as Johnson remained President, he would remember their conversations
and freshly realize that significant powers were determined to undermine
any real change in the South; and for a while, he subordinated his fear of the
possibility of "despotism" by a powerful central government in recognition
of the more immediate possibility of a kind of despotism supported by state
governments. As Congressman Rutherford B. Hayes wrote to a Cincinnati
newspaper editor opposed to Congressional Reconstruction on similar
principles, Nordhoff had told him that "if he had stayed in New York he would
have talked as you do, but now he gives it up."[12]
Nordhoff's assessment of Johnson's beliefs and actions was, according to
the judgment of most present-day historians, highly accurate: Johnson did
not, in fact, want to do away with white supremacy in the South; and in all his

11.   CN to William Cullen Bryant, February 21, 1867. Bryant-Godwin Papers, NYPL.
12.   Rutherford B. Hayes to Murat Halstead, 2/22/67, RBH Library, Fremont, OH.

actions, he undermined policies that had seemed reasonable enough at first glance.[13] In general, Nordhoff was clear-eyed when investigating a situation firsthand, though when surveying conditions from a distance, he was more prone to fall into unexamined dogma. He sensed the gravity of this failing, for his lengthy letter to Bryant recounting his encounters with Johnson was meant to justify a change in the *Evening Post*'s editorial policy in light of his new knowledge. Ruefully, he now saw that judging the situation from Paris and New York had led the *Post*'s editors to miss crucial aspects of Johnson's politics, to judge wrongly, in opposing Congressional Reconstruction, for more than a year past. "I think it was a grave mistake on our part," he wrote to Bryant, "that some one of us did not last winter (1865–66) visit Washington, so as to comprehend the real facts. I am convinced now, that while the President's policy was the best, he from the first made it impracticable." He regretted their criticisms of Congress. "I do not blame congress for not agreeing with him, & insisting on a policy of its own," he continued with feeling. "It did right, did so from a knowledge of facts wh. we had not in our possession." They hadn't had those facts simply because they hadn't bothered to investigate the Washington scene themselves. Johnson's policy "needed a man behind it, as much as a soul needs a body, & Mr. Johnson was not the man," and credible people believed that Johnson "from the first used his policy to further the ends of slavery & oppression." One of Johnson's old acquaintances told Nordhoff that Johnson had told him "that he never was opposed to slavery, for the slaves, that the blacks were happiest in that condition or some one near it, that white men alone must manage the South, &c." Filled with regret, Nordhoff considered the implications of all this information. "Mr. Johnson administered the government & managed his policy against the interests of liberty, against true democracy, and congress saw this—which I did not," he concluded grimly. "It makes all the difference in the world."[14]

Without waiting for Bryant's reply, Nordhoff wrote an editorial for the *Evening Post* of the next day, recapitulating his new judgment on Johnson and Reconstruction. He did not say, however, that he was repeating in print substantially what he had said to Johnson himself of the necessity that he sign the Reconstruction bill. Congress was only reflecting the popular will as demonstrated in the recent election, he decided, far from being motivated by the simple "centralizing" power-mongering he had previously discerned in the

---

13. See Foner, op. cit.; Eric McKittrick, *Andrew Johnson and Reconstruction* (Chicago: University of Chicago Press, 1960); Kenneth Stampp, *The Era of Reconstruction* (N.Y.: 1968); and Michael Les Benedict, *The Impeachment and Trial of Andrew Johnson* (New York: 1973).

14. CN to William Cullen Bryant, 2/21/67. Bryant-Godwin Papers, NYPL.

Radical measures. Rather than a dispute between two branches of government, Nordhoff now saw the battle between Johnson and the Congress as one between the President and the people. Johnson had appealed directly to the people in the campaign of 1866, "and he was beaten."[15]

There were limits to Nordhoff's radicalism. As expected, Johnson vetoed the Reconstruction bill, which Congress then passed over his veto. Throughout the remainder of 1867, Nordhoff and the *Evening Post* adhered to a moderate line, reproving military officials when they overstepped the limits of their authority, cautioning Johnson to comply with the spirit of the Act as well as its law. By the approach of autumn, Nordhoff's editorials began to exhibit the weariness with questions of race that was eventually to undermine Northern support of the Reconstruction effort. He counseled the Democrats to abandon their race-baiting tactics, eliciting howls of outrage from Republicans for trying to help the Democrats, and from Democrats for trying to undermine their traditional base of support. Nordhoff insisted that his advice was above partisanship and aimed only at restoring some balance to political life. If the Democrats would support universal manhood suffrage, he reasoned, they would be as likely as Republicans to gain votes from enfranchised blacks. Racial barriers to the suffrage had to be dismantled "because it is right, just, safe and best that this government shall be a government of the whole people, and not of any class or part." The persistence of the bitterness engendered by bigotry, which might well keep African-Americans from voting for Democrats in light of their history or keep Southern whites from considering themselves obligated to respect the rights of their former slaves, always eluded Nordhoff's full comprehension. It was a fatal lack, but the consequences of this blindness would be delayed for some years.[16]

Though Nordhoff continued to express his hope for a color-blind society, questions of race would not go away. During the summer of 1867, Johnson not only "suspended" Secretary of War Edwin Stanton, but also began the wholesale removal of military officials who took too hard a line with Southern whites. Nordhoff called for the president's impeachment should he continue on his fractious course. It made no difference that Johnson's actions were within the letter of the law. "Let Mr. Johnson beware," Nordhoff wrote ominously. "He is a literalist; he cons very closely the letter of the Constitution; we advise him not to forget that it also has a spirit," one which required him to "execute, and not obstruct and defeat the laws." Reluctant as he was to see federal power extended and strengthened, Nordhoff saw more basic issues at stake: justice, equality, liberty. The violence being inflicted on Southern blacks struck at the

15.   [CN,] "Why the President Ought to Sign the Bill," *Evening Post*, 2/22/67.
16.   [CN,] "Suffrage Once More," *Evening Post*, 7/25/67.

very heart of the national purpose, but Johnson seemed willfully oblivious to that fact. "He knows that justice is not done to a very large class of people in some of the southern states, except when the United States forces interfere," Nordhoff wrote. "It is a pity and a disgrace that it is so," but such was the truth. Johnson "might talk what nonsense he pleases about tyranny, about centralization, about military despotism," but "he, Andrew Johnson, is chiefly to blame." The president's intransigence encouraged Southern demagogues to resist, denounce, and obstruct the law, and his appeals to racism were all too clear. "Mr. Johnson is very full of sympathy for 'the South,' by which he means only the whites there," Nordhoff pointed out. If Johnson continued to stand in the way of peace, then Congress "will have to impeach and remove him."[17]

But the *Evening Post*'s editorial policy seemed to be of two minds on the issue of impeachment, and more conciliatory editorials followed these angry lashings out. Whether the more measured commentaries were the product of Bryant's influence or of Nordhoff's own second thoughts must remain a matter of speculation. One such editorial acknowledged that Johnson's course could drive people "to sanction extreme and unreasonable proceedings; and to approve, out of alarm and irritation, what they would not under other circumstances for a moment tolerate."[18] Although it wavered on Reconstruction, the *Evening Post* held firm to the ideal of equal civil rights for African-Americans, and Nordhoff continued to write pointed editorials favoring the passage of the Fifteenth Amendment to grant them the suffrage.[19]

By 1867, Nordhoff had struck up a correspondence with Boston Brahmin Edward Atkinson, a Republican businessman, the owner of textile mills dependent upon Southern cotton; he wanted to see stable business conditions restored, and that meant a federal retreat from enforcing the new policies. This was not an uncommon attitude by 1867, but Nordhoff believed the priorities were misplaced. The country, he told Atkinson in one letter, "is actually in anarchy; any thing may happen, & business & industry must languish till we get over this, & are back under the constitution."

> To me reconstruction is the *first* work. . . . A dozen impeachments would not be so bad or dangerous as to have a fuss about the Presidential election. I would remove the President at once

---

17. [CN,] "Does the President Court Impeachment?" *Evening Post*, 8/7/67.
18. [CN or WCB?] "The President and Reconstruction," *Evening Post*, 8/27/67.
19. [CN,] "The Fairness of Universal Suffrage," *Evening Post*, 9/2/67; [CN,] "Suffrage and Its Conditions," *Evening Post*, 11/22/67.

when Congress meets, if by that means we could have all the
United states fairly in for the Presidential election.[20]

But perhaps because Bryant had returned from Europe, the *Evening Post*
opposed impeachment when the President was actually brought to trial in
the spring of 1868.[21] The President deserved "censure" only, and the *Post*
applauded the decisions of the seven Republican Congressmen who voted to
acquit.[22]

The retreat of Nordhoff and the *Evening Post* from the Radicals continued.
Having laid all his eggs in the basket of political equality, Nordhoff viewed the
1870 ratification of the Fifteenth Amendment, which granted black men the
vote, as the longed-for consummation of the entire antislavery effort. With
full citizenship, the former slave was "no longer the proper object of special
legislation, for or against his interests." Nordhoff assumed, with a naiveté born
of wishful thinking, that the former slaves' new legal status would be respected
by their former masters and other Southern whites, thereby freeing him of the
dilemma of choosing between the principles of equal justice and decentralized
government.[23]

Now, he hoped, racial issues would no longer stand in the way of other
needed reforms. The major question for Nordhoff was this: what next for
the Republican Party, whose mission had at last been completed? Protective
tariffs raised the cost of living for the average American while enriching the
wealthy capitalist, an "iniquitous and monstrous oppression" badly in need of
reparation, and Nordhoff proposed free trade as the next standard for the
Republican Party to bear. He ignored the fact that the Republican coalition
included both protectionists and free traders. Economic equity was the logical
extension of antislavery.[24]

Unfortunately, Southern whites interfered with Nordhoff's envisioned
institution of a new platform. New violence in the South, and attempts to
intimidate black voters, erupted as the real consequence of the new voting
rights supposedly enjoyed by blacks. In response, Congress passed measures,
called by their enemies "Force Laws," which allowed the use of federal troops

---

20.   CN to Edward Atkinson, 9/9/67, Atkinson Papers, MHS.

21.   The Impeachment of Mr. Johnson," *Evening Post*, February 27, 1868; "A Word of
      Caution," *Evening Post*, April 26, 1868.

22.   "Coercing a Court," *Evening Post*, May 13, 1868; "The Acquittal of the President,"
      Evening Post, May 18, 1868.

23.   [CN,] "What Next?" *Evening Post*, April 1, 1870.

24.   [CN,] "What Next?" *Evening Post*, April 1, 1870.

to ensure that voting in the South was not subject to white manipulation and terrorism.

Nordhoff held stubbornly to his belief that the Fifteenth Amendment had placed the powers of self-protection and equal justice within the hands of Southern African-Americans. So keenly did Nordhoff resist the idea of centralized government and so fervently did he want to see an end to the disruption and rancor of Reconstruction and the South's resistance to it that he ignored the degree to which his panacea of equal voting rights might be undermined by recalcitrant local whites determined to prevent blacks from voting. Passage of a federal bill to protect Southern African-Americans from the Ku Klux Klan elicited only his disapproval. The time had come, he wrote in March 1871, for "strict deference to constitutional powers, duties and limitations," for if "a few mobs in country villages" posed a threat to the republic, "what becomes of it when the Constitution is repealed, and the general government usurps alike the powers of all the local and municipal authorities?" The potential for abuse, for the U.S. government to become merely the "armed guardian of ... the party which happens to control it," was too great to be tolerated.[25]

The *Evening Post*, which in 1867 had derided Andrew Johnson for his "pleas ... about tyranny, about centralization, about military despotism," in the face of local governments that took "no cognizance of crimes against one half their population" was, in 1871, voicing sentiments with the ring of awful familiarity. Nordhoff's egalitarianism had been satisfied by the bestowal of voting rights upon black men, but the dangers of centralization seemed to him to loom ever larger. Nineteenth-century liberalism, in questions of politics and race, was a double-edged sword.[26]

"I believe God leads us in this wilderness," Nordhoff wrote to Parke Godwin in June of 1868, "-- only he has the advantage of living longer than we poor mortals, & can afford to wait." He was swallowing his disappointment over the Democratic Party's decision to play on racial animosities during the 1868 election, rejecting civil rights advocate Salmon P. Chase's bid for its presidential nomination.[27] The Democratic campaign of Horatio Seymour and Frank Blair degenerated into an ugly racist harangue while the Republicans "waved the bloody shirt," referring constantly to Democratic disloyalty during the war. By September, Nordhoff was thoroughly disgusted with the Democrats, who

25. [CN,] "The Kuklux Bill," *Evening Post*, March 8, 1871; [CN,] "Does the End Justify the Means?" *Evening Post*, March 20, 1871.
26. "The Force Bill," *Evening Post*, April 7, 1871. Many of the post-1870 editorials are difficult to attribute with certainty to either Nordhoff or Bryant.
27. CN to Parke Godwin, June 26, 1868, Bryant-Godwin Papers, NYPL.

cried "about their sufferings, their dishonor, the tyranny before which they are prostrated," when "it is not their own rights they seek to insure," but only the ability "to rob other men of their rights."[28]

Like many Republican reformers, Nordhoff regarded the election of U.S. Grant to the presidency as an augury of good government and better times to come. Henry Adams recalled the circle of journalists with whom he allied himself, naming Nordhoff and several others: "all reformers, and all mixed and jumbled together in a tidal wave of expectation, waiting for General Grant to give orders."[29] Projecting his own wishes onto the silent figure of the General, Nordhoff predicted that Grant would be "his own man," maintaining his independence and rectitude. As he wrote enthusiastically to Godwin a few weeks before Grant's inauguration, Grant "has a very simple policy—down with the plunderers, economy & retrenchment," and he believed that "with so calm and well-regulated a man as Grant" as president, "we shall have a chance to discuss real questions."[30] In contrast to Johnson ("an unmitigated curse to the country"), Grant would bring peace.

The reality proved otherwise. Within a year of Grant's inauguration, Republican reformers generally regarded his administration as a disaster, an orgy of corruption and "plundering" by Grant's associates of which the president seemed blandly unaware. Liberal Republicans began to caucus in an attempt to reassert in their party the principles of laissez-faire government, an end to graft and wasteful "jobbery," withdrawal of federal troops from the South, and the institution of Civil Service reform. Nordhoff had become disillusioned with postwar Republicanism for some time, alienated from the "centralizing" and Grantism that seemed to have accompanied the party's purposelessness and slide into moral vacuity. Nor could he stomach the Democrats, flagrantly racist as its campaigns continued to be. He joined with the Liberal Republicans in the hope that a new rigidly principled and meritocratic governing party might be formed.[31]

The task of weaning old guard Republicans away from their party would not be an easy one, as illustrated by the response of Nordhoff's friend, Rutherford B. Hayes. Hayes, whose fidelity to party would be rewarded with the presidency six years later, insisted that reform would have to be undertaken within the existing Republican party, and he advised against any attempt to

---

28. [CN,] "No Disfranchisement in the Southern States," *Evening Post*, September 11, 1868.

29. Henry Adams, *The Education of Henry Adams* (Boston: 1922), 255.

30. CN to Parke Godwin, February 16, 1869. Bryant-Godwin Papers, NYPL.

31. John Sproat, *"The Best Men": Liberal Reformers in the Gilded Age* (NY: Oxford, 1968) remains the best explication of the Liberals' goals and motivations.

organize a third-party movement. The "great body of the Republican people," he maintained, still backed the Grant Administration's Southern policy; and all other differences were secondary so long as Democrats remained allied with defiant ex-Confederates. Nevertheless, the reformers began to meet and strategize.[32]

Journalists played a prominent role in these discussions.[33] Unhappy as he was with the postwar Republican Party, which seemed to him to symbolize protectionism, governmental giveaways to corporations, wild annexation schemes, profoundly corrupt associations, and unduly centralized power, Nordhoff was a bit more skeptical of the reformers' possible success than many of his colleagues. As a practical measure, he didn't want to see reform relegated to a fringe group cut off from the party mainstream, and he insisted to Carl Schurz that they must be "recognized as the true leaders of the Republican Party" rather than breaking off on their own. More prophetically than he knew, he added, "if we are not that, we are nothing."[34]

By the opening of the Grant Administration, Nordhoff had solidified his connections with federal officials. Nineteenth-century journalists could be powerful political allies, and their assistance could be freely given and gratefully accepted. With Nordhoff's virtual equation of journalism with politics, albeit politics of a public-spirited kind in his own eyes, he was an extreme example of the type, helping his allies and undermining his adversaries in numerous ways, large and small. In one instance, he would counsel a Congressman to postpone a controversial speech until his seat on the powerful Ways & Means Committee was assured; in another he would solicit information from a political activist with which the *Evening Post* might damage the Congressional candidacy of a political enemy.[35] Persistent in a cause he believed in, Nordhoff's zeal was

---

[32] CN to Rutherford B. Hayes, April 1, 1870; Hayes to CN, 4/5/70 and 3/13/71. RBH Library, Fremont, Ohio.

[33] One meeting included Henry and Charles Francis Adams, who were then engaging in exposures of the unscrupulous tactics of Jay Gould and his cronies; Nordhoff; E. L. Godkin of the *Nation*; Samuel Bowles of the *Springfield Republican*; Horace White of the *Chicago Tribune*; William Cullen Bryant; David Ames Wells; and a dozen others. Henry Adams to Jacob D. Cox, November 28, 1870, in *Letters*, Samuels et al., eds., 91–2.

[34] CN to Carl Schurz, 12/21/70. Schurz Papers, LC. See also [CN] "The New Departure," *Evening Post*, April 12, 1871, and [CN] "How to Destroy a Party," *Evening Post*, July 13, 1871.

[35] CN to Edward Atkinson, 9/15/68 and 10/23/68, on the article aimed at discrediting Benjamin Butler; CN to Atkinson, 3/14[/68], on delaying a speech by Senator William B. Allison of Iowa.

limited only by his growing circle of Washington contacts. In 1870, for example, he introduced free trader David Ames Wells to Grant to nudge Grant into proposing a revenue reform measure to Congress. First, Grant said he would informally suggest some tariff changes to a Congressional leader. Nordhoff told him that it would be more effective for him to send a formal message to both Houses. ("That, I have been told, he has been pondering ever since.") As Grant considered what he would do, Nordhoff went to the Secretary of the Interior, the Secretary of State, the Secretary of the Treasury, and the Speaker of the House, asking them to put pressure on Grant to follow Wells's advice. As if that were not enough, he canvassed Congress and wrote to party stalwart Rutherford B. Hayes, then Governor of Ohio. "The men like Garfield, Blaine, Daws [sic], &c. in the House" supported revenue reform, he wrote to Hayes; "& will, they told me, carry any bills wh. the Pres. will recommend." He hoped that the Governor would also write to Grant, but Nordhoff added it was best that Grant not know the extent of his own maneuverings. "You may ... say that I wrote you about his seeing Wells," he instructed Hayes, "... except of course that I saw the Cabinet; that he ought not to hear at second hand."[36]

Nordhoff's access to highly placed government officials was almost unlimited. Two of Nordhoff's closer friends among the Washington establishment during the Grant Administration were Secretary of State Hamilton Fish, widely regarded as the most honest and ablest member of a notably corrupt Cabinet, and Massachusetts Senator Charles Sumner, long-standing antislavery advocate and a symbol of the moral impetus behind the early Republican Party. Fish wrote Nordhoff several respectful, if exasperated, letters about the *Evening Post*'s reporters and articles, on one occasion exchanging with him unflattering analyses of the character of a mutual acquaintance, in a manner that suggested considerable confidence between the statesman and the editor.[37]

On another occasion, the *Evening Post*'s young Washington reporter, Scott Smith, angered Fish with a "splenetic" article complaining of the inaccessibility of the Secretary of State to the press. As there were no press offices, correspondents would simply roam about the various government offices, trying to buttonhole Cabinet officers or anyone else who might provide them with information. Smith was apparently too persistent. "I have in general, given him all the information that could properly be given to the press," Fish complained, "but when there has been nothing, he seems to have fancied, that the Department should ... invent or guess something." The new emphasis

[36]   CN to Rutherford B. Hayes, May 12, 1870. RBH Library, Fremont, Ohio.

[37]   Hamilton Fish to CN, 9/23/70, vol. 203, 582 ff.; CN to Hamilton Fish, 9/25/70, Fish Papers, vol. 72; Charlton I. Lewis to Hamilton Fish, 9/24/70, Fish Papers, vol. 72. Library of Congress.

upon "news" in the postwar period as a commodity to be produced placed many reporters under considerable pressure to hunt up "items" (although the *Evening Post* was less oriented toward "news" than toward opinion and features), and both reporters and their subjects frequently chafed at the situation. As he often did, Fish alluded to the higher expectations he held of the *Evening Post* than of other newspapers, and the consequent bruised feelings its criticisms caused in him. "I do not think that I am very thin-skinned," he wrote Nordhoff, "certainly I ought ... to be well covered with a callus, as tough as the Rhinoceros hide, but I confess that it would be less disagreeable to be misrepresented in some other journals than in the Post." He finished the letter on a conciliatory note, remarking that he was always ready to provide the *Post*'s reporter with any available information.[38] Nordhoff, in turn, was willing to assist Fish, as in the case of the settlement of the *Alabama* claims, when he offered to help "prepare the public mind" for the result. "If you think it would be useful to say or suggest any thing at any time, let me know it," he added.[39]

On other issues, however, he was in firm and public opposition to the Secretary of State, the most notable of these being the proposed annexation of San Domingo. Nordhoff's anti-imperialism made its first appearance during the contretemps over San Domingo, but it was an issue that he would argue repeatedly in years to come. In this case, Grant, without the knowledge of Fish, had authorized a friend to negotiate an annexation treaty with the island nation, citing in justification the desirability of having a naval station in the Caribbean, the ostensibly great natural resources of the island, the Monroe Doctrine, and the Dominican people's desire to join the United States.

As chairman of the Senate Foreign Relations Committee, however, Charles Sumner, in a much-publicized break with the president, grew more strongly opposed to the idea the more he investigated it. To annex San Domingo would be to assume a costly debt, to take on a country where civil war was already raging, and to undermine the autonomy of the black republic of Haiti. Furthermore, there was evidence that Grant's friends stood to benefit financially from annexation through their ownership of Dominican land and bonds. Worse still, the plebiscite that supposedly indicated the people's consent had been conducted under the shadow of American gunboats and threats from the Dominican dictator that those voting against annexation would be executed or banished. It was a situation that would be roughly paralleled in Hawaii twenty years later, and Nordhoff's reaction to the possibility of Dominican annexation

---

[38]   Hamilton Fish to CN, 10/1/70, Fish Papers, vol. 203, 611 ff.

[39]   CN to Hamilton Fish, January 18, 1871. Fish Papers, vol. 75, Library of Congress.

foreshadowed his much more public role in defeating the annexationists of 1893.[40]

Sumner was joined in opposition to annexation by Democrats and the reformist wing of the Republican Party. Grant was convinced that Sumner had promised his support and then betrayed him, and he began to systematically undermine Sumner's influence in the Senate and the Republican Party. It all added up to an ugly brouhaha in which personal attacks and partisan appeals predominated.

The *Evening Post* had taken the position that the annexation was being forwarded too hastily and without sufficient justification by the Administration. Fish, used by now to having the *Post*'s support, wrote to Bryant and Nordhoff inquiring about their opposition. Nordhoff answered candidly. People wanted to know "'what shall we do with it, if we buy it. How shall we govern it,' &c." He added that Bryant was not inveterately opposed, but "he too would like to know. So would I. Can we not let that cat out of the bag?" he asked Fish. "Ought we, to change the figure, to buy a pig in a poke?"[41]

Captured by the alternative idea of a protectorate, which had already garnered Sumner's support, Nordhoff wrote enthusiastically to Sumner only a few days later. "If we can start a system for San Domingo ..., we shall have settled the whole future of the West Indies," he wrote, "& kept them out of our arms where I at least do *not* want to see them." The question, to him, was not so open as he had intimated to Fish.[42] Nordhoff's opposition to the annexation was, like the attitudes of many nineteenth-century antiexpansionists, motivated by an amalgamation of distrust of an expanded government and the patronage involved in establishing far-flung outposts; a genuine concern that native peoples be allowed to run their own governments; and a fear of absorbing populations, which for cultural or racial reasons, seemed to be unassimilable. In contrast to his insistence on the full equality of America's former slaves, Nordhoff indulged in blatantly racist attacks on the idea of Dominican annexation, a scheme to foist upon the United States a "small collection of colored semi-barbarians." He also questioned the financial interests of Grant's friends in annexation, recalling the handsome profits some speculators had made off the annexation of Texas. Democracy demanded a fuller discussion of the plan than the Grant Administration had hitherto provided.[43]

---

40. On the San Domingo question, see Foner, *Reconstruction*, 494–7, and David Herbert Donald, *Charles Sumner and the Rights of Man*, 435–480, 509–515, 537–8.
41. CN to Hamilton Fish, 5/11/70. Fish Papers, Vol. 69, LC.
42. CN to Charles Sumner, 5/13/70, Sumner Papers, Houghton Library.
43. [CN,] "The United States as a Benevolent Institution," *Evening Post*, May 20, 1870.

Nordhoff continued to send exhortatory notes to Sumner—not a man who needed exhortation—as the political sanctions exacted by the President harshened. "I hope you will stick out agst. the San Domingo treaty," he wrote. "The President I think cuts up a little rough about it." He had heard rumors of bribes being offered to Congressmen in return for their support and had sent a reporter to investigate. As an ally of Sumner, Nordhoff was disturbed by rumors that Sumner had first promised to support Grant and then reneged, and he wrote to Fish in an attempt to get at the truth of the matter before publishing anything about it. Other newspapers had been filled with stories of the quarrel, but Nordhoff protested that he didn't like "mere gossip & scandal" though journalism, as practiced at other newspapers, had lowered "its standards to that wh. sometimes make me determine to leave the press entirely."[44]

Fish shot a letter back to Nordhoff advising against publishing the story although he acknowledged that Grant was angry with Sumner, and he denied that the dismissal of a Sumner protégé from his diplomatic post in London had anything to do with the disfavor into which Sumner had fallen. This was the official story that scarcely anyone believed; but Fish was a loyal member of the administration, not about to tell a newspaperman—even one with whom he had cordial relations—that Grant was, in fact, being vindictive. As for another story about Fish's son receiving a patronage position, Fish wrote that he would be pained should it be publicized and asked that the article be suppressed. Nordhoff did so. Clearly, public officials had as much interest in keeping the press happy as the press did in maintaining cordial relationships with its sources.[45]

Nordhoff's apparent cooperation with Fish did not affect his relationship with Sumner, and he continued to strategize with the Senator against the annexation treaty. Grant was "shrewd & pertinacious, & I think unscrupulous," he wrote in one letter and suggested ways in which a Senate resolution calling for a full investigation might derail the effort. To so question the President would be political dynamite, Nordhoff realized. "I don't think *you* ought to do this, but some other," he cautioned, proffering some plausible justifications for an inquiry. He closed on a more personal note, acknowledging that the idea might seem nonsensical to Sumner, "but I am losing patience with U.S.G., and a little counter attack might bother him." He doubted that even Grant "believes in his own public reasons."[46]

He had, indeed, lost patience. The questions and doubts of early editorials on San Domingo were replaced by unequivocal attacks upon the whole

---

44. CN to Hamilton Fish, 10/12/70. Fish Papers, vol. 73. Library of Congress.
45. Hamilton Fish to CN, 10/13/70, Fish Papers, vol. 205, 194 ff. Fish Papers, LC.
46. CN to Charles Sumner, 12/21/70, Sumner Papers, Houghton Library.

enterprise. Allegations had surfaced that U.S. military force was being used to coerce the Dominican people and that the pro-annexationist president of San Domingo was simply a dictator, propped up by the support of the United States. Questionable financial transactions threw suspicion on Grant's colleagues as well. Within three weeks of Nordhoff's suggestion to Sumner, in January 1871, the Senate amended a motion to send a commission of inquiry to the island with a denial that this inquiry implied any approval of annexation, and there the movement died.[47]

But the ramifications for the Republican Party, and for Charles Sumner in particular, did not cease in January of 1871. Sumner and the "old radical" element of the party, along with the growing liberal reformist wing, diminished in power as organizational politics overtook ideology. Sumner was stripped of the chairmanship of the Foreign Relations Committee, which incensed Nordhoff. In his opinion, if Grant "& his tools" were to succeed in their efforts, the Republican Party would be destroyed.[48] In late March, a scathing editorial attacked Grant, accusing him of sanctioning illegal extragovernmental diplomacy, interfering with Dominican internal affairs in violation of international law, and using naval forces against the will of Congress to "uphold a usurper against his own people," in defiance of the Constitution. In short, Nordhoff editorialized, "it is proved that our republic has been made to appear before the world ... as arrogant, insolent, regardless of public law and of its own Constitution, and as a violent trespasser upon the rights of its neighbors." The *Evening Post*'s break with Grant was complete.[49]

"It is not easy to make a pleasing paper, when one has almost continually to criticize," Nordhoff wrote to Parke Godwin in 1869. "Mr. Bryant asked the other day if we could not find something to praise, but it is hard to find it."[50] At odds with much of the *Evening Post*'s traditional Republican constituency, he continued to berate the affluent and respectable for their acquiescence in municipal corruption as well as the Tammany politicians and ward heelers.

In editing the *Evening Post*, he was accustomed to deferring, to a degree, to William Cullen Bryant, who was not only the editor in chief but half owner of the newspaper as well. Bryant's principles were largely in accord with Nordhoff's own, and although he tempered some of Nordhoff's more radical impulses, he did not often contradict them. Their differences should have

---

47. [CN,] "News From San Domingo," *Evening Post*, January 6, 1871.
48. [CN,] "Senator Sumner and the President," *Evening Post*, March 9, 1871; CN to Charles Sumner, March 10, 1871, Sumner Papers; Sumner to [CN,] March 10, 1871, Sumner Papers.
49. [CN,] "Senator Sumner's Speech," *Evening Post*, March 28, 1871.
50. CN to Parke Godwin, 2/16/69, Bryant-Godwin Papers, NYPL.

become less significant as Bryant, more and more, distanced himself from the daily operations of the *Evening Post,* removing to his estate on Long Island for days on end, spending summers in Massachusetts. But there were signs of strain. Bryant's circle of friends, exemplified by Peter Cooper, were often the subject of Nordhoff's editorial denunciation when their attempted reforms seemed to him antidemocratic or when they seemed to abdicate all responsibility for city government to the despised Tammany ward heelers. In taking a stand against Civil Service reform, the *Evening Post* was at odds with many members of its traditional audience. And as Bryant distanced himself from the paper, the presence of its other owner, Isaac Henderson, loomed ever more imposingly.

Henderson, a shrewd businessman, had made the *Evening Post* an enormously profitable concern and Bryant a wealthy man. In 1866, when he was indicted for taking kickbacks as the U.S. Naval agent in New York, Henderson so offended Parke Godwin that Godwin left the paper while Nordhoff threatened to do so, in the belief that Henderson's questionable financial transactions were compromising the newspaper's ability to fight corruption. By 1870, Henderson began to interfere with Nordhoff's editorial work. The two men were on a collision course.

In "What Is Best?" the little story about an amoral journalist that he had published in 1861, Nordhoff had held up the spectre of an editor who willingly molded his newspaper to fit the demands of the public. The protagonist "had one vast advantage over other men, ... that he did not believe in anything but his career." Nordhoff was an ambitious man and uneasy with that ambition, but he held to his beliefs even as they endangered the hitherto meteoric trajectory of his own career. His journalist-gone-astray had explained, in his parable, just how the world of journalism worked. "One man sells cotton, and another sells newspapers, and it is the business of each to be successful," the editor insists, "... to gain the best profit he can from his investment." Newspapers, in this view, did not lead public opinion, pretend though they might. "Conscience, do you say?" Nordhoff's editor replies to the remonstrance of his old professor. "But ... conscience has nothing to do with it. ... Of course we all want to do what is right. But a newspaper is not a moral agent; it is a commercial speculation, where the only duty is success." Ten years after he had written this passage, Nordhoff found himself confronted by a publisher who seemed to hold it as his guiding principle.

City Hall, in New York and other cities, patronized many newspapers, purchasing advertising and placing job-printing orders with their presses although these contracts constituted a conflict of interest in the eyes of some contemporary critics. James Parton considered these arrangements in an 1874 article on "Falsehood in the Daily Press." Noting the increasing influence of the "counting-room" over the editorial content of newspapers, he stated that

the convict Tweed was well aware of this new fact in
newspapers, the supremacy of the counting-room…. The
number of newspapers upon the pay-roll of the Ring was
eighty-nine, of which twenty-seven so depended upon this
plunder for subsistence that when the Ring was broken they
gasped and died…. There never was a period during the
thirty years' reign of thieves in New York when the press could
not have brought them to naught, if its counting-rooms had
been disinterested or its editors in command.[51]

The *Evening Post* was not immune from the "supremacy of the counting-
room," as one of Nordhoff's employees recalled, stating many years later that
the *Post*'s advertising manager, William Boggs,

was the most familiar representative of the publication in
the editorial rooms, and manifested a special interest in the
suppression of any paragraph, or allusion, that might offend
the dispensers of political advertising, which in those days was
an important source of revenue.[52]

Untroubled by such considerations, or at least undissuaded by them,
Nordhoff had been engaging in editorial attacks upon the city government
and its collusion with Albany politicos. He particularly criticized the various
city charters that allowed officials virtually a free hand in dispensing city
business. One of his chief complaints about the municipal government was
that it effectively concealed responsibility. Anyone who tried to find the source
of corruption would find it a "hopeless" effort, for the "system of checks and
counter-checks" made it easy to conceal responsibility. Nor did he lay the
blame solely at the feet of Tammany Democrats. The city was governed, "not
by a party, but by a conspiracy of men of both parties," he wrote. "We are all
at the mercy of political caucuses and secret cabals." In effect, he argued that
well-to-do Republicans colluded with Tammany Democrats, allowing graft to
go unchecked while vital public services were neglected. The beginnings of
a reformism based on populist principles had surfaced in Nordhoff's work,

---

51. James Parton, "Falsehood in the Daily Press," *Harper's Monthly* 49 (July 1874): 274.
   On the press and Tweed, see also Frank Luther Mott, *American Journalism* (NY:
   Macmillan, 1941), 382–4. Mott's survey, though occasionally dated, remains one
   of the more thoughtful and useful surveys of journalism history.
52. John Ranken Towse, *Evening Post 100th Anniversary* (New York: 1901).

a political attitude that ill accorded with the civil service reformism of most affluent Republican reformers of the day.[53]

Not himself a city resident, Nordhoff was nevertheless outraged at the waste of taxpayers' money in graft and kickbacks, and he gave prominent play to any proof of this waste that came to light. One report by the Citizens' Association—a group with which he had battled fiercely over popular government—included, he editorialized, "the singular fact" that in eight months, "five-hundred and thirty-nine dollars have been spent for feather dusters for the city offices." This, he added sarcastically, raised a question or two. And why was the city charged $48 for printer's ink that might be bought for one-third as much at any stationer's in town?[54] When a new city charter was forwarded in 1870 with the backing of the Citizens' Association, Nordhoff opposed it unequivocally, pointing out various loopholes in its articles concerning multiple office-holding questionable tax exemptions and blurred responsibilities.[55]

In 1870, he had remarked that the *Evening Post*'s continued exposures of malfeasance had incurred "the enmity of those who are concerned in the wrong," attacking it and complaining to the publisher.[56] By early 1871, Nordhoff's voice seemed to be muted on the subject, and it seems likely that the powerful people whom he had accused of collusion with corruption had exerted some pressure on the publishers. Bryant's friend Peter Cooper presented a report by the ubiquitous Citizens' Association purporting to demonstrate the benefits resulting from the changes instituted the previous year with the "Tweed charter." "Now, it does not belong to us to defend the new charter," one editorial on the positive Citizens' Association report began. "We opposed its passage." Grudging in its support, the column suggests nothing so much as a man forced to write what he did not believe, trying under duress to say as little as possible. If the charter had "produced any good result," it went on, it was "only honest" to let others defend it. In carefully qualified and tentative language, the editorial continued:

> It is not claimed by the Citizens' Association that all corruption has been extirpated from the city government…. But they assert--and nobody has so far appeared to contradict them— that in nine of the most important departments of the city's government honesty, economy and efficiency now prevail.[57]

---

53.   [CN,] "Can This City Govern Itself?" *Evening Post*, 5/8/67.
54.   [CN,] "$539 for Feather Dusters," *Evening Post*, 9/4/67.
55.   [CN,] "The Tweed Charter," *Evening Post*, 3/31/70.
56.   [CN,] "The Cuban Investigation," *Evening Post*, July 11, 1870.
57.   [CN,] "New York Under the New Charter," *Evening Post*, 3/18/71.

Certain stylistic tics identify the writing as Nordhoff's, but in substance, it seems a reluctant performance, hedged and undercut in every possible way.

It seems likely that such forced recantations were indicative of an increasingly uncomfortable situation for Nordhoff at the *Evening Post,* and perhaps it was the strain of working in such conditions that induced him to plan a long vacation away from the paper that spring. A few weeks after the editorial praising the charter, he notified friends that he would be heading to California at the end of April, taking Lida and their two oldest children, Walter and Amy.[58] Having made the decision to leave for two months—with what resolutions for the future it is impossible to know—Nordhoff reverted in his predeparture editorials to his more heartfelt opinion of the city government. "It is not difficult to make a tale of abuses in the present city administration," he wrote in early April. He elaborated in no uncertain terms.

> It is a fact that the tax collectors build fine houses while the taxpayers are fleeced; it is a fact that men who hold offices under the city procure their own election to the legislature; it is true that as the taxes increase we get less for our money; that the Ring first robs in the city and then legalizes or hides the robbery at Albany; that the jobbery in the city is supplemented by new and greater jobbing in the legislature; and that no party will give us reform.

Once again, he blamed the affluent: people of the sort who belonged to the Citizen's Association, people of the sort who were Bryant's closest friends. "New York is badly governed, largely because the men of wealth, and the employers of labor, do not care how it is governed," he charged.

> It is the more or less conscious conclusion of the "comfortable" people that they would rather surrender to the Ring a certain proportion annually of their gains than take the trouble which is necessary to secure good government, which makes to a large degree the strength and safety of the Ring.

He reiterated his democratic refrain. Why would they not listen? What impelled the wealthy to their irresponsible course? Aside from the lack of energy or devotion to civic responsibility that the well-to-do betrayed in their neglect, there was also their "dread of the people—a belief ... in the rich houses, that the poor are corrupt and ill-designing." Because of this antidemocratic

---

58.   CN to Edward Atkinson, 4/5/71, Atkinson Papers, Mass. Hist. Soc.

animus, all kinds of stratagems had been resorted to. "New York has been ruled in Albany; it has been ruled by commissions...," Nordhoff pointed out, "but it has never been governed by its people under a simple charter which would enable the people to make their local government as good or as bad as they chose." But every such antidemocratic scheme had only "increased the jobbery and corruption."

To leave no doubt about the subject of his attack, Nordhoff mentioned the collusion of those who insisted on ignoring the evil. "One of the strongest illustrations of the present condition of New York is seen in this," he wrote: that despite "monstrous and acknowledged abuses," a meeting aimed at discussing and correcting such wrongs "should find opposed to it a large number of the most wealthy, public-spirited and respectable citizens."[59] It was a pointed reference to the Citizens' Association and their ilk—in a total reversal of the unwilling endorsement he had provided Cooper's approval of the Tweed government but a few weeks before. And with this parting shot, Nordhoff left for the West Coast.

While gone on his nine-week tour, he sent back frequent lengthy articles on his observations. He was deeply impressed. It was a journey that every American ought to make, he declared, now that the transcontinental railroad had been completed. To Hayes, he exclaimed wonderingly, "It gives one new ideas ab[ou]t his country. Uncle Sam has a big farm, & I never saw the best of it till I made this journey." He rhapsodized on all they had seen and done, the beauties and unspoiled richness of California, "& more pleasures than I imagined could be crowded into 9 weeks."[60]

The return from paradise to New York was a rude shock, and the contrast may have stiffened a growing resolve in Nordhoff's mind. Within two weeks, as he neared his fortieth birthday, he had given notice at the *Evening Post*, and he wrote to Atkinson he would leave before the end of the summer. "The reasons why I'll tell you when I see you," he added darkly. "...I may tell you, generally, that Tweed & the N.Y. Ring are too powerful here" at the *Evening Post*. "I am glad of the change," he continued, "have had a disagreeable fight here for a year past. It does not embarrass me, & I am just beginning to think what I shall do next." He asked Atkinson to keep the news to himself.[61]

Over the next few weeks—his remaining ones as editor—Nordhoff renewed his attacks on the city government with redoubled fury, borne, perhaps,

---

59. [CN,] "City Reform," *Evening Post*, 4/7/71.
60. CN to Gordon L. Ford, 6/3/71, Ford Papers, NYPL; CN to Rutherford B. Hayes, 6/8/71, Hayes Library, Fremont, OH; CN to Gordon L. Ford, 6/26/71, Ford Papers, NYPL.
61. CN to Edward Atkinson, 7/10/71, Atkinson Papers, Mass. Hist. Soc.

out of bitterness at the result of his ten years' service at the *Evening Post*. If
Henderson and Bryant had been ordering him to soften his attacks, he was
now freed of all obligation to them. Furthermore, he had returned from his
cross-country trip with a fresh impression, after an absence of the dirtiness,
congestion, poverty, and meanness of New York City, and an accompanying
impatience with its denizens. After a bloody riot on July 12, between Irish
Catholics and Irish Protestants or "Orangemen," who were parading in honor
of Boyne Day, celebrating Cromwell's defeat of Catholic Ireland, Nordhoff,
in a series of particularly vituperative editorials, raged at the authorities for
ordering the Orangemen to cancel their celebration rather than enforcing the
peace, equating such action to antebellum rulings forbidding the gathering of
antislavery groups for what seemed to be similar reasons. It was but another
instance of governmental failure to treat citizens equally and ensure the rights
of all.

Meanwhile, he busied himself in planning for the future, and his letters
expressed a growing sense of liberation. The pressures of producing a daily
newspaper had prevented him from tackling many projects in the past. For all
his devotion to the ideal of a free press as an instrument of democracy, it could
be a maddening and frustrating duty. As he had once written to Atkinson, "[t]
he devil has a good deal of life in him; & I am glad I am poor, or I would be
tempted to go into the country & let him flourish." If he were able to concentrate
on the subjects that interested him most—cooperatives, for instance, or revenue
reform, "I would be a happy man; but I have to do a hundred things besides; &
have to be daily called a liar by Greeley, in the bargain—wh. is the hardest of
all."[62] Well, here was an end to all that.

His friends rallied around him as word spread of his resignation. Several
friends, he wrote Atkinson, to his surprise "understood my worries here"; he
didn't fear the future. While in Chicago, he had discussed working at the
Tribune with Horace White. He did not intend to lay down the standard, for,
he told Atkinson, "work is the only real justification we have for being alive"; if
he did return to California, as he contemplated, it would not be for "a flowery
bed of ease." Atkinson had suggested the editorship of a Boston newspaper—
among his friends, surely it could be arranged—but Nordhoff, for the moment,
declined. "I mean to be in no haste," he wrote. "...Providence--if we only use
our own judgments & save patience--decides many things for us," and he was
considering a variety of possibilities before him. "I sh[oul]d like of all things
a year's liberty." Reassuringly, he wrote to his friend, "Somewhere I shall fall
in—& work; I don't fear."[63] Governor Hayes, upon receiving the news, had

62.   CN to Edward Atkinson, 1/27/18[69]. Atkinson Papers, MHS.
63.   CN to Edward Atkinson, 7/13/71, Atkinson Papers, Mass. Hist. Soc.

reached the same conclusion. "I am sorry—very sorry that you leave the Post," he wrote to Nordhoff. "But you 'still live' and must *be* or *go* somewhere."[64]

There was, that July of 1871, no public announcement of the reasons for Nordhoff's resignation. A notice appeared in the *New York Times* that tersely stated the fact of his resignation and provided his new mailing address.[65] Rumors spread, however. Several years later, an item appeared in a Maine newspaper, "a grossly false statement" as the *Evening Post* huffed, maintaining that Bryant had "sternly rebuked" Nordhoff for an editorial against Tweed, which was "calculated to injure the business of the paper." Nordhoff, upon learning of the article, sat down and wrote a careful note to Bryant. "Dear Sir," he began. Their relationship had never been other than formal. "A friend has sent me a paragraph from the Portland *Press*, relating a story concerning you & myself, which is false," and he wanted Bryant to know that he had written to the editor of the *Press*, "telling him that he has been deceived into publishing what is untrue; & saying that I wrote the Tweed statue article with your consent; that you read it in proof & approved it; & that it was inserted with your consent." He would not "allow a false statement regarding you, or my relations with you to be circulated, or to go uncontradicted," he added.[66]

The *Evening Post* published Nordhoff's letter as a refutation of the Portland newspaper's charge. But the letter was confined to the specific item under question: the one article that Bryant had or had not wanted suppressed. It made no mention of Henderson or Boggs or of other cases. Nordhoff, a man of emphatic decision, usually denounced falsehood in the most sweeping of terms, expanding from the particular to the general, including hypothetical cases, past history, likely future events. He would not lie to the Portland editor about the history of the specific article, nor would he say a word about the larger issues implied in the case. Twenty-five years later, the *Evening Post*, memorializing Nordhoff, admitted that Nordhoff was "one of the first to attack mercilessly the Tweed ring, and it was a difference of opinion as to the line to be taken that brought his connection with the *Evening Post* to an end."[67]

---

64.   Hayes and Nordhoff exchanged amiable jokes in most of their letters, and the seriousness of Nordhoff's situation did not deter Hayes from concluding his letter by remarking that he had been in New York for a few hours, between trains, but had not looked Nordhoff up. "I thought of you, and didn't bore you. You owe me." Rutherford B. Hayes to CN, 7/27/71, Hayes Library, Fremont, Ohio.

65.   *New York Times*, 7/20/71.

66.   CN to William Cullen Bryant, 4/20/76, Bryant-Godwin Papers, NYPL; "A Falsehood Nailed to the Counter," *Evening Post*, 4/21/1876.

67.   "Charles Nordhoff: Some Reminiscences of the Man Who Edited the Evening Post Through the Period of the Civil War," *Evening Post*, 12/7/1901, 25.

And what of the *Evening Post* after Nordhoff's departure? Within two months of his resignation, Samuel J. Tilden, the reform-minded New York Democrat, wrote an unhappy letter to Parke Godwin. "With the inexperience of the present writers for the *Evening Post*," he observed, along with the "influences" borne on them "through the mere business agents, who can not be expected to look on public questions with the eye of statesmen"; and in the absence of Bryant "as a counterpoise, & in emergencies a control of the policy of the paper," the *Evening Post* was "drifting badly." Credible men of "high tone" had told Tilden that "confidence is becoming weak in the *morale*" of the paper; "-- articles find their way into the editorial columns which seem connected with patronage given to the job office." It would be "lamentable," Tilden concluded, if the "renown acquired by forty years of uprightness, honor and courageous sacrifice of interest should be surrendered by Mr. Boggs and Mr. Henderson." And even if the proprietors of the *Evening Post* did only care about profit, it was still bad policy to thus baldly discard all their ideals, for "if the paper should sink into such a concern as the *Commercial Advertiser*, its value as a property even would be much reduced."[68] Its value for Nordhoff had already sunk to zero.

After he left the *Evening Post*, Nordhoff immediately began writing for other newspapers, including a lengthy Letter to the Editor of the *New York Times* on the graft-ridden new courthouse—he had not relaxed his reformist zeal one whit—and a series of articles for the *Tribune* about another trip to California. He was at last free from the demands of a workaday job and the pressures of producing a daily newspaper. In a burst of creativity, he wrote four books in the succeeding three years. Nordhoff had left the *Evening Post* under duress, if with his head held high, and yet the leave-taking was to bring him the happiest years of his life.

---

68.   Samuel Tilden to Parke Godwin, 9/14/71, Bryant-Godwin Papers, NYPL.

CHAPTER 5

The Golden State

"The editor's life is a bundle of broken attempts, a perpetual beginning without finishing," wrote one observer of the press in 1867. "The energy and constructive ability which might, with time and leisurely study granted, write something worthy of living, is frittered away on little details."[1] The words might have been Nordhoff's own, for they echoed his long-standing complaint about the ceaseless demands of daily journalism. And now he was free. Several newspapers had offered him editorial positions after his resignation from the *Evening Post* in 1871, any one of which would have provided him with security, a steady income, and a ready pulpit from which to continue his "preaching." But rather than settling down once more into what had become for him a dreary and frustrating life, Nordhoff went his own way, travelling and writing books about the subjects that interested him most. The first of these, *California: For Health, Pleasure and Residence*, was an impressive beginning, regarded by contemporaries as enormously influential, destined to remain a best seller for decades to come, and spawning a sequel, *Northern California, Oregon, and the Sandwich Islands*. Characteristically, Nordhoff used *California* to editorialize away from the editor's desk, mingling sharp social criticism with simple boosterism. Over a century after its first publication in 1873, new editions of *California* continue to be published, a testament to the book's appeal. To Nordhoff, California represented new beginnings, for himself as well as for the country as a whole.

"I have, you will be glad to know, several openings," Nordhoff wrote to his friend, Gordon L. Ford, three weeks after having resigned from the *Evening Post*, "but am much inclined for a little waiting. They want me on the *Times*, but I think I shall commit the impudence of not going there."[2] As he weighed

---

1. Julius Wilcox, "Journalism as a Profession," *Galaxy* 4 (November 1867).

2. CN to Gordon L. Ford, August 14, 1871, Ford Papers, NYPL.

his options, Nordhoff's mind kept turning back to California, which had so impressed him that spring: the glorious climate, the openness of the society and the richness of the resources, the renewed sense of possibility he had felt there. Although he continued to publish articles on political affairs, he was planning a very different project for himself, beside which newspaper work seemed a poor alternative.[3]

By October of 1871, Nordhoff was planning to spend the winter in California. He had noted in one of his April *Evening Post* articles that the lack of useful information about California prevented many Americans from traveling to the state, a lack that he suggested the railroads might find it profitable to fill.[4] The idea recurred to him in September, and he approached C. P. Huntington of the Southern Pacific Railroad with a proposal. He would write a book to publicize the attractions of California if Huntington would finance the project. Huntington, hoping that such a book might sell more train tickets or even real estate from the SPRR's extensive California holdings, readily agreed. The Harpers would serve as publishers, their unparalleled marketing and distribution system at the ready.[5]

While the contracts were being drawn up, a declining New York daily was put up for sale, and several of Nordhoff's friends urged him to buy it. He resisted the idea; he was "very very *sore* abt. newspapers" and "dread[ed] the chances of a publisher" who might put him through the same ethical wringer as had Henderson at the *Post*. "I love my liberty," Nordhoff wrote to Atkinson. He didn't need "fame," he added; "I would like to be a sheep farmer in California."[6] And so the trip to California was settled. Nordhoff, Huntington, and the Harpers signed a contract in late November, Nordhoff promising to provide articles and books for the Harpers to publish, and Huntington for the Southern

3.   CN, "The Misgovernment of New York," *North American Review*, October 1871, 321–343, also published as a pamphlet (NY: American News Company, 1871). See also Nordhoff's letter to the editor of the *New York Times*, "A Visit to the New Court-House," July 26, 1871, published less than a week after Nordhoff left the *Evening Post*. He also alludes to freelance work for the New York *Tribune* in a letter to Whitelaw Reid, October 9, 1871, Reid Papers, LC.

4.   C[harles] N[ordhoff], "The Luxury of Travel: Pullman's Moving Palaces," New York *Evening Post*, 5/22/71.

5.   Nordhoff made a trip to Huntington, Virginia, in September 1871; and by early October, he wrote Atkinson of his California plans. See letters to Atkinson, September 17, 1871; October 9, 1871; to Gordon L. Ford, September 17, 1871. Ford Papers, NYPL; Atkinson Papers, MHS.

6.   CN to Edward Atkinson, November 14 [1871], and November 20, 1871. Atkinson Papers, MHS.

Pacific Railroad, agreeing to pay Nordhoff $8,000 with free railway passes for himself and his family.[7] Because of this contract, some writers later assumed that *California* was a simple piece of paid propaganda. In fact, the book was Nordhoff's idea. Huntington was secondary to the scheme, simply a means of financing Nordhoff's already determined-upon end. Much of the book was only a slight reworking of articles published in the *Evening Post* the previous April. But the railroad's money was useful, particularly to a man who, with nerves rubbed raw by ten years of editing a New York daily, desperately wanted time and independence for himself despite the need to support his wife and five children.

"I knew nothing" of California, Nordhoff wrote, "though I had read up about it." His *Evening Post* articles, drawn from his observations of the state, had "sent many persons there, to my knowledge, who had before hesitated from fear of hardship and a barbarous people and discomforts." He would be filling a real gap in public information. Most books on California before 1872 (only a few years after the completion of the transcontinental railroad) were published in San Francisco, by small publishing houses having little of the prestige or marketing apparatus of the Harpers, and it is doubtful that many of them attained a substantial audience in the East. The few descriptive volumes on California published in the East were singularly dry, most of them lacking illustrations or any apparent attractions for a mass audience.[8]

---

7.   Contract dated 11/22/1871. Harper Brothers Papers, Columbia University Library.

8.   The California collections at UCLA and the Huntington Library contain the following volumes published prior to 1871: Samuel Bowles, *Across the Continent* (Springfield: Samual Bowles Co., 1866); idem, *Our New West* (Hartford: Hartford Publishing Co., 1869); Charles Loring Brace, *The New West; Or, California in 1867-68* (NY: Putnam, 1869); J. Ross Browne, *Resources of the Pacific Slope* (NY: D. Appleton, 1869); California Immigrant Union, *All About California, and the inducements to settle there* (San Francisco: C.I.U., 1870); [A. J. Carr], *Illustrated Handbook of California* (London: S. Low, Son, & Marston, 1870); William L. Cole, *California: Its Scenery, Climate, Productions and Inhabitants* (NY: Irish-American Office, 1871); Titus Fey Cronise, *The Natural Wealth of California* (San Francisco: Bancroft, 1868); Bentham Fabian, *The Agricultural Lands of California* (San Francisco: H. H. Bancroft, 1869); John Shertzer Hittell, *The Resources of California* (San Francisco: Roman, 1866 (2nd edition); Samuel Kneeland, *The Wonders of the Yosemite Valley, and of California* (Boston: A. Moore, 1871); George W. Pine, *Beyond the West....* (Utica: T. J. Griffiths, 1870); Harvey Rice, *Letters from the Pacific Slope; or, First Impressions* (NY: D. Appleton, 1870); Oscar Tully Shuck, *The California Scrapbook* (San Francisco: H. H. Bancroft, 1869); and Marshall Pinckney Wilder, *California* (Boston: Wright & Potter, 1871). Of these publishers, only Appleton's, and perhaps Putnam's, can be compared

When it appeared in the autumn of 1872, *California, For Health, Pleasure, and Residence: A Book for Travellers and Settlers* became an immediate best seller. Before ten years had passed, it would go through five printings, and a second revised edition would be planned for 1882. The author's name was used as a marketing device by a developer who platted the town of "Nordhoff" in the Ojai Valley two years after *California* was first published.[9] It has been claimed that *California* sold three million copies—a probable exaggeration that itself attests to the book's reputation. As a piece of salesmanship, and a counter to the then-prevailing negative image of California, the book is a masterpiece.[10]

Nordhoff combined in *California* clear writing, skilled observation, and statistically convincing detail with an optimism and enthusiasm only slightly born of (and perhaps tainted by) Southern Pacific Railroad money, all presented with proselytizing zeal. Too many Americans went to Europe before they had seen the grandeur of America, and no such person could, in his judgment,

---

with the Harpers in terms of mass marketing. Most of these books are not bad, but compared with Nordhoff's, they are obscure.

9. "Nordhoff" is now the town of Ojai; its residents decided during World War I that Ojai sounded more patriotic than the original, suspiciously German, name. Nordhoff Peak continues to loom over the valley. See Baur, "Charles Nordhoff: Publicist Par Excellence," and Patricia L. Fry, *The Ojai Valley: An Illustrated History* (Ojai: Matilija Press, 1983).

10. Kevin Starr, in *Inventing the Dream: California Through the Progressive Era* (NY: Oxford, 1985), 26, states that *California* "single-handedly stimulated significant migration from the East and Europe." In *Americans and the California Dream* (NY: Oxford, 1973), Starr uses Nordhoff to exemplify his thesis: "The hope raised by promotional writers, such as Charles Nordhoff ... was the simple yet subtle hope for a better life animating America since its foundation." Morrow May gives the book "more credit for sending people to California than anything else ever written about the section" in *Los Angeles* (1933, 70). In the standard *Bibliography of the History of California* compiled by Robert Ernst Cowan (San Francisco: The Book Club of California, 1914), 162, Cowan states that Nordhoff's descriptions of California "were considered the best of their time and much esteemed." The publication figure of three million is from John Baur, "Charles Nordhoff: Publicist Par Excellence," *Ventura County Historical Society Quarterly* XIX #4 (Summer 1974), 6. The SPRR had a pamphlet version of *California* translated into French, German, and Spanish to attract European immigrants: *La California par Charles Nordhoff* (Londres: La Chemin de fer du Pacifique du Sud, 1883); *California als ziel der auswanderung* (London: W. G. Kingsbury, [1881]); *Guia de California, el estado del oro, por Carlos Nordhoff* (Londres: La Compania del ferro-carril del Pacifico del Sud, 1883).

claim to have "seen his own country, or that he even has an intelligent idea of its greatness."[11] Though it was left to Charles Lummis, a journalist one generation younger than Nordhoff, to coin the phrase "See America First," this was the basic conviction of Nordhoff's *California*. He also scorned the chauvinism of New Yorkers who believed themselves to be living "at the center of civilization," all his weariness with life in the city informing his description of its drawbacks. After six weeks in California, he asserted, one would conclude that New York was the real frontier, and California the most "complete ... civilization" in America.[12]

His argument found a receptive audience. In the words of one contemporary Californian, Nordhoff's book "did more ... than any similar work to spread the fame of the Southland throughout the East," and upon Nordhoff's death in 1901, the California obituary pages generally credited him with spurring the regional development boom of the 1870s and '80s. Western booster Lummis regarded *California* as Nordhoff's most important work for "introducing California to the American public as a livable country." "It is literally true," he added, "that Nordhoff was the first man to give an adequate idea of the superiority of California as a home," and the book was "the most effective that

---

[11]   CN, *California: For Health, Pleasure, and Residence* (Ten Speed Press reprint edition, 1973), 19. In addition to the numerous nineteenth-century editions of *California* (beginning with the Harper's edition of 1872) and this Ten Speed Press reprint, a new edition has recently been released under the title of *Nordhoff's West Coast: California, Oregon and Hawaii* (New York: Kegan Paul International, 1987), with an introduction by Kaori O'Connor. All citations below are to the Ten Speed Press reprint.

[12]   CN, *California*, 18. Nordhoff's reference to a "semi-barbarous foreign population" was, perhaps, an instance of playing to his audience; but two pages later, he is singing the praises of the Chicago stockyards, where the cattle, sheep, and hogs "are so well cared for that many a poor human being supposed to have an immortal and amenable soul, living in a New York tenement house, is neither so cleanly lodged nor so well protected against harm or cruelty." He probably did think the slum populations were "semi-barbarous," but a firm believer in the conditioning force of environment, he also seems to have held responsible those who continued to inflict miserable living conditions upon the poor. Though he might undercut his own reformism, Nordhoff's aspersions on the immigrants weren't absolutely inconsistent with his understanding of how cultures, rather than inherent inferiority or weakness of character, shaped behavior.

has ever yet been written in its actual results upon immigration to the Pacific Coast."[13]

As December 5, 1871, the day of the Nordhoffs' departure for the West Coast neared, Charles confessed to "a little cowardly pang at going"; for he was taking a leap into the unknown, more encumbered with responsibilities than he had been when he took a similar leap at the age of fourteen. Still, "I have done my duty," he declared to Atkinson, "& what is before me is pleasant, & only unpleasant because it is only a step." The world was fresh with possibility, and "I dream dreams of the future."[14] His pangs soon subsided, to be replaced with euphoria. Receiving a letter from Atkinson with question after question about his plans, Nordhoff gleefully enumerated the answers.

> 1st I shall ride 500 miles on horseback in Southern California.
> 2d I shall see the strangest parts of it.
> 3d I shall write down letters & magazine articles.
> 4t I hope to return in May.

Then his thoughts shifted from the practical to the philosophical.

> 6t. We do more good than we sometimes realize, but the Devil is *not* dead.
> 7th. Don't think severely of the human race.
> It has mean members; but on the whole it is pretty good, though abominably ignorant; & the more intimately you know poor people, the higher you will think of yr. fellow men. It is I think the *mean* rich who make us hopeless sometimes; but I know some very rich men who are as good as though they were not "worth a cent."
> 8th. Don't let us forget each other....

---

13. Charles Lummis, "In Western Letters," *Land of Sunshine* 15 [October 1901]: 237; and Harris Newmark, *Sixty Years in Southern California: 1853-1913* (Boston and New York: Houghton Mifflin, 1930), 624. Lummis, in citing the *Herald* as the first publisher of the California essays, was repeating an error made originally, it seems, by the Los Angeles *Times* in its eulogy of Nordhoff's work. Clearly, the editor of the *Times* assumed that Nordhoff was writing for his later employer, and many subsequent authors have followed suit. The original articles did not appear in the *Herald*, however, but in the *Evening Post*, the *Tribune*, and *Harper's Magazine*, as has been noted above. Nordhoff's preface to the book states as much.

14. CN to Edward Atkinson, 11/25/71, Atkinson Papers, MHS.

Atkinson's queries had continued. Which of his family—Lida and five children, ranging in age from two to thirteen years—were going to California with him? "9th. *All* go with me. We have never been separated, & don't want to be." And what did Lida think of all this? "10th. I am glad I married a brave woman." Would they ever meet again? "11th. And that I know a few good men & love them."[15]

In many ways, travel was Charles Nordhoff's escape from his own sense of duty. The seven-day transcontinental rail trip gave him a sense of being suspended beyond all responsibility. Once safely on board at Chicago, "you leave care behind in the depot."[16] The journey west, with the panorama of the plains and mountains unrolling outside the windows of the train, delighted Nordhoff. He and his family had made their car a cozy domestic nest, with Lida sewing and children playing on the carpeted floor or laughing at the antics of the prairie dogs that somersaulted as they passed.[17] It was all highly satisfying to one of Nordhoff's temperament: though restless and a wanderer by nature, he always longed for the comfort and security of a settled home and family life. His portrayal of California itself owed much to this juxtaposition of the domestic with the sublime. It made him happy to have his wife and children constantly near, seeing the country with him and learning about it. He would not leave them behind when he toured stockyards or surveyed the Chinese theater; the entire family went camping together, riding on horseback for miles, stopping whenever some natural wonder or human contrivance caught their eyes. They all grew tanned (in an age when pale skin was the fashion, their

---

15.   CN to Atkinson, 12/5/71. Atkinson Papers, MHS. The degree of Nordhoff's intimacy with Atkinson must remain a matter of speculation, but his expressions of affection are startling, and sometimes verge on the erotic. In this letter, Nordhoff concludes, "But can you not go to California with me? I believe I have for some years experienced an increasing affection for you-- wh. I suppose you will perceive; leads me to press you a little sometimes." See also CN to EA, 11/14[/71]: "Say not a word to any soul, if you love me," and 7/27/72: "I kind of ache to see you, old fellow...." This may simply indicate the sort of shift in conventional language that led one historian to interpret Eleanor Roosevelt's somewhat heated (to modern eyes) expressions of affection for a female companion as indicative of lesbianism, when in fact such language was conventional among women of their generation. Nevertheless, Nordhoff did spend most of his youth in the almost exclusively male preserve of the sailor's forecastle and seems to have retained an intense need for male companionship.

16.   CN, *California*, 23.

17.   CN, *California*, 25.

complexions "ruined for all city purposes").[18] Charles had rejoined his family after a six-week tour "to find my fragile lily of a baby, a rosy, boisterous strong slip of a girl"; and despite Atkinson's misgivings, he was confident that he was giving his children the best education possible. "Pray how were you educated?" he demanded of his friend. "I for my part went to sea at 14, & left off at 23," and he had "served my day & generation better than John College bred men I have known." He reminded his friend that "education comes from *Educe,* to draw forth," a fact that he thought most schools seemed to forget; "they merely cram in."[19]

On the way to California, the Nordhoffs disembarked several times to tour the passing scene. In Chicago, he gathered his wife, young sons and daughters, and headed for the stockyards. "I do not know of a more instructive or remarkable sight for tourists," he commented and praised the organization and humaneness of the operation. Nearby, the planned suburb of Riverside Park attracted his attention as an example of what organized, planned, cooperative action might accomplish.[20]

A side trip to Salt Lake City (through "the grandest, strangest, and rudest scenery—like a long opium dream") allowed Nordhoff to assess Mormonism and its leader, Brigham Young. Young, he wrote, resembled a "hearty, beef-eating English squire ...—until you come to look into his pale blue, keen eyes," which hinted at a capacity for "showing his teeth." He remarked upon the unembarrassed way in which one Mrs. Young referred to another Mrs. Young and regarded Young's walled-off houses as having "the air of an Eastern harem."[21] Too, Nordhoff was struck by the "odd frankness, if it was not mere heedlessness," which had led Young to mark the gates to his houses and factories with "a bee-hive, the symbol of industry, in the claws of an enormous and rapacious-looking eagle."[22]

The work required to reclaim and maintain this garden in the desert struck Nordhoff as wholly unnecessary, a product of Young's selfishness.[23] He perceived "an air of strain and hardship about every thing" in Salt Lake City: the houses were shabby, the youngsters pale and thin. "Moses led his people through the wilderness," Nordhoff concluded, but "he landed them in Canaan, flowing with milk and honey. Brigham was a very poor sort of Moses." Polygamy was the only reason the Mormons were not welcome in other states, he declared,

18. CN to Edward Atkinson, 4/18/1872. Atkinson Papers, MHS.
19. CN to Edward Atkinson, April 18, 1872. Atkinson Papers, MHS.
20. CN, *California,* 21–23.
21. CN, *California,* 39–40.
22. CN, *California,* 41.
23. CN, *California,* 41–2.

and it was "to polygamy, then, that the long journey and the lasting hardships, the too severe toil, the undersized children, have to be charged."[24] In general, a man tolerant (for his time) of religious diversity, Nordhoff could not abide polygamy, in part because it bore a distinctly class-based tinge, not unlike the slavery of the old South. Working men could not afford multiple wives and multiple homes for them. "It was for the luxury of the favored few," he declared unequivocally, "in order that they might gratify their bestial propensities, that this cruel migration was set on foot." And ultimately, it was all for naught. The coming of the railroad would end the Mormons' splendid isolation, and with it, Nordhoff predicted, the institution of polygamy as well.[25]

In opening the book with a polemic against Brigham Young, Nordhoff made it clear that this was to be no innocuous travel book. He had contracted to do certain things: promote tourism to California, describe the natural resources awaiting development there, and sing the praises of its healthful climate. All this he did, and did well. But he also used the book as a forum for a great deal of sharp social criticism. The book was indeed paid for by the railroad, but it was not entirely bought. The clearest evidence of this double nature can be found in the juxtaposition of acute social commentary—mostly aimed at far more popular institutions than polygamy—with a glowing portrait of the comforts of travel by rail and a breathless, even fawning account of the "five country merchants" who had built the Southern Pacific. Nordhoff had never been in favor of the huge land grants doled out to the railroads by the federal government, but in discussing the executives of the Southern Pacific, he avoided any mention of such touchy issues, preferring to dwell upon the remarkable feats of engineering that had carried the railroad over the High Sierras.[26]

Throughout the book, when discussing California's underdeveloped agricultural land, Nordhoff asserted that the coming of the railroad and consequent access to wider markets would result in higher productivity and profits; the small, poor farmer would grow rich. He blithely ignored the monopolistic aspects of the Southern Pacific's role in California commerce. Public awareness of the rapaciousness of the railroads, and the consequent agrarian discord and revolts, lay some years in the future; by the 1880s, Nordhoff would be a relentless enemy of the railroads.[27] But like many people early in the 1870s, Nordhoff wanted to believe that such corporations might be

---

24.   CN, *California*, 42–43.

25.   CN, *California*, 43.

26.   CN, *California*, 47–52.

27.   For Nordhoff's optimistic pronouncements upon the impact of the railroad, see, for example, *California*, 195–6, 207.

a force for good, providing stability and order, planning and technical expertise to an increasingly complex world. In ending California's isolation, surely the railroad had benefited America.

But Nordhoff's strongest sympathies were not with the corporation heads. He chose to end his chapter with a valedictory, not to Huntington, Hopkins, Crocker and Stanford, but to the eight railroad workers who had laid ten miles of track in one day, "eight giants" who "walked ten miles that day and lifted and handled one thousand tons of rail bars each."[28] For all the owners' canny management and shrewd business practices, Nordhoff seemed to say, do not forget: it was the labor of anonymous workingmen that really built the transcontinental railroad.

The sweep and grandeur of the final leg of the trip, down the Sierras and into Colfax, was the fitting climax to a trip that made Nordhoff wonder at the fate of so large and varied a nation. From the harsh winters of Maine to the gentle climate and chimneyless houses of Los Angeles, America encompassed striking contrasts, all transcended by the cultural unity of America: "One people, speaking the same language, reading the same books, holding a common religion, paying taxes to the same government, and proud of one common flag," he wrote, "pervades these various altitudes and climates, intervisits, intercommunicates, intermarries, and is … fused constantly more closely together as a nation." His more complex vision, of an America that had to tolerate and accommodate diversity, was swept away by the overpowering landscape. But California itself was not going to reinforce this image of a homogeneous culture.[29]

Enthralled as he was by nature, Nordhoff found California a wonderland. As he had often commented in his early books on leaping dolphins or dancing seabirds, so he missed little while journeying from one California settlement to another. Sometimes he travelled with his family and sometimes alone, cooking his dinner in Indian huts, sleeping at Spanish "ranchos" or "on the green grass, with my horse staked out, my feet near a fire, and my body wrapped in overcoat and blanket."[30] Regarding the land, he joined the careful scrutiny of a scientist with the lyricism of a romantic. Grasses, flowers, wild geese, he described them all, lovingly and vividly; but nature was also for use. "Three antelopes ran a race with the hand-car on which I made part of my journey to the San Joaquin River," he noted, "and kept up with us for nearly two miles." These glorious animals were so close to them, he added, "that if there had been a rifle at hand

---

28.   CN, *California*, 58.

29.   CN, *California*, 32.

30.   CN, *California*, 123–4.

we should have dined on antelope steak, which is very good meat."[31] Nordhoff could be as unsentimental as an engineer.

Surrounded by his family, able to think his own thoughts, he settled himself in Santa Barbara and comfortably wrote to the poor wretches stuck back in the Northeastern January. "I am writing this on an open piazza," he opened one letter to Atkinson, under bright skies with "flowers (17 different kinds)" abloom all about him, happily remote from the East and Easterners, whose world "seems to me an eternity away up somewhere too near the North Pole."[32] It took over a month for letters to reach them in Southern California, but this was an isolation in which he reveled. He did not look forward to their return east. "I dread the old life in advance," he confessed. "It seems like slavery to look forward to."[33]

California itself presented many marvels. Those for the amusement of tourists, though impressive, were the least important. In a book of twenty-six chapters, only two were devoted to pure sightseeing; Nordhoff's mind was drawn to less ephemeral purposes. But he enjoyed seeing exotic new places; he had a curious nature, and these things were instructive. In an age without film or television, sightseeing could be one's only chance to see a living sea lion or a five-hundred-year-old sequoia. "A seal in Barnum's Museum was a strange beast," he noted, but sea lions made "the strangest sight my eyes ever beheld," and "if Gustave Dore could see them, he would add another weird picture to his chamber of horrors."[34] Having left behind the darkening Eastern winter—a season that usually left him feeling depressed and harassed—he was delighted to ponder camellias and eight-foot-high geraniums.[35]

The greatest marvel was Yosemite. In the face of its beauties, Nordhoff was chastened, even awed. He had a conservationist's eye on the park and suggested an Olmsted-type plan of improvement largely to forestall a free-for-all of entrepreneurial depredations in the Valley. "[A]buses are creeping in already," he warned. A toll bridge had been built over the Merced River, the owner demanding fifty cents per crossing, and he learned that some renowned sugar pines had been cut down for timber instead of "jealously preserved."[36] The State should therefore purchase all the land in the valley. Aggressive governmental action was required, for Yosemite would either be improved according to a well-thought-out plan "or it will become a wreck, denuded of

---

[31]   CN, *California*, 190.

[32]   CN to Edward Atkinson, 1/21/1872, Atkinson Papers, Mass. Hist. Soc.

[33]   CN to Edward Atkinson, 2/22/1872.

[34]   CN, *California*, 62.

[35]   CN, *California*, 66.

[36]   CN, *California*, 78.

fine trees, cumbered with enterprising toll-takers, and made nauseous by the taint of selfish and sordid speculation."[37]

He perceived this short-sighted profit-mongering sensibility to be particularly egregious in the old gold-mining regions. Although Nordhoff believed limited mining, undertaken in a systematic way, could be viable, lucrative, and beneficial to California's long-term health, for the most part, he viewed the work of miners with disapproval. Not only had gold- and silver-mining fostered a feverish "boom" mentality, short-lived and vicious in effect, but the miners had despoiled the land to a shocking extent. The same mentality that would cut down Yosemite's trees for timber had been at work in the gold region as well, paying little regard to nature or even long-term utility in the mad scramble for easy money.

"If any one asserts that gold and silver have been an unmixed benefit to the people of the State, I should say he was mistaken," Nordhoff judged. Because of placer-mining, he wrote, "a large region of the country about Sonora has been denuded, and lies still a rocky desert." Hydraulic mining, "placer-mining on a gigantic scale," carried on not by the independent prospector but by large corporations, was resulting in a broader-scale rape of the California hills. Mining corporations would "wash away immense hills hundreds of feet high, confident that at the bottom, they will find their reward."[38] The old gold-mining region, littered with ghost towns, was a desolated wasteland that ill reflected its former beauties. "You can not realize how the country looked before our miners came to disturb it," Nordhoff wrote. "They washed away hills, they shoveled away broad, elevated plains; dozens of square miles of soil disappeared, and were driven off into lower valleys that they might exhume the gold."[39] The displaced soil was wreaking its own environmental havoc, "filling up the Yuba River," turning it from "a swift and clear mountain torrent," into "a turbid and not rapid stream," its bed raised fifty feet since the arrival of the miners in 1849. "It once contained trout," he noted, "but now I imagine a catfish would die in it."[40]

Nordhoff used his western travels to refine his sense of what constituted the good society. Worse than its effect upon the landscape, gold mining's most pernicious legacy was the gold-seeking mentality that seemed to sap people of their ambition. Sonora was a good example. The people, "kindly, generous, free, easily approachable," would idly pass their days sitting on their

---

37.   CN, *California*, 80.

38.   CN, *California*, 93.

39.   CN, *California*, 96.

40.   CN, *California*, 102.

doorsteps.[41] The easygoing atmosphere was seductive; the Sonorans did not keep the Sabbath, and on the Sunday that he visited the town, Nordhoff, "overcome by or saturated with the local atmosphere," nearly joined one of its citizens in a bar. The men constantly reminisced about the gold rush and "live[d] on with but little purpose, apparently, in their lives, except to sun themselves and to enjoy the climate," Nordhoff wrote. A sort of reverse natural selection operated: they had come to seek their fortune in the gold fields; the successful miners left with their gold, and the unsuccessful remained in Sonora. This failure of the work ethic that was the center of Nordhoff's ideology dismayed him.

There was a hint of envy beneath his disapproval. Nordhoff's ambitions, ideas of morality, and high expectations of himself precluded this form of contentment, and he knew it. The played-out miners lived simply, "contented, thinking of the happy old days; with enough to eat, ... and no cold winters to dread, nor prosperous people to make them unhappy."[42] Still, he maintained, gold "has been the curse of the town, and remains its curse still." The people were still obsessed with gold; it formed the focus of the community, if community it could be called. One merchant tore down his store in the center of town and searched for gold among the foundation stones. "It is strange to see," Nordhoff commented, "how even the presence, the known existence, of gold in the soil seems to paralyze men's energies," keeping them from all other pursuits.[43] Men would work at a mine for year after year, with a return that ultimately amounted to little more than the wages of a day laborer. "'Does every body in this town own a quartz-claim?' I asked a citizen, and he laughingly replied, 'Oh no, I don't, for instance,' adding, after a pause, 'that is to say, I do, but it is not worth any thing.'" The gold, Nordhoff declared, "is still a curse, a clog; if it were all gone, men, women, and boys would cease to think of it" and would earn their livings "by some industry useful to the general public."[44]

The past glory of Sonora might be renewed, however, if its agricultural wealth were cultivated as assiduously as the mines. "I do not doubt that the temptation held out by the mines has retarded the development of the agricultural wealth of the State," he concluded. For all his mistrust of corporations, he admired the enormous ranchos of Southern California and the foresightedness of a large landowner who would plant his acreage with orange trees. "It is not so long since the opinion was common that California was valuable only or chiefly

41. CN, *California*, 97.
42. CN, *California*, 97–98.
43. CN, *California*, 98–99.
44. CN, *California*, 98–99.

for its mines."[45] But with the expansion of markets accompanying the railroad system, that state of affairs was soon to be a thing of the past.

To "domesticate" the image of California, as Kevin Starr has phrased it, Nordhoff faced a multipronged task. He had to convince readers that a viable living, sufficient to maintain a middle-class lifestyle, might be obtained in California; that the disreputable days were over, and families would be welcome and comfortable; that violence was a minor problem. He tackled the first of these issues with alacrity; it gave him a chance to study a variety of farming enterprises, which seemed to be a source of fascination to him, and he flourished the facts and figures he gathered in persuasive, if numbing, detail.[46] With accurate information on the aberrant California growth cycle and a willingness to experiment, a farmer could easily prosper, and Nordhoff accordingly spent many pages of his book discussing the various crops that were found to flourish in the California sunshine. The possibilities were so wondrous that he feared Easterners would think he was exaggerating, and he was careful to avoid an air of omniscience in his writings. "I believe," "it was told to me," "I noticed," "the testimony of every farmer in the region is," "I was assured by the farmers," and "it seems to me"—all were phrases that couched virtually every pronouncement he made on the profitability of California agriculture.[47]

He tended to gloss over the problem of the water supply. Irrigation was amply supplying all the farms he had visited; compared to the profit-making potential, irrigating expenses seemed minor, and he was delighted to find a town in which a hundred farmers had cooperatively built their own irrigation canal, which they called "the People's Ditch." If all newcomers would so "join hands," the water problem could be managed.[48] "Eighty acres will make an industrious farmer rich in this climate," he wrote and blamed overly ambitious purchasers for their common failures. Small farms represented an ideal that went back to Jefferson, and beyond: independence, close ties to the land, moderation, and contentment with subsistence conditions. But when Nordhoff

---

[45.] CN, *California*, 104.

[46.] In trying to counteract the prevailing negative image of the state, Nordhoff indulged in his fondness for Dickensian names. "California has been ... regarded by Eastern people as the lady thought of the gallery of the Reverend Mr. Phydle D.D.'s church," he wrote: a respectable enough but inferior place. At the time that Nordhoff was finishing up *California*, the Beecher-Tilton scandal was causing a public uproar. Nordhoff knew Beecher, followed the trial with avid amusement, and considering his sharp dislike of anything that smacked of religious hypocrisy, the Reverend Mr. Phydle D. D. may have seemed a fine stand-in for Henry Ward Beecher.

[47.] CN, *California*, 144.

[48.] CN, *California*, 119, 140.

dreamed of establishing his own farm or ranch in California, he generally thought in terms of twenty thousand acres and more.[49]

California enjoyed a rich and varied ethnic mix. Nordhoff observed that "three races—the Indians, the old Spaniards, and we 'Americans'—live there harmoniously together."[50] (Notably, he did not mention Asians as part of the harmonious community.) He made a point of visiting the ranch of one of the "old Californians of wealth." The owner of the forty-thousand-acre ranch was one "Senor M.," who "looked at my curiosity with mild contempt. I offered him a rather good cigar," Nordhoff added—it was one of his customary propitiatory gestures to the unfriendly—"whereupon he became a little communicative."[51] The "contented man of great wealth" lived poorly, according to Nordhoff's standards, in a three-room adobe house.

He was more interested in "a range of open shanties, which … I had innocently taken for cattle sheds" where the Native Americans lived., and he looked to the inscrutable Senor M. for his pronouncement on these tenants.[52] "'They are poor creatures,' said Senor M., with a shrug of his sholders; 'poor creatures, but quiet; not good for much, but useful.'"[53] Shown a shed "which I had imagined to be the chicken-house," in response to a query as to the Indians' living quarters, Nordhoff saw "what we should call careless disorder and litter." He was relatively silent upon the living conditions of the Indians. They made good workers, he noted, and pleased the large farmers for whom they worked; but here, as with the Spanish, Nordhoff's inability to speak or understand their language was a barrier to understanding. In the early morning hours, he went out to watch the Indians, who seem to have ignored him; and he went to the trouble of visiting one of their dances, at which he noticed the little courtesies and customs they observed. "Altogether it was an extremely decorous and common-place affair," he noted, the anthropologist in him paying close attention. A young man would break a decorated egg over "the head of some girl he admired. Then I saw that it had been filled with very finely-cut small pieces of colored and gilt paper, which fell all over the girl's head, and shone like spangles."[54]

Nordhoff was disposed to grant the Spanish Catholic missionaries a great deal of credit. Civilization meant Christianity, and property holding, and hard

---

49. CN, *California*, 144–145, and passim. Nordhoff's ambitious thoughts of a large ranch in California may be found in his letters to Edward Atkinson of 1872.

50. CN, *California*, 123.

51. CN, *California*, 148–149.

52. CN, *California*, 150.

53. CN, *California*, 150.

54. CN, *California*, 158.

work, and these gifts the Dominicans had provided to the Indians.[55] But their training had been incomplete; they were now under a subjection that might have been avoided, if only the Spanish fathers had inculcated in them a "love of wealth and ownership." "No doubt they made happy communities," he allowed, but "the children of the missions never grew ... to the stature of men of our century."[56] This failure was not exclusive to the Indians, however; the "Americans" who had come to California before the gold rush were also doomed, and Nordhoff echoed his verdict on the Indians in describing them. "I do not doubt that it was a happy life they led—these old Californians," he wrote. "But it did not belong to the nineteenth century."[57]

The pluralism of Southern California both intrigued and puzzled Nordhoff. He approved of the education the Spanish children received, but he was disconcerted by the mixing—not melding—of cultures in the public schools. "In many cases it is necessary to carry on the school in Spanish," he wrote; the children spoke Spanish during recess while they would return to their classroom "to sing together, and with surprising readiness, 'My Country, 'tis of Thee,' or some other American song."[58] He did not precisely disapprove of these bilingual schools; but they were, he felt, a relic of the past, part of the transition to a fully "American" culture. Nevertheless, he continued to place quotation marks around the word "American." California could not support too many presumptions about what, precisely, that word meant.

Of all the advantages that Nordhoff perceived in California in 1872, one was paramount: it was not the South. Possessing a beneficent climate and rich agricultural land, as did the former Confederacy, California was not war-ravaged, not racked by violence and vigilantism, not suffering from a bitter legacy of a racist, class-bound, and inequitable social system. Or so it seemed.

But as full of promise and opportunities as this new Eden seemed to Nordhoff, he could yet perceive a serpent among the orange trees. Chinese immigration, which had been occurring for decades and which had supplied the sparsely populated state with much of its labor force, was at the center of growing controversy; for the completion of the Central Pacific railroad in 1869, which had been largely built with a workforce of over ten thousand imported Chinese laborers, and the passage of the Burlingame Treaty in 1868, which allowed unlimited Chinese immigration to the United States, had resulted in greater competition for jobs between the Asian immigrants and unskilled

---

55.   CN, *California*, 158.

56.   CN, *California*, 159.

57.   CN, *California*, 245.

58.   CN, *California*, 151.

whites. By the 1870s, approximately 25 percent of all wage workers in California were Chinese.

Predictably, the presence of the Chinese, whose culture seemed far more alien to European-Americans than that of the troublesome Irish and German immigrants who clogged the Eastern cities, aroused bitter hate campaigns. "Anti-coolie" clubs had sprung up among the white working class, demanding that the Chinese be expelled; boycotts of Chinese-made goods, facilitated by the use of a "white label" to denote acceptable products, had begun. The 1867 platforms of both the California Republican/Union Party and the Democratic included calls for immigration restriction. But State attempts at shutting the door to further immigration, contrary to federal law, were struck down, and the war of invective flared. One official, a regent of the University of California, declared that "I believe the Chinese have no souls to save, and if they have they are not worth saving." Henry George, whose concern for the welfare of the working class was unquestionable, accused Chinese labor of "accentuat[ing] the drive toward monopoly" and referred to the Chinese as (among other things) "utter heathens, treacherous, sensual, cowardly and cruel."[59] Amid such heated rhetoric, it was not surprising that violence broke out. Just months before Nordhoff's arrival, a vicious riot had erupted in Los Angeles between Anglo and Mexican Angelenos and the Chinese community, in which at least nineteen Chinese were murdered.[60]

Nordhoff was himself uneasy about the influx of immigrants from Asia. Liberal democracy demanded as its necessary complement, in his view, a strong religious or ethical belief in the mutual obligation of each to all, and this he equated with Christianity. He knew that Asians had their own sophisticated belief system, and he knew something of Confucianism, which was the Chinese state religion; but these did not, he believed, include the Golden Rule as a fundamental tenet or anything resembling it. Nordhoff placed great emphasis upon the formative effects of culture. And while people such as African-Americans had been raised in a familiar Christian culture and therefore, he thought, ought to be as well-equipped for the duties of citizenship as any white American, the Chinese were another question altogether. Had their society prepared them for participation in a liberal democracy? He was not sure.

---

[59]   Henry George, quoted in Alexander Saxton, *The Indispensable Enemy: Labor and the Anti-Chinese Movement in California* (Berkeley: University of California Press, 1971), 102.

[60]   See Saxton, passim. The quotation (by Frank Pixley) is in David Lavender's *California: Land of New Beginnings* (Lincoln: University of Nebraska Press, 1987): 302. Lavender summarizes the situation in the early 1870s on pages 301–303.

But as the racial hatred intensified in California, it seemed to him terribly reminiscent of old battles he had fought as a young man. The marginalization and subjugation of one race to another had, in the South, not only stunted the development of what ought to have been a richly productive region, but it had also dragged the entire nation into a bloody civil war, of untold cost in human lives, suffering, and bitterness. California, relatively untouched by the Civil War, seemed to have a chance to escape the poison that had so complicated life in the East; but now it looked as if it might be setting off on the same path toward bitterness. Others also perceived a parallel between the racial conflict then occurring in California and that of the South; the conclusion drawn by the anti-immigration forces was that in order to avoid such a fate as the South had suffered, the state should rid itself of this troublesome foreign race, of the "serfs and their masters" who replaced "intelligent [white] freemen."[61]

Nordhoff's first pronouncements upon the Chinese situation in California were the product of his flying trip through the state in early 1871 and were published first in the *Evening Post*.[62] Recounting the praise "John" received from employers as "not the image, the very presence of the best-trained and quickest-witted servant in the world"—helpful, orderly, clean, economical—Nordhoff added, "Of course, you say, everybody has Johns." But he continued, somewhat ambivalently:

> Well, no; people have prejudices and fears. You have two or three Johns in the house, and when you go out—if you are the lady of the house—you take the children along. There have been unpleasant occurrences.[63]

His anthropological propensities stirred, Nordhoff commented upon the Chinaman's quarters, diet (more varied and much preferable to that of white laborers), hygiene, and recreation. In many ways, he was favorably impressed. When he took his family to the Chinese theater, he noted that they were able to leave late at night with "not a rude or disrespectful word or gesture ... seen in the whole crowd" despite the fact that the theater was a gathering place for the lower classes. "I can't say that I would have ventured into a place of the same kind, or out of it, in New York, without anxiety."[64] This same decorous behavior reigned inside the theatre as well. As he and his family sat and watched in their alien surroundings, the audience remained orderly, and Nordhoff took pains

---

[61].   Saxton, 19 ff., 101.

[62].   CN, *California*, 84–85.

[63].   CN, *California*, 85.

[64].   CN, *California*, 85–86.

to draw parallels to theaters in the East, from the clowns to the vendor selling snacks.[65]

Although far from being a cultural relativist (for he believed in the superiority of America over most other cultures), Nordhoff did attempt to understand the Chinatown theatricals by the standards of the Chinese. He conceded that the orchestra kept time well enough, there was some "excellent tumbling," and the players "shrieked, and gesticulated, and sang, with …the careful and studied precision of men doing their best." But the heightened artifice of Chinese theater left him, used to more naturalistic western plays, dissatisfied. "There is something dry and overstrained in their attitudes, gestures, and tones," he wrote, trying to puzzle out the play's apparent appeal to its audience.

> It is as though they had been refining and refining for centuries, until at last they had got every natural tone and movement off their stage…. Not one of the players—not even the clown—was even for an instant betrayed into a movement or tone of voice proper and natural to him or any other human being; and after we had sat for an hour, listening and looking, we could not help but admire the atrocious perfection of their unnaturalness.[66]

The Nordhoffs' own decorum suffered accordingly despite Charles's apparent earnestness in trying to fathom an alien culture; the lead singer's "quaver or trill" caused them to burst into "uncontrollable laughter" in the theater.[67]

But a stroll through Chinatown on a Sunday amused Nordhoff much less. All the usual activities of the week were being carried on: buying and selling, accounting, cigar manufacturing, dining at restaurants, and gambling. What was worse, all this Sabbath breaking went on with the collusion of the white community. "'It is a great convenience,' said a gentleman to me, 'to have servants who don't want to go to church.' Perhaps," Nordhoff continued grimly, but this was for him the very heart of the "Chinese problem": it was not a "convenience" to harbor "a multitude of heathen" in the community, who led the whites to break Sabbath with them.[68] But Hamlet-like, Nordhoff immediately backed away from the implications of what he was saying. Making the Chinese a pariah

---

65. CN, *California*, 86.

66. CN, *California*, 87.

67. CN, *California*, 87.

68. CN, *California*, 89–90.

class was not the answer.[69] The Chinese had to be brought to conform with Christian culture "and not live among us disordering and disorganizing our own society."[70]

The parallel between the situation of Asian immigrants in San Francisco and that of Irish immigrants in New York was unmistakable. Chinatown was "a blot on the city," worse than New York's Five Points; and as in the Five Points, the vilest tenements were "the property of men who call themselves respectable, whose children attend church, and who are not ashamed to draw their living from this vice and wretchedness." He commented sadly that such a situation prevailed in New York, but that he had hoped for better things in so young a city as San Francisco and not to find "the same unconcern for the poor, the same carelessness of how your neighbor lives, the same heedless, cold, godless disregard of whatever passes outside of our own respectable doors and comfortably carpeted houses, which is the curse of an overgrown and old city like New York."

This was the great pity of it all: that the sins of the past seemed about to replay themselves in what ought to have been the land of the future. Americans ignored the poor, the marginalized, at their own peril. Yes, it would be injurious, as many in the anti-Chinese movement declared, for a "serf" class to be instituted in California. But no people ought to be made serfs, and no people ought to be expelled because of the exploitation that they suffered. "If free government is to continue among us, we can not afford to have a 'lower class,'" Nordhoff declared; "we can not afford, for our children's sakes, to suffer men, women, and children to live like beasts, for they will in time act like beasts—they will bite."[71]

History could not be reversed, but the future—the future still might be molded by the deeds, or misdeeds, of the present generation. "John is inevitable," Nordhoff wrote. "He has discovered America, and finds it a good

---

69. CN, *California*, 90.

70. CN, *California*, 91. Compare this statement with the 1869 reply of John Stuart Mill (whom Nordhoff admired a great deal) to Henry George's attack on the Chinese. Mill acknowledged that there might be economic difficulties associated with the influx of Chinese labor, but asserted that the answer lay not in exclusion, but in assimilation: "The institutions of the United States are the most potent means that have yet existed of spreading the most important elements of civilization down to the poorest and most ignorant of the laboring masses. If every Chinese child were compulsively brought under your school system, … and kept under it for a sufficient number of years, would not the Chinese population be in time raised to the level of the Americans?" Quoted in Saxton, 103.

71. CN, *California*, 91, 139.

country. We shall not keep him out." It was up to white Americans to determine the Chinese's role in their society. To expect people to live virtuously in the Chinatown slum, to expect them to bring their wives and children to such a place, was not reasonable. Himself a devout Protestant, Nordhoff was forthright in the role he saw for his religion in the America that he dreamed of. He closed his chapter on "John" with an urgent plea to those who professed the Christian faith. Liberalism required brotherly love, and the Gospel was not an exclusionary text, but a social document by which real Christians lived. "If we treat [the Chinese] as Christianity teaches that we ought to treat our fellow-men," Nordhoff exhorted his readers, "if we do unto him as we would that others should do to us, … he may become a useful part of us." But "if we choose to pass him by on the other side; to let him live among us as an alien from our manners, habits, customs," Nordhoff warned, "John may prove a more troublesome and dangerous creature than any we have yet taken on board our ship."[72]

Taking a piece of ostensible boosterism and turning it into a work of social criticism, as he did in *California*, was characteristic of Nordhoff's general outlook on reform, a combination of idealism and pragmatism. He would accept certain conditions and constraints as a given, working within those constraints toward the better world he envisioned, a world that might be reached by incremental steps rather than revolutionary change. This was the case with partisan politics as well.

To a large extent, Nordhoff was alienated from conventional politics, and he was happy enough to spend the first half of the election year of 1872 travelling about the West, for all practical purposes cut off from political action. He continued to watch his reformist friends from a distance, encouraging their efforts even as he doubted their efficacy. As the Liberal Republicans organized their schismatic convention for Cincinnati, he was content to remain on the sidelines. Any change from a Grant presidency would be a change for the better.[73] "I am a Republican," he wrote to Carl Schurz, who spearheaded the Liberal movement, "but I will not vote for Grant." Yet he was doubtful that the Cincinnati convention would have any real effect upon national politics.[74]

"When, in yr. last, you asked what shd be done with Greeley," he wrote to Atkinson on the third of May, "… surely none of us thought to make him President." But so it was; the delegates, split between too many candidates and too many factions, had settled on Greeley as the most popular and, they

---

[72]   CN, *California*, 91.

[73]   CN to Edward Atkinson, April 18, 1872. Atkinson Papers, MHS.

[74]   CN to Carl Schurz, April 17, 1872. Schurz Papers, LC.

hoped, electable man available.[75] But Greeley, an avid protectionist and former Whig, espoused many principles antithetical to the ostensible purposes of the Liberal reformers. Nordhoff's mind kept returning to the absurdity of it all. "My perverse imagination falters on this idea," he wrote. "Suppose some industrious mouser shd. extract from the *Tribune* of the last six years all that H.G. has said ... of Schurtz, of Gratz Brown, of Wells, of you, of me, & dozens of others. What a droll exhibit he would make; & what a lot of godless scamps they would show H.G. to be acting with."[76]

Nordhoff concluded that Greeley must have made a bargain with the Democrats in order to secure the nomination; he would still support the editor in preference to Grant. He sent a few political tips to Whitelaw Reid, Greeley's lieutenant at the *Tribune*, who had also been publishing some of Nordhoff's work.[77] But Atkinson and other reformers rebelled, and there was talk of finding yet another candidate to bear the liberal standard. Nordhoff deemed this a bad idea. "I believe Greeley can beat Grant," he wrote to Atkinson, "and I don't believe two men can. ...& I don't see, now, that there is any other choice."[78]

Atkinson finally responded to Nordhoff's letters with a curt note; evidently, Nordhoff's jibes had stung him more than he had intended. "I wonder if you have lost yr. temper with me," Nordhoff wrote back conciliatingly. "Don't do that; friends are not abundant in this world; & you & I are too old to quarrel, I hope." But Nordhoff insisted that it would be a mistake for the liberals to repudiate Greeley's nomination. His mood of hilarity came upon him again. He regarded politics as a serious business; his entire life demonstrated that. But the antics of reformers unwilling to listen to political reason brought out his sarcastic temper. "To bolt from a bolt is to play baby," he insisted, "and the *Nation*'s notion that the new party shd. contain *only* honest men would I believe have made it too small for success." Wasn't the main goal to replace Grant? "It would have been delightful to put the angel Gabriel in his place—but Gabriel will want better managers than you fellows."[79]

The presidential campaign of 1872 quickly took on an ugly tone, with Democratically backed Greeley at least tacitly condoning the party's race-baiting tactics. By mid-July, Nordhoff had concluded he could support Greeley

---

[75].   For a detailed account of the political maneuvering that led to Greeley's nomination, see Matthew T. Downey, "Horace Greeley and the Politicians," *Journal of American History* 3 (1967): 727–750.

[76].   CN to Edward Atkinson, May 3, 1872. Atkinson Papers, MHS.

[77].   CN to Whitelaw Reid, May 7, 1872. Reid Papers, LC.

[78].   CN to Edward Atkinson, May 26, 1872.

[79].   CN to Edward Atkinson, June 3, 1872. Atkinson Papers, MHS.

no more than Grant. Finishing up *California* and going over the galley proofs for Harpers late that summer, he seemed disinterested in the election and only hoped for "a thorough disorganization of parties next year."[80] On election day, he dutifully went to the polls, voted on state and local issues, and then "I cut the electoral part of my ticket," refusing to cast a vote for either presidential candidate.[81] Grant's landslide victory filled him with "disgust," and he thought of retreating once more to California, going so far as to "make a business proposition abt. sheep" to one acquaintance. Like many of his contemporaries, Nordhoff contemplated the fate of the Republic with despair. "I have been amusing myself by reading Gibbons's Decline & Fall of Rome," he told a friend, "& it is melancholy reading."[82]

One result of the fractured election of 1872 was a shift in the alliances of various newspaper editors and politicians. Some editors, disgusted with the public's disregard for their opinions, asserted that their newspapers were no longer partisan, but independent of politics. Murat Halstead and Horace Greeley (in the weeks between the election and his death) adopted this course. The alignment of Liberal Republicans and Democrats against Grant and Republican Stalwarts resulted in some very strange bedfellows within the journalistic community. In New York, Greeley's *Tribune* found the despised *Herald* firmly on its side; the *New York Times* and the *Evening Post* opposed such erstwhile allies as Horace White's Chicago *Tribune*. This was Nordhoff's world, like it or not, and the topsy-turvy election of 1872 only deepened his alienation from Republican newspapers like the *Times* and the *Evening Post*; and he could no longer dismiss the *Herald* out of hand.[83]

"Everything looked very beautiful on our return," Lida Nordhoff wrote to one of her friends in mid-July of 1872, "and we felt no desire to exchange Overlook for the beauties and climate of California."[84] Charles had not persuaded her that life on a California sheep ranch would be preferable to their cozy home

---

80.   CN to Edward Atkinson, July 15, July 30, 1872. Atkinson Papers, Mass. Hist. Soc.

81.   CN to Gordon L. Ford, November 8, [1872], Ford Papers, NYPL.

82.   CN to Edward Atkinson, November 12 and 27, 1872.

83.   See Hans L. Trefousse, *Carl Schurz* (Knoxville: University of Tennessee Press, 1982); Glyndon Van Deusen, *Horace Greeley* (Philadelphia: University of Pennsylvania Press, 1953); Sproat, *"The Best Men"*; Donald W. Curl, *Murat Halstead and the Cincinnati Commercial* (Boca Raton: University Presses of Florida, 1980); Michael F. McGerr, "The Meaning of Liberal Republicanism," *Civil War History* 28 (December 1982): 307–23; and Foner, *Reconstruction*, 510.

84.   Lida Nordhoff to Mrs. Gordon L. Ford, [July 13, 1872], Ford Papers, NYPL.

and long-standing social connections above the Hudson River.[85] Despite Lida's apparent lack of enthusiasm for the idea, Nordhoff still regarded the possibility of a move to California as his only hope of true independence, "a fulcrum for my lever." "I have not genius enough of the money-making kind," he reasoned, and almost every New York daily was "controlled by its publisher. I suppose you know what that means. I am still sore with the knowledge."[86] Newspaper journalism had proven a disappointment, hampered as it increasingly seemed to be by publishers' concern with profits and losses. Nor could he see himself as successful in a more literary career; that November, he had agreed to let Harper & Brothers destroy their remaining stock of *Cape Cod and All Along Shore*, a compilation of his magazine stories and his only published book of fiction. It had been a commercial failure, and this too was a disappointment. "My stories are, I think, good --," he had told Atkinson, "but one of them diluted into a novel would have brought me money, and perhaps reputation—all together came to neither."[87]

The publication of *California* forestalled the question of Nordhoff's career, for the book was an immediate success and prompted the Harper brothers to contract with Nordhoff for a follow-up volume on the rest of the Pacific coast and Hawaii. Whitelaw Reid also asked Nordhoff to serve as the *Tribune*'s Hawaiian correspondent, but Nordhoff declined. "I don't care for *news as news*," he informed the editor; for him, analysis and interpretation of events was far more interesting than simply recording the events themselves, however entertaining many people might find them to be. He meant to look into conditions in Hawaii in depth, and Reid agreed to publish his analyses in the *Tribune*.[88]

He wrote to a prominent California banker proposing an arrangement similar to that he had had with Huntington to finance the research. "I want it understood that I shall tell the truth, as I did in the present book," he told the banker, but that truth would be favorable to California and the west.[89] The

---

85. Lida Nordhoff to Mrs. Ford, [7/13/72], Ford Papers; and CN to Atkinson, 7/15/72, Atkinson Papers. Nordhoff seems to have involved himself with his children to a great extent, observing, in this instance that "My little Elsie [aged three] had a painful & tedious but not dangerous turn.... She bore what must have been real agony, with great courage, so that she is really a very respectable infant."

86. CN to Edward Atkinson, Atkinson Papers, Mass. Hist. Soc., 12/7/1872.

87. CN to Atkinson, 11/14/71; Contract releasing Harpers from further responsibility for *Cape Cod*, dated November 30, 1872, in *Contract Book* 2, 186, Harper Brothers Papers, Columbia University.

88. CN to Reid, 12/31/1872. Reid Papers, LC.

89. CN to William C. Ralston, 12/19/1872. Ralston Papers, Bancroft Library.

Californian agreed to provide $2,000 and contacted Huntington about the proposal as well, but whether Nordhoff was able to come up with the full $8,000 he sought is unclear.[90] He signed a contract with the Harpers on the second day of the new year, and once again, the entire family headed west, arriving in Honolulu in early February 1873.[91]

Grant "means empire," he had written one friend in 1872, and there was talk that the United States would annex Hawaii. It was this issue that prompted Nordhoff's eagerness to see the islands.[92] But *Northern California* was as negative a picture of the Pacific Rim as *California* had been positive, the latter meant to attract and the former to repel. Like the preceding volume, *Northern California, Oregon, and the Sandwich Islands* was as much a political tract as a guidebook; but Nordhoff did not neglect the "guidebook" aspects of the work, and he provided extensive practical information for travellers. Much of this information dovetailed with the principal agenda of his book: to demonstrate the unfitness of the islands for annexation to the United States. Privately, Nordhoff reveled in the tropical climate and wildlife of Hawaii. "We breakfasted on strawberries & guavas," he wrote to Whitelaw Reid in February, "...& I go about in white, & look just like an angel in a red neck tie, who don't care a cent whether it snows in New York or not."[93]

He began the book by recounting his version of Hawaiian history. "The Hawaiian people, when they first became known to the world, were several stages removed from mere savagery," he stated, with "a tolerably perfect system of government and of land tenure."[94] Under this benevolently feudal system, the chiefs owned the land and its products; and the people, obliged to work two days a week, lived by his sufferance and their own toil. Habits of deference had been inculcated, which outlasted the system itself. One "Hawaiian lady, a chiefess, but the wife of an American, and herself tenderly nurtured and a woman of education and refinement," was seen "boxing the ears of a tall native, whom she had caught furiously abusing his wife." When asked why the man bore such treatment, she answered that "He knows I am his chief" and would not even think of casting an angry look her way.[95]

[90.] Note from William C. Ralston to C.P. Huntington, [1872], Ralston Papers, Bancroft Library.

[91.] *Contract Book* II, 189–90 and 264, 1/2/1873. Harpers Brothers Papers, Columbia University; CN to Gordon L. Ford, 1/24/1873, Ford Papers, NYPL.

[92.] CN to Carl Schurz, June 13, 1872. Schurz Papers, LC.

[93.] CN to Whitelaw Reid, February 17, 1873. Reid Papers, LC.

[94.] CN, *Northern California, Oregon, and the Sandwich Islands* (Berkeley: Ten Speed Press, 1974, reprint of the 1874 edition), 78–9.

[95.] CN, *Northern California*, 80.

Nordhoff viewed these bygone days, with the common people under the care of benevolently paternalistic chiefs, as a golden age. What made the system work, in the old days, was the impossibility of exploitation in a precapitalist world. Paternalism and mutuality were the rules by which all people—rulers and ruled—lived. The chiefs protected their people and took pride in keeping them happy and prosperous. "Food was abundant; commerce was unknown; the chief could not eat or waste more than his people could easily produce for him; and until disturbing causes came in with Captain Cook, no doubt feudalism wrought satisfactory results here."[96] Such a halcyon age was destroyed, however, when the chiefs' wants were no longer so circumscribed: when white intrusion brought with it the evils of a crass modern age. As commerce began, "as money came into use, the feudal system began to be oppressive," Nordhoff wrote, as the chiefs became avaricious for "money, or for what the ships brought," and made their people work harder and harder to produce goods for trade.[97] The only solution to this deteriorated state, and one rightfully arrived at in 1848, was for the king to divide up the chiefs' land into individual holdings, which "relieved the people of a sore oppression, and at a single blow destroyed feudalism."[98]

The whites who had come to Hawaii struck Nordhoff as more at peace with themselves than mainland society, and this he attributed to their isolation from the world at large. They received their mail and news only once a month; in a world without telephones and with no telegraph lines yet established to the islands, the Hawaiians were spared the ceaseless up-and-down turmoil of daily events that plagued their mainland cousins. "To a New Yorker, ... this will seem deplorable enough," he wrote of the Hawaiians' isolation, "but you have no idea how charming, how pleasant, how satisfactory it is ... to feel that for a month at least the world must get on without your interfering hand."[99] Watching the steamer depart, "a great burden falls from your soul, because for a month you have not the least responsibility for what may happen in any part of the planet," and "you say to yourself, 'Who cares?' Let what will happen, you are not responsible."[100]

In his travels about the Hawaiian Islands, Nordhoff thought a great deal about his ideal community and the various permutations Hawaiian society had undergone. A wistfulness pervaded his consideration of the Hawaiian culture, so recently transformed from a tribal, feudal society into an individualistic commercial one. The transformation was far from complete or monolithic,

96. CN, *Northern California*, 82.
97. CN, *Northern California*, 84.
98. CN, *Northern California*, 85.
99. CN, *Northern California*, 36.
100. CN, *Northern California*, 36.

and this heightened Nordhoff's sense of the gains and losses such a change entailed. That there were gains was not to be doubted: at least not initially. But his pride in the efforts of missionaries was tempered by a perception that the relentless activities of these New Englanders, the moral rigidity of "incorrigible Puritans," their "remorseless determination," was not altogether appropriate to the Hawaiian culture. Once one viewed the schools, the churches, the "well-managed charities," Nordhoff thought,

> it will be revealed to you that the reason why all the country looks so familiar to you is that it is really a very accurate reproduction of New England country scenery. ... The whole scene has no more breadth nor freedom about it than a petty New England village, but it is just as neat, trim, orderly, and silent also. ...You do not need to look deep to know that [the missionaries] were men of force...; men and women who had formed their own lives according to certain fixed and immutable rules, who knew no better country than New England, nor any better ways than New England ways, and to whom it never occurred to think that what was good and sufficient in Massachusetts was not equally good and fit in any part of the world.[101]

Still, however cramped and tunnel-visioned he might suspect the missionaries to have been, he at first insisted that on balance, what they had wrought was all to the good. They had come to "civilize a savage nation"; they gave the Hawaiians a written language, schoolbooks, translations of the Bible, and gathered them in schools and churches.[102] It was only to the Hawaiians' own benefit that they be exposed to and transformed by the superior values of liberal democracy and Christianity, and he characterized the precontact Hawaiians as "vile," amoral, "prone to murder and pillage," and "debauched."[103]

In such passages, Nordhoff was uncritically reflecting what he had heard from his earliest contacts in Hawaii: white planters and the descendants of New England missionaries. Following such moralistic outbursts, however, his propensity for anthropological inquiry took over; and he spent much time sympathetically discussing the Hawaiians' language, their dress, their food, their ways of earning a living, and the routine rituals of their lives. His respect for them grew tremendously. Not all of their ways compared unfavorably to

---

[101.] CN, *Northern California*, 23.

[102.] CN, *Northern California*, 25.

[103.] CN, *Northern California*, 26–27.

American culture; "the unconstructed dress, lei, bare feet and flowing hair of a Hawaiian woman "compares very favorably with a high-heeled, waspwaisted, absurdly-bonneted, fashionable white lady."[104]

The luau was a colorful native custom, its rituals entrancing the visiting journalist. The stewards of the luau which Nordhoff attended, all dressed in green shirts and crimson trousers with wreaths upon their heads, "presented a truly magnificent appearance," he wrote; and he found the simple pleasure Hawaiians exhibited in the spectacle, and the food, amusing. "They eat, and eat, and eat," he wrote. "They beat their stomachs with satisfaction; they talk and eat; they ride about awhile, and eat again; they laugh, sing, and eat." He described "the extremely dramatic meles" or chants "the tones of which have a singular fascination for my ears."[105] A *mele*, he explained, involved a man and a woman singing with "a shrill kind of drone" while gesturing and telling a tale, with passionate motions and "tragic intensity" of looks. The natives' attitude toward Nordhoff, watching their festivities, seems to have been one of benevolent amusement. He could understand the sense of the mele, and it did not seem altogether alien; he likened it to the Song of Solomon. "On one occasion I was told they sang a mele for me," he added, "and I judged, from the laughter some parts of it excited, that my feelings were saved by my ignorance of the language."[106]

Noting their fondness for making flower leis and wreaths for the head, he looked on with a peculiar double consciousness, wishing to understand them from within and yet unable to keep from standing apart, determinedly unswayed by the romance of a scene, noting both the beauty of leis and the "air of dissipation" they gave to the older people once the flowers had wilted.[107] He evaluated the life of the Hawaiian native with a degree of envy; the "primitive" held a strong attraction for the nineteenth-century Westerner, mixed though that attitude was with condescension. "Two days' labor every week will provide abundant food for a man and his family," he wrote; and the Hawaiian could read, play cards, ride horseback, sleep, and in general enjoy life. He implied that despite the benefits of literacy and infrastructure brought by the white missionaries, very little "civilization" might be enough for the Hawaiians. "It would hardly do to compare the Hawaiian people with those of New England," he concluded one chapter, alluding to the New Englander's reputation for education and high culture; but the Hawaiians compared favorably with most of the European peasantry. Ambitious, driven, and wearily anticipating his return

---

[104.] CN, *Northern California*, 31.
[105.] CN, *Northern California*, 87.
[106.] CN, *Northern California*, 87.
[107.] CN, *Northern California*, 88.

to the workaday world, Nordhoff wondered, wistfully, "if, after all, in the year 2873, our pushing and hard-pushed civilization of the nineteenth century will get as great praise as it gets from ourselves, its victims."[108]

Despite the gentleness of its people, the Hawaii portrayed in Nordhoff's book is not a hospitable or gentle place. It is characterized by narrow trails of jagged lava, more apt to maim a horse than not, of precipitous canyons, flukish climatic zones, simmering volcanoes, poor soil, inadequate markets, and an unalterably alien population. Annexation of such a land to the United States would be a disastrous mistake. "The islands are utterly worthless!" he exclaimed in one letter, "mere rocks," without arable land, "a wretched hole." To ensure that his findings received proper attention, he had copies of his *Harper's* articles sent to Secretary of State Fish and later wrote to Charles Sumner his opinion that "to annex would be a blunder for us, & a crime agst. them."[109]

The volcanic origins of the island had left it scattered with dead craters and cones, its fields nothing more than masses of jagged volcanic rock. "Very little soil is needed to give vegetation a chance in a rainy season," he admitted, "and the decomposed lava makes a rich earth. But ... nothing seems really to thrive."[110] This was the crux of the matter: agriculture was the measure of a land's value to Nordhoff, commerce and urban pursuits seeming only to fatten the "non-producers" of the world; and Hawaii showed few prospects for agricultural development. Sugar planters had made a modest profit, but the difficulties and costs of transportation and marketing left Nordhoff dubious as to the long-term viability of such pursuits. The United States already enjoyed every economic advantage conceivable from its implicitly colonial relationship with Hawaii, without the burden of including the islands within its polity. "If our flag flew over Honolulu we could hardly expect to have a more complete monopoly of Hawaiian commerce than we already enjoy," he observed with satisfaction.[111]

Annexation would encumber the United States with a costly outpost, an unassimilable population, and no outlet for the industrious emigrant. Plainly, much of Nordhoff's objection to annexation was based on racist assumptions: it was not in American interests to "take into our family" the islands' "mixed population of Chinese and other coolies."[112] Nordhoff was oblivious to the racism of his position, although he had argued vehemently against unthinking

---

108. CN, *Northern California*, 88.
109. CN to Hamilton Fish, 8/6/73. Fish Papers, volume 96, Library of Congress; CN to Charles Sumner, 11/15/73, Sumner Papers, Houghton Library.
110. CN, *Northern California*, 49.
111. CN, *Northern California*, 90.
112. CN, *Northern California*, 96.

xenophobia in the case of the California Chinese. But the Chinese were already in California: there was no escaping that fact, no reversing the clock. Hawaii was a different issue altogether. Here, the infiltration of America by undesirable elements might be avoided. And their undesirability was not due to the incompatibility of liberal democracy with a non-Christian belief system, for the Hawaiians, as he noted with care, were thoroughly Christianized.[113] Like most nineteenth-century anti-imperialists, his motives were a mélange of racism, respect for native autonomy, and a distrust of the extension of government necessitated by far-flung outposts. He would repeat many of the same arguments against Hawaiian annexation in 1893 with explosive effect.

After spending February, March, and half of April 1873 in Hawaii, Nordhoff left his wife and children in Honolulu while he travelled back to the mainland to work on the Northern California/Oregon section of his book.[114] An air of lassitude pervades his writing on this region, punctuated by occasional bursts of irritation. He had seen some of this territory before in his 1872 trip and found little of new interest. Being separated from his family probably contributed to his depression, for he had never been away from them for long before; he had even taken Lida with him on some of his excursions to Union military camps during the Civil War. Additionally, the question of his future career was once more upon him, with no clear answers in sight. He was prone to such periodic downturns of mood; during these black periods, life seemed dreary and effortful, and he found little to admire in the human race.

In the year since he had first visited California, Nordhoff had had time to think over the "Chinese problem." As an eminent journalist, Nordhoff travelled among the wealthy and powerful, and his opinions were heavily influenced by elites. In California, men who owned large farms or factories generally opposed the movement against Chinese immigration. Nordhoff's new observations reflected this perspective although he would add a greater element of social concern for the fate of the Chinese than many of their employers would demonstrate.

"The Chinese as Laborers and Producers," the fifth chapter of the book on Northern California, presented a more solid affirmation of the necessity and morality of equal rights for the immigrants, unweakened by the ambivalence and hedging that had given his earlier piece such a schizophrenic air. To refer to any people as "laborers and producers" was, of course, the highest accolade

---

113. CN, *Northern California*, 96–7.

114. CN to Whitelaw Reid, April 21, 1873. During this period, Nordhoff apparently solidified a friendship with Daniel C. Gilman, the educational reformer and founding president of the reorganized University of California, later president of Johns Hopkins University.

in Nordhoff's vocabulary. He now viewed the anti-Chinese movement as only a variation of the bigotry against African-Americans, which he had witnessed in the East. No longer did he refer to the Chinese immigrant as "John," which, perhaps, he had come to realize was condescending. Nordhoff leveled his most scathing condemnations instead at the white "Hoodlums" who were seeking to deprive the Chinese of their rights and the careless wealthy who were content to leave the Chinese community as a breeding ground for social ills.

The people agitating against the Chinese were not the working class, he insisted. They were "Hoodlums," and "the people who actually earn the bread they eat do not persecute the Chinese."[115] He would not believe that there was any real economic conflict between poor whites and the Chinese or that both egalitarianism and the welfare of working-class whites could not coexist without compromise.[116] He no longer seriously doubted that the Chinese might be assimilated to the benefit of the United States, but he saw the corrupting taint of bigotry spread from the "Hoodlums and demagogues" to the larger society so that "the proscribed race," be it Asian or African, was roughly treated in the courts "and gets scant and hard justice dealt out to it."[117] More than many of his contemporaries, who viewed poverty and other social ills as the products of individual immorality, Nordhoff saw social problems as stemming from the interrelationships of wealth and power, oppression, and greed that seemed to plague American cities. Noting the similarity of problems between Chinatown and the Five Points, he suggested that the names of slumlords be published, a tactic later to be effectively used by Progressive-era muckrakers.[118]

Despite the complaints that the Chinese laborer sent his pay home to China, he insisted that "he does not and can not send off the work he has done for it, the ditches he has dug, the levees he has made, the meals he has cooked, and the clothes he has washed and ironed," which continued to enrich America, "to make abundance where, but for his help, there would be scarcity."[119] He concluded once more with an exhortation against religious hypocrisy. No matter what effect the Chinese might have on California, he insisted, "it is shameful that he should be meanly maltreated and persecuted among a people who boast themselves Christian and claim to be civilized."[120]

White Indian relations also came under Nordhoff's scrutiny. He was appalled by the nonchalant murderousness the whites displayed. One

115. CN, *Northern California*, 142.
116. CN, *Northern California*, 143.
117. CN, *Northern California*, 142.
118. CN, *Northern California*, 142.
119. CN, *Northern California*, 143.
120. CN, *Northern California*, 148.

"thoroughly kind-hearted man" related "with the utmost unconcern and as a matter of course how they used to shoot down" Indians. These men seemed determined to ignore the fact that the Indians were fellow human beings. His conversation with one army general took a distressing turn. When the general, a "kindly, honest, good fellow," described, even as he patted a little boy on the head, cold-bloodedly killing one Native American, "I confess I was dumb with amazement," Nordhoff wrote. "The tragedy had not even the dignity of an event in this man's life. He shot Indians as he ate his dinner, plainly as a mere matter of course."[121]

The reservation system was an ostensibly more benign solution to the "Indian problem"; but Nordhoff, who had long opposed special treatment of the Indians, advocating that they simply be given their citizenship and left alone, declared that the one reservation he visited demonstrated the government's abdication of a responsibility it had taken upon itself. In Nordhoff's view, the government had adopted the role of "guardian" to Indian "wards" and then had abandoned the concomitant responsibilities. The reservations provided their residents with sufficient clothing, food, and shelter; but no effort was made to educate them or "to form in them those habits which might elevate at least their children."[122] Nordhoff was himself a guardian with a ward: his son Laurence had been adopted as a matter of social responsibility. But paternalism, for Nordhoff, was a means to an end, and that end was the eventual independence of one's children or one's ward. Viewed in this light, the government's actions fell far short. Compulsory schooling, which Nordhoff regarded as essential to any good society, was notably lacking; discipline was generally nonexistent. The Modoc Indians who fought against being removed knew that they would be "bored to desperation by such a life as this" and understandably "preferred death to remaining on the reservation."[123]

As for Northern California and Oregon in general, Nordhoff had little good to say. Perhaps it was the accumulated weight of witnessing the whites' attacks upon the Chinese and the mistreatment of Indians by both violence and neglect that colored Nordhoff's view of the Pacific Northwest; perhaps it was the three months' absence from his family. The note he most often struck was one of disappointment. Astoria, Oregon, was not the "romantic" spot he had imagined, but a "narrow, broken, irreclaimably rough strip of land." And when one came to the "forest primeval," he found it "dreary and monotonous in the extreme." Although he had often delighted in natural scenery, he found nothing to admire in the green forests of Oregon. "The interminable,

121. CN, *Northern California*, 185.
122. CN, *Northern California*, 164.
123. CN, *Northern California*, 165.

apparently impenetrable thicket of firs" only exercised "a gloomy, depressing influence," their beauties of color and form not making up for "their dreary continuity of shade." Astoria's sawmill was "sawing away for dear life," Nordhoff added, "because if it stopped the forest would doubtless push it into the river."[124]

Nor did the natural landscape alone meet with his disapproval; he made the names of places the targets of his scorn. "When, at Kahuma, you enter Washington Territory, your ears begin to be assailed by the most barbarous names imaginable," he wrote. The man who blithely accepted Hawaii's Kilauea and Molokai could not stomach the Washington names, singling out "Skookum-Chuck," "Newaukum," "Tumwater," "Toutle," "Snohomish," "Cowlitz," and "Nenolelops" as among the worst offendors. "They complain in Olympia that Washington Territory gets but little immigration," he observed, "but what wonder? What man, having the whole American continent to choose from, would willingly date his letters from the county of Snohomish, or bring up his children in the city of Nenolelops?"[125]

Nordhoff departed from San Francisco in late July, probably with a sense of relief, to meet his family in Honolulu. They spent the remainder of the summer in the islands, enjoying the mild climate, and the entire family headed home in late September after nearly eight months of travel. Nearing San Francisco, the steamer carrying the Nordhoffs was shipwrecked. All escaped unharmed; the incident disturbed Nordhoff's equanimity somewhat less than the names "Snohomish" and "Toutle." "My wife & the youngsters conducted themselves with the most perfect composure & courage, & every body praises them," Nordhoff wrote proudly to David Wells. "The little Elsie was a little trump." They departed San Francisco for the long train ride back east on the twenty-fifth of October 1873.[126]

"I have learned one thing thoroughly this winter," Nordhoff had written to Atkinson in 1872, "-- that there are other places in the world, besides New York." He had met Californians "who don't give a --- for N.Y., & though at first I shuddered at their profane thought, I have lately begun to laugh."[127] He had met "rough people, of different races & long ways," generous and public-spirited, far from the dangerous barbarians of mythical California. "And I have seen multitudes of men live at ease, with no anxious thoughts...," he went on, "with a certainty for their children's future, with open doors to the stranger; & with a free outdoor life wh. in some cases does not prevent them from reading The

---

124. CN, *Northern California*, 210–211.
125. CN, *Northern California*, 221–2.
126. CN to David Ames Wells, 9/20/73, Wells Papers, LC; see also CN to Gordon L. Ford, 9/20/73 and 10/15/73, in the Ford Papers, NYPL.
127. CN to Edward Atkinson, 4/18/1872. Atkinson Papers, MHS.

Nation, The Spectator, The Pall Mall, &c."[128] If environment was the key to human behavior, as Nordhoff believed, then Edenic California might renew the simple goodness that he had thought forever lost to America. The good society was possible, if only one could discover the conditions that would let brotherly love flourish, hard work receive its just reward, and material well-being provide a seedbed for spiritual growth.

He contemplated the direction and purpose of his life, three thousand miles removed from his old environs, and began to think that his editorial work had not really amounted to much of real good. "What I feel in your work & mine," he wrote to Atkinson, "is that we preach & preach to a vast careless audience, & I half suspect that half of my old pleasure in my work arose from a mere selfish gratification, about 'great public influence,' wh. is bosh." Some more immediate and direct influence upon people's lives might prove, in the end, a worthier effort than all his journalistic "preaching." "I have a dream," he wrote soberly,

> I am not sure but the best thing a man of moderate fortune in
> these days could do, for himself & for the world, would be to
> go out into such a new country as this, buy a large lot of land,
> & gather abt. him a certain number of the poor industrious
> unintelligent of the East; & train them & their children to the
> best thoughts he had in his own heart.

This would not be "a charitable institution," for "every man shd. buy his land, & earn his living," but these poor industrious men would be enabled to win their independence by the benevolent employment practices of the founder. "Your factories would answer," he continued, with a slight dig at Atkinson's business practices, "but such people have to work too many hours; they are not prosperous; they are not attached to the site; they are wanderers; you cannot get enough hold of their lives."[129]

Resembling a feudal domain, this version of Nordhoff's ideal community contained internal contradictions, for his insistence that the inhabitants of such a community would be landowning and independent undermined his sense that the leader, teacher, boss, or lord of such a village had to have "hold" of the occupants' lives. Perhaps he meant a transitory authority, enabling the poor to earn their independence, instructed in the habits of industry, thrift, and sobriety, which might enable them to do so. Nordhoff, contemplating the open and rich agricultural land of Southern California, believed it was possible,

---

128. CN to Edward Atkinson, 4/18/1872. Atkinson Papers, MHS.
129. CN to Edward Atkinson, 2/28/1872, Atkinson Papers, MHS.

even inevitable. "If life shd not offer anything useful in the East," he dreamily supposed, "I am capable of trying such a project within the next three years."[130]

When Atkinson obtained a patent for one of his contrivances, Nordhoff congratulated him with assurances that he was sure to become a millionaire. When he was rich, he should experiment with his factories, "& see if you can make cotton goods without deteriorating the human race." The rich had to take care of the poor for the good of the Republic, live near them, engage themselves in their lives. He thought of a paternalistic planned community in England. "It is not with the brains alone, but with the heart too," he reminded Atkinson, "that men build successful Saltaires."[131]

All this was in the realm of the speculative, and Atkinson asked Nordhoff what he planned to do after completing his book. "It was ungracious of you to ask me what I propose to do," he admonished Atkinson. (Then remembering that his touchy friends did not always appreciate his sense of humor, he interlined an apologetic, "This is a joke.") "I don't know & I don't care," he stated flatly. He had enjoyed his winter, "learned much," had done some good work, and he would have enough money upon his return East "to keep the little ones in bread & clothes." In the fresh and uncluttered air of Santa Barbara, Nordhoff was ready to foreswear journalism altogether and follow his heart. "And if I find that my career seems to have come, without fault of mine, to a natural close in the East," he wrote, he would return to California, where he could "build myself up an estate, ... which will leave my hands free to do the best things I can for mankind."[132]

It was not to be; Nordhoff could never free himself from the demands of a day-to-day job, doing work not of his own choosing. But by late 1873, resources dwindling, he knew what he wanted to do with his precious remaining liberty. If he could not create his own perfect community, perhaps he could discover models already in existence, lacking followers only because they were so little known, and he might do for these model communities what he had done for California. Upon his return home, he almost immediately tackled his next project, a labor of love and an enduring social document: *The Communistic Societies of the United States*.

[130.] CN to Edward Atkinson, 2/28/1872, Atkinson Papers, MHS.

[131.] CN to Edward Atkinson, 4/18/1872, Atkinson Papers, MHS.

[132.] CN to Edward Atkinson, 4/18/1872, Atkinson Papers, MHS.

CHAPTER 6

A Commune Is but a Larger Family

After almost ten months of travelling about California and Hawaii, Charles Nordhoff and his family arrived home in mid-November of 1873.[1] Having no commitments before him, and seeing the devastation wrought by the recent "panic" and ensuing depression, Nordhoff decided to write the book that he hoped might hold out to the working class the promise of a better life. Cooperation, or non-Marxian socialism, seemed to be flourishing in small little-known enclaves of America, lightening the lives of people who otherwise might have remained trapped in insecure, unprofitable, and deadening jobs. Unionization, Nordhoff believed, required a mistaken admission on the part of the laborer that he would forever be a wage laborer, and the need for some alternative mechanism to improve workers' lives was manifest.

In fact, as he set off on his tour of socialist communities, Nordhoff was not simply searching for more equitable economic arrangements between labor and capital, but for the ultimately good society, one in which physical well-being and beneficent social organization would combine to enable members to grow and flourish intellectually and spiritually as well as materially. But his thinking was largely anachronistic, based as it was in the idea of small insular communities, peopled by artisans, motivated by a common religious bond, while the problems that troubled him so deeply were the problems of the modern industrial city, an impersonal and secular place, a world where artisanal skill was largely redundant. Although he hoped that communitarianism would spread among the poor, he was modern enough in his own aspirations that he forever gave up the idea of founding a community of his own. And yet, his commitment to social causes needed some outlet, some means of action. There was nowhere

---

[1] See CN to Charles Sumner, 11/15/73, for the date of the Nordhoffs' return. Sumner Papers, Houghton Library.

for him to turn but to the world of daily journalism that he had so happily abandoned three years before.

Nordhoff's interest in social organization dated from his youth, when sailing ships provided microcosms that he studied keenly, while his journalistic forays to the Carolina Sea Islands, California, and Hawaii bore similarly sociological intent. He had long been intrigued by cooperative organizations of various kinds; some of his oldest friends had studied and written on communitarianism.[2]

Labor unrest showed signs of taking the place of slavery as the most violent and disruptive force in American life, destabilizing a society whose people, exhausted by the Civil War, craved stability as little else. Imbued with a sense of urgency deepened by the darkening depression, Nordhoff wasted little time in embarking upon his investigation of the "communistic societies." Adhering to an antebellum producerist ideology, Nordhoff wanted to believe that hard work still opened the doors of opportunity in America, and the growing evidence to the contrary troubled him. Only the hope of upward mobility kept the poor from demoralization, he believed. "Take away entirely the grounds of such a hope," he wrote, "and a great mass of our poorer people would gradually sink into stupidity, and a blind discontent which education would only increase, until they became a danger to the state."[3]

This dark possibility was only strengthened, he thought, by trade unions. The union member "is taught to regard himself … as a hireling for life," resigned to that state, with unions "only demanding better conditions of their masters." Nordhoff objected to Marxist ideology, refusing to see "necessary and eternal enmity between labor and capital" where he believed a true harmony of interests, rightly understood, reigned. "Communistic efforts" could provide the needed outlet for the dissatisfied worker, even after the imminent closing of the frontier.[4] If only trade unions directed their resources away from rabble-rousing and "futile efforts to shorten hours of labor" and toward publicity on the possibilities of cooperation, "they would have achieved some positive good." And so he stepped into the breach.[5]

---

[2]   Parke Godwin, *A Popular View of the Doctrines of Charles Fourier* (NY: J. S. Redfield, 1844). Lossing's article has been republished in book form: Don Gifford, ed., *An Early View of the Shakers: Benson John Lossing and the Harpers Article of July 1857* (Hanover: University Press of New England, 1989).

[3]   CN, *The Communistic Societies of the United States; From Personal Visit and Observation* (New York: Hillary House Ltd., 1960, reprint of the 1875 Harper & Brothers edition), 11. All subsequent citations will be to this edition.

[4]   CN, *Communistic Societies*, 13–14.

[5]   CN, *Communistic Societies*, 13–14, 17.

He began with a discussion of Amana, an Iowa community. Nordhoff adopted a dry and, at times, sardonic tone in his descriptions, with a delicate way of stating the more potentially salacious details that neither exploited them nor veiled their nature. Overall, it was with respect and tolerance that he described the Amana Inspirationists and other communitarians.[6]

An inescapable factor in nearly all the communities Nordhoff visited was their frequently unorthodox attitudes toward sex and marriage, and as a happily married man, he viewed these departures from convention with a certain fascination, if not disapproval. In Amana, marriage was allowed, but regarded as sinful. "The [female] sex, I believe, is not highly esteemed by these people," he observed, "who think it dangerous to the Christian's peace of mind" (implying that the Christian was a male), and they kept the sexes rigidly segregated. Nordhoff looked askance on these arrangements, and he happily noted their futility. For all their efforts, "love, courtship, and marriage go on at Amana as elsewhere in the world." He disapproved of such relentless repression, which seemed to him an unnecessary impoverishment of life. Even more disturbing were the Inspirationists' attitudes toward marriage and family life in general, for "matrimony is not regarded as a meritorious act." This was a foreign concept, indeed.[7]

He dwelled on the impact of ethnicity on the communal experiment, attributing much of the Inspirationists' contentedness to their low expectations, which he explained as typical of "German peasants." The degree of detachment with which Nordhoff dissected the German character was remarkable for he was proudly aware of having been born a Prussian, but it is an index of how thoroughly he considered himself as an American. If he described different races on occasion as if they were different species, it was no less true that he did the same with every ethnic or social group he encountered.

> I think I noticed at Amana, and elsewhere among the German communistic societies, a satisfaction in their lives, a pride in the equality which the communal system secures, and also in the conscious surrender of the individual will to the general good, which is not so clearly ... felt among other nationalities.

From the Germans' contentedness with Amana, a society that struck the restless Nordhoff as confining and oppressive, he surmised that the German's

---

6.   CN, *Communistic Societies*, 19–22.

7.   CN, *Communistic Societies*, 35–36. On the communitarians' various sexual arrangements, see Laurence Foster's *Religion and Sexuality* and Louis J. Kern's *An Ordered Love: Sex Roles and Sexuality in Victorian Utopias* (Chapel Hill: 1981).

"lower passions" could be easily subdued, and "certainly he is more easily contented to remain in one place"—clearly, he was not including himself as a typical German. An innkeeper was interested to learn that Nordhoff had recently been to Hawaii and questioned him closely about the islands. "He returned to the subject again and again," Nordhoff wrote, "and evidently looked upon me as a prodigiously interesting person"; and yet the man "sat serenely in his place, and was not moved by a single wandering thought."[8]

Nordhoff ended his consideration of Amana with praise for their instruction of children, which inculcated "piety, orderly habits, obedience, politeness, cleanliness, kindness to others, truthfulness, cheerfulness, etc."; but he tacitly condemned the rigidity of the separation of sexes as propounded to children. On balance, Amana provided a decent enough life for people of the German "peasantry," of few needs or aspirations. But it was clearly not the rich society—in material or intellectual terms—which he hoped to find.

Nordhoff next turned his attention to the Harmony society's Economy. Economy was magnificently sited on the Ohio River, a quiet town of rectilinear streets, handsome brick houses, and the "prevailing characteristics" of "neatness and a Sunday quiet." "Once it was a busy place, for it had cotton, silk, and woolen factories, a brewery, and other industries," he noted elegiacally, but these were gone, and people there were surprised "at sight of a strange face; for ... visitors are not nowadays frequent in Economy."[9]

Two factors had led to Economy's prosperity, Nordhoff believed: leadership and a written covenant. He had a legalistic turn of mind. The law was almost sacred, for it was the embodiment of the people's will: always subject to alteration if the public so desired, but not to be wantonly disregarded. The bad management of cooperative or communitarian societies was, he judged, the chief reason for their failures, and might be avoided by clearly spelled-out agreements. In the case of Economy, he included in his report a verbatim copy of the Rappites' "Articles of Association," taking up three closely printed pages as if it were intended to serve as a model for others.[10]

The rule of celibacy was followed by the entire village, and the population was diminishing accordingly. But they continued to live as families, with men, women, and children sharing their homes as they had before celibacy was instituted. To Nordhoff, this was evidence of an almost awe-inspiring degree of self-control.

---

8.   CN, *Communistic Societies*, 41–42.

9.   CN, *Communistic Societies*, 64–65.

10. CN, *Communistic Societies*, 81–84.

> "What kind of watch or safeguard… do you keep over the
> intercourse of the sexes," I asked in Economy, and received for
> reply, "None at all; it would be of no use. If you have to watch
> people, you had better give them up."

And they had forsaken tobacco at the same time that they had adopted
celibacy, "a deprivation," wrote Nordhoff, probably puffing on a cigar as he
penned the words, "which these Germans must have felt as severely as the
abandonment of conjugal joys."[11]

In Nordhoff's account, George Rapp had served not only as the "organizer"
of the workforce, "but he was also their preacher and teacher." This leadership
was essential to the community's success. "He appears to have avoided
ostentation and needless forms and ceremonies," Nordhoff recounted with
admiration. Rapp eschewed "any uniform dress or peculiar form of speech,"
avoiding "merely formal differences" from the world at large. There were
criticisms of Rapp as "tyrannical and self-seeking," and he had been accused of
gathering together ignorant people "in order to rule them," Nordhoff reported.
He disagreed, for the society members that he had met were far from ignorant.
"They are simple and pious people," he judged, "but not incapable of taking
care of their own interests."[12]

"Its large factories are closed," he noted, for Harmony's population had
diminished as the members, enabled to accrue capital, now employed laborers
of their own "at a distance from their own town." This then was the desired end
to the communal experiment: that the workers gain their independence and in
turn employ others, creating prosperity for all about them.[13] The implications
of a society dependent upon the labor of outsiders did not seem to bother
Nordhoff, and when he encountered similar arrangements elsewhere, he
viewed them as confirmation of the benevolence of cooperation.

Another group of dissenting Germans made up the Separatist community
at Zoar, Ohio. To maintain a community in a rampantly individualistic world
was no easy task, Nordhoff acknowledged; he was struck by a scene he witnessed
in a Zoar schoolhouse:

> On the blackboard, when I visited the school, a pupil had just
> completed an example in proportion, concerning the division
> of property among heirs; and I thought how remarkable it is
> that the community life ever lasts, … when even the examples

11. CN, *Communistic Societies*, 74.
12. CN, *Communistic Societies*, 92.
13. CN, *Communistic Societies*, 90–94.

by which children of a community are taught arithmetic refer
to division of property, and individual ownership, and every
piece of literature they read tends to inculcate the love of
"me" and "mine."

But he was unimpressed by the accomplishments of the Zoar residents,
more members of "the peasant class of Southern Germany." He found the
Separatists lacking in energy or ambition, and he saw this as a failure of the
leadership so crucial to a community's success.[14]

Their founder had not left any "marks to show that he strove for or desired a
higher life here" or that he valued beauty or comfort. The town was haphazardly
designed and ill maintained, with no sidewalks or other improvements, and the
town breathed "a general air of neglect and lack of order, a shabbiness, ... which
shocks one who has lately visited the Shakers and the Rappists." It was a place of
missed opportunities, and he damned the community with faint praise. "The
Zoarites have achieved comfort—according to the German peasant's notion—
and wealth," he acknowledged; they did not toil severely or fear the future.
"Much more they might have accomplished; but they have not been taught
the need of more." The condition of Zoar confirmed his already well-formed
notions of "the extreme importance and value ... of leaders with ideas at least
a step higher than those of their people."[15]

More often than not, Nordhoff found his communities' leadership wanting.
The leader of Aurora, an Oregon community, was one Dr. Keil, a Prussian, and
he did not escape Nordhoff's critical eye. He visited Aurora while working on
Northern California, Oregon, and the Sandwich Islands, and the irascibility reflected
in that book can also be discerned in his treatment of Aurora. The community
was a pecuniary success, without a doubt, but Nordhoff saw too many ways in
which it seemed yet another example of missed opportunities, of complacency
born of simple material prosperity to the detriment of intellectual pursuits.

The model for social organization of Keil and his followers was the strong
patriarchal family; their interests and property were all held "absolutely in
common" while the family structure was maintained in its conventional form.
The government itself was autocratic: Keil was the president and chose four
advisors to assist him. "In the management of affairs he consults these,"
explained Nordhoff drily, "whose opinions, I imagine, usually agree with his."[16]

Their efforts had yielded much. Their orchards were the most extensive
and profitable in the state, along with numerous artisanal shops and eighteen

14. CN, *Communistic Societies*, 104–107, 109.

15. CN, *Communistic Societies*, 110.

16. CN, *Communistic Societies*, 309–310.

thousand acres to call their own. They had accomplished all of this, noted
Nordhoff, "without any peculiar religious belief, any interference with the
marriage or family relation, without a peculiar dress, or any other habit to
mark them as Separatists," and they had done so "without long or exhausting
or enforced labor." Was this not the ideal model, replicable by any American
community? Their existence was based upon simple principles of Christian
fellowship, and material needs were abundantly provided for; they even owned
their individual plots of land. "The extraordinary feature of the Bethel and
Aurora communities is the looseness of the bond which keeps the people
together," Nordhoff observed. "They might break up at any time; but they have
remained in community for thirty years."[17]

And yet Aurora was curiously incomplete, Nordhoff commented, with
"little room for poetry or for the imagination." "What is not directly useful is
sternly left out," he explained. There were no carpets or cushioned furniture
although "provision safes, flour-bins, barrels" filled the hallways. Even in Dr.
Keil's own home, there were virtually no books, "no pictures--nothing to please
the taste." Nordhoff found himself being reproved for his attention to such
superfluities while there were social needs to be filled. When he "urged them to
lay out the village in a somewhat picturesque style, to which the ground would
readily lend itself," he wrote, "and explained that a cottage might be plain and
yet not ugly,"

> the reply invariably came: "We have all that is necessary
> now; by and by, if we are able and want them, we may have
> luxuries." "For the present," said one, "we have duties to do:
> we must support our widows, our orphans, our old people
> who can no longer produce. No man is allowed to want here
> amongst us; we all work for the helpless."

This stripped-down functionalism in the service of society seemed to
Nordhoff unnecessary, a quirk of the personalities involved. "It was a droll
illustration of their devotion to the useful," Nordhoff wrote, "to find in
the borders of the garden, where flowers had been planted, these flowers
alternating with lettuce, radishes, and other small vegetables."[18]

This single-mindedness was personified in their aging President, Dr. Keil.
As in other visits, Nordhoff's fluency in German was an asset for Keil spoke
no English. The leader "seemed excitable and somewhat suspicious," he wrote,
unread except for the Bible "and that only as it helped him to enforce his

---

17.   CN, *Communistic Societies*, 312, 330.
18.   CN, *Communistic Societies*, 318.

own philosophy." Keil's eyes were lit with "a somewhat fierce fire," Nordhoff noted, "and I thought I could perceive a fanatic, certainly a person of a very determined, imperious will, united to a narrow creed."[19]

A true liberal, Nordhoff disliked what he perceived as fanaticism; he believed cool reason to be the only avenue toward truth, secular or divine. But he listened to Keil with growing compassion. "He said it was desirable and needful so to arrange our lives as to bring them into harmony with natural laws and God's laws," reported Nordhoff; "... that we all needed his protection" and they then turned into a "little inclosure" with five adults' graves, set close together. "'Here,' [Keil] said,

> "lie my children—all I had, five; they all died after they were men and women, between the ages of eighteen and twenty-one. One after the other I laid them here. It was hard to bear; but now I can thank God for that too. He gave them, and I thanked him; he took them, and now I can thank him too." Then, after a minute's silence, he turned upon me with sombre eyes and said: "To bear all that comes upon us in silence, in quiet, without noise,... or useless repining—that is to be a man, and that we can do only with God's help."[20]

If Keil was not the image of Nordhoff's perfect leader, perhaps his failings were born of a hard life, one not calculated to produce the broad-mindedness that Nordhoff sought. How could one expect leaders from an initially resourceless group of people?

Nordhoff assessed the Auroral community with disappointment. "What they have secured is neighbors, sufficient food ..., and a distinct and certain provision for their old age, or for helplessness." He believed—perhaps optimistically—that such security might have been easily obtained by an individual farmer, "if he had labored as steadily and industriously, and lived as economically as the Aurora people have." The real answer to their content, he thought, was spiritual as well as material, born of fellowship and mutual care. This was a chief benefit of the communal life.

> It is probable ... that in the minds of most of them, the value of united action, the value to each of the example of the others, and the security against absolute poverty and helplessness in

---

19. CN, *Communistic Societies*, 318.
20. CN, *Communistic Societies*, 318–319.

the first years of hard struggle, as well as the comfort of social
ties, has counted for a great deal.

They were, if reports were to be believed (as Nordhoff apparently thought
they should), fortunate in many ways, freed even from evils that had little
connection to political economy. Aurora had no criminals, no jail, no lawsuits
or lawyers; no insane, or blind, or deaf people; and no poor. In the face of
such facts, his concern for intellectual culture seemed almost irrelevant. This
stable society apparently did not suffer from the lack of a library. Still, he could
not help noting, "its members ... lack even the most common and moderate
literary culture" beyond functional literacy; and "from the president down it
is absolutely without intellectual life." They seemed culturally impoverished,
with no social life worthy of the name, no organized gatherings of any kind.[21]

Keil's successor might have "intellectual culture enough to desire to lift
them up to a higher plane of living." There was a flaw in Keil's system, however,
for it "produces no such man." Real leadership, Nordhoff believed, would
develop future leaders, not a passive and complacent mass.[22] And democracy
would work only when individuals were challenged and given high aspirations.
In the world of Dr. Keil, Nordhoff saw attendance to material needs without
any attention to what he saw as the "higher" aspects of life: a fatal confusion
of means and ends.

He continued his quest. "Etienne Cabet had a pretty dream," he began in
his account of the Icarian Community. "This dream took hold of his mind, and
he spent sixteen years of his life in trying to turn it into real life." Nordhoff
had had dreams of his own, but he felt contempt for ill-considered schemes
that seemed to cause suffering, which led people astray. In Icaria, the failure
of leadership was of even greater import than the dead hand of Dr. Keil in
Aurora. He respected the efforts of Cabet's hapless followers, he wrote, but he
concluded that Cabet himself was "a vain dreamer."[23]

Cabet's "Utopia" (a term Nordhoff never used in describing the other
communities he visited, connoting as it did the impossible) began with "the
only element indispensable to success—a large number of followers." One of
Cabet's pamphlets, issued in Nauvoo and titled "If I had half a million dollars,"
set forth his dreams of the good he might do were he to be provided with
sufficient capital. The very idea elicited Nordhoff's scorn. "The fact that four
years after [Cabet] came to Nauvoo," he wrote, "he should have still spent his
time in such impracticable dreams shows, I think, that he was not a fit leader

21.   CN, *Communistic Societies*, 321–322.

22.   CN, *Communistic Societies*, 323.

23.   CN, *Communistic Societies*, 333.

for the enterprise." Attention to the incremental steps by which utopia might be gained was the missing key.[24]

Cabet's willingness to go into debt was another black mark on his record, and his idle dreams angered Nordhoff because it seemed to him, innocent people who couldn't be expected to know better had sacrificed much at his behest.

> Alas for the dreams of a dreamer! I turned over the leaves of his pamphlet while wandering through the muddy lanes of the present Icaria, on one chilly Sunday in March [1874], with a keen sense of pain at the contrast between the comfort and elegance he so glowingly described, and the dreary poverty of the life which a few determined men and women have there chosen to follow, for the sake of principles which they hold both true and valuable.

"The living is still of the plainest," he continued, after their eighteen years in Iowa. One member acknowledged the austerity of their life, "'but we are independent—no man's servants—and we are content.'" Nordhoff judged the Icarians to be poor managers and businessmen, but granted their "abundant courage and determination."[25]

Admonished by an acquaintance to "deal gently and cautiously with Icaria," Nordhoff drew his conclusion: "I am far from belittling the effort of the men of Icaria." But their sad plight, he insisted, "only shows how important, and indeed indispensable ..., it is to have an able leader, and to give to him almost unlimited power and absolute obedience." The tension in Nordhoff's thought between his democratic ideals and his low estimation of the capacity of an untutored populace was hard to deny in considering these little communities. That the Icarians had given Cabet power and obedience had, of course, been their downfall; but Nordhoff hoped that Americans would show greater wisdom in picking their leaders than had been shown by the followers of Cabet. His own idea that powerful leaders would always demonstrate wisdom and benevolence was, in fact, as utopian as any scheme by Etienne Cabet and far more dangerous.

"I find I am drifting a little further from home than I planned when I set out," Nordhoff wrote to a friend from Buffalo in mid-December. "...I have seen much that is curious & valuable & think even more than I did of my project."[26] He was preparing to visit the Shakers, prominent and successful

---

24. CN, *Communistic Societies*, 334–5.

25. CN, *Communistic Societies*, 335, 337.

26. CN to Gordon L. Ford, December 17, 1873, Ford Papers, NYPL.

communitarians whom he made a special effort to investigate. *Communistic Societies* is a lopsided work, with well over a quarter of its pages devoted to the Shakers, testament to his fascination with their societies. They left him in awe of their lack of care for the pleasures of the world, impressed by the material advantages of their organization and yet uneasy with a regimented social system that damned family life as contrary to divine law. Much of this chapter was composed simply of verbatim transcriptions of various Shaker documents, without editorial comment, as if the material contained therein were either self-explanatory, or defied explanation, or perhaps so compelling that he felt it should be preserved for further study. Nordhoff's treatment of the Shakers was generally respectful, but there is no doubt he found them an alien people.[27]

He arranged to meet the Shakers' chief public spokesman, Elder Frederick Evans, who resided at the Mount Lebanon village in New York. He recalled the visit vividly. "It was on a bleak and sleety December day that I made my first visit to a Shaker family," he began. An eerie calm pervaded the place.

> As I came by appointment, a brother...received me at the door, opening it silently at the precise moment when I had reached the vestibule, and, silently bowing, took my bag from my hand and motioned me to follow him. ...We entered another house, and, opening a door, my guide welcomed me to the "visitors' room." "This," said he, "is where you will stay. A brother will come in presently to speak with you." And with a bow my guide noiselessly slipped out, softly closed the door behind him, and I was alone.

He inspected his surroundings. The room was simple, neat, and clean; there was an unusual arrangement of the window sashes contrived to keep the room ventilated without drafts. His guide soon appeared, a former university student from Sweden. "His voice was soft and low," Nordhoff noted, "his motions noiseless, his conversation in a subdued tone, his smile ready; but his expression was that of one who guarded himself against the world, with which he was determined to have nothing to do."[28]

Nordhoff felt himself a stranger in this milieu, an intruder. His general impression of the village was of otherworldliness, an atmosphere so subdued and orderly ("an eternal Sabbath stillness") that it made him uneasy, even as he admired the Shakers' systematic and controlled organization. He soon met with Elder Frederick Evans, the Society's principal spokesman to the outside world,

---

27.   CN, *Communistic Societies*, 117.

28.   CN, *Communistic Societies*, 115, 152.

who wrote for him a letter to other Shaker societies. Evans explained Nordhoff's purpose, calling him "an influential Writer and Editor of high Standing in the Republic of Letters" and "an honest & honorable man," and asked the Shaker societies to treat him hospitably.[29]

The Shakers' religion, an adaptation of Christianity that stressed the dual male and female nature of the deity and which held "the lustful gratifications of the flesh as the source and foundation of human corruption," Nordhoff found he could explain best by recording their hymns. Folk songs had always been one of his chosen sources of social analysis, perhaps because of their democratic character and, as a journalistic device, for their illustrative quality. The Shaker songs were powerfully evocative of the ascetic and antisexual nature of the celibate community. After quoting one series of verses that pointed to celibacy as the "way of regeneration" ("Dead unto a carnal nature, / From that tyrant ever free"), Nordhoff noted a bit of context that seemed pertinent: Ann Lee, the founder of the Shakers, had been unhappily married and lost four infants before founding her religion.[30]

The communities were certainly ascetic, with customs designed to "mortify the body." Of all the societies he had visited, the Shakers seemed the most astringent. "One [woman]," he noted, "thought it would be an improvement to abolish the caps, and let the hair have its natural growth and appearance --but I am afraid she might be called a radical." The list of forbidden pleasures was a daunting one: Shakers were allowed no dogs, no meat, no children to play with, no tobacco, no romance, and no sex. Nordhoff (who seems to have enjoyed all of these things) was impressed with their rigor. "To a man or woman not thoroughly and earnestly in love with an ascetic life and deeply disgusted with the world, Shakerism would be unendurable," he wrote, "and I believe insincerity to be rare among them. It is not a comfortable place for hypocrites or pretenders."[31]

But to the inhabitants, who spent much of their energy in contriving ways to save labor, paring life down to a simplicity that was, in practical terms, easily ordered and maintained, the life was well-suited, if comparable to the fussy manners of "a parcel of old bachelors and old maids." Nordhoff hinted that he thought their strictures were out of proportion to their significance: he referred to the emphasis on "personal comfort, neatness, and order" as "minor morals." But the social system, for all its deprivations, allowed the Shakers a more comfortable, if regulated, life than many a factory operative outside the

29. CN, *Communistic Societies*, 152–3; Frederick Evans "To the Elders of the Shaker Societies," 12/22/73, miscellaneous manuscript collection, Library of Congress.
30. CN, *Communistic Societies*, 123, 125.
31. CN, *Communistic Societies*, 167, 204.

order. "Shakers do not toil severely," Nordhoff noted. They were unplagued by the ambitions of the worldly. Their labor-saving contrivances were ingenious, their "arrangements for working are of the best and most convenient." With their leisure time, they learned hymns, read the newspapers ("crimes and accidents being omitted as unprofitable"), read and wrote letters, and engaged in conversation.[32]

"As to books and literature in general," he stated, "they are not a reading people," and he noted that the Elder's library contained almost no books. Always, the lack of literature indicated to Nordhoff a certain shallowness of thought, however deeply held the Shakers' religious convictions might be. He asked the former college student about the scarcity of books and was told that the man felt any lingering desires for books to read indicated "something wrong about him, dragging him down from his higher spiritual state." This was an astonishing admission to the bookish Nordhoff, a total inversion of his own belief in the value of the written word.[33]

The Shakers' world-view was so different from his own that Nordhoff had trouble even framing questions that could be taken on their own terms, without having his words redefined by his subjects. They were, in a profound sense, at cross-purposes. He didn't want to believe that socialism in this small-scale form, even when it was a manifestation of an ascetic religion, required such a diminishing and regimentation that it necessitated the elimination of books, of art, of fine architecture. "Considering the homeliness of the buildings, which mostly have the appearance of mere factories or human hives," he wrote, "I asked Elder Frederick whether, if they were to build anew, they would not aim at some architectural effect, some beauty of design." The question elicited a strong reaction from Evans, for whom "beauty" had an entirely different meaning, akin to the socially minded functionalism Nordhoff had encountered in Aurora. Evans "replied with great positiveness, 'No, the beautiful, as you call it, is absurd and abnormal. It has no business with us. The divine man has no right to waste money upon what you would call beauty, in his house or his daily life, while there are people living in misery.'" Evans's standards for any future building were those of good ventilation, lighting, insulation, and "protection and comfort, because those things tend to health and long life," Nordhoff recounted. "But no beauty."[34]

32. CN, *Communistic Societies*, 142, 149, 211.

33. CN, *Communistic Societies*, 164–5.

34. CN, *Communistic Societies*, 164–5. Evans's ideas concerning the social responsibilities of utilitarian architecture were not unlike those developed in the early twentieth century by the German Bauhaus school, essentially socialist in intent, their designs intended to serve the working classes' need for cheap housing. The

Nordhoff approved of any religion that inculcated, as he said, "the practical virtues of honesty, industry, frugality, charity, and temperance." Of the Shaker proverbs, such as "Put your hands to work and your hearts to God," he noted that they "are not remarkable, except as showing that with [Ann Lee's] religious enthusiasm she united practical sense." Their social organization, of novitiates and church families, had proven "a complete and judicious system of administration." But it was emphatically not a democracy. Members of the Ministry, which decided upon the organization and allotment of labor and the allocation of resources, were appointed by elders who had themselves earlier been appointed by elders, in a self-perpetuating theocracy.[35]

The entire question of the relationship of men to women was central to the Shaker's social order, and in this the control of the Society was absolute, an insistence on "separate spheres" with a vengeance. In addition to their segregated workforce, "being celibate, they use proper precautions in the intercourse of the sexes," never allowing men and women to touch one another or shake hands, depriving all of the privacy of separate bedrooms. "The sexes even eat apart; they labor apart; they worship, standing and marching, apart; they visit each other only at stated intervals and according to a prescribed order," Nordhoff noted, "and in all things the sexes maintain a certain distance and reserve toward each other."[36]

This strict arrangement of the lives of men and women, meant to keep them apart, seemed emblematic of the lack of spontaneity and personal autonomy, which proved to be the price of the order and affluence of the Shakers' society. The visits of sisters to the brethren were "[l]ike all else in their lives," Nordhoff wrote, "... prearranged for them"; their business meetings were notable for "arousing thought." At one meeting, he heard some of the women complain of "the too great monotony of their own lives," a judgment in which he shared. If his ideal system was to provide more than a regimented, unfree, and self-limiting life, then the socialism of the Shakers held no keys to success.[37]

The greatest test of Nordhoff's tolerance came in his visits to the Perfectionists, who had, in their early days, been widely vilified for their

---

mid-twentieth-century rediscovery of the merits of Shaker architecture was largely the result of the ascendancy of a "functionalist" aesthetic. What Evans would have thought of the modern vogue for Shaker designs among the circle of art connoisseurs is impossible to determine, of course; although he might have welcomed a wider appreciation for the virtues of Shaker design, the use of such designs as emblems of taste and status probably would have troubled him greatly.

[35]. CN, *Communistic Societies*, 129, 130, 139.

[36]. CN, *Communistic Societies*, 166.

[37]. CN, *Communistic Societies*, 170, 203.

practice of "complex marriage," which was incorrectly equated by outsiders with free love. Such a prominent and materially successful community could not be ignored, and Nordhoff's report of their Oneida, New York, community was, if anything, drier and more laconic than the others.

Aside from their odd organization of sexual relationships, Nordhoff found their community system admirable. Their farm and factories were well-run and profitable, their administration "perfect and thorough," one of the few that was able to provide him with facts and figures at his request. There were committees to manage everything from heating and education to patent rights and haircutting, and though it seemed "cumbrous," the organization functioned efficiently and well. Furthermore, it was democratic, all actions requiring the "general consent of all the people." The committees were run by women as well as men, and they had no honorary titles for any members, all being called either Mister or Miss. ("It was somewhat startling to me to hear Miss --- speak about her baby," Nordhoff admitted.) As with the affluent citizens of Economy, these communitarians had prospered to the extent that they now employed outsiders to perform their drudgery so that their burden of labor was not arduous.[38]

All the children were placed in a general nursery as soon as they were weaned. "The children I saw were plump, and looked sound," Nordhoff wrote doubtfully, "but they seemed to me a little subdued and desolate, as though they missed the exclusive love and care of a father and mother. This, however, may have been only a fancy," he added, anxious to be fair to the Oneidans;

> though I should grieve to see in the eyes of my own little ones
> an expression which I thought I saw in the Oneida children,
> difficult to describe—perhaps I might say a lack of buoyancy,
> or of confidence and gladness. A man or woman may not find
> it disagreeable to be part of a great machine, but I suspect it is
> harder for a child. However, I will not insist on this, for I may
> have been mistaken.

He suspected his own ability to be objective in such a case and mocked his own somewhat sentimental tendencies, comparing his reaction to the children of Oneida with that he had once had to "a lot of little chickens raised in an egg-hatching machine, and having a blanket for shelter instead of the wing of a mother." He had thought he could tell that they missed their mother. "But

---

[38.]   CN, *Communistic Societies*, 278–281.

after all they grew up to be hearty chickens," he wrote, "as useful as their more particularly nurtured fellows."[39]

As for the character of the Oneidans, he was struck with "the amount of ingenuity, inventive skill, and business talent developed among men from whom, in the outer world, one would not expect such qualities," betraying his generally low opinion of the average American.[40] The Perfectionists were particularly clever in starting up new factories simply by having one of their members observe an already-operating example. Furthermore, they were "kind, polite to each other and to strangers, cheerful, and industrious," working and living, some two hundred people, without confusion or undue clamor.[41]

As Perfectionists, the Oneida colonists aimed at "immediate and total cessation from sin." As part of that standard, they embraced "community of goods and of persons" as "taught and commanded by Jesus." Herein lay the aspect of Perfectionism that offended so many outsiders, and Nordhoff explained the reasoning behind it. "The community system" in which no individual held private property, was extended to marital relations as well. "Complex marriage" was regulated by "certain religious and social restraints," but the Oneidans insisted that "there is 'no intrinsic difference between property in persons and property in things; and that the same spirit which abolished exclusiveness in regard to money would abolish ... exclusiveness in regard to women and children.'"[42]

The enterprise was suspect to Nordhoff. "It is an extraordinary evidence of the capacity of mankind for various and extreme religious beliefs," he wrote wonderingly, "that many men have brought their wives and young daughters into the Oneida Community." He spelled out the arrangements, rhetorically treading on eggshells: men and women could "freely cohabit," and exclusive attachments were discouraged as sinfully selfish; such attachments were always broken up by the community. To Nordhoff, who maintained an evenness of tone throughout his discussion of "complex marriage," the system seemed cold-blooded, even cruel. Such a ban on a couple's desire to be "true to each other" had caused "suffering" in his belief. But he did not doubt their sincerity or their intention to keep out people with base motives. "The Perfectionists are sincerely and almost fanatically attached to their peculiar faith," he asserted, "and accept new members only with great care and many precautions."[43]

---

39. CN, *Communistic Societies*, 281–2.

40. CN, *Communistic Societies*, 285.

41. CN, *Communistic Societies*, 287.

42. CN, *Communistic Societies*, 271–2.

43. CN, *Communistic Societies*, 276–7, 289.

Another peculiarity of the Perfectionist life was "Criticism." Instituted as a means of preventing intrigues, backbiting, and animosities from undermining the community's solidarity, "Criticism" involved one community member voluntarily having his faults pointed out to him by a company of his peers ("with," Nordhoff noted, "...an astonishing and often exasperating plainness of speech"). It was "a most important and ingenious device, which Noyes and his followers rightly regard as the cornerstone of their practical community life." He was allowed to attend one session.[44]

"Fifteen persons besides myself, about half women, and about half young people under thirty, were seated in a room. The young man to be criticized, whom I will call Charles, sat inconspicuously in the midst of the company," Charles Nordhoff wrote. Acutely sensitive to others' feelings, Nordhoff recorded the proceedings in detail, and was, perhaps, feeling that the criticisms being leveled at the young man were not far afield from those with which he berated himself. One man

> remarked that he thought Charles had been somewhat hardened by too great good fortune; that his success in certain enterprises had somewhat spoiled him; if he had not succeeded so well, he would have been a better man; that he was somewhat wise in his own esteem; not given to consult with others, or to seek or take advice.

Other members chimed in, agreeing with the first. A second man remarked that Charles was mistaken in arrogantly crediting himself with his successes, for others had helped him a great deal. It continued in this vein, with members telling "Charles" of his bad table manners, his rudeness of language, his being a "respecter of persons," his irreligiosity. Taking notes, Nordhoff did not fail to perceive how painful the procedure was to the young man. "Amid all this very plain speaking, which I have considerably condensed," he commented, "... Charles sat speechless, looking before him; but as the accusations multiplied, his face grew paler, and drops of perspiration began to stand on his forehead." After all had finished, John Humphrey Noyes, the aging leader of the Oneida community, spoke up, summarizing what had been said and adding his own comments: "Charles," he said, had

> "fallen under the too common temptation of selfish love, and a desire to wait upon and cultivate an exclusive intimacy with the woman who was to bear a child through him. This

---

[44.]   CN, *Communistic Societies*, 289.

is an insidious temptation, very apt to attack people under such circumstances; but it must nevertheless be struggled against." ...Charles had determined, and [Noyes] agreed with him, that he ought to isolate himself entirely from the woman, and let another man take his place at her side; and this Charles had accordingly done, with a most praiseworthy spirit of self-sacrifice. ...Taking all this in view, [Noyes] thought Charles was in a fair way to become a better man, and had manifested a sincere desire to improve, and to rid himself of all selfish faults.

"All that I have recited was said by practiced tongues. The people knew very well how to express themselves. There was no vagueness, no uncertainty," Nordhoff wrote with some anger. "Every point was made; every sentence was a hit—a stab I was going to say, but as the sufferer was a volunteer, I suppose this would be too strong a word." He admitted, however, that the process had its utility, and possibly might benefit both "Charles" and the critics, "for if there had been bitterness in any of their hearts before, this was likely to be dissipated by free utterance." But he had no praise for Noyes's contribution, which disclosed, he wrote, a "strange and horrible ... view of morals and duty."[45]

Leaving such questions aside, however, he was modestly positive about the Perfectionist's results. "The people seem contented, and pleased with their success, as well they may be, for it is remarkable," he wrote. "...They struck me as matter-of-fact, with no nonsense or romance about them, by no means overworked, and with a certain, perhaps for their place in life high average of culture." And yet they seemed, somehow, uninteresting. If they had found the way to contentment on earth, Nordhoff was not at all sure that it was not, in some perverse way, too easy, too perfect, too deadening. They seemed to him "a common-place company," but he regarded it as almost inevitable that they should be so, "people whose lives are removed from need, and narrowly bounded by their community; whose religious theory calls for no internal struggles, and ... very little self-denial; who are well-fed and sufficiently amused, and not overworked, and have no future to fear." Their existence seemed to lack profundity. "The greater passions are not stirred in such a life."[46]

Nordhoff believed, as he often stated, that life's challenges were meant by God to bring out the best qualities in people: stated tritely, that suffering built character. The Oneidans were guilty not only of too easy a life, but of too easy an acceptance of what struck Nordhoff as highly troubling doctrines. Fittingly,

---

[45]   CN, *Communistic Societies*, 291–293.

[46]   CN, *Communistic Societies*, 288.

in concluding his account, he quoted one of the hymns that the men and women sang to each other at a Sunday gathering, which chorused that "the love of God is better" than any love humans might hold for one another.

Nordhoff knew well the condemnation that the Oneidans' unorthodox sexual relationships had incurred, and in so closing his chapter with this hymn, he seems to have placed his objections on grounds different than sheer illiberalism. The implication was that "complex marriage," as practiced at Oneida, was a singularly passionless affair, subsumed into a religiosity that drained intimate human relationships of much of their meaning. Their material prosperity seemed less significant than the blandness and complacency that seemed to mark the place. "Thus ended Sunday at Oneida Community," he wrote, seeing no need for further elaboration, "and with this ... I may conclude my account of these people." And there he closed the door.[47]

Although his analyses of the individual communities had often pointed out serious flaws (the book somewhat resembling *Rasselas* in its unsatisfying tour of belief systems), Nordhoff's conclusion was decidedly more positive. More and more, the principles he derived from his investigations resembled his own idea of the perfect society, often with interpretations only tenuously linked to the facts he had recorded.

All the communes were bonded together by religious belief. For a commune to "exist harmoniously," he concluded, all members had to be "of one mind upon some question" that was either religious or took the place of religion. Such a transcendent belief might take many forms, such as the Aurorans' belief that the essence of Christianity was unselfishness or the Icarians' belief in Cabet's social ideas. But "I do not think that any of these people can be justly called fanatics," he added. "Fanaticism" was a term of opprobrium to Nordhoff, and he exempted the communitarians from the charge. Almost desperately hoping that he had found a universally palatable solution to labor problems (or perhaps a means of restoring lost simplicity and the small communities of antebellum America), he deemphasized the extremist character of the communitarians' belief systems, projecting onto them his own liberalism instead. They had "each a very positive and deeply rooted religious faith," but could not be called fanatics "except by a person who holds every body to be a fanatic who believes differently from himself." Such an intolerant person was the real fanatic, in contrast to his communitarians; for "none of these people believe that they are alone good or alone right; all admit freely that there is room in the world for various and varying religious beliefs and that neither wisdom nor righteousness ends with them." In fact, none of the communities was open to people of faiths different than their own, and thus Nordhoff glossed over a primary

---

[47.]   CN, *Communistic Societies*, 300–301.

difficulty in applying their example to American society at large, a society with an increasingly diverse population.[48]

Despite evidence to the contrary, he was also anxious to acquit them of the charge of "oppos[ing] family life." "This, too, is an error," he insisted. Only the Perfectionists had established "what can be fairly called unnatural sexual relations," and most of the others kept families intact. "The Shakers and Rappists are celibates," he acknowledged, and so might have dispelled his vision of life as usual under a communal organization. But there were many examples of communities with conventional family structures to counterbalance the celibates. Thus, he insisted, these issues presented no obstacles at all to the would-be communist: one need not be a religious fanatic or practice "unnatural" sexual relations in order to form a successful commune.[49]

As inventors and as businessmen and women, Nordhoff believed the communitarians deserved nothing but praise. Their neighbors benefited from their proximity; as with all communities, the expanded markets, increased employment, and example of frugality and skill enhanced their neighborhoods. "A commune is a fixture," he observed. "Its people build and arrange for all time; and if they have an ideal of comfort they work up to it." He also asserted that the communes fostered the development of talent (ignoring his harsh judgment of Aurora in this regard) and that the most able members did, rightly, assume positions of leadership. "Nothing surprised me more," he maintained, "...than ...the ease and certainty with which the brains come to the top." That the leadership be wise, that the systems be meritocratic, was all the more important because of the relative position held by the rank and file. "The fundamental principle of communal life," he declared, "is the subordination of the individual's will to the general interest or the general will," which meant "unquestioning obedience by the members toward the leaders, elders, or chiefs of their society."[50]

The system was not one of arbitrary dictatorship. The leaders would not act without "the unanimous consent of the membership." But acting in the interest of their followers, he emphasized, did not mean that the leaders were simply to execute their designs as competent managers rather than thinkers and initiators. He envisioned less a democratic government than one in which the natural leaders held an almost mystical bond of understanding with their subjects—the sort of contented hierarchy long praised by classical conservatives, from Burke to Carlyle. Nordhoff found the Icarian system, which he called "as

---

48. CN, *Communistic Societies*, 387–8.

49. CN, *Communistic Societies*, 388–9.

50. CN, *Communistic Societies*, 390–2.

nearly as possible a pure democracy," to be "the worst" political system of all he
had encountered. As he explained,

> The president ... is simply an executive officer to do the will of
> the majority, which is expressed or ascertained every Saturday
> night, and is his rule of conduct for the following week. "The
> president could not sell a bushel of corn without instructions
> from the meeting of the people," said an Icarian to me—and
> thereby seemed to me to condemn the system of which he was
> evidently proud.

In contrast to such rampant democracy, the Shakers and Amana
communities gave their leaders—who were not elected, but appointed "by
the highest spiritual authority, ... almost, but not quite, unlimited power and
authority"—the only reins on that power being their obligation to preserve
harmony and conform to the general principles of the societies that they
headed. Such a leader formed the "habits, not only of daily life, but even of
thought, of those whom he governs," Nordhoff believed, "just as a father forms
the character of his children in a family."[51]

Despite the fact that power was concentrated in the leadership, Nordhoff
denied the hierarchical nature of such government and stoutly maintained
that "in a commune there is absolute equality. The leader is only the chief
servant; his food and lodgings are no better than those of the members." This
was an odd sort of equality when some had control over labor and resources,
while others simply acquiesced in that control. "In a commune no member is
a servant," he declared. "If any servants are kept, they are hired from among
the world's people." The implications of such an arrangement, which in fact
solved no labor problems but rather displaced them onto an extraneous group,
did not seem to shake Nordhoff's belief that here might be found a new,
more functional social system. In fact, the spread of tightly knit communities
that relegated the hardest or most distasteful tasks to outsiders would have
resulted in substantially the same conditions that Nordhoff was hoping to
alleviate: the affluent and comfortable retaining their affluence through
their exploitation of others' need for wage labor. Nordhoff never disavowed
capitalism, and he approved of the hiring practices of the communitarians in
part because they were proverbially kind and generous employers. Still, the goal
he ostensibly sought for the common laborer was not benevolent employment,
but independence. His own years of daily labor had impressed him with how
confining such a life inevitably would be. "Any one who has felt the oppressive

51.   CN, *Communistic Societies*, 393, 396.

burden of even the highest and best-paid kinds of service," he wrote, "will see that independence and equality are great boons, for which many a man willingly sacrifices much else." It was with some dread that he considered his own future. How long could he continue to support his family on cobbled-together projects?[52]

But his dream of independence, which he held so crucial to the moral as well as material well-being of any man or woman, was not an all-inclusive one. Nordhoff ignored the outsiders and continued to explicate the benefits of communitarianism, not the least of which was "order and system" (even if purchased at the "expense of variety and amusement"). This was particularly attractive when Nordhoff thought of New York, which had often driven him to rage and nearly to despair. As he said, "a man or woman born with what the Shakers would call a gift of order"—and surely Nordhoff was such a man—"finds ... a singular charm in the precision, method, regularity, and perfect system of a communal village." It was as if "an eternal Sabbath" reigned therein. "There is no hurly-burly," he wrote. "This systematic arrangement of life ... gives a decency and dignity to humble life which in general society [it] is too often without."[53]

"I have found myself constantly falling into the error of comparing [communitarian life] with my own, or with the life of men and women in pleasant circumstances in great cities," he acknowledged. All the successful communes were "composed of what are customarily called 'common people.'" There were no "highly educated, refined, cultivated, or elegant men or women," no "exalted views of humanity or destiny; they are not enthusiasts; they do not speak much of the beautiful with a big B," he wrote. "They are utilitarians." Their utilitarianism was all-pervasive. "Some do not even like flowers," he noted; others rejected music, and while their buildings were solid, "they care nothing for architectural effects. Art is not known among them; mere beauty and grace are undervalued, even despised."[54]

The benefits of communal life were several: security, varied and easy employment, wholesome enjoyments, independence, and relief from "a great mass of carking cares." This was crucial, for such benefits were the very basis of communal life. Although religion certainly played an important role, in Nordhoff's judgment, the communal impulse resulted from "a deep-seated dissatisfaction with society as it is constituted"; they were people who "by adverse circumstances, oppression, or wrong, [have] been made to feel very keenly the need of something better." Thus, peasants often succeeded in such

---

[52]   CN, *Communistic Societies*, 394, 412.

[53]   CN, *Communistic Societies*, 395.

[54]   CN, *Communistic Societies*, 399–400.

efforts while the well-educated and well-off usually failed. There was, in fact, an inverse relationship between the success of a commune and the previous successes of its members: "If education or intellectual culture are important forces," he noted, "the unsuccessful societies had these, the successful ones had them not." Such success depended upon "a feeling of the unbearableness of the circumstances" of the members' lives outside the commune. "The general [prejudice] of modern society is blindly right at bottom," Nordhoff concluded. "Communism is a mutiny against society."[55]

Furthermore, communes were, in Nordhoff's equation, essentially the product of a Protestant consciousness, the orderly obverse of (Roman Catholic) anarchism. If communism was, indeed, a "mutiny against society," then

> whether the communist shall rebel with a bludgeon and a petroleum torch, or with a plow and a church, depends upon whether he has not or has faith in God—whether he is a religious being or not. If priestcraft and tyranny have sapped his faith and debauched his moral sense, then he will attack society as the French commune recently attacked Paris— animated by a furious envy…, and an undiscriminating hatred toward every thing which reminds him of his oppressors, or of the social system from which he has or imagines he has suffered wrong.

Thus, French communists, and by extension the restive Irish immigrants in New York City, might well have had genuine grievances; but their means of redress were all wrong. The well-instructed Christian—by which Nordhoff meant the Protestant—would seek refuge in more peaceful, in his view more positive ways. He was a clear believer in the social obligations imposed by Christian faith, if he acted upon those obligations in a way far different from the communists, and he sympathized with their fidelity to principle. If the rebel had faith in God and hope in "the social theory which Jesus propounded," then he would "seek another way out" than violence, "each giving his own interpretation to that brief narrative of Luke in which he describes the primitive Christian Church: 'And all that believed were together, and had all things in common; and sold their possessions and goods; and parted them to all men as every man had need.'" "These words," Nordhoff wrote, "…form the charter of every communistic society of which I have spoken." Thus, communism was not subversive at all, but yet another form of Christian resolution.[56]

55. CN, *Communistic Societies*, 406–8.
56. CN, *Communistic Societies*, 409.

"Some things the communist must surrender," he ruminated, "and the most precious of these is solitude." If he had ever contemplated joining such a community himself, his new knowledge would have quickly ended that ambition, for he had an almost desperate need for privacy. As a youth, in the claustrophobic world of sailing ships, he would escape to the spars alone, periodically, to read or to think; as an adult, he built a little stone gazebo on the edge of the cliff near his house, a retreat from the family he loved nonetheless. His peace of mind demanded as much. "The man to whom at intervals the faces and voices of his kind become hateful, whose bitterest need it is to be sometimes alone," he wrote, "—this man need not try communism." Communal living demanded that everything--time, space, thought—be shared. "You are part of a great family, all whose interests and all whose life must necessarily be in common." The example of Moses recurred to him, an exemplar of the pain of leadership. "Moses, wandering over the desert with his great commune," he pondered, "occasionally went up into a mountain; but he never returned to the dead level of the Israelites without finding his heart filled with rage and despair." Nordhoff, whose descents from his Alpine home to the "hurly-burly" of New York were often occasions of despair, felt himself more akin to Moses than to the hapless, faceless Israelites. "Fortunately," he added, "to the greater part of mankind the faces and voices of their kind are necessary."[57]

His ideal commune would be a small homogeneous village, coreligionists living in separate houses, deferring to the judgment of their leaders. Women would enjoy political equality; laziness would not exist among the members. A mutual "interchange of thought and experience" was a significant aspect of the experiment; the strength of example, not to mention the constant surveillance, would "check and control" any "slight tendencies to evil in any member." The social advantages of good schools and churches were important ones.[58]

But the communities he had visited had not made the most of their opportunities. Though some were ascetics, and though frugality was clearly necessary in the early years of any such establishment, Nordhoff's concept of the economy was based on ever-expanding abundance, and he protested that

> I can not see why a prosperous commune should not own the best books; why it should not have music; why it should not hear the most eloquent lecturers; why it should not have pleasant pleasure-grounds, and devote some means to ...fine architecture.

[57.] CN, *Communistic Societies*, 410–11.

[58.] CN, *Communistic Societies*, 413–416.

This was their great failure; as with the common farmer, their children would grow restless and leave them for the more vital and variegated urban centers. Farmers could not help the dullness of their surroundings, but Nordhoff couldn't see how the finer things in life "would be dangerous to the success of the commune."[59] Their insularity, the fact that the communes did not exchange information among themselves, was also a disappointment to him.

But his ultimate verdict, however measured, was a positive one. Compared to the life of an ordinary American farmer or worker, "the communist life is so much freer from care and risk, so much easier, so much better in many ways, and in all material aspects, that I sincerely wish it might have a farther development in the United States." Communistic societies would not rapidly increase in number, he allowed; but as examples, they were important, one more "way by which the dissatisfied laborer may, if he chooses, better his condition."[60] To his mind, establishing a commune ought not to have been impossible for any determined group of persons. An implicit critique of industrial capitalism's harsher aspects, Nordhoff's communism was, in a way, only a new twist on the frontier thesis—equally buoyant in its optimism, equally blithe in its disregard of the lack of skill or capital possessed by the vaunted beneficiaries of such opportunities. Whether forging ahead of the Western line of settlement or beyond the limits of conventional social arrangement, ways could be found for people to pull themselves up into a better life. This was America, after all.

Nordhoff's study of communitarianism was a deeply personal book. He undertook the project before securing a publisher for it; not until July of 1874, after the book was substantially completed, did he sign a contract with the Harpers for its publication.[61] *The Communistic Societies of the United States* was first issued by Harper & Brothers in late 1874. A second edition, and the last until the plethora of reprints appeared nearly a century later, was published in 1875, unfortunately priced at $4—well above the means of the common laborer.

There was widespread interest in the topic for America was still in the grips of the depression that had begun in 1873, and with the mounting misery of the poor grew the apprehension of the better-off, haunted by the specter of the Paris Commune of 1871. *Communistic Societies* received considerable attention

---

59.   CN, *Communistic Societies*, 416–417.

60.   CN, *Communistic Societies*, 417–18.

61.   A February 24, 1874, letter to Whitelaw Reid refers to asking a third party to "get a publisher for me," implying that the Harpers were not eager to publish *Communistic Societies*. Reid Papers, LC. A contract was signed with the Harpers on July 1, 1874, for the book. Harper Brothers' Papers, Contract Book II, page 253, Columbia University.

from nationally circulated publications and was reviewed in the *New York Times*, the *Nation*, and the *North American Review*, then being edited by Henry Adams.[62]

The last of these, by Franklin B. Sanborn, was mixed but positive.[63] "We suppose it useless to expect or express the wish that Mr. Nordhoff should be more methodical in his books," Sanborn began and proceeded to criticize Nordhoff for "beginning in the middle, and leaving off at both ends." Nordhoff, he believed, had not given enough attention to questions of the role of mysticism in communistic attempts, but as he correctly noted, Nordhoff's intentions had led him in other directions. His argument that "a wholesome communism is possible," Sanborn said, was made "with some success" although the reviewer disagreed with Nordhoff's contention that the communities might add "more refined attractions" to their successes. "A more careful study of the elements of successful communism would probably convince him," Sanborn wrote,

> that it is not self-gratification, but self-denial, that makes the strongest bond among the members; and that the further the rigid idea of duty was removed, and the more it was replaced by that of even innocent pleasure, the greater would be the danger that the community would fall apart.[64]

But Sanborn believed (with more than a hint of condescension) "much [could] be learned" from Nordhoff's "entertaining volume."

Communistic Societies was also noticed in the *New York Times*, this time not as an insufficiently scholarly exegesis, as in the *North American*, but more as the overtly political work that Nordhoff had intended it to be. The reviewer paraphrased Nordhoff's verdict: "Communists, Mr. Nordhoff tells us, are cleanly, honest, humane, and charitable, temperate, principled against debt, contented, and even cheerful." But the *Times* concluded, communism "kills social ambition and represses the love of the sexes, the spur to most of the exertion which results in the development of the human race, and the

---

[62]   See the *New York Times*, March 8, 1875; the *Nation*, January 14, 1875; the *North American Review*, January 1875.

[63]   The reviewer was Franklin B. Sanborn although Adams had at first asked Arthur Latham Perry to write the review. See J. C. Levenson, Ernest Samuels, et al., eds., *The Letters of Henry Adams* (Cambridge: Belknap Press/Harvard, 1982), volume 2, p. 208, n. 4.

[64]   [Franklin B. Sanborn], Review of *The Communistic Societies of the United States*, in *North American Review*, January 1875, 226–9.

advancement of civilization."[65] The reviewer approved of Nordhoff's opposition
to trade unions' "suicidal tendencies" and referred the reader to his extensive
bibliography for further information.[66] The *Times* was not about to recommend
the spread of communism, no matter how laudable the virtues ascribed to it.

A young Henry James reviewed the book for the *Nation*, evidently having
read it with great interest. Nordhoff wrote, he thought, "in a friendly spirit,"
tending "to dip his pen into rose-color" though "he professes to take the
rigidly economical and not the sentimental view." James had a low opinion of
the societies described by Nordhoff. "It would have been possible, we think,"
he wrote,

> for an acute moralist to travel over the same ground as Mr.
> Nordhoff and to present in consequence a rather duskier
> picture of human life at Amana, Mount Lebanon, and
> Oneida; but his work for our actual needs would doubtless
> have been less useful.

As to whether a higher intellectual life could be made available to the
communists, James had his doubts. The people were "common, uneducated,
unaspiring," and "if their ignorance has often hardened into queer, stiff,
sterile dogma, the sacrifice of intelligence has not been considerable." The
psychological aspects of the communists struck James as more interesting
than the economic. If Nordhoff had tried to understand the internal logic
governing their lives, to James, the people thus described were impossibly
eccentric: inexplicable, amusing curiosities. "One is struck," he wrote, "...with
the existence in human nature of lurking and unsuspected strata, as it were,
of asceticism, of the capacity for taking a grim satisfaction in dreariness." But
James found Nordhoff's account of Dr. Keil beside the grave of his children
worth quoting. The lengthy chapter on the Shakers was interesting as well,
explaining "everything indeed in the matter but one—how twenty-five hundred
people, that is, can be found to embrace a life of such organized and theorized
aridity," and he cited Nordhoff's conversation with Elder Evans on architecture
as evidence of their life of "negatives." Of the Oneida Perfectionists, James

[65] The unorthodox sexual relationships obtaining at "intentional communities" were
central to their attempts to get back to first principles of Christianity, however
ill understood these efforts might have been. See Lawrence Foster, *Religion and
Sexuality: Three American Communal Experiments of the Nineteenth Century* (NY: Oxford
University Press, 1981).

[66] "New Publications: Communism in the United States," *New York Times*, March 8,
1875.

was highly critical. "Its industrial results are doubtless excellent; but morally and socially it strikes us as simply hideous." The description of "Criticism" "upon the young man Henry" (an interesting mistake of James's, for Nordhoff had called the subject "Charles") provoked a verdict of "fathomless depths of barbarism," "an attempt to organize and glorify the detestable tendency toward the complete effacement of privacy in life and thought everywhere so rampant with us nowadays." But he concluded that Nordhoff's book had demonstrated that communism, "under certain conditions and with strictly rational hopes," could be a "paying experiment."[67]

By January of 1880, Nordhoff's *Communistic Societies of the United States* had been in print five years, going through two Harper editions.[68] But it had not sold well, and it had not penetrated the thinking of the working class; no wellspring of cooperation had ensued, as its examples of material prosperity remained models of nothing but their own peculiar selves. Nordhoff had by then struck up a correspondence with Henry George, the journalist reformer whom he had met, briefly, during his 1872 tour of California. Appleton's was about to publish *Progress and Poverty*, George's own effort to solve the paradox that had prompted Nordhoff's earlier investigations. Nordhoff had seen one of the advance copies and wrote to George enthusiastically of it. With his congratulations, however, Nordhoff warned George of the possibility that his book, like Nordhoff's own, might not have the influence that George hoped for it. George, however, was sanguine, and he wrote to Nordhoff some consoling words. "As to your 'Communistic Societies' I think you underate [*sic*] its influence," he wrote.

> And certainly in other books and ways you must have exerted much influence. But how much can you see? Have you never when, reading, a spark has been struck in your mind, thought how little the author could know of his influence on you. And so you do not see who is taking your book from a library shelf, or stealing a read from a secondhand book stall, or turning over, it may be some broken pages, in country inn or

---

67. James's review is reprinted in *Henry James: Literary Criticism: Essays on Literature, American Writers, English Writers* (NY: Library of America, 1984), 560–567.

68. Twentieth-century reprints of *Communistic Societies* include the 1960 Hillary House (NY) edition; a 1965 Schocken Books edition, introduced by Franklin H. Littell; and the Dover Books reprint, introduced by Mark Holloway, which has been in print continuously since 1966. No reprints prior to 1960 have been located.

Indiaman's forecastle. Still less can you see the influence. It
may only show after many days.[69]

   This was the beginning of a deep friendship between George and Nordhoff,
for they shared many assumptions: the division of society into "producers" and
"non-producers," the sympathy for the working class that nevertheless insisted
that directed change must originate with strong leaders, the moral necessity
of striving for positive change. But *Progress and Poverty* went on to phenomenal
success, eventually drawing George into politics and spawning a national
movement. George had not limited his scheme to small-scale communities or to
the religiously fervid. Nordhoff could not even conceive of the good society on
the large impersonalized scale of urban industrial America; there was nothing
that working people could do to follow his model, except leave the cities (and
jobs) permanently behind, conceptually as well as geographically. And while
Nordhoff denied that religious "fanaticism" was necessary to communal success,
nevertheless it was the motivating force behind every one of his examples.

   There is limited evidence that Nordhoff's message was heeded by at least
a few; people applied for admission to his communities, telling them that his
portrait had attracted them to do so.[70] Furthermore, one historian has recently

---

69.   Henry George to Charles Nordhoff, Jan. 31, 1880 [mistakenly dated 1879], Henry
     George Papers, NYPL. In a letter dated Dec. 21, 1879, George thanked Nordhoff
     for his encouragement regarding *Progress and Poverty*. "It pleases me that you
     remembered me, and it pleases me that you like my book," George wrote. "Your
     friendship and your opinion I value very much. ...I have derived so much from you
     that it pleases me *very* much that my book interests and pleases you."

70.   See letters in the Nixon family papers, Collection 680, Box 2, folder 17, Ohio
     Historical Society Library, Columbus, Ohio for letters of application to the Zoar
     community. Sylvester Brewer of Lewisburg, Kentucky wrote (June 19, 1876), "I have
     been reading Nordhoff's Book on Communities and amongst all that he wrote
     about I like yours the best...." In November of 1876, A. W. Birkbeck of Enfield New
     Hampshire, wrote, "all that We Know of Zoar peopel is wat We read in Mr Charles
     Nordhoffs Book on Communistic Societies...." and one T. H. Rose of Marietta,
     Ohio, wrote in July of 1877: "I have been reading an account of your community
     in Nordhoff's book and have been captured by it." In German, Carl Archutz [?] of
     Philadelphia wrote in April of 1876 that ".,. somebody brought me a book, where all
     the communist societies are explained (by Nordhoff), yet ... yours is the only one
     that agrees with my insight." All these writers were applying to admission to Zoar;
     there are also letters of 1876 and 1877 that do not mention Nordhoff by name, but
     mention having read about Zoar. Nordhoff's account of Zoar was hardly a glowing
     one, but seems to have caught people's imaginations nonetheless.

documented the ongoing vitality of communitarian movements in the post–Civil War period despite earlier assumptions that socialist communities were an antebellum phenomenon.[71] Still, Nordhoff's book had little obvious effect.

If *The Communistic Societies of the United States* failed to reach the people whom Nordhoff had hoped to affect—workingmen and women and, perhaps even more so, leaders willing to guide their efforts—it is easy to see why. For it was a book that he wrote for himself. He did not tailor the prose or tone down the learned allusions to the level that he assumed was intelligible to the average uneducated laborer. His references to the disabilities of "peasants" were not calculated to endear the book to the working class. Nor did he follow the schematic rules of mass publishing that had shaped his books on California; *Communistic Societies* is organized to the extent that the visits are described separately, and the whole introduced and concluded with Nordhoff's generalizations. But the chapters vary wildly in length: the section on the Shakers might have formed its own book while some communities merited only a page or two. In this, Nordhoff was following the dictates of his own interests. The lengthy verbatim passages from primary sources, the pages and pages of song verses laid out without comment, all reflect his sense of the value of recording, much as an anthropologist might, cultural artifacts in some permanent form. But they do not make for easy reading.

He may have been looking for answers to puzzles in his own life. If labor unions were not the answer, if coercion was always wrong, if democracy in fact was not an empty chimera born of a naive concept of human capacity, then what could he do, what plan could he forward, to restore opportunity and justice to the worker? How much was he willing to risk in his desire to be of use to society? He could never stomach the idea of standing for elective office, and perhaps this was as much due to a recognition of the intractability of the problems facing America as to his unwillingness to make himself available to all. On a more personal note, his considerations of the communists' social relationships—conventional family life, celibacy, or complex marriage—often bear an undercurrent of evaluation, of weighing the benefits against the costs, of measuring them, in short, as he admitted in his conclusion, against the life he had carved out for himself, the responsibilities he had assumed. When he wrote of the "man to whom at intervals the faces and voices of his kind become hateful, whose bitterest need it is to be sometimes alone," it is himself he is speaking of, and not without a degree of sadness. For all that he surrounded himself with a loving family and friends, he was an intensely lonely man.

[71.]   Robert S. Fogarty, *All Things New: American Communes and Utopian Movements, 1860-1914* (Chicago: University of Chicago Press, 1990).

But there was no denying the facts of communal life, and by extension any life that was to be of benefit to others. Nordhoff hadn't the temperament for a commune, and he couldn't have borne the public life of a politician. What, then, was he to do? His book was one attempt at leadership, at exerting some force for good in the world. But as he pondered the discoveries he had made in his journeys, there recurred to him a telling example. The leader of a commune, he had learned, must be both a strong-willed and forceful person and one who could tolerate being surrounded by people with whom he had little in common. Moses's descents from his mountaintop invariably caused him anger and pain, Nordhoff wrote. But leadership required such sacrificial descents, for the people would not tolerate a long-absent Moses:

> [F]or in the commune there must be absolute equality; there can be no special privileges; and when the great Leader, resting his spirit on the mountain, and enjoying the luxury of solitude and retirement from the hateful sights and sounds of human kind, "delayed to come down," his fellow communists began at once to murmur, "As for this Moses, the man who brought us up out of the land of Egypt, we wot not what is become of him."[72]

His California dreams of founding a quasi-feudal community of his own, where he would be intimately involved in instructing and molding the lives of the simple people on the land, could not last in the face of the realities of communal life, and he never again spoke in such terms. And three years had elapsed since Nordhoff's resignation from the *Evening Post* and his withdrawal from the world of daily journalism. Knowing that many of his old associates might "wot not what had become of him," he was, as he completed *Communistic Societies,* arranging to begin again down among the Israelites as a correspondent for the New York *Herald.*

[72.] CN, *Communistic Societies,* 410–11.

CHAPTER 7

Bennett's Ambassador

In 1874, Charles Nordhoff decided to rejoin the world of daily journalism, still an intensely partisan world in which alliances with newspapers were politically significant. Nordhoff had been a strong Lincoln Republican since the late 1850s, an allegiance based upon his opposition to the expansion of slavery and an adherence to free-soil ideology. But in the postwar years, the Republican Party was beginning to assume a new identity: more probusiness, oriented toward governmental support of corporate and infrastructural expansion; favoring the institution of the civil service and a government staffed by technical experts; and comfortable with the expanded power of the federal government, which it continued to control. All of these positions repelled Nordhoff, and as he considered the postwar political landscape, he edged away from his former allies. Accordingly, he could not take his place at any of the liberal Republican journals that courted him upon his return. He went to work instead for the mass circulation New York *Herald*, with its working-class constituency and Democratic leanings, and settled into a position as a Special Correspondent in Washington. There, he learned that the workings of government bore little relation to his ideals of democracy.

Before consigning himself once again to a day-to-day job, Charles Nordhoff completed the fourth and last book written during his three years as a freelance: *Politics for Young Americans*. With chapters ranging in subject matter from the meaning of society to the divinely ordained necessity of free trade and hard currency, the little volume spelled out Nordhoff's credo in the form of a secondary-school civics textbook.[1]

An unqualified success, *Politics* went through fourteen editions between 1875 and 1899, most of them in a textbook-style revision, and it received a

---

[1] Contract Book II, 375–6, dated October 1, 1874. Harper Brothers Papers, Columbia University.

favorable review from the *New York Times*. Argentinean and Mexican editions were published and presumably used in the schools of those nations. Written for young people, the book explained the meanings of "liberty, law, government, and human rights" and was intended to provide schoolchildren with the basic knowledge a good citizen needed to know. It included the usual descriptions of the branches of government, separation of powers, and a copy of the U.S. Constitution. But the book was not consistent. Nordhoff's more idiosyncratic ideas, informed by experience, often contradicted more conventional, comfortable recitations of patriotic truisms. The widespread acceptance of *Politics* is all the more remarkable because of Nordhoff's blunt pronouncements on then-controversial issues such as protectionism, the currency, and the rights of labor unions.[2]

Nordhoff insisted on the necessity of politics to good government, declaring nonpartisan government "the dream of weak and amiable men," a utopian notion suitable only for a world without selfishness. It was every citizen's duty to participate in politics at every level, to influence nominations and prevent civic wrongdoing. Citizens were also obliged to expose any corruption they might discover—a duty which a crusading journalist was particularly well-equipped to fulfill. Without the clash of opposing political parties, government would become monolithic, with no opposition to point out its shortcomings.[3]

Political participation went beyond voting to the formation of and attendance at caucuses, where political "preparatory work" was largely done. Caucuses were morally neutral; their morality depended upon the people involved. Nordhoff had no objections to these "silent, secret, but not therefore necessarily evil" councils. Where did such cabals leave democracy and the popular will? Largely as a force to approve or veto measures conceived by those clever enough, and connected enough, to form caucuses.[4]

---

[2] "New Publications: Politics for Young Americans," *New York Times*, January 10, 1875. CN, *Politics for Young Americans* (NY: Harper & Brothers, 1875), v–vi, 11. All citations will be to this edition. *Politics* went through numerous editions: Harper's editions in 1875, 1876; Harper's "revised for schools and colleges" every year between 1877 and 1884, and in 1886, 1887, and 1890. The American Book Company of Cincinnati published an edition in 1899. A Spanish translation by Eduardo Ruiz was published in 1885 and 1890 titled *La ciencia administrativa al alcance de los jovenos: Obra escrita en ingles por Charles Nordhoff, tr. al castellano, y arreglada a las instituciones y al caracter del pueblo mexicano por el Lic* (Mexico City: Oficina tip. de la Secretaria de fomento). An Argentinian edition was published in 1891 under the title of *Politica para los jovenes americanos, traducido del ingles por Gabriel Zendequi* (Buenos Aires: Felix Lajouane, 1891).

[3] CN, *Politics*, 48, 158–160, 176, 187.

[4] CN, *Politics*, 182.

Nordhoff was sanguine about the quality of American politicians. Compared to other free countries, American politics were relatively free of corruption. "There is a good deal of irritating ignorance and some corruption among our political leaders," he wrote, "but not nearly so much as there is in England or France; it vexes us more because we meet it face to face." Americans exposed governmental corruption, and it was well that they did; it would be even better if legislatures required corporations to submit reports for public inspection. Such exposure would allow the people to act and was the key to progress.[5]

A great many pages of *Politics* decried centralized government as an evil, sure to deprive the people of their liberty, and a practice to be avoided even at the cost of disorder. In the America of 1874, this argument was far from abstract, as the policy of federal intervention in the South came increasingly under attack. This fear of centralized government overrode, for all but the most radical of Republicans, concern for the safety of the freedmen. Federal intervention was "unwise and dangerous," Nordhoff wrote, liable to render the people unfit for self-government. With his view of society as an aggregate of individuals, he did not take into account the special hazards of a situation in which racial hatreds allied a majority against a minority. Southern lawlessness, he thought, ought to be reprehensible to the "orderly part" of Southern society, regardless of the targets of attack. He seems to have been blind to the intentions of the "orderly part" of the Southern white population, who intended, no less than the KKK, to restore the white supremacy endangered by reconstruction governments.[6]

The citizenry, therefore, must look out for themselves; guards could not be posted at every door. Did this not imply that against determined oppression, the weak had no right to help from government? Nordhoff insisted that justice always triumphed where courage prevailed; power did not enter into the question. Immediately after the Civil War, he wrote, the freedmen had been threatened by "the intolerant and ignorant part of the Southern whites," and the government tried to protect them. But "this was soon seen to be impossible." Still, all was well: the African-Americans "presently learned to defend themselves," and wherever they demonstrated courage, "their persecutions have ceased." This was nonsense, but Nordhoff desperately wanted to believe that peace was not being purchased at the price of justice or that any infringement of Southern whites' "liberty" was necessary.[7]

---

5.   CN, *Politics*, 158, 160, 181.

6.   CN, *Politics*, 23.

7.   CN, *Politics*, 24–26.

With unintended irony, Nordhoff insisted that "*the chief object of a constitution is to limit the power of majorities.*" But what then of having a constable at every door? Unlimited majority rule would be "the most grinding of tyrannies," for "the minority ... would be mere slaves whose rights to life, property, and comfort no one who chose to join the majority would be bound to respect." This was a very good description of the evolving order in the South, but Nordhoff would not see it.[8]

If Nordhoff had been, as he told Atkinson, "very very *sore* abt. newspapers," by late 1874, he had sufficiently recovered from his bad experience with the New York *Evening Post* to conclude that his aims might best be served by once again joining the fray of daily journalism. Although he had been offered a job on the *New York Times*, freelanced extensively for the New York *Tribune*, and would have been welcomed by Horace White on the Chicago *Tribune*, the journal he chose to work for was the New York *Herald*. No paper could have presented a greater contrast to the *Evening Post*, *Times*, or the two *Tribunes*, all bastions of Republican respectability, than did the *Herald*. Allying himself with the *Herald* was a clear statement of Nordhoff's disaffection with postwar Republicanism and with Radical Reconstruction, and a reaffirmation of his faith in democratic principles.

The *Herald* was universally acknowledged to be preeminent in its news-gathering capability, and its circulation far exceeded that of any other American newspaper. Its huge readership of well over one hundred thousand, substantially composed of the poor and working class, was a great attraction to Nordhoff. No one could ignore the *Herald*, although many wished they might. In a critique published in 1866 in the *North American Review* (yet another stronghold of the Republican elite), James Parton recounted the career of the newspaper's founder, proprietor, and publisher, James Gordon Bennett, as one that balanced a brilliantly innovative grasp of news gathering with a totally unprincipled editorial voice. Parton viewed the *Herald* as a harbinger of what journalism was to become: a means of gathering news, not of directing public opinion. "It is impossible any longer to deny that the chief newspaper of [New York] is the New York Herald," he wrote. "No matter how much we may regret this fact, or be ashamed of it, no journalist can deny it."[9] Bennett's success spoke clearly to Parton of the true function of journalism, for the *Herald* grew ever more popular as the years went on despite "the fixed disapproval of every public-spirited human being who has lived in the United States since [Bennett] began his career." During the war, Bennett had taken the Democratic line, antiwar and verging on proslavery, and his loyalty was accordingly suspect.

---

8.   CN, *Politics*, 58–59.

9.   James Parton, "The New York Herald," *North American Review* 102 (April 1866), 379.

In Parton's opinion, if the U.S. flag had been replaced by the Confederate banner above New York's city hall, "it would not have cost this isolated alien one pang,—unless, perchance, a rival newspaper had been the first to announce the fact." To Bennett, "*nothing* was sacred, or august, or venerable, or even serious." Believing in nothing, he could attack others' beliefs with impunity, but he himself "could not be hit at all."[10]

But, Parton insisted, it was not the *Herald*'s editorials, with their "vein of Mephistophelean mockery," which ensured the newspaper's success, but rather "that amazing variety and fulness of intelligence [i.e., "news"] which often compelled men who hated it most to get up at the dawn of day to buy it."[11] From its beginnings in 1835, the *Herald* had demonstrated Bennett's strengths and his weaknesses and in 1866 continued to exhibit them: "immense expenditure and vigilance in getting news, and a reckless disregard of principle, truth, and decency in its editorials." Even in 1866, Parton judged, the paper was still "profoundly odious" and would not, could not change, so long as James Gordon Bennett controlled it.[12]

By 1874, however, the founder of the *Herald* had been dead for two years. Sole control of the newspaper was left to his son and namesake, James Gordon Bennett, Jr., who at the time of his assumption of full ownership was only thirty-one years old. The younger Bennett was not held in high esteem in Nordhoff's customary circles. "[I]n the fall of 1874," Nordhoff would recall many years later, he was "a man at that time singularly misunderstood and undervalued." Bennett had a reputation for traveling in "fast" circles; his wealth, sophisticated upbringing in France (whence his mother had fled when the opprobrium heaped upon her husband grew unbearable), and abilities as a sportsman earned him entree to the Union Club and the highest social circles of postwar New York. Admiring contemporaries often conjectured that his privileged and isolated upbringing had somehow kept him from developing the greatness that he otherwise might have achieved; his enemies simply discounted him as a spoiled, capricious bon vivant, a man who inherited a position of authority but who ill deserved the power he wielded.

In fact, Bennett Jr. found his way into public notice both for his alcoholic binges and for his apparent determination to live up to his father's example in making the *Herald* the greatest news-gathering journal of the day. It was the younger Bennett who commissioned Henry Stanley to look for British missionary David Livingstone in 1869 and then made Stanley's reports into a gripping real-life drama that boosted circulation and made the words "Dr.

---

[10]   Parton, 399, 400.

[11]   Parton, 380–381.

[12]   Parton, 397.

Livingstone, I presume?" an enduring catchphrase. Bennett sponsored several expeditions of this type: to Africa, to the North Pole, to find the Northwest Passage; and he was canny enough to exploit the dramatic potential of such created news stories to the hilt. In succeeding decades, Joseph Pulitzer and William Randolph Hearst would be the modern masters of the manufactured event, but it was the younger Bennett who invented the practice. He had an eye for talent, too, and hired people such as Mark Twain, Walt Whitman, Richard Harding Davis, and numerous lesser luminaries to fill the pages of the *Herald* with prose that was lively, interesting, and above all else, marketable.[13]

Nordhoff could never have worked for the elder Bennett, who represented so clearly everything Nordhoff despised about journalism: opportunism, scandal-mongering, the seeming triumph of sales figures over principle. In fact, the argument of his soulless editor Stoffle in the 1861 parable on the moral dangers of modern journalism, "What is Best?" might have been taken from the editorial pages of the New York *Herald* itself. But in 1861, Nordhoff had accepted the view that the greatest danger to editorial integrity lay in "pandering" to the masses for the sake of high circulations; and in 1874, his perspective had shifted, locating the corrupting influence not in appealing to the public, but

---

13. Accounts of James Gordon Bennett Jr.'s life and career are few and, unfortunately, tend to focus on the superficial (and sensational) aspects of his personal life, while paying scant attention to his journalistic efforts. Since Bennett left no papers behind and the *Herald* business records no longer exist, historians have relied upon newspaper accounts of Bennett's doings, which naturally focus on his wild social life. The result is that very little is known about Bennett's work as the publisher of the *Herald* although accounts agree that he kept an iron grip on the newspaper as long as he lived. What Nordhoff has to say about Bennett contradicts the standard picture of Bennett, which may be found in the following accounts: Don C. Seitz, *The James Gordon Bennetts, Father and Son* (Indianapolis: Bobbs-Merrill, 1928); Gerald Carson, "The Czar of Herald Square: James Gordon Bennett, Jr.," *Timeline* 6 (February–March 1989): 14–27; Richard Luger, *The Paper: The Life and Death of the New York Herald-Tribune* (NY: Random House, 1986); Richard O'Connor, *The Scandalous Mr. Bennett* (NY: Doubleday, 1962); Jean-Christophe P. Gourvennee, *Un Journal Americain a Paris: James Gordon Bennett et le New York Herald, 1887-1918* (Paris: Musee D'Orsay/*International Herald Tribune*, translated by Patricia Valicenti, 1990); and Steven D. Lyons, "James Gordon Bennett, Jr.," in Perry J. Ashley, ed., *American Newspaper Journalists, 1873-1900* (Dictionary of Literary Biography volume 23; Detroit: Gale Research Company, 1983): 7–16. Another of Bennett's reporters, foreign correspondent Januarius McGahan, has been revived from obscurity by Dale L. Walker, *Januarius MacGahan: The Life and Campaigns of an American War Correspondent* (Athens: Ohio University Press, 1988).

in undue solicitude to the moneyed interests that all too often controlled a newspaper's fortunes. And if there was one thing that Nordhoff had learned from his work at the *Evening Post*, it was this: a newspaper might have the most principled editor in the world—for who could doubt the principles of William Cullen Bryant?—but if the owners demanded certain concessions for the sake of courting advertisers or palliating influential community leaders, it might as well be edited by an open mercenary.

Bennett Jr. had not earned the "odious" reputation of his father in 1874. Newspaper critics howled when a front-page story about the escape of "wild beasts" from the Central Park Zoo, the elaborate fiction of a bored editor, was described as fact, complete with scenes of carnage: only the final paragraph admitted that the story was a fabrication. For years, whenever anyone wanted to impugn the veracity of the *Herald*, the phrase "wild beasts" was a byword and a reproach, emblematic of the paper's irresponsible conduct; but it might be noted that the story only produced a panicked reaction because of the general credibility of the *Herald*'s reporting.

In Nordhoff's recollection, Bennett Jr. held high ideas of the *Herald*'s mission, with "a thoroughly independent judgment" and a "strong desire and determination" that the *Herald* should "serve and advance the cause of good government and good morals and the true interests of the whole country."[14] The fact that Bennett had opened a soup kitchen in the slums during the depression of 1873–74, with soup delivered from Delmonico's; had established a "free ice fund" for the poor during the sweltering summers; and contributed $100,000 toward famine relief in Ireland, all demonstrated a degree of sympathy for the unfortunate by no means typical of publishers at the time. And to Nordhoff's satisfaction, there could be no conflict between the counting room and the editorial offices of the *Herald* as there had been at the *Evening Post*; Bennett controlled them both, as sole owner, publisher, and de facto editor in chief.[15]

Bennett was an autocrat. He ran the *Herald* like a despot over a small country, and not always benevolently; or as Nordhoff would have preferred to phrase it, as the Captain of a ship, with no possible divisions of responsibility or authority. Stories of his eccentricities, apocryphal or not, abound. He would hire and fire on a whim or cable staff members to come to Paris and then send them home again without seeing them. He hired Stanford White in the 1890s to design a Renaissance palace for the new *Herald* offices and then lined the cornice with stone owls whose eyes blinked red at night. The owl he took as

14. CN, *Reminiscences of Some Editors I have Known* (San Diego: 1900): 11–12.
15. CN, *Reminiscences*, 13.

his personal emblem, and when he died in 1918 at the age of seventy-seven, his headstone bore no inscription: only two owls perched in the corners.[16]

For all his idiosyncratic ways, Bennett inspired immense loyalty, and even love, in some of his employees. "I would have come near going to Hell because of my real affection for him," wrote one veteran of the *Herald*.[17] Nordhoff was similarly devoted. He liked strong leaders, whether they were communitarians or ships' captains, mayors, presidents, or newspaper publishers. It was the waffling evasion of responsibility, the wrangling over authority, which made him feel rage and frustration.[18] The *Herald* was feudal, but then, Nordhoff admired some forms of feudalism. Bennett asked Nordhoff to act as the *Herald*'s "Special Correspondent" in Washington beginning in the autumn of 1874, and after some discussion, he agreed, apparently extracting an agreement from Bennett that he never be asked to write editorials against his own principles.[19] It is clear that initially at least, he accepted a place at the *Herald* without fully respecting its character. The emphasis on news gathering, which so many critics singled out as its great contribution to the future of journalism, left Nordhoff bored. Crime stories, fires, and scandal held little interest for him: how could such stuff make the public better informed in any real sense of the word? Samuel Bowles, the editor of the Springfield *Republican*, wrote him early in 1876 to suggest that the *Herald* needed much improvement, which Nordhoff

---

16. Setz, *The James Gordon Bennetts*, and Richard O'Connor, *The Scandalous Mr. Bennett*, passim. See also memoirs of Bennett's subordinates, Joseph I. C. Clarke, *My Life and Memories* (NY: Dodd, Mead and Co., 1925), and Albert Stevens Crockett, *When James Gordon Bennett was Caliph of Baghdad* (New York: Funk & Wagnalls, 1926). The dog story is in Crockett.

17. Albert Stevens Crockett, quoted in Carson, "Czar," 15.

18. CN, *Reminiscences*, 13.

19. Don C. Seitz, *The James Gordon Bennetts*, 242: "The chief editorial writers of the *Herald* in the palmy days ... were the Reverend Doctor George H. Hepworth, ... and Charles Nordhoff. Hepworth ... abased himself at the feet of his proprietor and tried to meet every whim of his swift-changing mind. Not so Nordhoff. He was a sturdy and much beloved character in American literary life. As an editorial writer on the *Herald*, he stood up stoutly for the things he believed to be right. He would come to work with a large supply of pencil stubs with which he always wrote his copy. ...Bennett ... ordered Nordhoff to write a leader coming out for Harrison [in the election of 1888]. He quietly declined, remarking that the agreement under which he came to the *Herald* prescribed that he should never be asked to write in support of things to which he was opposed. To this Bennett gave cheerful assent and instructed [John Russell] Young, a Republican, to produce the editorial. This he did. It was put into type, but never printed."

might—in a management position—see instituted. "You are right," he shot back in reply, but he wouldn't want to undertake such a task. "That place does not interest me; I can't make up my mind to care abt. *news.*" He continued, saying that the *Evening Post*, "while I managed it, & while it was the most successful, was not a newspaper. I can't take any interest in the tons of rubbish wh. enterprising people call news."[20] In another letter, this time to Whitelaw Reid, he referred to the New York *Tribune* as "the best paper in the world," adding parenthetically, "this is treason for me I suppose."[21]

Nordhoff wore three hats in his new position: he wrote editorials and generally assisted in editing the paper from its New York central office; while Congress was in session (in those days often less than six months of the year), he managed the *Herald*'s Washington Bureau; and during those sessions, he served as its "Special Correspondent" in Washington. Contemporary accounts mentioned, in the 1880s, that he was the highest paid of all Washington correspondents, at $10,000 per year, an enormous salary for the time.[22]

What did Bennett intend Nordhoff to do in Washington? "The Special Correspondent of a great newspaper possesses for the time being something of the influence of an Ambassador," the publisher was quoted as saying.

> Now, according to Machiavelli, an Ambassador should endeavor to make himself *persona grata* with those to whom he is accredited, if only thereby to gain the best opportunities

---

20. CN to Samuel Bowles, 1/16/1876, Bowles Papers, Yale. Nordhoff was, at this time, still in good enough favor with Henry Adams and other reformers who were trying to buy the *Evening Post* that they considered him a likely editor: "Please also make some enquiry about Nordhoff. Is he again in Washington on the Herald? ... If [Horace] White refuses and our negotiation continues for the Post, we may settle on Nordhoff if he will come. I know no one else so good." Henry Adams to Henry Cabot Lodge, February 27, 1876, in Samuels et al., eds., *Letters of Henry Adams* (Cambridge: Belknap Press, 1982), vol. 2, p. 256.

21. CN to Whitelaw Reid, April 14, 1875. Reid Papers, LC.

22. See Charles Nordhoff, *Reminiscences of Some Editors I Have Known* (San Diego: 1900), 11–32; Fred A. Emery, "Washington Newspaper Correspondents," *Records of the Columbia Historical Society* 35–36 (1935), 278: "Charles Nordhoff was a famous head of the New York Herald Bureau." The salary of $10,000 is mentioned as the highest salary paid to a Washington correspondent in T.C. Crawford, "The Special Correspondents at Washington," *The Cosmopolitan* 12 (January 1892), 356. Nordhoff's salary is reported in "News Gathering at Washington," *The Journalist* (December 22, 1888).

for obtaining every possible information and to be able to
report events in a broad impartial spirit.[23]

This was precisely what Nordhoff proceeded to do. His memory of forty
years' later was that Bennett, recognizing the growing importance of the
national capital, emphasized to Nordhoff his idea of Nordhoff's new role: Aside
from his reporters, Bennett had said, he wanted "a man of acknowledged ability
and experience." Such a journalist of "brains and character" would "gain a great
deal for the paper with which he is connected, by the intimate knowledge of
public affairs he will get in Washington." Bennett recognized Nordhoff's larger
ambitions and, as Nordhoff recalled the conversation, continued to predict
that "'you, sitting in your office and seeing public men on equal terms and at
your leisure there or in society, will always know much more of what is going
on, of *real* importance than all the reporters.'" Added Nordhoff, "In this he
was right."[24]

As a "Special Correspondent" in Washington, Nordhoff was a great
deal more than a reporter. In 1900, seventy years old and long since
retired, he spoke of his career with pride. He had learned, he said, that a
correspondent who knew "intimately and on equal terms half a dozen men
on each side" and had gained their trust "that he will not publish or talk to
others about what they say to him in confidence," then he would "always be
prepared beforehand for coming events."[25] The "Special Correspondent"
was a creature now extinct, although modern-day investigative reporters and
editorial-page columnists perform many of the same functions. A "Special"
was the correspondent who, privy to behind-the-scenes maneuvering,
was able to furnish his newspaper with cogent political analyses and
prognostications.

His effectiveness largely depended, as Nordhoff knew, upon the degree
to which powerful politicians could trust him to be discreet. His position was
not unique. As a contemporary longtime Washington correspondent, Henry
Van Ness Boynton, remembered, accusations of the press's "sensationalism"
were misplaced, for what reporters knew "in regard to the inside of national
affairs and the doings of public men, and do not print, would constitute the
real sensations." Boynton continued,

---

[23]   James Gordon Bennett, Jr., quoted in Lucy Maynard Salmon, *The Newspaper and the
       Historian* (NY: Oxford, 1923), 182.

[24]   CN, *Reminiscences*, 13.

[25]   CN, *Reminiscences*, 13.

> If any half dozen of the older correspondents in Washington
> should agree to sit down and send to the country ... their
> knowledge of such [political] affairs..., their narratives, which
> should not vary from the truth in any particular, or be in any
> sense exaggerated, would come as near pulling down the very
> pillars of the temple as anything that could be put in print.[26]

Nordhoff's newspaper columns were one product of his work in Washington, but only one, and it seems likely he did not consider them the most important product. They were a way of reaching the masses, true; and he clung to his belief in the efficacy of journalism as an educative force: a tool of persuasion to make the great clunky engine of democracy move forward. But his dispatches were also read by Washington insiders; and as such, he used them to drop hints, to cajole and persuade, and if necessary, to embarrass legislators when he saw them engaging in what he considered breaches of the public trust. And his position gave him access to all the prime movers and shakers in the capital, a situation that he exploited to the hilt.

And there was nothing unethical in this, by the standards then current. Before the McKinley administration in the 1890s, there were no institutionalized means of passing information from the government to the press. Although twentieth-century journalistic ethics frown upon close relationships between journalists and politicians (with, it might be added, little effect), in post–Civil War America it was assumed, even required, that Washington correspondents form intimate connections with members of Congress and the executive branch. Reporters would simply make the circuit of the Capitol, government offices, and the Executive Mansion, conversing with officials and cementing the symbiotic relationship between press and politicians that the mutual need for sources and favorable publicity produced. A man fortunate enough to have an office, like Nordhoff, often received visits from Congressmen, who had no workplace other than their desks on the House floor.[27]

To wield influence behind the scenes was a mark of a journalist's wisdom, not of duplicity. *Harper's Weekly*, in its laudatory obituary of Nordhoff, proudly

---

[26] Henry Van Ness Boynton, "The Press and Public Men," *Century Magazine* 43 (October 1891): 853–862.

[27] Donald A. Ritchie, in *Press Gallery: Congress and the Washington Correspondents* (Cambridge: Harvard University Press, 1991), argues that this "symbiotic" relationship, almost inevitable due to the interdependence of politicians and the press, is far more characteristic of press-government relations than an adversarial one. Ritchie documents a long history of precisely these kinds of relationships and discusses Gilded Age Washington journalism in some depth and with great cogency.

mentioned him as "not only one of the few correspondents in whom public men confided, but one of still fewer whom they consulted."[28] In contrast to the old disrepute in which antebellum reporters had been held, a Special Correspondent, as one journalist wrote, needed "much candor and sweetness so that [officials] will admit him everywhere and talk to him unrestrainedly." These correspondents "must be and are welcome at the houses, clubs, and business places of the men who lead in public affairs."[29] As a well-informed, influential, and intelligent man, Nordhoff's easy friendships with Congressmen and other high-level officials are not surprising. Aside from his personal qualities, however, Nordhoff was in the right place at the right time. The 1870s were auspicious years for any knowing outsider in the national capital, as institutional inadequacies were compensated for on an ad hoc basis. Unlike the modern-day Congress, the federal legislature in the 1870s was the home of amateurs, overwhelmed with newly increased demands on the federal government without any institutional support. As an indication of the expanded scope of governance, for example, the number of federal employees increased by nearly 40 percent between 1861 and 1871 and over 170 percent between 1861 and 1881. The average number of bills introduced in Congress in one year during the 1860s was 1,847; this increased to 6,171 per year in the 1870s, and to well over 12,000 each year in the 1880s. As Margaret Thompson and David J. Rothman have noted, governmental structure was woefully anachronistic, characterized by noncareerist Representatives: men who, new to Washington, hadn't the foggiest notion of federal parliamentary procedure, the workings of the nascent federal bureaucracy, or their colleagues' interests and capacities. Except for the chairs of committees, no Congressman had an office in which to work or any staff to assist him. And since few members stayed on past one or two terms, institutional memory was dim: every Congress before 1900 was made up of over 70 percent freshmen, who busily reinvented the wheel every two years.[30]

To this inexperience and the lack of institutional support of Gilded Age Congresses, Thompson attributes the enormous postwar rise in lobbying. Lobbyists, she notes, at least provided some information—however skewed to favor their clients—which might assist an overworked Congressman in making legislative decisions and which might help in winnowing out claims to be

[28]   H.L.N., "Charles Nordhoff," *Harper's Weekly*, 7/27/1901.

[29]   Julian Ralph, "The Newspaper Correspondent," *Scribner's Magazine* 14 (August 1893), 150–156.

[30]   Margaret Susan Thompson, *The "Spider Web:" Congress and Lobbying in the Age of Grant* (Ithaca: Cornell University Press, 1985): 19, 46, 48, 87, and passim; David J. Rothman, *Politics and Power: The United States Senate, 1869-1901* (Cambridge: Harvard University Press, 1966).

acted upon from those to be ignored. Journalists played their part as well. Well-informed, highly politicized, and well-connected to home constituencies, good Washington correspondents almost always lasted longer in the nation's capital than did the men on whom they were reporting. A savvy journalist could provide invaluable instruction to a freshman Congressman on procedures, personalities, and where certain political bodies were buried. Additionally, as Washington correspondents sought out officials and cultivated them as sources, those officials were equally anxious to gain the ear of journalists who could help them with publicity and, through the judicious use of leaks and innuendo, with a political weapon of no small importance.[31]

In this curiously laggard world of official Washington, tackling postwar problems with prewar institutions, Nordhoff was in his element. He was better known than most Congressmen, respected for his logical mind and wide-ranging knowledge, and able to discuss burning public issues with the very men who might decide national policy. His tenure lasted sixteen years: compared to most nineteenth-century Congressmen, by the end of his career, Nordhoff was a Washington institution in and of himself.

In his 1866 article on the New York *Herald*, James Parton expressed the hope that nonpartisan reporting would be the standard of the new journalism, and he cited coverage of the postwar South as an example of the unsatisfactory character of the political press. One had to read several newspapers, of different political persuasions, to get a balanced picture of conditions there. "This is pitiful," he declared. "This is utterly beneath the journalism of 1866," and the newspaper of the future would "soar far above such needless limitations as these, and present the truth in *all* its aspects, regardless of its effects upon theories, parties, factions, and Presidential campaigns."[32]

James Gordon Bennett, Jr., who gained control of the *Herald* the year that Parton's critique was published, might have tried to follow Parton's prescription, for shortly after hiring Nordhoff, he asked him to tour the South and send reports to the *Herald* "on the actual condition of affairs in those states," as Nordhoff recalled, stipulating that "'I want only the truth, without fear, favor or prejudice.'"[33] The New York *Herald* had, from its beginnings in 1835, declared itself to be an independent newspaper, unlike most of its contemporaries;

[31.] Donald Ritchie, *Press Gallery: Congress and the Washington Correspondents* (Cambridge: Harvard University Press, 1991), passim. See especially the chapter on Uriah Hunt Painter for an example of a journalist serving as a paid lobbyist and paying for it in public condemnation and the chapter on Henry Van Ness Boynton, who exercised significant influence on legislators, apparently out of motives of public service.

[32.] James Parton, "The New York Herald," 412.

[33.] CN, *Reminiscences*, 15.

others were subsidized by political parties, but the *Herald* was beholden to none for financial support or ideological guidance. It had through the years, however, an emphatically Democratic air to it, appealing as it did to a mass audience composed for the most part of immigrants and the working class.

Nordhoff was comfortable enough with such an affiliation. Unlike the Liberal Republicans, who praised political independence in principle while almost invariably rejecting the Democracy and favoring Republicans, Nordhoff wavered in his party allegiances. He was a man dedicated to working within the party system, and yet both parties left him slightly queasy, the Republicans for their elitist tendencies and blatant federal corruption, the Democrats for their race-baiting, copperhead legacy, and blatant municipal corruption. Often he was reduced to choosing the lesser of two evils, for he regarded a vote for a third-party candidate as a vote thrown away.

On the issue of Reconstruction, Nordhoff was increasingly at odds with the more radical faction of the Republican Party. Ten years had passed since the end of the War, and he was tired: tired of reports of violence within the South and animosity between the sections, tired of the Republicans' assumption of greater national power than the federal government had ever before possessed, and tired of thinking about race, believing that with the right to vote, the African-Americans had achieved sufficient parity to pull themselves up by their own effort and will.

During the Congressional session of the winter of 1874–5, Nordhoff's first season in Washington for the *Herald*, the issue of Reconstruction was heatedly debated. Already, as he wrote, he was "in more or less intimate friendly relations with many of [Congress's] leading members, of both parties," and he listened to private as well as public discussions of the "Southern question" with growing impatience. None of the opinions he heard seemed to be based on facts.[34] "Objectivity," as a journalistic concept, had not been fully formulated in 1875; and Nordhoff himself had always stressed the interpretive nature of the journalist's mission. "A fact," he had written early in his career, "is not only a stubborn thing; it is a stupid, dead, inanimate, worthless piece of carrion, which lies there, supine, till some one comes and breathes a soul of meaning into it."[35] But he clearly believed one might rise above partisan shaping of facts: truth transcended perspective, if one were only fair-minded and intelligent enough to find it out. And this, in the case of the South, was what he intended to do.

---

34.   CN, "Preliminary," *The Cotton States in the Spring and Summer of 1875* (Burt Franklin Research and Source Works Series #90, reprint of the 1875 edition; New York: Burt Franklin, n.d.): 9.

35.   CN, "What is Best?" in *Cape Cod and All Along Shore*, 65–66.

Between March and July of 1875, he toured in succession most of the South's hot spots of racial strife. His findings, as he wrote in introduction to a collection of his articles, became "the subject of contentious discussion in the journals of both parties"; and he proudly added that he had failed to please "partisans" of any stripe. "It was probably inevitable that [the reports] should offend those whose preconceived views or whose interests they did not advance," he added philosophically, and with a touch of smugness, "for I sought only for facts, and did not care what side they favored." He expressed surprise to find "opinions and conclusions imputed to me ... which I did not and do not entertain." He was responsible for the selection of facts presented, but he had tried to present a balanced picture, and everywhere he found others using his Southern portrait, in a warped and distorted form, to serve their own purposes. "I see that my Mississippi letters have started a Republican howl," he wrote to David Ames Wells in June, "& some of the brethren already raise the bloody shirt. It is very disgusting, but I must tell the truth."[36]

In the states he had visited, he stated, there was no hostility toward the North or any desire to reenslave the African-Americans or hope of "in any way curtailing the rights of the blacks as citizens."[37] What of reports of violence between the races? Gross exaggerations, according to Nordhoff. The few disturbances there were in Mississippi, for example, resulted from the heightened tensions of an election in which Democrats were "trying to rid themselves of the justly hateful rule of a corrupt faction" and from the failure of the Republican Governor to use "the usual means of preserving the peace."[38]

What of the ascendancy of the old Confederate elite? Well, it was only natural that "the Southern man who fought and believed in" secession should hold to his principles, and continue to follow the admired generals who had led him during the war. And since "it is a fact that the men of brains, of intelligence, ... did, almost to a man, consent to secession, and take an active part in the war against the Union," and since they had as a consequence "paid a heavy penalty for their mistake" in the loss of their riches, it was unfair of the North "to demand that they shall be reviled and put down by their own people." Loyalty and deference to leadership were apparently higher values for Nordhoff than forced renunciations of a lost cause.[39]

It was, in this view, not racial hatred but Republican corruption that caused "what has been called the 'color-line' in politics" for property-owning, taxpaying whites naturally preferred the Democrats while propertyless, illiterate blacks

---

36.   CN, *Cotton States*, 9; CN to David Ames Wells, June 10th, [1875], Wells Papers, LC.

37.   CN, *Cotton States*, 10.

38.   CN, *Cotton States*, 10.

39.   CN, *Cotton States*, 11.

"easily misled by appeals to their fears" were strong Republicans. In short, Reconstruction had been necessary immediately after the war, but it had outlived its usefulness. The Radical Republicans were like physicians who provided a remedy to a critically ill patient and then insisted on continuing the treatment after the patient's recovery.[40]

More perceptive on issues of class than those of race, Nordhoff recognized the great disparity between rich and poor among the Southern whites. The poor whites, "a kind of people unknown among [Northerners]," were "in a dread of having social equality with the negro imposed upon them."[41] Didn't this suggest a long-term problem, not to be rectified in a few short years? No. Violence by poor whites against blacks was, he judged, instigated by demagogues, and strict enforcement of the law would put an end to it. But such "extermination" of a "criminal class" was the duty of State, not Federal, government.[42]

The reaction to Nordhoff's Southern letters was swift and bitter. Most vocal in opposition was the *National Republican*, a Washington, D.C., organ of the Republican Party. It first accused the *Herald* of a vindictive smear campaign against President Grant and his programs, for Bennett had launched an editorial campaign against a third presidential term for Grant. With this baseline of animosity, Nordhoff became the object of attack. The criticisms of the *National Republican* included ad hominem diatribes and pointed disparagement—not without justice—of Nordhoff's journalistic skill in separating lies from truth about the South.

In June of 1875, when the last of his letters on the South was appearing, Nordhoff was described in the *National Republican* as "known to fame as an unprincipled writer of sensational trash." Rebuffed by Grant, the *National Republican* reported, he had "sunk to his proper level," as a purveyor of sensationalism for the "Ishmaelite Detective Press."[43] Calling Nordhoff a "sycophant," the *National Republican* printed a letter from one H. C. Myers, a Southern Republican official who disputed Nordhoff's characterization of him as a corrupt and "bad man." He had shown Nordhoff several documents, Myers wrote, including both a White League newspaper containing allegations of corruption and the findings of a commission including George F. Hoar (a Radical Republican from Massachusetts and an advocate of an activist federal government) that he was innocent of any "malfeasance." Myers had also shown Nordhoff the auditor's report on the school system of which he was superintendent, which pronounced the books in order. "There was not

40. CN, *Cotton States*, 16.
41. CN, *Cotton States*, 18.
42. CN, *Cotton States*,. 17–18.
43. "The New York Herald and President Grant," *Daily National Republican*, June 4, 1875.

the slightest evidence, primary or circumstantial, to support the charge of ...
malfeasance in office" leveled at him by Nordhoff, Myers maintained.[44] It
isn't clear what additional evidence, if any, Nordhoff examined to reach his
conclusion; if Myers was correct, he was guilty of willful distortions.

Furthermore, when he included a statement from a Democrat on the need
for a Democratic federal administration to "disorganize the colored vote,"
which he seems to have interpreted (with a breathtaking naivete or lack of
candor) as a wish for a nonracialized political climate, Nordhoff was obscuring
some grave implications, the *National Republican* declared, should a Democratic
administration come to power. This intention to "disorganize" the "colored
vote" meant simply that the African-Americans were to be disfranchised. "The
laws of reconstruction are to be trampled underfoot," it declared, "and the
colored man will have no more rights hereafter that the white man is bound to
respect than he had when held in the bonds of slavery."[45]

The newspaper admitted that Nordhoff had included facts damaging
to the Democrats' case as well, but claimed that he and Democratic papers
failed to make much of them or indeed to notice them at all.[46] Nuance and
emphasis were skewed, if not the facts, in Nordhoff's work. But the *National
Republican* could not confine itself to criticizing the accuracy of Nordhoff's
Southern reports. It attacked his reputation. There were those, it commented,
who thought Nordhoff was "a Republican, a gentleman," the former editor of
the eminently respectable New York *Evening Post*. "This is a mistake," it declared.
"It is true that he at one time wrote for the *Post*; but it was as any Hessian would
have done the same thing." How to explain this seeming lack of integrity? The
National Republican resorted to ethnic slurs in its attempt to discredit Nordhoff's
credibility, which, as this piece suggests, was stubbornly persistent among many
otherwise respectable Republicans. Nordhoff was no Republican "and could
not be one if he tried, because, as his name indicates, he is a Dutch Jew" who
had come to America "simply because he knew that he might be called upon
to do the kind of work he is now engaged in, and that no respectable journalist
of native or foreign birth would descend to compete with him."[47]

Having come to America at the age of five, Nordhoff obviously had not
had such dubious motives in immigrating. More importantly, the ugliness of
the anti-Semitism at last provoked Nordhoff's response. In a letter sent to the
Republican national committee and reprinted in the New York *Tribune* and other
papers around the country, he began with tightly controlled anger. "I have been

---

44. "Nordhoff's Pilgrimage," *National Republican*, June 9, 1875, 2.

45. "Disorganize the Colored Vote," *National Republican*, June 14, 1875, 2.

46. [Untitled Editorial], *Daily National Republican*, 6/23/75, 2.

47. [Untitled Editorial], *Daily National Republican*, June 16, 1875.

so unfortunate as to displease the central and chief organ of the Republican party," he wrote to the chairman of that party, and that newspaper had told its readers that he was not to be believed—"not because I have misstated facts, or am an incapable or inaccurate observer—but on the ground that I am a 'Dutch Jew,' 'Dutch' standing here, of course, for German."[48] The *National Republican* was evading the real issues in its opprobrium:

> Now, if I were, in the Organ's elegant phrase, a "Dutch Jew,"
> I don't see what that has to do with the creditability of my
> statements. I am, in fact, a German, and am proud of my
> descent from a people who have been the faithful supporters
> of liberty on two continents. I am not a Jew, but if I were, I
> should not be ashamed of it; for the Jews in this country are
> an intelligent, industrious and peaceable body of citizens.

The attack was not simply factually incorrect, evasive, and bigoted. It was stupid, impolitic, and, for the Republican Party, inexpedient. "Speaking in the name of the Republican Administration, whose mouthpiece it is," Nordhoff wrote, "it has the folly to assert that if a man is a Jew by religion, he is thereby unworthy of confidence." Didn't the Republican Party realize that this was an insult to an important constituency? "You ought to muzzle your dog the *National Republican*," Nordhoff went on; "...he is snapping at the heels of your friends." Was it not "an insane folly" to so "fling a gratuitous insult in the face of several hundred thousand German and Jewish voters," to drive them away and provide fodder for the Democrats in their own campaign? If the Republican Party did not dispose of the *National Republican*, Nordhoff concluded, "you ought to change its name. You might call it the *National Idiot*. I make you the suggestion as a sincere and earnest Republican."[49]

Nordhoff recognized some forms of bigotry when he saw them, and he had not lost the ability to write a scorching attack upon it. The *National Republican*, for its part, clearly saw Nordhoff's writings as a serious threat. Although it had some cogent criticism of his work, in its descent to ethnic slurs, it diminished its own credibility.

---

[48] See the copy of the letter in the Gordon L. Ford Papers, with a note that Reid was to publish it. The letter is reprinted in "A Political Letter of 1875," *Western States Jewish History* 19 (April 1983), 231–2, which notes that it was reprinted in the Santa Barbara *Daily Press* on June 28, 1875. The *Daily Press*, like most small newspapers of its time, openly "clipped" items from the bigger national papers, and its use of the letter suggests that other newspapers might have done the same.

[49] "A Political Letter," 232.

Nordhoff was badly mistaken on the Southern issue. How could he have been so wrong? The verdict of history, imperfect though it may be, is that the Southern Democrats consistently engaged in terrorism, violence, and dishonest manipulation of laws to intimidate and disenfranchise the African-Americans. As soon as federal involvement in the South ended, Jim Crow laws established segregation as a way of life in the South for the first time; "grandfather clauses" and unfairly administered literacy tests kept blacks away from the polls while their (mostly uneducated) white brethren solidly voted into office conservative and segregationist Democrats.[50]

First, although Nordhoff cited many interviews with African-Americans and quoted them expressing dissatisfaction with Republican rule, there are indications that he interviewed these people in the presence of whites, whom he probably asked to introduce him to some "representative" freedmen. Nordhoff had been keenly sensitive, in his first extended Southern explorations in the Sea Islands of 1863, to the impact of power relationships upon an individual's ability to be candid on sensitive subjects. In his legalistic mind, the fact that the African-Americans had gained the vote removed them from the category of the oppressed, and he therefore thought there was less need for caution. But his willingness to accept at face value statements by blacks made in the presence of whites betrays an almost willful blindness to existing conditions.

Second, Nordhoff was democratic in his conscious ideology, but elitist in his practical inclinations. When it came to matters of polity, the educated, the propertied, and the well-established enjoyed his esteem and trust over the poor and uneducated. His own life, in which hard work and intelligence had resulted in high position and financial security, led him to suspect (though he would have denied it if directly questioned) that the poor and powerless simply did not have the capacity to rise or the concomitant capacity to govern. His lifelong insistence upon the centrality of good leadership to democratic government was one manifestation of elitist tendencies; his willingness to believe well-placed Southern whites was another. "Demagoguery," the evil side of the good leadership coin, seemed to him an enormous danger and the chief cause of black Southerners' discontent. When Southern Democrats assured

---

50. See Leon F. Litwack, *Been in the Storm So Long: The Aftermath of Slavery* (New York: 1979); Eric Foner, *Reconstruction*; Eric Foner, *Nothing But Freedom: Emancipation and its Legacy* (Baton Rouge: LSU Press, 1983); Morton Keller, *Affairs of State: Public Life in Late Nineteenth-Century America* (Cambridge: Harvard University Press, 1977); William Gillette, *Retreat from Reconstruction, 1869-1879* (Baton Rouge: Louisiana State University Press, 1979); C. Vann Woodward, *The Strange Career of Jim Crow*; Edward L. Ayers, *Vengeance and Justice: Crime and Punishment in the Nineteenth-Century American South* (New York: 1984).

northerners that they would, if only left to themselves, take care that the rights of the former slaves would be respected and upheld, Nordhoff, and many public officials, believed them.

Third, Nordhoff believed in the basic goodness of American values and refused to believe that men born and bred in America—even if it were antebellum Southern America—would continue to act in ways that seemed to him irrational and wrong. "We of the North do not always remember," he wrote somberly, that the Southerners were "Americans, like ourselves, having, by nature or long training a love of order and permanence" and therefore certain to rebuild their society in accordance with the new order.[51] Nordhoff seems to have expected a passivity from Southerners that ill accorded with his vision of their vigorous "reconstitution" of society. The partisan *National Republican* noted that Nordhoff seemed "unable to find a respectable colored Republican in that section" and asked, "Is it possible that the blacks are all scoundrels or demagogues?"[52] In this aspect of Nordhoff's work, one detects racism, more subtle than that of many of his contemporaries, but racism nonetheless. It undeniably colored much of his judgment and in the end distorted his vision.[53]

On a more personal level, Nordhoff, who could be courageous and outspoken in defense of what he believed to be right, was also capable of bending himself (however unconsciously) into agreement with the powerful. He was, by his midforties, the ultimate insider, as descriptions of his job as "Special Correspondent" attest: privy to the quiet maneuverings of those who knew how to work the system, confidant of Congressmen and Cabinet ministers, scold to Presidents. But he was an insider with the mentality of an outsider, possessed of a peculiar double perspective. His memory of maltreatment as a sailor was a double-edged sword. At times, it might make him an astute cultural critic—as he continued to be for many years to come—but it also could so disorient him in the world of the securely comfortable that he accepted the conventional wisdom with little scrutiny. The pull of one side toward appeasement, longing for acceptance, and the memory of injustice pulling him in an opposite direction often exhausted his energy and made him weary of his fellow human beings.

Though he firmly declared his accounts to be purely factual, Nordhoff would not deny that he held opinions. "But I do not wish to be misunderstood," he insisted; and in prefacing the collection of his letters, as if switching from the news columns to the editorial page, he tried to explain that point of view, which he believed he had so successfully concealed in the reports themselves. "It is proper to say that I am a Republican," he stated,

---

51.   CN, *Cotton States*, 16.

52.   [Editorial, untitled], *Daily National Republican*, June 23, 1875, 2.

53.   CN, *Cotton States*, 18.

and have never voted any other Federal ticket than the Republican; I have been opposed to slavery as long as I have had an opinion on any subject except sugar-candy and tops; and I am a thorough believer in the capacity of the people to rule themselves, even if they are very ignorant, better than any body else can rule them.[54]

All of this was absolutely true, if disingenuous. In 1872, Nordhoff had not voted for the Republican candidate for president; he had not voted for anyone. His antislavery credentials were long-standing ones; that he felt compelled to defend them is telling testimony to the generally understood meaning of his letters. And his belief in democracy was real enough.

But the last sentence of this declaration exemplified the way Nordhoff's statements might easily be claimed by both sides. In this carefully phrased statement, in the United States of 1875, which "ignorant" people did he mean? The white Southerners desiring to end federal intervention? The freed slaves, so newly enfranchised? He meant, in fact, both. That he would not see the contradiction involved—the issue of conflict between unmatched powers that might overwhelm his abstract democracy—was all too typical of Northerners who, for various reasons, simply did not want to see.

In 1875, in his new career in the national capital, Nordhoff was still exhilarated by the Washington scene. "I've been very busy," he wrote to an old Brooklyn friend. "...I don't get to bed before 12, and Lida stays up for me," he added, glad that the Congressional session would soon be over, "though I can't say it is entirely disagreeable."[55] By early 1876, at the end of observing his second session of Congress at close hand, Nordhoff no longer found his job such a joy. "I hope you enjoyed your New Years," he glumly wrote to a friend. "I have had no rest & somewhat dread the meeting of congress."[56] And but a few weeks later, "These politics are horribly dead barren. I'm tired of my life here."[57] Clearly, the bloom was off the rose.

He had, however, by that time made himself persona grata (as Bennett had put it) with many of the top politicians in Washington. His private letters are sprinkled with references to conversations with the Attorney General, the Secretary of State, and other Cabinet officers as well as the Secretary of the Smithsonian and innumerable Senators and Congressmen. The information he gleaned he shared with selected friends. "I tell you this in strict confidence,"

---

54. CN, *Cotton States*, 10.
55. CN to Gordon L. Ford, January 13, 1875. Ford Papers, NYPL.
56. CN to Gordon L. Ford, January 3, 1876. Ford Papers, NYPL.
57. CN to David Ames Wells, April 24, 1876. Wells Papers, LC.

he cautioned in one letter to Hayes, in which he repeated one official's opinion that Grant favored Hayes as a successor, "--as from me, I mean, for I shd lose [the Attorney General's] confidence if he knew I blabbed."[58]

The closer he got to national politics, the less Nordhoff liked it, for both parties seemed to him gravely unfit to govern. "If the Democrats had a little more sense, I would not care, for reform would then come through them, & I would urge everybody to support them," Nordhoff wrote to Carl Schurz; but the more he saw of them, the less he liked the idea of their holding power. "I would rather have them than Grant, or than *Grantism*, for the next four years," he admitted, "but the alternative is not pleasant."[59] Politics had to improve and would; it required only public exposure through the press and the parties in opposition "attack[ing] & expos[ing]" each other.[60] Schurz apparently had little patience with Nordhoff's urgings that he help to purge the Republican Party. "Schurz is down on me," he wrote to a staunch Republican friend, and he likened himself to "a private soldier, who fortunately has a sort of independence in out post duty, but no influence with the commander in chief; so that almost any body may take a kick at me, & some do." He tried to be philosophical. Perhaps, as a lone journalist, he could serve the public better than the politicians. At the very least, "I do my duty in my own sphere, & say what I think when I say anything," he concluded. "And that's all that is absolutely necessary."[61]

By the summer of 1876, the Republican Party was so divided that Rutherford B. Hayes was nominated as its Presidential candidate on the negative attribute that he was the least likely of any candidate to give offense.[62] Nordhoff knew Hayes as a fellow Ohioan, a Republican who had served valiantly in the Civil War, and the husband of one of Lida's old schoolmates. From the time that Nordhoff was at the *Evening Post*, they exchanged frank letters on political

58. CN to Rutherford B. Hayes, 1/11/1876, Hayes Papers, Hayes Library, Fremont, Ohio. For other examples, see letters dating from Nordhoff from 1875 on in the Gordon L. Ford Papers, Samuel Bowles Papers, Edward Atkinson Papers, David Ames Wells Papers, Whitelaw Reid Papers, and Samuel Langley Papers.

59. CN to Carl Schurz, 1/26/76, Schurz Papers, LC.

60. CN to Carl Schurz, March 8, 1876, Schurz Papers, LC.

61. CN to Mrs. John Davis, May 9, 1876, Rutherford B. Hayes Library.

62. Ari Hoogenboom, *The Presidency of Rutherford B. Hayes* (Lawrence: University of Kansas Press, 1988), 14–16. See also Kenneth E. Davison, *The Presidency of Rutherford B. Hayes* [the title must have a nice ring to it] (Westport, CT: Greenwood Press, 1972), chapter 2; and the most detailed analysis of the entire election of 1876 and its aftermath, Keith Ian Polakoff, *The Politics of Inertia: The Election of 1876 and the End of Reconstruction* (Baton Rouge: Louisiana State University Press, 1973), passim.

issues.[63] Hayes was, by all accounts, a kindly and genial man, and like Nordhoff, he had a well-developed sense of humor. Their letters, following Hayes's election as Governor of Ohio in 1869, show their friendship to have been a warm one.[64]

Hayes's victory in Ohio was given ample publicity in Republican journals across the nation, including a front-page article in the newspaper-like *Harper's Weekly*. "I am sincerely glad you gained the day," Nordhoff wrote Hayes, but unable to sustain the serious tone, he continued:

> & I judge by the picture of you, wh. appears in *Harper's Weekly*, ... that you had a hard squeak for it; & that you were, on the morning before Election day—when I suppose this was taken—very badly demoralized. You look, in this picture ... about sick enough to throw up your Commission, and almost any thing else you had about you. Pray tell Mrs. Hayes that when she lets you be taken, she ought to make you look a little pleasanter—or get ... somebody to sit for you. This picture of you is a libel on the State of Ohio; if you were really quite so ugly as that I think I shd electioneer agst you, on principle.[65]

Hayes shot back a quick retort. "I like the picture," he wrote. "It got me your letter. ...Lucy thinks she has seen worse looking pictures, but she can't remember where or when, and I'm glad she can't."[66] Nordhoff replied shortly thereafter. "I told Joe Harper on Friday that when you got done with yr. annual message you meant to sue them for slander. He thought I was joking—but I think you have a fair case against them." Knowing his friend to be more of a Party loyalist than he himself was, while more and more corruption within the Grant Administration was coming to light, Nordhoff continued his gibes. A pious elderly woman, a friend of the Hayeses and the Nordhoffs, had lost her pocketbook. "I hear she was with you in Columbus," he noted significantly. "Is it possible the Republican Party in Ohio has become so corrupt as to--but there, I'll say no more ab[ou]t it."[67]

Nordhoff's sense of humor could be so cutting that it sometimes hurt his friends, which always surprised him. "Be sure that I did not mean to hurt, but only to tease you," he once wrote to David Wells, after Wells had reacted badly

---

63.   This controversy is treated above, in chapter 3.

64.   See Harry Barnard, *Rutherford B. Hayes and His America* (NY: Bobbs-Merrill, 1954), 239–241.

65.   CN to Rutherford B. Hayes, Oct. 29, 1869. Hayes Library, Fremont, Ohio.

66.   R. B. Hayes to CN, 2 November 1869. Hayes Library, Fremont, Ohio.

67.   CN to Rutherford B. Hayes, 11/20/69, Hayes Library, Fremont, Ohio.

to one of Nordhoff's sardonic letters; "...you shock me when you say I was 'caustic.' Forgive me."[68] But these witticisms amused Hayes, and the Hayeses and Nordhoffs continued on cordial social terms. Nordhoff never failed to visit Hayes when on one of his frequent trips to Cincinnati.

The election of 1875, when Hayes ran once more in the Ohio gubernatorial race, earned the entire Nordhoff family's wholehearted support for their old friend. "Hurrah for Ohio! I always thought well of the state," Lida wrote in congratulations. They had all been worrying about the outcome, she added, and "even my little girls clapped their hands in glee, when the victory was announced." While she wrote, she added, "my irrepressible Charles Nordhoff is walking up and down the room in a state of excitement ..., and engaged in delivering political lectures to this audience of one."[69]

Despite their long-standing alliance, Nordhoff greeted his friend's nomination for the presidency in 1876 cautiously. He wrote to Hayes soon after the convention, warning him that he couldn't predict the *Herald*'s editorial stand, "and I have not much influence in the office."[70] However, when Hayes asked him for suggestions as to what to include in his letter of acceptance (virtually the only campaigning a presidential candidate could respectably do at that time), Nordhoff wrote back a lengthy missive, phrasing several predictable positions in the unctuous manner of a true politician. On the South, he advocated that Hayes pull out the federal troops and restore it to local control. He also advocated a return to hard currency and free trade, economy and retrenchment in government, and (surprisingly for Nordhoff) a strong statement on the necessity of Civil Service Reform. This was not simply Nordhoff mouthing what he held to be Hayes's beliefs: he seems to have become a firm advocate of Civil Service reform himself after living in Washington and seeing the havoc wrought by the descending throngs of office seekers every two years.

He reminded Hayes that he had to win over at least part of the white South. "The darkies you'll have any how," he explained with an uncharacteristically crude slur, "the white Whigs are what you want to capture." He labored considerably over the letter and added a demurral. "I'll bet you will say what a

68. CN to David Ames Wells, January 15 [no year]; Wells Papers, LC. This probably refers to Nordhoff's merciless tweaking of his reformist friends over the outcome of the 1872 Liberal Republican convention, which he did, indeed, find "absurd."

69. Lida Nordhoff to Rutherford B. Hayes, appended to CN to Hayes, 10/13/1875, Hayes Library, Fremont, Ohio.

70. Nordhoff continued, "But Mr. Bennett is personally kind to me; & if you shd chance to want to see me, I fancy he would let me come to you at any time almost." CN to Rutherford B. Hayes, June 22, 1876, Hayes Papers, RBH Library.

cheeky fellow this Charles Nordhoff is," he concluded, "& you will never know that I sat here perspiring at every pore, and with a handkerchief about my neck to save my collar," to write the letter. "Stick it in the wastebasket." He also invited Hayes to come talk with him the next time he was in Washington. Hayes might even stay with the Nordhoffs, he wrote following the furor over *Cotton States*, though it might be "imprudent to stay with so notorious a person as myself. It would cause remark."[71]

For all his willingness to offer advice, Nordhoff was far from an ardent Hayes partisan, and he admitted to David Wells that he was "on the political fence." Throughout the campaign, he vacillated. He liked and trusted Hayes, but he was "staggered" by the activities of the Republican Party and would not commit himself. Tilden he cared little for, but he believed that Hayes could do nothing to rid the Republican Party of its "scoundrels" singlehandedly.[72] Tilden's relatively weak campaign letter, however, swung Nordhoff back to Hayes. Tilden lacked "grip." There was, in fact, little to choose between the two candidates: a reformist Democratic governor or a reformist Republican governor. Nordhoff was weary of politics. "I am worn down with this long session," he closed an August letter, "& need a rest."[73]

But the "bloody shirt" campaigning of the Republicans and the continued use of federal force in the South, repelled Nordhoff from supporting his old friend. By the last day of September, his dispatch in the *Herald* warned of the dangers of the continued governance of a corrupt Republican Party, even under Hayes's presidency. "I could not persuade myself to consult you abt. the writing before-hand," Nordhoff wrote to Hayes. "I don't know whether you will be pleased, or displeased. If the latter, you can easily cause some one to declare me an ignorant meddler, & I shall make no reply." He emphasized, once again, that he could not control the *Herald*'s editorials, which strongly supported Tilden.[74]

[71.] CN to Rutherford B. Hayes, 7/3/1876. Hayes Papers, RBH Library.

[72.] CN to David Ames Wells, July 13, 1876, Wells Papers, LC.

[73.] CN to David Ames Wells, August 7, 1876, Wells Papers, LC. See also Nordhoff's letter to one of his oldest friends: "I send you by this mail a couple of caricatures of Lincoln, which I found in an old bookstore here. It seems to me like a look into the very far past, to see the great Lincoln treated like a common mortal. ...[T]he extreme & prostrating heats here & the long continued session have abt. worn me out, & left me with very little energy. ...Tilden's letter was a great disappointment to me. Wells & Hewitt had boasted to me that it would be a bold & statesmanlike document; it seems to me timid & shuffling. I shall go Hayes." CN to Gordon L. Ford, August 9, 1876. Ford Papers, NYPL.

[74.] CN to Rutherford B. Hayes, 9/30/1876, Hayes Library.

The defection of liberals such as Nordhoff drew sardonic comment from Hayes's advisors. Such sunny views of the Southern situation, should the federal troops be withdrawn, appalled radicals who saw persistent and grave dangers in the region. "There are some cultured gentlemen of great worth, of noble theories and less practical wisdom. Some writing for you, some against you....," wrote one to Hayes. "But Stalls & Godwin and Nordhof & Bowles are not so wise as the plain western farmer-soldier who is not willing in a rush of sentimentality to put the keeping of the good cause in rebel hands." The seekers of Southern home rule were dangerously close to advocating what had been the Confederacy's wish in 1860.

> Mr. Nordhoff says that the only thing wrong in the south is Federal interference—this withdrawn all will be sunny—16 years ago Jeff Davis said let us alone. I know that there has been bad government down South--The rebel element sullenly stood aloof --the Negro element was untrained. The wonder is that things were not worse. The former take hold rigorously.... If there is no Federal interference this [disfranchisement of the former slaves] will take place, can we permit this? Can we break our faith to freedmen?[75]

By mid-October, Nordhoff was even more convinced that a Republican administration would mean several more years' unwarranted use of force by the Federal government. "What is most often, and very frequently expressed to me," Nordhoff wrote to Hayes, resorting to the journalist's trick of placing one's own opinions in the mouths of others,

> who am known as friendly to you, is a fear that, granting your good intentions, you may in fact, if elected, be a mere prisoner in the hands of the men who are now carrying things with so high a hand; that the [Radicals] will justly say that they showed their hand clearly and you were elected on a coercive and revolutionary policy, to which the country committed itself.

If Hayes acquiesced in the actions of Southern Republican governments, it might well lose him the election, Nordhoff warned. "People here are very desirous of peace," he wrote, "very reluctant at severe measures, or measures of doubtful constitutionality."[76] That same day, he wrote virtually the same

75.   W. M. Dickson to Hayes, 10/2/1876, Hayes library.

76.   CN to Hayes, 10/15/76, Hayes Papers, RBH Library.

criticism to Samuel Bowles, this time acknowledging the beliefs as his own. The Republicans would stop at nothing to retain power. "The show of force," he wrote, presciently, as it turned out, "...will, I believe, be used on the count of Electoral votes, as a pretext for throwing out those states, if they shd go Democratic." He was not "one who fears vague dangers," he added, "but everything in the present Republican management looks like desperation." If Hayes did not repudiate the federal action in the South, he would vote for Tilden. Furthermore, the country should give Tilden "as large a vote as possible, & as many northern states as possible, so as to prevent any dispute in the Electoral count."[77] It did not turn out so simply.

The contested election rested upon questionable vote counts in Florida, Louisiana, and South Carolina. Nineteen electoral votes were at stake. The Democrats claimed that Republican Returning Boards had fraudulently thrown out entire (Democratic) districts' votes to ensure a Republican victory. The Republicans claimed that the eliminated Democratic votes were the result of fraud and intimidation of African-Americans who would have otherwise voted Republican. If all the disputed votes were awarded to Hayes, he would win by a single electoral vote while Tilden had a comfortable margin requiring that only one of the uncertain electoral votes be declared Democratic.[78]

So virulent were the charges being thrown back and forth, accusing both parties of attempting an illegal seizure of power through fraudulent means that tension mounted and some feared a second civil war might break out. Fanning the flames were the partisan journals, some of which called for violent action to preserve whichever victory suited them best (one journalist even advocating the assassination of Hayes), but the *Herald* struck a conciliatory note in its editorials and in Nordhoff's columns. Calmness and reason should prevail, the *Herald* counseled, for one of the candidates would be defeated, one elected, and the country would have to peaceably live with the result.[79]

Hamilton Fish, Grant's Secretary of State, wrote Nordhoff a letter several days after the election. The two often corresponded, sharing information. The election was on Fish's mind, and he unburdened himself to Nordhoff. All was "doubt & uncertainty" as to the outcome, he wrote, and praised the *Herald*'s editorials as "nice & Patriotic. Leading journals," Fish continued,

> should tend to [dampen] the tendency to excitement & extravagance—Our *future* depends on moderation, &

---

[77]   CN to Samuel Bowles, October 15, 1876, Bowles Papers, Yale.

[78]   See Hoogenboom, chapter 2; Davison, chapter 3; and Polakoff, passim.

[79]   See especially CN's Christmas column, December 25, 1876, calling for Christian forbearance in the face of disappointment.

calmness, & the discouragement of the violence to which
the hopes of the present possession of Government (on both
sides) & unquestionably the minimum...amount of money, at
stake on the result of the election, seem to bring the public
mind.

Fish believed that the danger facing the nation was real. "For God's sake
let us not have another Civil Commotion within our generation," he closed his
letter. "I trust never—but at least not in our day."[80]

"I am very uneasy about the immediate future," Nordhoff replied. He
reaffirmed the *Herald*'s intention to keep a moderate tone, a course, he
said, which had been dictated by Bennett himself. Nordhoff hoped that a
Congressional decision might yet be avoided, and he thought the Administration
might further such a result if it would acknowledge "the bad character of
the Returning Boards, & held them, as the public does, as objects of just
suspicion."[81] Fish mildly demurred. "An honest return," he wrote, "...should
not be questioned because made by bad men."[82]

Another five weeks went by, and there was no sign that any simple recount
might resolve the conflict. Nordhoff lost his conciliatory tone. "There is reason
to believe," he wrote in the *Herald*, "that the republican extremists are making
very desperate efforts to prevent a fair and full count in Florida," exciting "both
suspicion and disgust" among "many republicans here, who hold that their
party cannot afford to gain by trickery or evasion," but that "the honor of the
party and the safety of the country are compromised by such acts."[83]

Nordhoff was, no doubt, among the foremost of the suspicious and
disgusted Republicans to whom he referred. As soon as Congress settled upon
a plan for the Electoral Commission, Nordhoff wrote of the decision with
obvious relief. There had been a feeling that a failure to come up with a plan
would be "equivalent to declarations of civil war," which had "depressed and
alarmed" most knowledgeable people. Though the agreed-upon plan was,
as yet, kept a secret from the public, yet "enough has dropped from various
persons in various ways" that Nordhoff was able to describe the Commission's

---

80.   Hamilton Fish to CN, November 17, 1876. Fish Papers, LC, v. 218, 336.

81.   CN to Hamilton Fish, November 20, 1876. Fish Papers, LC, vol. 117.

82.   Hamilton Fish to CN, November 25, 1876. Fish Papers, LC, vol. 219, pp. 68–9.

83.   CN, "Washington. How the Habeas Corpus Programs Failed in Florida, [etc.]," New
       York *Herald*, January 2, 1877, 8.

makeup with remarkable accuracy. This was the sort of situation in which his friendships gave him a journalistic edge.[84]

He could not believe that the Commission might ignore all evidence that pointed to Republican fraud or even to the need for an investigation of the returns. As he explained in one column, certain Republicans held that whatever decision the Louisiana Returning Board had submitted—however fraudulent it might be openly acknowledged to be—was the decision that would be adhered to as a matter of law. It was outrageous.[85]

But the issues now at stake were ones which at least mattered to Nordhoff: Truth versus falsehood, Democracy versus despotism. He thrived on his outrage; his pleasure in his work resurged. Writing to one friend, he commented on the historic nature of events then transpiring. "We really had a narrow escape from another civil war," he added. "...It has been an extremely exciting & busy winter so far for me; but I get sleep enough, & seem to do well."[86]

The first decision of the Electoral Commission stunned him. The Republicans had insisted "that, no matter what rights or wrongs were shown by investigating, no matter how clearly it was proved that the Tilden electors had a majority," the decision of the Florida Returning Board was final and unquestionable. Worse, that same Returning Board "had openly confessed fraud," not denied by the Republicans, and thus "the State was undoubtedly carried for the Tilden electors, and ...the Returning Board by omissions and changes of votes, all contrary to the law which created and defined its duty, gave the vote to the Hayes electors."[87] It was likely that the other contested states' votes would be decided in the same peremptory manner.

In danger of losing an important contact, not to mention a friend, Nordhoff set about trying to mend his fences with Hayes, making conciliatory overtures to intermediaries.[88] Resigning himself to the likely result of the electoral count, Nordhoff nevertheless resented the arbitrary way in which the matter was being settled. He began making sarcastic comments in letters. Recommending a hotel to a friend, he wrote, "The Arlington is nearest us; & if I were an Electoral

---

84.   "The Grand Committee is to consist of five members of the Senate and five of the House, ...and, besides these, of four members of the Supreme Bench....These four are to select a fifth. To the committee of fifteen members, thus composed, are to be referred the questions relating to the disputed States.... [CN,] "Washington: Light on the Electoral Question at Last. [etc.]," New York *Herald*, January 18, 1877.

85.   [CN,] "Washington. Illegal Action of the Louisiana Returning Board [etc.]," New York *Herald*, January 23, 1877.

86.   CN to Gordon L. Ford, February 2, 1877. Ford Papers, NYPL.

87.   [CN,] "Florida for Hayes," New York *Herald*, February 10, 1877.

88.   CN to Charles Foster, February 15, 1877. Hayes Papers, RBH Library.

Commission, I shd refuse to receive evidence, & decide for the Arlington. Being however an incorruptible Democrat, I must tell you that the Rigg's is the newest."[89] To Samuel Bowles, he wrote of having to deny his youngest daughter a visitor thus: "This is not a paternal government, as you might guess, but I found myself immediately obliged to go behind the returns & throw out the vote by which this little girl had been returned." Despite his irritation, Nordhoff eventually grew philosophical. "Yes," he wrote Bowles, "it is an outrage ... to put in Hayes—but what a piece of history it is, too."[90]

The Democrats tried to delay what seemed Hayes's certain election by filibustering, but the count was finally finished at four in the morning on March 2, two days before the inauguration. Hayes was elected President. Rumors flew about a clandestine bargain having been struck between the Southern Democrats and the Hayes camp, the gist of which was that if Hayes were allowed to assume the Presidency, then he would restore home rule in the South. That spring of 1877, Nordhoff tried to deny that there had been any quid pro quo, the belief in which might damage the effectiveness of the new President. "The Southern men did not ask for an 'agreement,'" Nordhoff insisted in one *Herald* column and argued that though there might have been discussions between Hayes lieutenants and Southerners as to his intentions, they didn't "make or attempt to make any bargain with Mr. Hayes,... or with any one for him."[91] The Southern "Whigs," he insisted, had simply favored Hayes's election because Tilden was well known to oppose federal funding of a Southern Pacific railroad. By modern standards, Nordhoff was highly accurate in his reporting, even on an issue that so filled him with resentment. Though the idea of a conspiratorial "bargain" persisted for decades, later studies have, in fact, demonstrated that the Southern politicians' peaceable acquiescence in the outcome was secured for precisely the reasons that Nordhoff attributed to it.[92]

A week after Rutherford B. Hayes was sworn in as eighteenth President of the United States, Charles Nordhoff sat down to write a letter to his friend, economist David Ames Wells. "Hayes opens admirably," he wrote and added that he would give Hayes his full support. But, he continued, "I don't think... there is much genuine reform possible to him"; Nordhoff had already expressed his opinion that Hayes would be but a tool in the hands of the "centralizers" of the Republican Party. He went on,

---

89. CN to Gordon L. Ford, February 18, [1877]. Ford Papers, NYPL.

90. CN to Samuel Bowles, February 21, 1877. Bowles Papers, Yale University Library.

91. [CN,] "Hayes' Southern Policy," New York *Evening Post*, March 29, 1877.

92. C. Vann Woodward, *Reunion and Reaction* (Garden City, NY: 1956).

while I shall do all I can to further every good, & to help
him, I am not inclined to go back to the Republican party,
or to overlook or condone the rascally fraud by which the
Republican leaders grabbed the election. I don't think the
country ought to forget them; it ought to vote them down,
wherever they raise their heads.[93]

Nordhoff tried to live up to his pledge to support Hayes in his efforts at
reform, but their friendship had been damaged. Although Lida and several
other old schoolmates of Lucy Hayes were invited to the White House shortly
after the inauguration, weeks later Nordhoff admitted to a friend that he hadn't
yet been able to see the new President. He was out of favor, he knew, for he had
asked if he might see Hayes and been immediately rebuffed. "I hear privately
that he took it hard that I went Tilden," he added, but brushed the matter off.
"I suppose he will get over it by & by"; he would continue to support him, &
their estrangement "leaves me a little freed" to retain his independence. Still,
he kept trying to renew the old tie. He wrote a letter to Carl Schurz in April,
praising the new administration's actions regarding the South. "I hope when I
get back to Washington I shall be allowed to see His Excellency," he added, "who
is to me so far like the Grand Lama of Thibet, a being profoundly venerated,
but unseen."[94]

But he swore he was through with the Republican Party as a whole. He
would support Hayes, he insisted. "But I mean to stick religiously & through evil
as well as good report to the Democratic party," he wrote to Wells. "I never felt
so comfortable in my life as now that I have got into the party where I belong,
& I mean to stick."[95] When a movement was made that summer to indict the
Louisiana Returning Board for fraud, it won Nordhoff's hearty approval.[96]

Hayes's hurt feelings faded somewhat by that summer. "We are on the best
of terms now with Nordhoff again," he wrote to an Ohio friend. "I hope this
time we shall get on without interruption. He is so capable, interesting and
good that it is a vexation to be out with him on some silly crotchet."[97] In a less
benign humor, Hayes wrote to another mutual friend, with some sarcasm, "You
must be glad to know that Nordoff [sic] has stuck now lo! these five months!"

---

93. CN to David Ames Wells, March 12, 1877. David Ames Wells Papers, Library of
     Congress.
94. "Capital Society Gossip," New York *Daily Graphic*, 3/12/77. CN to David Ames Wells,
     March 20, 1877. Wells Papers, LC; CN to Carl Schurz, 4/19/77. Schurz Papers, LC.
95. CN to David Ames Wells, April 22, 1877. Wells Papers, LC.
96. CN to Carl Schurz, July 6, 1877. Schurz Papers, LC
97. Rutherford B. Hayes to Dr. John Davis, July 8, 1877. Hayes Papers, RBH Library.

But Nordhoff had done so, he added, in "a most effective, manful and generous way." Nordhoff's shifts in stance throughout the campaign and the electoral controversy, which he regarded as only the honest judgments of an independent man, earned another name in the mind of Hayes. "We must forgive his panicky fickleness of last year," wrote the new president. "When he is right he is very right."[98]

Nordhoff's dilemma in 1876, facing the Hobson's Choice of Tilden or Hayes, was dramatically resolved by the contested election and the indefensible actions of the Republicans on the Electoral Commission. And yet, as he observed the new Democratic Congress at work, he began to think that he had only exchanged a party of knaves for a party of fools. Nothing in Washington seemed to work very well, and the question of why this should be so would puzzle him for some years before he reached several very grim conclusions.

[98.]   RBH to Mrs. John Davis, August 6, 1877. Hayes Papers, RBH Library.

CHAPTER 8

Perpetual Outpost Duty

Charles Nordhoff's outrage at the result of the electoral controversy of 1877 reflected not only idealism, but a certain naivete as well. He could foresee the attempt to steal the election; he was well used to regarding politics as partly the purview of greed, but on balance, he had always supposed that right would ultimately prevail. As he wrote in *Politics for Young Americans*, American politics only seemed corrupt because of the openness of the American system, allowing criticism to flourish, which made corruption appear rampant. That openness, that criticism freely aired, he believed, would ensure that the public good would triumph.

Nordhoff had faith in the free market, in the people's representatives, in American democracy and its institutions. In his vision of democracy, political parties were mechanisms by which different principles and policies might contend for a popular mandate. But never before had he had such an intimate and sustained view of how those members might wield power. New York's municipal government under Tweed had been emblematic to Nordhoff of corruption and incompetence, but he had supposed the United States Congress to be composed of men of a substantially different order than Tweed. After observing Washington life for several years, however, he found his faith in politics, politicians, and the good faith of the powerful both North and South begin to erode. Democracy required wise leaders, but he sought them with diminishing confidence that they might be found in the federal city.

Nordhoff did not blame Rutherford B. Hayes personally for the electoral commission's perfidy. Seeing that the president had distanced himself from the wheeling-and-dealing that resulted in his victory, and presented with the fait accompli of a Hayes administration, Nordhoff pragmatically made the best of the situation. By the summer of 1877, he had mended his fences with his old friend and felt no compunction about using the insider status he had attained to make his voice heard by the new administration.[1]

"I am greatly delighted that the Pres[iden]t takes so little hand in the riots," Nordhoff wrote to Carl Schurz that July. The country was in the midst of a nationwide railroad strike. Hayes had been pursuing a moderate legalistic course: he would send federal troops only when requested to do so by state authorities, and then only to prevent violence rather than to break the strike and restore train traffic. There were those—including (not surprisingly) railroad magnate Tom Scott, U. S. Grant, and most Republican newspapers— who advocated federal intervention to put down the strikers by force, and their urgings prompted Nordhoff's letter. "It seems to me nothing would be less prudent," he wrote Schurz, "than any positive action by the Administration, such as calling out volunteers or declaring Martial Law in a state."

Nordhoff disliked lawlessness, but the strikers, he implied, had been driven to it by the railroad managers; the uprising had begun with a cut in the workers' wages, which they could ill afford. If Hayes did anything at all, it should be "to privately tell the RRd men they had better come to terms with their people. ...The companies are by no means without blame in the matter."

Nordhoff, who had always maintained that strikes hurt only the strikers, had modified his view. He now believed that some good might come of the strike, for "it will bring the Corporations to their senses, & some of them to a settlement." Corporations needed to be "brought to their senses"; their frequent cuts in the subsistence-level wages of their unskilled employees, made while retaining sizable profits for their stockholders, were not only unchristian (bad enough in Nordhoff's eyes), but clearly drove desperate workers into violent protest.[2]

Nordhoff tended to view all labor-capital problems, in 1877, as the result of the "derangement" of industry caused by protective tariffs. Most people with conservative economic views (adherents, like Nordhoff, of the ideas of Adam Smith) believed that there were certain immutable laws that governed the economy and against which it was not only futile, but downright detrimental, to legislate. In this view, the tariff disrupted the natural equilibrium that free-market forces would otherwise bring about, with unfair prices and unfair wages as the result. Classical liberal economics could encompass no

---

[1]   Nordhoff seems to have persuaded Hayes to purchase some Palisades land not far from Nordhoff's own home, indicating a friendly relationship. CN to Webb Hayes, June 11, 1878, Rutherford B. Hayes Library, Fremont, Ohio.

[2]   CN to Carl Schurz, July 25, 1877. Schurz Papers, LC. Unfortunately, it's impossible to identify CN's newspaper writings during the summer of 1877, as he had no byline when Congress was not in session.

remedy for labor problems other than a more perfect policy of governmental noninterference. In an age without minimum wage laws or any acceptance of collective bargaining, "protection," to free traders, meant artificially boosting the profits of manufacturers without any benefit to those who worked for them.[3] Nordhoff had no doubt that an absolute adherence to the principles of laissez-faire would benefit workers.

After a week of ugly confrontations across the northeastern states, the strike ended. But the strike, which precipitated cries that communism was threatening the free institutions of the United States, did not alarm Nordhoff greatly. He didn't interpret it as a sign that labor troubles, in an age of rapid industrialization, might become a chronic problem, and he saw nothing inherently oppressive in mechanization. On the contrary, he jeered at the dreamy nostalgia for manual labor of well-heeled literatteurs.[4]

"Now that the Great Fuss is over," he wrote sardonically to editor Samuel Bowles, "let me ask you if *you* ever swung the cheerful scythe?" Bowles had written an editorial on the joys of old-fashioned manual labor—labor of a kind, which, Nordhoff suspected, Bowles himself had never undertaken. But Nordhoff had worked with his hands for many years, and he mocked Bowles's romanticism. The editorial was "very well done—but *I've mowed & with a scythe.*" He had done all kinds of work, he reminded Bowles: "rolled cotton on the New Orleans levee," "hauled lumber out of a down East bark's hold in Sumarara," and "pulled a boat after whales from daylight to dark."

[3.] A brief and useful summary of the spectrum of economic thought during this period can be found in Paul F. Boller, Jr., *American Thought in Transition: The Impact of Evolutionary Naturalism, 1865-1900* (Chicago: Rand McNally, 1969), chapter 4. The conventionality of Nordhoff's pre-1880 views is ubiquitous throughout his work, but is most explicitly treated in *Politics for Young Americans*, q.v.

[4.] CN to Samuel Bowles, 7/30/77, Bowles Papers, Yale University Library. On the Hayes Administration's reaction to the strike, see Ari Hoogenboom, *The Presidency of Rutherford B. Hayes* (Lawrence: University of Kansas Press, 1988), 79–91. Nordhoff didn't disapprove of the Arts and Crafts movement being propounded by William Morris et al. His daughter, Evelyn, was trained in craft bookbinding by the Morris-Sanderson shop in England and apparently went on to do respected bindery work in New York before her premature death in the 1890s. (CN to Edward Atkinson [March 1889] and April 7, 1889, Atkinson Papers, MHS.) She seems to have had her father's full support although craft bookbinding was more an aesthetic luxury for the few than a return to the lost integration of work and life, which the Arts and Crafts theorists hoped for. See also Eileen Boris, *Art and Labor: Ruskin, Morris, and the Craftsman Ideal in America* (Philadelphia: Temple University Press, 1986).

I declare to you I'd rather do any of these again, than swing
the cheerful scythe. If you want any fellow to hurrah for
mowing machines, you want to get a fellow that has mowed
by the day with a scythe. I'll bet you something he don't see
no romance about it. But your article was very nice—to read
as you sit on a patent mower's spring seat; or whistle to your
horses. When I was a boy at sea we used to sing

> For to plow & to mow
> To reap & to sow
> And to be a farmer's boy-oy-oy-oy
> To be a farmer's boy.

But I never seriously thought of farming until
I read a description of a mowing machine.[5]

Nordhoff was impatient with those who carelessly theorized on labor
without having lived a workingman's life. His own experience gave him, he felt,
authority to speak for the working class; and as he chafed at the constraints of
his job, he continued to feel himself akin to laborers of all kinds. He appreciated
his privileged position in having gained a forum, unlike the worn-out and ill-
educated sailors he had once lived among; and he tried to use that forum as a
spokesman for the voiceless.

The very problems that prompted Nordhoff's investigation of
communitarianism had long undermined his serenity in, if not his adherence to
the tenets of classical economics. The events of the succeeding decade, during
which violent strikes occurred with increasing frequency amid widespread
unemployment, eventually eroded this adherence. His loss of certitude,
however, was a slow and uneven process. Although he had, by 1877, conceded
the possible utility of strikes, Nordhoff's columns of the late 1870s still referred
mockingly to populist rhetoric about "bloated aristocrats," still held that labor
and capital shared mutual interests, and generally spoke uncritically of the
enterprise of businessmen. An early Congressional bill proposing government
oversight of interstate commerce (i.e., of railroads) was simply "foolish," he
wrote, the product of ignorance and the craven kowtowing of Congressmen
to the demands of the Granger movement. Even as late as 1880, Nordhoff
wrote with assurance that "the time has not yet come for any definite action by
Congress" to solve the "railroad problem." The free market, the "necessities and

---

5.   CN to Samuel Bowles, 7/30/77, Bowles Papers, Yale University Library.

rivalries of the railroads are in themselves solving many important questions," and government could not hasten the process.[6]

In fact, so thoroughly did Nordhoff distrust government intervention on the federal level that in 1878 he praised the Congressional session just ended for having done almost nothing. The purpose of Congress, he wrote, was to debate and deliberate, at length, educating the people in the process, rather than to make quick, "blundering" attempts at needless legislation. The Republican Party (which he regarded as having outlived its reason for being) was the party of "paternal interference generally," and a more damning phrase in his vocabulary would be hard to find.[7]

Gilded Age Washington was still largely a seasonal town. As it swelled with the sessions of Congress to accommodate Senators, Representatives, their families, and hangers-on, "society," cramming a year's activity into a few winter months, took on a pace that verged on the frenetic. Even his eight-year-old daughter, Elsie, Nordhoff wrote, had been "infected with the fashionable follies of Washington." Dinners and parties and teas provided occasions for open lobbying, subtle and not so subtle. Nor were high-ranking officials cloistered or their attendance at social functions at all unusual. The Nordhoffs appear to have participated fully in the ever-changing social milieu. "This kaleidoscopic life presents many new faces in place of the old," Lida Nordhoff wrote to a friend upon their annual relocation to DC, and their "friends coming on, threw us into a small round of dissipation from which we are just emerging."[8] In such a setting, politics and personal relationships were hopelessly tangled.

---

6.   [CN,] "Washington: The Thurman Funding Bill Passed by the Senate," N.Y. *Herald*, April 10, 1878; "Washington: Senator Blaine's Revival of Sectional Agitation," N.Y. *Herald*, December 12, 1878; and "Washington: Feeling in the House on the Tariff Question," January 13, 1880. Any number of Nordhoff's pre-1880 articles demonstrate these attitudes. [CN,] "Washington: Senator Blaine's Revival of Sectional Agitation," N.Y. *Herald*, December 12, 1878. [CN,] "Washington: Feeling in the House on the Tariff Question," N.Y. *Herald*, January 13, 1880.

7.   [CN,] "Washington: Review of Remarkable Session of Congress," N.Y. *Herald*, June 17, 1878.

8.   CN to Samuel Bowles, February 21, 1877, Bowles Papers, Yale University Library; Henry Adams to Henry Cabot Lodge, December 2, 1877, which mentions a dinner at which Schurz, Abram Hewitt, William Story, and Nordhoff were present; and Henry Adams to Mary Dwight Parkman, February 20, 1879, mentions an evening at which Hayes dropped in on Adams, Schurz, Godkin, and Senator L.Q.C. Lamar; both in Levenson et al., eds., *Letters of Henry Adams*. CN to Mrs. Henry Dawes, February 2 [n. y.], Dawes Papers, LC; Lida Nordhoff to Mrs. Gordon L. Ford, 11/12/77, Ford Papers, NYPL. On Washington during the Gilded Age, see Constance M. Green's

Life in late 1877 and the spring of 1878 seemed grim to Nordhoff, the demands upon him more than he could bear. Politics were barren. Journalism was a wearisome effort; time was slipping away, and his sense of possibility with it. "I am I think somewhat greyer," he wrote pensively, "& I fear somewhat less elastic & more dull in my treadmill." Despite Lida's robust strength as a young woman, her health began to fail during the Nordhoffs' first years in Washington. She took occasional trips away from Washington's "malarial" atmosphere while Charles remained at his post, growing gloomier and gloomier in her absence and at her ill health. Meanwhile, his friend Edward Atkinson seems to have suffered a nervous breakdown in 1877 and wrote Nordhoff despairing letters that could only have been disheartening to his old friend. Nordhoff's mood continued to darken, and by late May, he wrote his friend unhappily, "I was so near down that I couldn't stand it any longer, without a little look at the sea," and he fled to the Delaware shore for a weekend's escape from politics and duties. "I am really more used up than I ever was in my life," he confessed.[9]

Washington: Village and Capital, 1800-1878 (Princeton: Princeton University Press, 1962) and *Washington: Capital City, 1879-1950* (Princeton: Princeton University Press, 1963); J. Kirkpatrick Flack, *Desideratum in Washington: The Intellectual Community in the Capital City, 1870-1900* (Cambridge: Schenkman Publishing Co., 1975); Kathryn Allamong Jacob, "High Society in Washington During the Gilded Age, 1865-1900: Three Distinct Aristocracies," Ph.D. dissertation, Johns Hopkins University, 1986. Colorful contemporary accounts are found in Benjamin Perley Poore, *Perley's Reminiscences* (Philadelphia: Hubbard, 1886); George Alfred Townsend, *Washington, Outside and Inside: A Picture and a Narrative* (Hartford: James Betts & Co., 1873); [Rollin H. Kirk], *Many Secrets Revealed; or, Ten Years Behind the Scenes in Washington City* (Washington: 1885); O. O. Stealey, *Twenty Years in the Press Gallery* (New York: by Author, 1906). Frances Hodgson Burnett's *Through One Administration* (New York: 1883) and Charles T. Murray's *Sub Rosa* (New York: 1880) present fictionalized accounts of the blend of lobbying, politics, and society that characterized Washington life; I am grateful to Donald Ritchie for pointing me toward the latter two works.

9.   CN to Gordon L. Ford, December 23, 1877; CN to Gordon L. Ford, March 17, 1878; CN to Gordon L. Ford, 3/17/78, Ford Papers, NYPL; CN to Ford, January 3, 1879; CN to Gordon L. Ford, May 22, 1878. Edward Atkinson to CN, May 10, 1877, MHS. The only full-length biography of Atkinson (Harold Francis Williamson, *Edward Atkinson: The Biography of an American Liberal*, Boston: Old Corner Bookstore, 1934) is far too reverential to mention any mental instability, but judging from this letter, Atkinson was no stranger to depressive breakdown: "I don't want to be remiss or shirk but I am compelled to seek relief in rest, thankful that it is possible. I am

Carl Schurz had been named to the Hayes Cabinet as Secretary of the Interior, and Nordhoff freely wrote Schurz letters on current events, with apparent confidence that his views were welcome and given serious consideration. In turn, Schurz called upon Nordhoff and the New York *Herald* as a defender against more hostile newspapers. Nordhoff was only too happy to help Schurz, for his fellow German-American was working for the reforms that he himself believed in: civil service, new Indian and Southern policies, a return to hard currency. Since he believed that the real function of newspapers was to inform and guide the public, the idea that the *Herald* ought to take no sides in political controversy would have struck Nordhoff as absurd. The truth had to be told, no matter how controversial that "truth" might be. He offered to defend Schurz as well as other allies from political assault in the *Herald*, "whenever the attack upon you becomes serious," and cooperated with officials in other ways, as well. Hamilton Fish, for instance, called upon him to quash rumors that he was being considered for a diplomatic post in Prussia. For strategic reasons, he was not always open about his political involvements, and he cautioned one correspondent that "it is not best that I should appear to anyone to be meddling in party politics." But such alliances and involvements were highly valuable. In return for his efforts on their behalf, Nordhoff relied upon officials as sources of information as well as contacts with which to further the appointment of friends to office. In one case, Bennett asked Nordhoff to ask Schurz to ask Hayes to promote one of Bennett's friends: a fine example of the attenuated functioning of the insiders' network.[10]

Nordhoff resisted manipulation, refusing to use the *Herald* as a forum for petty squabbling between writers and critics, for example, or scornfully deriding an obvious gambit to release erroneous information in order to boost the price of worthless stock. For his own part, influence peddling was an integral part of business. The price of influence? He did not see himself constrained by his close contacts with Washington politicos; in an age of still highly politicized

---

again where I was several months ago, becoming incapable of … sound judgments from depression and nervous exhaustion—In the daytime or when I have actual regular work I seem all right and almost feel as if the trouble was imaginary but it is far from being so." CN to Gordon L. Ford, May 22, 1878. Ford Papers, NYPL. See also CN to Ford, March 17, 1878.

10. CN to August Belmont, December 9, 1878, Belmont Papers, Columbia University; CN to Carl Schurz, August 15, [1877]; Trefousse, *Carl Schurz*, 241, details the attacks on Schurz during the summer of 1877. On favors and appointments: CN to Schurz, July 6, 17, and 29 [1878]; CN to Schurz, August 17, 1877, Schurz Papers, LC; CN to Gordon L. Ford, December 12 and 17, [1878], Ford Family Papers, NYPL; David Ames Wells to Rutherford B. Hayes, January 22, 1878, Hayes Papers, RBH Library.

newspaper writing, many journalists simply followed their own ideological bents. Their "principles" did not include objectivity. In Nordhoff's case, he could not be relied upon to let his personal friendships interfere with his editorial judgment—as Hayes had learned so well during the controversy over the election of 1876.[11]

Nordhoff's social connections may explain his changing reactions to conditions in the South. Upon taking office in March of 1877, President Hayes had almost immediately ordered federal troops at the Louisiana and South Carolina state capitals to return to their barracks, and a policy of noninterference was pursued in an effort to break "the Solid South" and make the Republican Party more than just a beleaguered minority in the region. All but the most radical Northern Republicans were happy to end federal involvement in the South, which seemed ineffectual at best and dangerous at worst. With white Southerners solemnly promising to protect the civil rights of former slaves, if only given "home rule," Hayes's Southern policy received widespread support.[12]

Nordhoff was among those supporters. He had been calling for an end to Radical Reconstruction since the early 1870s, largely out of his distrust of centralized government. A government strong enough to enforce unwanted social change was also, he believed, strong enough to become despotic. Since the white Southerners kept protesting that left to their own devices, they would protect civil rights for all citizens, black as well as white, Nordhoff saw all justifications of federal interference as mere power-grabbing by Republican

[11.] Henry Adams to Henry Cabort Lodge, February 1, 1878, in Levenson et al., eds., *The Letters of Henry Adams*, 333, relates his failure to get Nordhoff to "sass" a hostile writer; [CN,] "Washington: Feeling Over the Result At Utica," N.Y. *Herald*, February 26, 1880. Rutherford B. Hayes to J. M. Comly, October 29, 1878, copy in RBH Library, Fremont, Ohio. CN's articles applauding the Potter Commission's investigation of the election of 1876 include "Washington: Florida Exposures as the Work of Anti-Hayes Republicans," 4/26/1878; "Washington: The Electoral Frauds a Perplexity to Congress," 5/2/78; "Washington: Rumor of Another Presidential Investigation," 5/4/78; "Washington: Investigation of Electoral Frauds Determined Upon," 5/9/78; "Washington: The Potter Resolutions Passed by a Democratic Quorum," 5/18/78; "The Potter Committee," 6/2/78; "Washington: The House Judiciary Committee on the President's Title," 6/5/78.

[12.] See Eric Foner, *Reconstruction: America's Unfinished Revolution, 1863-1877* (NY: Harper & Row, 1988), 581–600; William Gillette, *Retreat From Reconstruction, 1869-1879* (Baton Rouge: Louisiana State University Press, 1979) chapter 14; and Ari Hoogenboom, *The Presidency of Rutherford B. Hayes* (Lawrence: University of Kansas Press, 1988) chapter 3.

politicians determined to retain their hold on the votes of black citizens through various spurious tactics. The justice of the new Southern policy depended on the good faith of the white Southerners, in which Nordhoff wanted to believe. It simplified matters enormously to do so.

The Congressional election of 1878 was the first to take place under full "home rule" by Southern governments and therefore was a test of the new conditions. Had peace and democratic government at last been restored? They had not. Reports coming from the South claimed that the election had swung to the Democrats with the help of fraud, intimidation, violence, discriminatory poll taxes and other stratagems—legal and extralegal—to keep African-Americans from the polls. White juries negated all efforts by federal marshals to punish those guilty of intimidation. This was the result of leaving Southerners in control of the canvass. "I am reluctantly forced to admit," Hayes said a week after the election, "that the experiment was a failure."[13]

Nordhoff was already in Washington in late November 1879, two weeks before Congress was to convene, and he had the latest information on the elections as the story emerged. He was appalled. But he could not believe that the men he knew, who had sworn so vociferously that they would protect the blacks' voting rights, might be responsible. The problem, he was sure, did not lie with the intelligent, reasonable Southerners he had come to know. "I saw several South Carolina Democrats," he wrote to Hayes a few weeks after the election, "-- good men, who feel bitterly what has been done there; & I judge that there is a pretty wide spread feeling of intense disgust & resentment among a large body of reputable Democrats." Hayes would be well-advised to exploit this split between "reputable" and disreputable Democrats, breaking at last the "solid South" and the color line in Southern politics.[14]

In a lengthy article published November 23 in the *Herald*, Nordhoff detailed the reported misconduct of the election. He blasted the South Carolina and Virginia elections in particular as "fraudulent," attacked SC governor Wade Hampton for tolerating fraud and intimidation, declared the activities a betrayal of the promises made by white Southerners, and called upon "decent, honest" democrats to denounce the election frauds.[15]

---

13. See Hoogenboom, *Hayes*, 72–73.

14. CN to Rutherford B. Hayes, 11/23/78. Hayes Papers, RBH library.

15. The entire headline of CN's article conveys the tone very well [CN]: "Washington: The Late Elections in Certain of the Southern States. Details of Outrages Reported. Interference with Federal Authorities in Enforcing the Law. Unnecessary Frauds Practised. Violence and Intimidation No Longer in Vogue." Headlines, of course, are not made up by newspaper writers, but by the typographers or editorial assistants; it is doubtful that Nordhoff would conceive of a "necessary" fraud.

But as Congressmen and Senators began to gather in the national capital in early December, Nordhoff apparently discussed the elections with some of his contacts, and his outrage was at first muffled and then dissipated altogether. The overwhelming victories of the Democrats in the South could be attributed, he then wrote in the *Herald*, not so much to malfeasance by the Democrats as to the African-Americans' avoidance of paying a poll tax (with which he found no fault) or even their selling off their votes to the highest bidder. The election frauds, though real in a few isolated cases, were not a systemic problem. Both parties were simply playing on the Southern issue for "selfish ends." The judicial system in the states was fully capable of dealing with the few malefactors, without Congressional interference.[16]

By December 6, he had heard enough to entirely disavow his column of November 23. He had been lied to, he said, as had Hayes. There were very few problems in the South. The Republicans, disappointed at their defeat, were playing politics; in fact, federal election officials, by their presence at Southern polls, had *caused* the disturbances in a cynical political maneuver. He was certain his new information was accurate; one source had been reelected in one of the allegedly fraud-ridden districts, Nordhoff related with astonishing credulity, and this man maintained there was no problem at all.[17]

The following spring, however, when it came time for the new Congress—controlled by Democrats for the first time in nearly twenty years—to pass appropriation bills, the Democrats insisted on attaching to the bills riders that would prevent enforcement of the federal election laws by prohibiting payments to federal election officials. Hayes made it clear that he would veto any such bill despite the possibility that Congress would "stop the wheels ... of government if I do not yield my convictions in favor of the election laws." He made good his threat, first vetoing an army appropriation bill in late April, insisting that every citizen had the right "to cast one unintimidated ballot and to have his ballot

16.   [CN,] "Washington: Premonitions Prior to the Opening of Congress," N.Y. *Herald*, 12/2/1878; [CN,] "Washington: Second Session of the Forty-Fifth Congress," N.Y. *Herald*, 12/3/78.

17.   [CN,] "Washington: The Effort to Revive the Southern Question," 12/6/78. See also "Washington: Report of the Committee on Army Reorganization," in which Nordhoff recalls frauds committed in the past by Republicans. Although he states, "a republican fraud in 1876 does not justify a Democratic fraud in 1878," this certainly is the implication of the article. In "Washington: The Southern Question Among the Politicians" (12/9/78) and in "Washington: Senator Blaine's Revival of Sectional Agitation" (12/12/1878), he repeats his opinion that it is Republican fear-mongering to gain political power.

honestly counted," and that the government had to be given the resources to protect that right.[18]

At first, during the appropriations battle, Nordhoff adhered to his view that alarmist Republicans were simply exploiting old animosities for political advantage. Several "influential republicans," he noted in one dispatch, had objected to these characterizations (clearly Nordhoff's column was read and considered important enough for politicians to worry about); but, he insisted, there was no basis for "the excitement and bitterness which are suddenly manifested here by republicans," for if the Democrats persisted in their course and left the government without appropriations, they would be committing "a revolutionary act" for which the country would soon turn them out. By now, Nordhoff had seen a Democratic Congress in operation, and he was not impressed.[19]

As he watched the maneuverings of Democrats, who insisted upon weakening the election laws even at the risk of bankrupting the government, Nordhoff began to reconsider his opinion of the Southerners. He had believed them when they protested their innocence in the fraudulence of the election the previous autumn; but now, in Washington, and able to see for himself the part the Southerners played in the appropriations contretemps, he became suspicious. The Southern Democrats, he wrote in one column, insisted in private conversations that they wanted to pass an appropriation bill and end the deadlock, but they didn't take any action. It seemed that they actually hoped the deadlock continued. At any rate, he was no longer able to accept their private protestations of innocence at face value.[20]

The session finally concluded at the end of June. Nordhoff ventured the opinion that "there was not, after all, much at stake in the ... struggle, and ...the three months and a half were spent, not in saving the country or destroying its liberties, but in maneuvering for political position." Nevertheless, he praised Hayes and ventured that the Republicans would be well-advised to eschew "bloody shirt" rhetoric, look to other issues, but also insist on the necessity of federal supervision of elections. He issued a warning to the South. "The politics of South Carolina and Mississippi will be carefully watched here," he wrote in one prognostication, for the Republicans would surely protest the votes of any states in which "the negroes are prevented from voting." The Republicans

---

18.   Hayes quoted in Hoogenboom, *Hayes*, 75. On Hayes's battle with Congress in 1879, see Hoogenboom, 72–77.

19.   [CN,] "Washington: The Work of President Making in Congress," NY *Herald*, 3/31/1879.

20.   [CN,] "Washington: Forthcoming Address of the Democrats on the Veto," NY *Herald*, 5/23/1879.

meant to make the public "understand plainly what is going on" in the Southern states "so as to create a public opinion which will require their exclusion from the Presidential contest unless there is a fair and full vote."[21]

It was all disheartening, and he thought—as he often did, those years in Washington—of simply leaving the whole sordid business behind. "Politics are so mixed as to be hideously disagreeable," he once confided to a friend, "& between us I often in these days feel as though I … could back out peacefully & say goodbye."[22] But he couldn't back out. The politicking and venality that he found so "hideously disagreeable" only reinforced his sense of the crucial role journalism would play in curbing the worst abuses of the people's trust.

Despite his faith in classical economics, Nordhoff was not blind to the hardships of the working poor and the unemployed. Economic conditions eased as the country began to recover from the depression begun in 1873, but one could not walk through Lower Manhattan (as Nordhoff did when working in New York during Congressional recesses) without perceiving a wretchedness that could not be regarded as an aberration. More open-minded than his friends, economist David Ames Wells and Boston businessman Edward Atkinson, he paid close attention to new ideas concerning economic issues. In 1879, he read a copy of Henry George's *Progress and Poverty.*

George's theory that land monopoly was the basic cause of poverty and that the solution accordingly was to establish a confiscatory tax on rent, the "single tax," struck Nordhoff as worthy of serious consideration. It certainly answered some troubling dilemmas of American society—want amid abundance, deepening poverty despite rapid progress—and it did so without fundamentally differing from the old idea of natural harmony. Nordhoff had met George on one of his earlier trips to California, and the younger author was familiar with his work. "Your friendship and your opinion I value very much," George wrote in reply to Nordhoff's letter. "…I have derived so much from you that it pleases me *very* much that my book interests and pleases you."[23]

Nordhoff had not been an uncritical reader; he suggested that George should have "but briefly stated the economic basis." George demurred; he intended the book as a primer for "those who have never read and never

---

21. [CN,] "Washington: Political Results of the Extra Session," NY *Herald,* July 4, 1879; [CN,] "Washington: Gathering of the Statesmen and Politicians," NY *Herald,* 12/1/1879.

22. CN to Gordon L. Ford, February 23, 1880. Ford Papers, NYPL.

23. Henry George to CN, 12/21/1879. George Papers, NYPL. On George, see John L. Thomas, *Alternative America: Henry George, Edward Bellamy. Henry Demarest Lloyd and the Adversary Tradition* (Cambridge: Belknap, 1983). Boller also summarizes George's ideas in op. cit., chapter 5.

thought on such subjects before."[24] Although it had deserted him during the composition of *Communistic Societies*, Nordhoff had a keen sense of publishers' marketing strategies (having learned them under the guidance of Fletcher Harper), and he advised George on issues to discuss with Appleton's, which was about to publish the first large printing of *Progress and Poverty*. George, though light of heart now that his opus was out of his hands, did as Nordhoff advised, for they faced a common problem: "the difficulty of reaching those most concerned in any social reform," the uneducated poor. "It is a general fact," George added,

> that those who suffer most are least able to help themselves. Perhaps it is the law of the universe; ...but it is certain that successful efforts for amelioration of the condition of the lowest class have come from above not below.[25]

Here indeed was a kindred spirit. Nordhoff and George shared a sense of the ultimate responsibility of the affluent and educated to lead the "lowest class," as well as the belief that, as George wrote, the "most terrible thing about unjust social enactments is not the physical suffering they cause, but the mental and moral degradation they produce." They also were both seekers after utopia: searching for the ultimate answer, the single adjustment which might, once and for all, establish the good society.

George shared Nordhoff's doubts about the efficacy of their efforts at reform. But they shared a faith in the transcendent meaning of their work as well, a deeply religious impulse underlay all their efforts. Perhaps their attempts would come to nothing, George acknowledged. "But who can tell," he added serenely, "and as you say, 'we are to work away all the same.' We *are*, as you say; we *are*." The call of duty, "in obedience to a higher power," ought to sustain them, however ineffectual their efforts might seem. One ought not to mind feeling as a voice crying out in the wilderness, George wrote. "Sometimes I think it must be 'the peace which passeth understanding.'"[26] It was not a peace that came easily to Nordhoff; he often complained of being on "perpetual outpost duty." The religiously based sense of duty that provided George with a certain equanimity and confidence regarding his work served at times to keep Nordhoff oppressed with a crushing sense of duties exacted of him, duties that

---

24. Henry George to CN, 12/21/1879. George Papers, NYPL.

25. Henry George to CN, January 31, 1879 [*sic*: George misdated his letter, which he wrote in 1880]. George Papers, NYPL.

26. Henry George to CN, January 31, 1879 [1880]. George Papers, NYPL.

morality required him to undertake. And unlike George, he could never bring himself to subject his family to poverty for the sake of an idea.[27]

Nevertheless, it is not surprising that Nordhoff found in George an ally, and he did what he could to encourage him. They became good friends; in 1880, Nordhoff even had George to Thanksgiving dinner. As *Progress and Poverty* grew in popularity, Nordhoff suggested George run for Congress (some years before the latter's unsuccessful New York mayoralty campaign of 1886), and they apparently saw each other socially with some frequency. He also provided George with a letter of introduction to James Bryce, who was beginning work on *The American Commonwealth*, a favor he would only have done for someone he believed to have ideas worth pursuing.[28]

When the House voted, in March of 1880, to change the rules of access for the press, Nordhoff blasted Congress in the *Herald*. Only former Congressmen, who (in Nordhoff's eyes) were using their connections to serve as lobbyists, would now be allowed onto the floor while "to disable the press from interfering with these favored lobbyists," the rule "rigorously excludes" the press not just from the floor, but from the cloakrooms as well. This action by the Democratic Congress would

> pave the way for all kinds of lobbying and jobbing and at the same time so thoroughly cripple the press in its efforts to

---

[27]   CN, *God and the Future Life* (NY: Harper & Brothers, 1883), 191–2: On Thoreau giving up pencil-making: "I think he was right. Being free of hand, having no one depending on his labors, he had not only a right to stop what had become mere mechanical drudgery, but it was his duty to himself to do so. Observe, if he had a wife and children or other helpless ones justly depending on him, his duty would have been to go on patiently and honestly making lead-pencils. I knew once a painter who, if he had had leisure, would have become famous.... But he had a wife and numerous family; to have cultivated his art would have been to expose them to want, or at least to deprivation of comforts, and being a good man, he deliberately gave up the work ... in which he might have won fame, and gave his life contentedly to bread-and-butter labors...." When he wrote this, Nordhoff was well-acquainted with Henry George. It is hard to judge whether he thought *Progress and Poverty* was worth the deprivation George's family suffered during its composition. He obviously thought George a "good man," but if one takes this passage at face value, he would not have approved.

[28]   CN to David Ames Wells, 11/29/80. Wells Papers, LC. Henry George to CN, June 11, 1881 and October 29, 1882, George Papers, NYPL; CN to James Bryce, 12/27/1883, Bodleian Library.

discover the tricks of lobbyists or get intelligent and satisfactory information concerning the business of the House.

The new rules "put it out of the power of the press to gain anything more than a very perfunctory knowledge of what may be preparing in the House." What about the press gallery? Nordhoff disdained the very idea of an intelligent journalist being sequestered above the House floor and the mischief-making Representatives below. Yes, there was a press gallery. However, it had never been meant to serve as the sole venue of the press, but as a convenience for stenographers trying only to record proceedings. "To secure any real information for the public of course the press gallery is useless," he insisted. "To obtain a knowledge of what is going on in the House, good, bad or indifferent, it is necessary to have some means of communication with members." Nordhoff had been used to moving freely among the Congressmen, on or off the floor, and the new restrictions offended his exalted idea of the role of the journalist. They only reflected the Congress's recognition of the press's effectiveness in foiling their schemes. "When in former days the lobby and the press were put on equal terms," he wrote,

> ... the correspondents of newspapers, who are both honest and alert, were able, in numberless instances, to get at and expose and defeat the schemes of the lobby. But in the new era of economy and reform, so-called, the democrats have, with curious care, both crippled the press and protected and encouraged the lobby.[29]

Within a few days, the House Rules Committee had amended their previous work—most likely because of the outcry from journalists—so that the press was to be allowed in the cloakrooms, after all. But former Congressmen still were the only non-Representatives allowed onto the floor of the House, and Nordhoff was not satisfied, damning the Congress as a nest of opportunists anticipating their elevation to the more lucrative ranks of the lobby. It was scandalous. And the Congress sank another notch in Nordhoff's already-dimming estimation.[30]

Nordhoff's great panacea, education of the public through journalistic exposure, was also undermined by the continuing reversion of the two Houses of Congress to secret sessions in which to deliberate and vote upon politically

---

[29]   [CN,] "Washington: Policy of the Democrats on the Election Laws... New Rules in the Interest of Lobbyists," N.Y. *Herald*, March 9, 1880.

[30]   [CN,] "Washington: Proposed Changes in the Rules of the House," NY *Herald*, March 18, 1880.

sensitive matters, and the committee system had similarly hidden from the public the "fools and extremists." What the House needed, Nordhoff asserted, was "free speech, and plenty of it." The old question of "executive sessions," during which the doors of the Senate were closed to the press and public while members deliberated, roused Nordhoff to new flights of indignation. It was further evidence of the duplicity of federal legislators, who conducted "star chamber" proceedings more to protect their cynical bargaining than to preserve any necessarily secret information. Why should the investigation of electoral frauds be kept from public knowledge? Why were nominations to federal offices not held in the open? Such measures were counterproductive for secrecy "has never answered any good public end ..., but the contrary," he wrote. "It confuses the public mind with garbled and incomplete reports, defeats the honest purpose of an inquiry and deadens the public interest in the subject."[31] Grave faults in a democracy! More and more, Nordhoff eyed the national legislature with suspicion.

The very machinery of government was going awry, it seemed. Congress was no longer a deliberative body, where genuine debate brought out the merits and demerits of a bill under consideration; it had become a stage for empty posturing, "the reading of stupid essays under the pretense of their being speeches." Congressmen brandished carefully crafted manuscripts adroitly designed to disguise the speakers' inability to think on their feet. Worse still, Nordhoff could no longer refer to the Congressional Record with confidence that it reflected what had actually been said on the floor. "An honorable and stupid gentleman gets the floor," he wrote indignantly, "reads over a page or two in an inaudible voice, and then ... asks 'leave to print,' which the House, rather than be bored to death, grants at once." Thereupon, the speech was printed in the *Record* as if it had been delivered, another "fraud on the public," an effort to substitute image for substance by "a set of incapables who have no business in a deliberative body," but who remained through "swindling" their constituents with falsified *Records* "into the belief that they can and do effectively address the House." He applauded an attempt by Abram Hewitt to do away with the practice, soon to be firmly entrenched, and insisted that to do so was only a matter of "common honesty."[32]

31.   [CN,] "Washington: Initiation of General Legislation Agreed Upon," NY *Herald*, April 10, 1879; [CN,] "Washington: Prospects for a Short Session of Congress," NY *Herald*, March 24, 1879; [CN,] "Washington: New Movement of the Electoral Investigating Committee," NY *Herald*, May 22, 1878.

32.   [CN,] "Washington: The Legislation Pending Before Congress," NY *Herald*, April 21, 1879; [CN,] "Washington: The Legislation Pending Before Congress," April 21,

He waged an ongoing crusade against Congressional secretiveness, mocking "that fearful and wonderful thing, the 'dignity of the Senate,'" which was often invoked against the frequent "leaks" of pending legislation. In one column, he noted that it probably "never occurred to you ... that the Senate had any dignity at all." But there was such a thing, and Nordhoff compared it to "a delicate woman" who "bears the most surprising strains and hardships without wincing and then some day falls into hysterics over a mosquito." He had seen enough to recognize the spuriousness of appeals to "dignity."

> It might not offend "the dignity of the Senate," for instance, if it were conscious that one, two, four, six, eight Senators were "drunk on duty".... It might not offend the "dignity of the Senate" if it should become conscious that an august Senator was carefully walking down one grand staircase in the Capitol to avoid a poor woman with a baby waiting for him at the foot of another grand staircase. It might not even alarm the "dignity of the Senate" to become aware that some august Senators speculated in Wall Street on the probable success of bills of their own introduction.... In fact, the stamina ... and even the toughness of the "dignity of the Senate" is wonderful, but then, just when everybody has stopped inquiring about its welfare, slap-bang it goes down on the floor in a fit.

What calamitous news had finally flattened this robust dignity? Merely the publication of a treaty. "Some muddle-witted and pretentious Senators" had decided that the treaty must be considered in secrecy, "without the knowledge of the people." The *Herald*, and several other newspapers, had published the document, and Nordhoff saw nothing unusual or improper in its doing so. Indeed, it was a necessary public service to publish such treaties, to circumvent the Senate's attempts to usurp the people's right to govern themselves. "It is surely a curious piece of impertinence in seventy-six men," Nordhoff wrote,

> very few of whom have more than average intelligence or ability, to assume to themselves the right to judge in secret of so important a public document to the exclusion of 51,000,000 of the people. ...Sensible Senators know from long experience that secret documents which ought to be made public always get out, and they are glad of it.

1879; "Washington: Falsification of the Congressional Record of Speeches," July 18, 1882.

This was not to say that everything that transpired on Capitol Hill should be published. But the relationship between Congressmen and reporters had always been one of cooperation in reasonable instances, not adversarialism. "Sensible Senators know, and many of them have said it," Nordhoff explained, that if any document truly had to be kept secret to protect the national interest, "it would be the surest means to this end to call the principal correspondents here into council," explain the need for secrecy, and rest secure in the knowledge that there was "no correspondent here of even moderate ability and influence who is not the constant recipient of confidential information, and such trust is never violated." Problems only arose when the Congress attempted to suppress information, which, in the judgment of the press, rightly belonged to the people. The press had become, for Nordhoff, more representative of the people's interests than the people's own elected representatives.[33]

The election of 1880 pitted Democrat Winfield Scott Hancock against Republican James A. Garfield, and despite his misgivings about the Democratic Party's capacity to lead, Nordhoff favored Hancock unequivocally. He knew Garfield well and judged him to be a weak man, who would, like Hayes, be putty in the machine Republicans' hands. Despite this lack of enthusiasm, he accepted Garfield's election without alarm and maintained friendly relations with his fellow Ohioan. When the Garfield family travelled by train to Washington in March of 1881 for the inauguration, Nordhoff was the only journalist not relegated to a separate car set aside for the press, but travelled in the Garfields' private car. He took part in their celebratory dinner and joined them in looking down at the gathered crowds as they passed stations along the way. But he was on a busman's holiday, responsible for writing a lengthy and colorful account of the inaugural trip for the *Herald*. Once more, he was the outsider allowed among the insiders, privileged and yet set apart. He felt keenly his anomalous status, closing his account with the image of the Garfields comfortably asleep in their berths while he, the "weary scribe," stayed up to finish his work.[34]

Garfield's election renewed Nordhoff's contempt for "reformers"—like Atkinson, Horace White, or George William Curtis—who either couldn't or wouldn't exercise political skill in their efforts. They talked reform, but

---

33.   [CN,] "Washington: Senators Hill and Salisbury on the Rampage," NY *Herald*, January 23, 1881. On cooperation between reporters and politicians, see Donald Ritchie, *Press Gallery: Congress and the Washington Correspondents* (Cambridge: Harvard University Press, 1991).

34.   CN to David Ames Wells, July 7 [1880], Wells Papers; CN to Edward Atkinson, July 17, 1880, Atkinson papers; CN to Edward Atkinson, November 29, 1880; [CN,] "Nearing the Capitol: Glories of the President-Elect's Progress," New York *Herald*, March 1, 1880.

their loyalty to the Republican Party was absolute, making a mockery of their vaunted "independence." What was needed, Nordhoff thought, was "a split in the Republican Party," but, as he asked Atkinson, "who is going to split? You don't; the independents don't; the free trade party don't; the reformers don't;—all fall in behind Conkling." Nordhoff may not have appreciated the degree to which cultural differences between the two parties could override other questions: the Republicans were supposed to be the party of the old-stock American, the affluent, the educated, the "respectable" citizen; the Democrats were regarded as the party of the immigrant, the ill-educated, and the poor. Nordhoff was bitter toward his supposed allies. "So long as you Independents think any Republican better than a Democrat," he admonished Atkinson, "you must expect to see the worst men in your party rule."[35]

"I don't see any future in politics," he wrote to Wells gloomily in June of 1881, "except for you & me to stick to the Democrats." His alienation ran deep, and partisan politics increasingly seemed a shabby and inconsequential game. "I have abandoned politics of course," he wrote to Atkinson matter-of-factly one week later; and he may even have believed what he said.[36]

With the election of 1880, Nordhoff still wished to reserve judgment on the question of Southern disfranchisement of African-Americans although he regarded Southern claims of rectitude as dubious. Hayes made an impassioned statement to Congress in December of 1880, which Nordhoff quoted at length, in which the President accused the South of "fraudulent practices" to prevent blacks from voting. Southerners objected to the accusation, Nordhoff wrote, "and there is a disposition to ask Mr. Hayes for the evidence on which he has founded so grave a charge." Reverting to his usual calls for an end to the color line in Southern politics, Nordhoff nevertheless was attentive to the enduring saliency of race as a factor. He no longer believed what any politician, Southern or Northern, said to him about conditions in the South without "evidence."[37]

Within a few weeks of this column, however, the allegations of fraud in South Carolina had become too persuasive to ignore. Nordhoff could not blink away the testimony of credible people that wide-scale intimidation had handed the South Carolina election to the Democrats. He had thought Southern

---

35. CN to David Ames Wells, November 29, 1880. Wells Papers, LC; CN to Edward Atkinson, November 29, 1880; and CN to Atkinson, April 14, 1881, Atkinson Papers, MHS.

36. CN to Wells, June 5, 1881; CN to Atkinson, June 13, 1881.

37. CN to Edward Atkinson, November 29, 1880. Atkinson Papers, MHS. Rutherford B. Hayes, quoted in [CN,] "Washington: Reception of the President's Message by Congress," NY *Herald*, 12/7/1880. [CN,] "Washington: Reception of the President's Message by Congress," NY *Herald*, 12/7/1880.

Democrats (that is, the majority of the white population) were honorable people—even if he no longer fully trusted their representatives in Washington. "It is not easy to believe that all the members of the democratic party in South Carolina can submit in silence to such accusations as these," he wrote in the *Herald*, for to do so "would be to acknowledge and to condone the grossest frauds," for Democrats to "reap the advantage of the vilest wrongs, although they may have kept their own fingers clean," and he insisted that there should be "courage and statesmanship enough" among the white residents of South Carolina to "assert the right of every man to vote as he pleases and have his vote counted as he cast it." But no courageous Democrat had made any such assertion. Nordhoff was shaken, and angry. "It is surprising and disgusting," he wrote, "that no man of standing influence and intelligence has so far appeared down there to take the side of the defenseless, and demand an honest and free election."[38]

Before the election of 1880, Nordhoff had generally blamed Northern Democrats for race-baiting tactics while crediting the Southerners with a more pragmatic acceptance of new social realities. In a complete reversal, he now saw that the Southern Democrats might be guilty of various electoral crimes; but Nordhoff insisted that the entire party, Northerners and Southerners, could not be so wholly corrupt as to deprive other citizens of their civil rights. He had, since 1877, thought of himself as a Democrat despite that party's racist elements; the electoral fraud perpetrated by the Republicans that year had pushed him beyond tolerance for what he saw as a party grown hopelessly corrupt. Were the Democrats no better? He would not believe it. "The South Carolina whites may as well understand," he warned, "that they cannot count on Northern democrats to defend or support them in claiming Congressional seats so tainted with fraud."[39] Here, he mistakenly identified the feelings of all Northern Democrats with his own. His political education was, as yet, incomplete.

38. [CN,] Washington: Latest Construction of the Cabinet Makers," NY *Herald*, January 4, 1881.
39. [CN,] "Washington: Latest Construction of the Cabinet Makers," NY *Herald*, 1/4/1881.

CHAPTER 9

To Expose Abuses and Redress Wrongs

The 1880s were a decade of crisis, of violent labor unrest and deepening social problems in the cities, as the toll of rapid industrialization was manifested in overcrowded, pestilential, and violent tenement districts populated by an immigrant community that seemed to outsiders unable to take advantage of America's opportunities. For Charles Nordhoff, widespread poverty and unemployment, and a sense that the poor were losing faith in the American dream, loomed as auguries of national destruction. He began to question his cherished beliefs in classical economics and to look in various directions for some satisfactory explanation of "why the world is so poor."

At the same time, his Washington columns castigated the federal legislature for its inaction in the face of serious threats to the national well-being. The New York *Herald* as a whole, partially under his direction, detailed the problems troubling the city, the state, and the country, using the methods and rhetoric, and proposing the solutions that would be adopted by the Progressive muckrakers of a later generation. Far from being the middle-class reformers credited with Progressivism, however, Nordhoff and his newspaper unmistakably identified themselves with the working poor. Disgusted with the Washington officials who would not listen to reason, alienating them with his blistering criticisms, Nordhoff rested his hopes for positive social change in journalism, even as he feared for the soul of a profession that seemed ever more forgetful of its public mission.

By the 1880s, Nordhoff's attitude toward journalism had soured considerably. Although he continued to believe in journalism's ability to "educate the people," the business itself was dreary, the work "hard & disagreeable toil."[1] He held himself aloof from the burgeoning press associations, from the bonhomie of

---

1. CN to Worthington Ford, "Sunday Evg.," [1884] Ford Papers, NYPL; CN to George Bancroft, June 5, 1885, Bancroft-Bliss Papers, LC.

the *Gridiron Club* and from discussions of the journalistic craft as a mere trade to be plied. For Nordhoff, journalism was first, last, and always a means of political action—and the nonpoliticized aspects of journalism seemed to him worse than useless. But the uglier aspects of political reporting had always depressed him, as he saw himself vainly attempting to hold up a standard that even his own newspaper sometimes failed to maintain and other papers seemed absolutely without any dedication to the truth whatsoever. "The *Tribune* and Philada. *Press* really astound me daily with reports on matters where I am well informed," he wrote in disgust to Atkinson in 1888, "which reports are wildly false." When a controversy "degenerated, as it has, in the *Tribune* & *Herald*, to mere billingsgate," he tried to hold himself above the fray. He insisted, "in what I have written I have appealed to reason & justice & the public good, but when the dirt flinging begins, I am silent, as other decent men are."[2]

Even *Harper's* was exhibiting craven tendencies. George Bancroft, the venerable old Jacksonian, found an article he had written rejected by a *Harper's* editor; and Nordhoff, who had become a good friend of Bancroft during his Washington years, looked into his reasons. "[Y]ou see he is afraid," Nordhoff wrote to Bancroft, "--not of the Supreme Court, but of his readers. What a pass we have come to when a correction of false & mischievous ... news is thought to be so unpopular that an editor is scared by the idea of it."[3] The business aspects of journalism, which so often ran counter to its public duties, seemed to Nordhoff to be in dangerous ascendancy.

But even as journalism became big business during the Gilded Age, and new streamlined methods of organization, production, and distribution were firmly entrenched, the content, and intent, of journalism retained its politicized orientation. While the need for large circulations rose, the question of how to gain those circulations—what kind of journalism the public would pay for—was the subject of heated debate. Fairness and balance were always highly praised, as was completeness of news coverage, though such platitudes could result in remarkably different results in different hands; but the myriad ways in which a newspaper might help or hinder certain causes—by selection, extent, and manner of coverage—were usually acknowledged. "No great journal can be a party organ," intoned one writer. "This was the cause of the inferiority of the *Tribune* and the *Times* ... to the *Herald*. The latter takes sides, but it is

---

2.   CN to Edward Atkinson, August 1, 1888 and May 12, 1881. Atkinson Papers, MHS.

3.   The editor at Harper's was a Mr. Alden. CN to Mrs. George Bancroft, October 3, 1884. Bancroft-Bliss Papers, LC; CN to George Mancroft, December 17, 1888. Atkinson Papers, Massachusetts Historical Society.

not restricted to one side."[4] George William Curtis, going further, equated partisanship with honesty. "We do not know one truly independent journal in the country whose sympathies are not with one of the two great parties," Curtis believed. "The man who thinks that both are equally bad, and does not care which prevails, is a man without opinions, or without principle, or without perception, and in either case is wholly unfit to be editor."

Bennett, according to Nordhoff, had declared that the *Herald* was not to be "any man's or any party's organ," but would continue in the tradition of independence established by his father. It would report the "facts" while making unmistakable judgments as to the implications of those facts: in political contests, one candidate could always be judged preferable to another without distorting the substance of their positions. Thus, while Bennett's rule was to attempt to cover all sides of an issue, the *Herald* made no pretense of believing all sides to have equal merit. Nordhoff himself explained the *Herald*'s policy during the campaign of 1884 to a young editor: Bennett leaned toward Arthur and opposed Blaine, but in supporting Arthur, the *Herald* only "stated facts & rectified misunderstandings of other papers—as the *Times*. The *Herald* ought to make known the truth abt. all sides."[5] "The Truth" was hotly contested, of

---

4. Various attitudes toward the profession are compiled in Charles Wingate, *Views and Interviews on Journalism* (New York: F. B. Patterson, 1875), passim. See also Hazel Dicken-Garcia, *Journalistic Standards in Nineteenth-Century America* (Madison: University of Wisconsin Press, 1989), 48–49, on the nineteenth-century "inability to conceptualize a nonpolitical role" for journalism. Dicken-Garcia, while delineating the growing calls for "independence," regards post–Civil War journalism as fitting a new paradigm, a "business model" replacing an antebellum "information model." By the end of the Civil War, she writes (p. 51), "the contours of a new business model were clear. Among such changes were the press's establishment as part of people's lives, subordination of opinion and partisanship to facts, modification of reporting form [into the standard 'inverted pyramid'], developments in news gathering, and adoption of organized business techniques to handle demand, supply and costs." All this is quite true, as far as the *process* of producing a newspaper is concerned; the "incorporation of America" certainly included journalism. The change in *content* and *intent* is less clear. But the "subordination of opinion ... to facts," though increasingly discussed, cannot be said to have triumphed in 1900 when muckrakers were advocating numerous changes and Hearst was plumping whatever political cause—such as war—caught his fancy. Dicken-Garcia takes a generally consensual view, as well as a Whiggish one, toward the evolution of journalism toward twentieth-century standards. See also Frederic Hudson, in Wingate, 135.
5. CN to Worthington Ford, April 17, 1884. Ford Papers, NYPL.

course, but that was essential to a democracy. Forthright debate was absolutely mandatory, with opposing newspapers squaring off in daily battle.[6]

Each newspaper, then, would in this view represent a segment of the populace, providing a public voice for the different, sometimes clashing interests of the community: interest-group politics was not an innovation of the twentieth century.[7] There were those, such as Whitelaw Reid, who denied that their newspapers had any ideological bent whatsoever, begging the entire issue of selectivity, and this was the view that was to triumph in the early twentieth century. But during the Gilded Age, a newspaper was judged, for the most part, not by its conformity to a bland neutrality—which, indeed, was usually disparaged as betraying a lack of principle—but by the positions it did take. There was disagreement as to whether newspapers actually led public opinion or merely reflected it, but the idea of being representative of a constituency of readers was pervasive. With politics as the standard of judgment, the reputations of more populist newspapers suffered accordingly among the conservative upper middle class, which succeeded in establishing the conservative and Republican New York *Tribune* and *New York Times* as the newspapers "of record," as opposed to the "irresponsible" reporting in the mass-circulation journals. The *Herald*'s politics—exhibited less on its editorial page than in its selection of stories—were not calculated to please those content with the status quo, but addressed the problems of the majority of its readers, the working poor.

The methods and attitudes that later generations would call "muckraking" were intrinsic to Nordhoff's work; he was constantly investigating rumors of perfidy so that he might present a compelling, factually based case for reform. He made considerable efforts to track down likely conflicts of interest, as in one case in which he suspected that American owners of Mexican mines were trying to manipulate American foreign policy for their own benefit.[8]

Henry George's idea that land monopoly was at the root of chronic economic troubles may well have focused Nordhoff's attention on the growing

---

[6.] George William Curtis, quoted in Wingate, 144; Bennett quoted in CN, *Reminiscences*, 12.

[7.] On the idea of newspapers as representing segments of the public, see Charles Wingate, *Views and Interviews with Journalists* (NY: F. B. Patterson, 1875), esp. as expressed by Henry Watterson, 17–18; Samuel Bowles, 45; Charles A. Dana, 62; David Croly, 84–85 and 340. Reid (p. 25–26) expresses an opposing view: the *Tribune*, he said, did not "represent" anything. It simply contained "every attainable fact of sufficient significance, affecting the social, political, intellectual and moral movements of the world."

[8.] CN to Col. Foster, May 21, 1877, Cincinnati Historical Society.

power of monopolies in general. Just as he was beginning to perceive that the concentration of power in the hands of corporate heads might pose a threat to the national welfare, along came Jay Gould, buying up all the telegraph lines.

Gould had long served as a lightning rod for public distrust of the emerging corporate order. In 1868, Henry Adams and his brother, Charles Francis, had produced a spectacularly damning account of Gould's machinations concerning the Erie railroad, which made his name a byword among reformers of the day, but this proved only a prelude to one of Gould's most audacious maneuvers. Adept at working Wall Street to his own advantage, Gould achieved national notoriety in 1869 when, in collusion with Jim Fisk, he had tried to corner the gold market and thereby precipitated a financial crisis of no small proportions.[9] During the 1870s, Gould had worked at increasing and consolidating his railroad holdings and emerged a major stockholder of almost every Southwestern railroad then existing, as well as of the Union Pacific.

Despite Nordhoff's 1871 contract with C. P. Huntington to write *California*, he was no great friend of the railroads. The efforts to bribe various federal officials, the use of watered stock, and the "land-grabbing" that they engaged in had discredited them in his eyes. But he felt that the general operations of corporations—as distinguished from blatantly criminal activity—ought not to be overseen or regulated in any way by the government. In 1881, Gould, already in control of a good part of the nation's railroad mileage, made deals with Huntington and William Vanderbilt, which left him in charge of the Western Union Telegraph Company. Worse, the new Gould-owned Western Union had just absorbed two smaller competing companies to form a monolithic lock on long-distance telegraphic communication across the United States.[10]

The telegraph system, in days before widespread use of the telephone, constituted a crucial means of communication when speed was important. It had been used to good effect in conveying military information during the Civil War, but by 1881, its chief users were the newspapers. The Associated Press had been formed to pool telegraph reports for the use of member newspapers, which kept the cost down and allowed many smaller papers to cover an unprecedented range of national and international issues in a timely manner. For the New York *Herald*, which prided itself on the enterprise and comprehensiveness with which it gathered news, the telegraph was of singular importance—as it was to the other big New York newspapers that aspired to a national audience.

[9.] For a detailed account of Gould's dealings throughout his life, see Maury Klein's *The Life and Legend of Jay Gould* (Baltimore: Johns Hopkins University Press, 1986). On the scheme to corner the gold market, see Klein, 99–101.

[10.] Klein, 279–82.

Placing the means of national communication under the control of a man like Gould, who was popularly perceived as power-mad as well as avaricious, shocked many journalists, who wasted no time in sounding the alarm in their editorial pages and news columns. One cartoon, published in *Punch*, showed Gould handing out AP dispatches signed with his name from the back of a wagon labeled "The Monopoly News Delivery" while editors of the *World*, *Herald*, *Sun*, *Star*, and *Mail Express* groveled below. (Significantly, the *Tribune* was not represented; it was already assumed to be in Jay Gould's pocket since he had financed Whitelaw Reid's purchase of the newspaper after the death of Greeley.)[11]

The growth in importance of the privately owned telegraph system had alarmed a few critics long before 1881; they saw nonpublic control of such a "natural monopoly" as dangerous. Nordhoff had resisted calls to nationalize the telegraph, noting in *Politics for Young Americans* the potential danger to civil liberties of allowing the government to control the nation's communications. The people needed to watch over their government, and they did this through their representatives in the press, who, Nordhoff believed, could transcend the petty political motives of all-too-many government officials to present news that was not objective, but intelligently critical from any number of perspectives. Left in the hands of the government, the telegraph might become the instrument of censorship and propaganda campaigns that would keep the people in ignorance.[12]

But if it was dangerous for the government to own the telegraph, how much more dangerous it would be for Jay Gould to control it! Appalled, Nordhoff wrote a column for the *Herald* in which he called for the government to step in against telegraph monopoly. There had emerged, he noted, a "new class of capitalists" who were "a danger to the people" and far too powerful for individual citizens to combat alone. Nordhoff's faith in the justice of free-market forces had at last been stretched too far, and snapped. "The telegraph consolidation has aroused a great deal of feeling in Congress," he wrote, as a bill to investigate the telegraph companies was introduced by William M. Springer of Indiana,

> and has persuaded some prominent men who hitherto were
> disinclined to government interference with corporations
> that it has become necessary for the defence of the people
> against monopolists, who, though they seem to quarrel for

---

11. Klein, illustration preceding, 375. Several other cartoons reprinted in Klein strike the same theme of a Gould-controlled press.

12. CN, *Politics for Young Americans* (New York: Harper & Brothers, 1875), 28–31.

a while, in the end always unite their forces against their customers, the people.[13]

Nordhoff, in his paraphrasing of any Congressman's arguments, usually made it clear whether or not he considered a given position just. In the case of the Springer telegraph bill, he elaborated on the reasoning behind the proposed legislation. Western Union was not a private concern, but a common carrier in the operations of which the people were vitally interested. Usually loath to provide publicity through lengthy quotations to positions he opposed or regarded as "buncombe," Nordhoff quoted the sponsoring Congressman at length.[14] The "'representatives of the people,'" Nordhoff recalled him saying,

> would not long suffer their constituents to be robbed by mammoth corporations when the remedy is in the hands of the law-making power. It is true there is great objection from some quarters to government interference ..., but such objections on abstract constitutional constructions ought not to stand for a moment in the way of the establishment of such reforms and legislation as will secure to the people reasonable and efficient facilities for the transmission of communications by telegraph.[15]

Resuming his own voice, Nordhoff noted that the idea of "interference and regulation" was gaining favor on Capitol Hill, for legislators saw the need to "protect the public rigorously against the constant selfish schemes of a few capitalists who play with public interest for the mere object of doubling and redoubling their millions." Rate-gouging and stock-watering were simply wrong and not to be endured. Existing law did "not protect the public," he insisted. Furthermore, "the recent gigantic consolidation proves that it never will." He continued:

> Private enterprise is powerless against the schemes of a few men with hundreds of millions in their pockets unless Congress will undertake to supervise and regulate their

---

13.   [CN,] "Washington: Opposition to Telegraph Monopoly in Congress," New York *Herald*, January 19, 1881.

14.   William M. Springer also wrote an article a few months after he introduced his bill: "The Telegraph Monopoly," *North American Review* 132 (April, 1881), 370–381.

15.   Congressman William M. Springer, quoted in [CN] "Washington: Opposition to Telegraph Monopolies in Congress," 1/19/81.

operations in the most rigid manner for the protection of the people.[16]

No longer could he conceive of the likes of Jay Gould and William Vanderbilt as representatives of "private enterprise," for they seemed to produce nothing in their machinations except watered stock and personal power. Nordhoff had always viewed society in terms of "producers" and "non-producers," a reflection of his Jacksonian upbringing, and the idea that monopolies were a perversion of America's open system was also of Jacksonian vintage. The unprecedented scale of corporate power, impossible to ignore in 1881, had breathed new life into the old antimonopoly tradition.

As government inaction continued, Nordhoff kept up his attacks on the telegraph monopoly. Various methods of dealing with the telegraph were proposed, and Nordhoff considered the possibility of a government-owned-and-operated telegraph system as an acceptable, if not optimal, solution. He advised a young editor on the *Herald* on how to attack the subject. "It strikes me we ought not to go so diametrically against a govt. telegraph; but say it has objections—true; but if we cannot have any other—such as a contract one then we want & must have a govt. lien."[17]

Rather than nationalizing the telegraph, Nordhoff preferred some limitations on governmental control. But his distaste for full government ownership was not absolute. "Whatever the objections to this," he told his protégé editor, "the hurt of the present monopoly is *greater*; & cannot & will not be endured." By so stating the matter, an editorial might thereby "help us to the contract lien," he added, "& it keeps up the Monopoly cry."[18]

Nordhoff had long viewed government as a potentially positive force in the community, but only on the local level, thus keeping it close to the people, its responsibilities easily seen, its errors readily corrected. In the 1860s, his *Evening Post* editorials called upon the New York City and State governments to enact and enforce laws to protect the public health and safety. Even in 1881, presented with chemists' reports on the commonplace adulteration of foodstuffs, he insisted on "stringent laws to expose and punish the poisonous adulteration of

[16]. [CN,] "Washington: Opposition," 1/19/81. See also [CN] "Washington: Movement Against Telegraph Monopolies," NY *Herald*, February 1, 1881.

[17]. [CN,] "Our Telegraph System: Western Union Monopoly Attacked and Exposed," NY *Herald*, January 15, 1884. [CN,] "Washington: A Measure to Create a Postal Telegraph Monopoly," NY *Herald*, January 14, 1884.

[18]. CN to Worthington Ford, [1884], Ford Papers, NYPL.

food," but only through state laws.[19] His approval of federal regulation of the telegraph was tentative, and as an abstract principle, he continued to distrust governmental interference with the economy.

In 1881, when the New York *Evening Post* was for sale after William Cullen Bryant's death, Gordon L. Ford approached Nordhoff about joining Wells, himself, and several others in buying and editing the newspaper. But the idea held no appeal for him: it would mean the loss of independence for the would-be partners were both "literary" and out to make a good profit, "all would want a finger in the pie"; and if there were disagreements over editorial policy, the whole arrangement would become untenable.

But even without these impediments, Nordhoff wrote, "I for one should long hesitate, & as I now feel, decline." To run the newspaper "would be to embark on years of very persistent hard work, no let up," and always with the possibility of losing everything. Nordhoff was content at the *Herald*, with no responsibility for the newspaper's finances, "and I have not for some years thought of going into any other paper." Ford was one of his closest friends, with whom he was always candid, and he added that he was "in very friendly & even intimate terms with Mr. Bennett, whom I greatly like & respect, & who does not conceal that he values me."

Nordhoff appreciated his situation at the *Herald*. "I have my fair influence in [Bennett's] councils," he continued, "& it has a large very large audience, which I greatly value" his job gave him "more liberty, as to time & continuous labor than I could look for in the *Post*." What he really yearned for was time, time away from doing other men's work. "If any one would offer me a moderate support for three days work in the week," he went on, "that would be a temptation, for it is leisure for other & more important work which I crave, as I get older. I see lots of it to do, & can't get the chance. ...I mean to stay where I am," he concluded, "& to have one master rather than a dozen, & some leisure, instead of none." Although he longed for financial independence, "I don't want to go into any undertaking wh. would swallow me up entirely, & will not." Wells would "think me a great goose I guess," he added ruefully, "but will forgive me, because he knows that I love you both, but am a sort of pigheaded ignoramus." He suggested that Carl Schurz be approached instead for the *Evening Post*'s editorial work, and soon Schurz was hired in his place.[20]

---

19. [CN,] "Washington: Startling Statements Regarding the Adulteration of Food." New York *Herald*, February 17, 1881.

20. CN to Gordon L. Ford, February 27, 1881. Ford Papers, NYPL. In another age, Nordhoff might have wound up in the academy. See also CN to Ford, April 11, 1881. The sanitized version of the change of editorship at the *Evening Post* can be found in the statements by Carl Schurz, Horace White, and E. L. Godkin in *The Evening*

When the new *Evening Post* was safely launched that June, Nordhoff wrote to Wells his opinion of the venture. Never one to engage in risky financial speculation, unsure of its morality even as he longed for the kind of quick financial boons it might provide, Nordhoff regarded his peers with some bemusement, not untouched by bitterness. "It seems funny enough," he concluded his letter to Wells, "to see the 'damn literary fellows' like Villard, White & you turning out capitalists & ...lords."[21]

And what of the "one master" whom Nordhoff preferred to the dozen? James Gordon Bennett, Jr., who had grown up in Paris, relocated there in the face of stark humiliation in 1877 and never again made the United States more than a temporary resting place. But according to subordinates, the *Herald* was no less under his control; Bennett continued to run the newspaper from Paris, freely using the telegraph to convey his orders to the New York staff and not infrequently summoning editors and writers to Europe for meetings. An enigmatic figure, Bennett's role in overseeing the *Herald* has generally been ignored in the light of his publicly dissolute social life. But his bemused and bedazzled employees remembered the intensity of their experiences with Bennett. He was "the benevolent despot, the occasionally unjust and suspicious employer, and yet the generous ... patron," wrote one former employee, "and the man for whom ... I would have come near going to hell."[22]

The character of the younger Bennett's *Herald*—pro-labor, antimonopoly— suited Nordhoff well. It was, above all, a good pulpit: he once said that the *Herald*, with its large national circulation, was "the best place in which to make public new ideas, new policies, or to expose abuses and redress wrongs."[23] As for Bennett himself, he had come to know him "intimately," and he regarded his employer as "singularly misunderstood and undervalued." His former employer, Nordhoff wrote some years after his own retirement, was "one of the most remarkable men I have known, and one of the ablest," a true "'statesman-journalist.'" Bennett held a "determination that the *Herald* should be used by him always to serve and advance the cause of good government and good morals and the true interests of the whole country."[24] Another serious journalist (and future Librarian of Congress), John Russell Young, declared Bennett to have

---

Post Hundredth Anniversary, November 16, 1901 (NY: Evening Post Co., 1902). The squabbling among the three editors can be found in their respective biographies: Logdon on White, Trefousse on Schurz, and Armstrong on Godkin.

[21]   CN to David Ames Wells, June 5 [1881]. Wells Papers, LC.

[22]   Albert Stevens Crockett, *When James Gordon Bennett was the Caliph of Baghdad* (NY: Funk & Wagnalls, 1926), 411.

[23]   CN, *Reminiscences of Some Editors I Have Known* (San Diego: 1900), 28.

[24]   CN, *Reminiscences*, 11–12.

"courage, clearness, a quick mind, a thorough knowledge of his profession, generous and resolute qualities, and great independence."[25]

As for Bennett's dictatorial ways toward his employees, Nordhoff did not object to strong leadership and readily acknowledged his own subordinate position in exchange for the intellectual independence Bennett granted him. Though he chafed at his job, Nordhoff didn't blame Bennett, who paid him an enormous salary ($10,000 per year in 1888, reputedly the highest of any Washington correspondent) and treated him magnanimously, it seems, at all times. "Mr. Bennett has generously given me six months holiday with *full pay*," Nordhoff wrote to Atkinson in 1881. "I am more grateful to him than I can tell you."[26] In 1888, he similarly allowed Nordhoff several months' paid holiday in Europe, where Nordhoff was able to see his grandson for the first time.[27] Simple gratitude may have colored Nordhoff's estimation of his employer, but his high opinion of Bennett never wavered.

Most importantly, he enjoyed virtually total freedom to say what he liked in the *Herald* and, just as importantly, to not say what he did not believe. Don Seitz, Bennett's contemporary and biographer, described two of Bennett's editorial writers, George H. Hepworth, and Nordhoff. Hepworth "abased himself at the feet of his proprietor," Seitz wrote, in contrast to Nordhoff, who "stood up stoutly for the things he believed to be right." When Bennett asked him to write an editorial favoring Benjamin Harrison over Grover Cleveland in the presidential contest of 1888, Nordhoff "quietly declined," according to one observer, "remarking that the agreement under which he came to the *Herald* prescribed that he should never be asked to write in support of things to which he was opposed. To this Bennett gave cheerful assent."[28]

As for the old problem of the counting room exerting influence over editorial policy—the problem that had ultimately driven Nordhoff from the *Evening Post*—this was never an issue at the *Herald*. Bennett was both proprietor

---

25.   John Russell Young, quoted in Seitz, *The James Gordon Bennetts*, 250.

26.   CN to Edward Atkinson, June 13, 1881, Atkinson Papers; and "News Gathering at Washington," *The Journalist*, December 22, 1888: "Chas. Nordhoff … is credited with drawing the heaviest salary paid in Washington—$10,000." He also mentions to Atkinson on another occasion going to Europe for a month "by Mr. Bennett's leave." CN to EA, 4/22/84.

27.   CN to Mr. Fairchild, April 3, 1888, mentions Nordhoff's departure on April 4 for Europe; Fairchild Papers, NYPL. On July 17, he wrote to Gordon L. Ford from Germany, that his anticipated date of return was August 2 or 3, making his trip four months long. This was a trip in which he travelled to his birthplace, Erwitte, in Prussia.

28.   Seitz, 241–2.

and de facto editor in chief, and so there could be no conflict in the paper's general purpose. Once, in the 1890s, two large advertisers wrote letters to the *Herald* saying that they would "appreciate" its support of their favored candidate in the New York mayoral election, a Tammany Hall politician. Bennett's response was to have both letters printed at the head of the editorial page, with an accompanying paragraph: "We are very, very sorry that we cannot comply with these requests, for even if George Washington came to life the *Herald* would not support him if he were Tammany's standard-bearer." (Pulitzer and the *World* remarked on the incident editorially, condemning the two businessmen's attempt to buy off the *Herald* and indirectly praising Bennett's handling of the matter.) Similarly, when Bennett offered a writing contract to Samuel Clemens, in Clemens's remembrance, he told the writer that "if I would I might have full swing, and about anything and everything I wanted to."[29]

Bennett Jr. had been apprenticed in the *Herald*'s various departments, his father having him serve time in the pressroom, the business office, and with the compositors before turning the *Herald* over to his twenty-five-year-old heir-apparent. Nordhoff commented more than once upon Bennett's detailed grasp of every aspect of running the paper, down to the important matter of purchasing the paper to be used. Because of this, he regarded Bennett as a true workingman, a producer, and of a totally different class than most publishers. He also credited the elder and the younger Bennetts with possessing both a "keen scent for news" and "the ability to mix the news with brains." Nordhoff had always disdained "news" detached from interpretation, but he believed the *Herald* managed to incorporate both. "A fact would suggest something" to Bennett.[30]

There was a dynamism, an energy about Bennett and his *Herald* that one *Herald* veteran, Albert Crockett, could not forget, and he ruminated on the low esteem in which Bennett was held both during his lifetime and after and blamed Bennett's public alcoholic binges for this neglect. "The Book of Fame is silent on the indiscretions of many of those it has enrolled," he wrote. "Some are loved or hated for those very faults," and he credited Bennett with advancing "science and invention and human knowledge" in the "guise" of running a newspaper. "What I assert is that the man did some things that were great— greater than have been accomplished by some the world calls great," Crockett concluded.[31]

---

[29]. Seitz, 226–7 and 365–6.

[30]. Seitz, 326–7, 365–6; CN, *Reminiscences*, 15–16, 19. See CN to Edward Atkinson, August 4, 1880, directing him to "Mr. Bennett. He is a working man...."

[31]. Crockett, op. cit., 410–11.

This was a verdict that Charles Nordhoff seconded. Bennett was "persistently and viciously misunderstood, misrepresented and calumniated," he wrote, because he was a "thoroughly and courageously independent and honest journalist" and "because he chose to live a life different from the ordinary."[32] But it was Bennett's political stance—his charities, his willingness to publicize the struggles of labor and the depredations suffered by poor city residents, his defiance of Jay Gould—that most won Nordhoff's respect.

Of course, the readership of the *Herald*—the largest mass-circulation newspaper of its time, one of the pioneers of the "penny press"—was composed in large part of German and Irish immigrants, and it was only good business for Bennett to exhibit a concern for the working class. The *Herald* gave full coverage to Irish politics, particularly Parnell's American tour of the 1880s, and Bismarck's exploits were well-publicized as well; the persistent nationalistic feelings of immigrants would have been gratified by the *Herald*'s attention to their homelands. There may have been a hint of noblesse oblige in Bennett's attention to the working class as well. Certainly Bennett, born to wealth, was less interested in currying favor with the affluent and "respectable" classes than were journalist-publishers like Whitelaw Reid. Reid, with few resources of his own, courted Jay Gould in order to finance his 1873 purchase of the *Tribune*; Bennett had a considerably different relationship with Gould.

In addition to giving a prominent forum to antimonopolist sentiments such as those expressed by Nordhoff, Bennett responded to Gould's purchase of the Western Union Telegraph Company by setting up the Commercial Cable Company, deliberately providing the only competition to Gould's transatlantic cable, breaking Western Union's monopoly and forcing it to cut its rates. Considering the extensive use the *Herald* made of the telegraph, Bennett's action certainly made sense financially, but contemporaries believed he had set up the company for altruistic reasons as well. The publisher "saw the public necessity and benefit very strongly" of the Commercial Cable Company, Nordhoff later wrote, "believing that a cable monopoly was sure to be oppressive to the public, and sure to lead to abuses." In response, Gould attacked Bennett, once sending a letter to all the other New York dailies; Bennett obtained a copy, had it printed in the *Herald*, and placed himself in the popular position of an enemy of the much-despised Gould.[33]

32. CN, *Reminiscences*, 14.

33. CN, *Reminiscences*, 28; Joseph I. C. Clarke, *My Life and Memories* (New York: Dodd, Mead, 1925), 141; Lyons, 13; Seitz, 363–4. Maury Klein, in *The Life and Legend of Jay Gould* (Baltimore: Johns Hopkins University Press, 1986), goes into some detail on Bennett's activities against Gould and attributes Bennett's hostility to the fact that his own telegraph company was in competition with Gould's Western Union. But

As Nordhoff continued to pillory the Democratic and Republican leadership in the *Herald,* he created enemies. Though Rutherford B. Hayes had somewhat recovered from his hurt at Nordhoff's "panicky fickleness" in 1876–77, when Nordhoff had decried in print the "rascally fraud" of the Republicans, not all the victims of Nordhoff's attacks were so forgiving. Probably, the most powerful enemy he created for himself was James G. Blaine.

By 1882, Nordhoff and Blaine had been neighbors and friends for some years, emblematic in their coziness of the general cooperation that was the rule between the press and politicians. But Nordhoff's loyalties were to ideals, as he conceived them, and not to particular politicians. In May of 1881, he had written to Atkinson of the need to collaborate with any politician who might further their cause. "I dislike & despise Conkling more probably than you do, & I like Blaine more than you do," he had written. "But what have personal like or dislike to do with a grave public question?"[34]

With his conversion to the Democratic faith, Nordhoff had become a political opponent of Blaine, the most powerful Republican politician of the postwar period. Their political estrangement hardened into personal animosity in early 1882, when a young Democratic Congressman, Perry Belmont (son of Democratic Party boss August Belmont) gave Nordhoff some letters obtained by the House Foreign Relations Committee. A scandal had begun to surface the previous fall concerning the State Department's policy toward Chile and Peru, which had been involved for some time in "the War of the Pacific" over contested territory. The United States' diplomatic policy regarding the war was characterized by peculiar reversals and inconsistencies and seemed to favor Peru by pressuring Chile to cede territory to its enemy. Blaine, the former Secretary of State, had done his best to lay the blame for any improprieties upon the late American minister to Peru, but the Foreign Relations Committee decided to investigate and requested that all pertinent State Department correspondence be turned over.[35]

Bennett didn't purchase the Commercial Cable Company until 1883, and by then, the *Herald* had for several years been pillorying Gould in news stories and editorials as well as Nordhoff's columns.

[34.] See Webb Hayes to Rutherford B. Hayes, June 12, 1876, RBH Library; Eliza (Mrs. John) Davis to Rutherford B. Hayes, June 23, 1876; and Hans Trefousse, *Carl Schurz* (Knoxville: University of Tennessee, 1982), 251, for mention of a meeting between Blaine and Schurz at Nordhoff's home in 1880. CN to Edward Atkinson, May 12, 1881. Atkinson Papers, MHS.

[35.] Perry Belmont, *An American Democrat* (NY: 1939). Belmont mistakes the date on which Nordhoff printed the letters, which was in fact February 18, 1882. A concise

Suspicious connections between Blaine, his Minister to Paris, a French banking organization, and an American guano dealer called "The Peruvian Company," made evident in the State Department letters, suggested that Blaine and his cohorts were financially interested in a favorable ruling on a certain claim before the Peruvian government. Various actions by the American minister and other foreign service officials persuaded Peru that the United States would intercede on its behalf in its war against Chile, provided only that it then act favorably on the claim under question.

Nordhoff had been reporting on the growing scandal for well over six weeks by mid-January of 1882 and had voiced his suspicions in no uncertain terms. He called for a full investigation into the matter. "There is no doubt that somebody in authority attempted to coerce Chile and persuade Peru into a recognition of the ...claims," he maintained, at a time when Peru was in no position to resist. America's "crooked diplomacy" had prolonged the war, damaged both countries and alienated them from the United States, and all "for the sake of furthering a prodigious scheme of claims." Someone had to be held responsible, and Nordhoff was not reluctant to fix that responsibility on Blaine.[36]

With the release of the Foreign Affairs Committee's evidence that month, Nordhoff concluded that if Blaine was not abysmally, unaccountably ignorant of the operations of his own subordinates, he was himself guilty of misconduct. The letters "must either cover Mr. Blaine with ridicule," he wrote in the *Herald*, "or convict him of designs which were injurious to his country and not reputable in themselves." Belmont, like many a denizen of Capitol Hill before and since, wanted further evidence to be made public and so he surreptitiously turned some classified correspondence over to Nordhoff and to Nordhoff's colleague at the NY *Sun*, Charles Anderson Dana. Nordhoff spelled out the letters' meaning in unmistakable terms. The State Department was in collusion with "a jobbing transaction," even at the risk of war. Twice in succeeding weeks, to document his accusations, Nordhoff devoted his column to verbatim transcripts of the pertinent letters, taking up five and six full columns of the *Herald*'s tiniest typeface. Blaine's proffered explanations of the State Department's actions were unconvincing, and Nordhoff meticulously listed all the inconsistencies and omissions in his statements. Nordhoff insisted that a "thorough inquiry" would prove ugly allegations against Blaine and his State Department. "But

---

account of the Peru-Chile imbroglio can be found in Thomas C. Reeves, *Gentleman Boss: The Life of Chester Alan Arthur* (NY: Knopf, 1975), 282–93.

36. See, for example, [CN] "Washington," NY *Herald*, December 19, 1881. [CN,] "Washington: Investigation of Our South American Diplomacy," NY *Herald*, January 10, 1882.

unless the country demands it," he added, "this House committee clearly means that nobody shall be hurt" other than minor functionaries.[37]

But ultimately, the Foreign Affairs committee circumscribed its investigation, declining to accept all the written evidence offered by a key witness and confining itself to narrow, predetermined specifics. The "thorough inquiry" that Nordhoff hoped the country would demand never took place. Blaine emerged from the scandal with his political viability intact, if not unscathed, and was to become the Republican presidential nominee two years later.

To Nordhoff, the manner in which the Blaine scandal had been disposed of was one more triumph of politics over justice. Never again could he rely upon Blaine as anything but an adversary. "Of course you know that Blaine *hates* me," he wrote to Edward Atkinson in 1890; "--on acc[oun]t of the old Peru-Chile-Shipherd matter wh[ich] I forced on public attention & did I think a great service to the country." For eight years, then, Blaine's hostility toward Nordhoff had simmered unabated; and in this, he was not alone. By the early 1880s, Nordhoff had seen enough—enough venality, enough special-interest legislation, enough hypocrisy, and enough abuse of power—to discard all caution. More and more, his *Herald* columns resembled less political analyses than criminal indictments.[38]

As the decade of the '80s wore on, the Nordhoffs' "kaleidoscopic" Washington socializing continued, the entire family benefitting from Charles's privileged position close to the seats of power. As Walter's new wife, Sarah, recalled many years later, she and the three Nordhoff daughters "went occasionally to the White House receptions, behind the barrier—while the crowd passed along in front." Frequent dinner companions at the Nordhoff home on K Street included L. Q. C. Lamar, the Mississippi Senator who was named to the Supreme Court in 1884; journalist-cum-railroad baron Henry Villard; astronomer Simon Newcomb; aeronautics pioneer Samuel Langley;

37. [CN,] "Peru-Chile. Diplomatic Correspondence Sent to Congress." NY *Herald*, January 27, 1882. [CN,] "The Peruvian Question: Mr. Shipherd's Diplomatic Correspondence Made Public." NY *Herald*, February 18, 1882.[CN,] "The Peruvian Imbroglio," NY *Herald*, January 28, 1882, and "The Peruvian Company: Mr. Shipherd's Diplomatic Correspondence Made Public," February 18, 1882. [CN,] "Washington: Omissions of Mr. Blaine's Explanation," NY *Herald*, January 31, 1882. [CN,] "Washington: Senator Butler on the South Carolina Census," NY *Herald*, February 8, 1881. [CN,] "Washington: The Chile-Peru Investigation Commenced," NY *Herald*, March 16, 1882. See also [CN,] "Washington: Shipherd's Refusal to Throw Light on the Peruvian Company," NY *Herald*, April 19, 1882.
38. CN to Edward Atkinson, June 7, [1890]. Atkinson Papers, MHS.

and Nordhoff's Alpine neighbor and friend William Walter Phelps. He was willing to exert himself to help his friends and the friends of friends through his contacts. George Bancroft, whom Nordhoff once thanked for his "long & unvarying kindnesses," upon occasion would receive Nordhoff's help with editors at *Harper's*.[39]

Nordhoff seems to have cared less for political agreement than for intelligent debate or knowledgeable scientific discussion, as the spectrum of his friendships attests. Phelps, for instance, an avid protectionist and a Republican, was close enough to Nordhoff to leave him $10,000 in his will. Nor was the socializing purely intellectual; his daughter-in-law, Sarah, remembered Langley, then the Secretary of the Smithsonian Institution, as "courting [Nordhoff's eldest daughter] Amy, who would have none of him." (As an old woman, Sarah mused that "[w]e gave little thought then to his preoccupation with airships—it seemed a mild form of insanity.") "There were breakfasts at nine o'clock at Mrs. George Kennan's," Sarah went on, referring to the wife of the famed writer on Siberia; there were "evening parties before balls," charity functions and dinners with Phoebe Hearst, the British minister and his wife, the Popes, the Whitneys, the Daweses, and "a flood of calling" by the women and the men. Elsie, at sixteen, was supposed to be a "particular friend" of President Cleveland.[40]

---

[39]   Lida Nordhoff to Phoebe Hearst, n.d., Phoebe A. Hearst Papers, Bancroft Library. See also CN to Gordon L. Ford, May 18, 1887, regarding his putting the K Street House up for sale. CN to Mrs. George Bancroft, October 3, 1884. Bancroft-Bliss Papers, LC; CN to George Bancroft, 6/5/1885, Bancroft-Bliss Papers, LC; CN to Edward Atkinson, "Tuesday" [1885]. The astronomer under question was Asa Hall "who," Nordhoff wrote, "discovered the satellites of Mars." Hall's discovery had made him famous, in Europe as well as in the United States, but had never received sufficient recognition, Nordhoff believed, and attendance at the meeting would garner him "a great reception." "Now then, can't you ask Mr. Forbes, & a few other rich friends to put their hands in their pockets - *without publication* you understand—& enable Hall & his wife to go? ...- [T]here must be no newspaper item about it, because Hall is poor, but proud."

[40]   Lida Nordhoff, two letters to Phoebe Hearst, Washington, no dates, Phoebe A. Hearst Papers, Bancroft Library; CN to Mrs. Dawes, Feb. 2, no year. Dawes Papers, LC. At this time, the Nordhoffs were living at 1732 H Street; they also bought a home, eventually, at 1731 K Street. Both these addresses are less than three blocks from the White House; in 1887, Nordhoff believed he could sell the K Street house for $50,000. CN to Gordon L. Ford, May 18, 1887. Sarah Cope Whitall Nordhoff, dictated memoir, in the possession of Walter Morrison of Sudbury, Massachusetts, and Franklin Nordhoff of Torrance, California, 22. Mr. Nordhoff believed the

Although Nordhoff preferred Washington to "the comprehensive brutal selfishness of N.Y.," with the accompanying "utter hopelessness of curing it," he was never content being tied down in either venue, churning out columns on a daily schedule that left him too drained to attempt other serious work. His desperate need for time away, he once wrote to Ford's son Worthington, "comes I suspect less from weariness than from an intense desire to finish some work which I have in my mind, & to which I must give a little consecutive thought, or burst." He occasionally resented even the public demand that kept him at his *Herald* routine. "I have not a moment at my command," he complained to one editor, declining to write an article on political matters. "...What a plague the invention of reading & writing—or rather the general spread of the thing, has become." He was, he explained, "a man who has more duties to perform than he likes; who just now gets no leisure, even to write a letter to a friend; and whose chief notion of Heaven is a place where we will be authorized to neglect & defy all his duties."[41]

Whenever he was feeling particularly trapped, Nordhoff's mind would turn to the tropics, far from Washington, New York, and "civilization" in general. "I must say the northern winter oppresses me more as I get older," he once wrote to Atkinson. "I read the other day an Arab proverb, 'it is dangerous to walk in an avenue of palms'—which is subtly true."[42]

Like many of his contemporaries, Nordhoff read Gibbons's *Decline and Fall of the Roman Empire* as a cautionary tale for America, for the country's prosperity during the early 1880s seemed to have no solid underpinnings. With the economic downturn of 1884, his worst fears seemed to be confirmed. Something was very wrong with the economy, and for the first time, he seriously questioned the explanations of economic liberals like Atkinson. In late 1884, after a trip to Paris at one of Bennett's frequent summonses, he wrote to Atkinson with a troubled mind. "I wish you'd turn your attention to a matter about which really thoughtful economists, as we pretend to be, ought to make a careful & thorough study," he began. "I mean the *universal* depression of industry." All explanations that blamed the American tariff system were inadequate in the face of international dislocations, nor did the profligacy and idleness of the poor seem the real culprits. He sent Atkinson an English newspaper clipping on the "dreadful conditions" of industry in that country. A

---

memoir had been written in the 1950s. CN to Daniel Lamont, March 17, 1885, Grover Cleveland Papers, LC.

41. CN to Edward Atkinson, October 18, 1882, Atkinson Papers, MHS. CN to Worthington Ford, [June] 1881, Ford Papers, NYPL. CN to J. M. Libbey [editor of the *Princeton Review*], October 12, 1882. CN Papers, NYPL.

42. CN to Edward Atkinson, January 6, 1884. Atkinson Papers, MHS.

French resident had told him, he added, "that the French people are poorer just now than he has ever known them," throughout rural France as well as its cities, and that this poverty had struck "people of all kinds—decent & respectable, who are ... pinched and reduced to-straights [*sic*] of economy beyond usual." He had heard the same report from Germans about Germany. Silk prices were dropping despite a war that ought to have driven prices up, and deflation was the rule. What had happened to the old law of supply and demand? "The peculiarity of the situation everywhere seems to me to be overproduction," he wrote. "Now overproduction means overabundance—& surely that cannot properly be a cause of prolonged suffering? But what then? Of course what is the matter is a general—almost universal *derangement* of industry. *But* what makes that is the question."

Perhaps the protective tariff was to blame for the American "derangement", "but it has not made it with England? Scarcely with France? & Bismarck's high tariff has not had time to have this effect in Germany." No, it was not simply the tariff. There was something systemically wrong with the new industrial order. There was a deeper problem, "a disease" which he believed "threatens what we call civilization." As if afraid that Atkinson would not believe him, Nordhoff added example upon example. "Why are there more ships now afloat than suffice to do all the carrying trade of the world, so that ships are a drag?" he asked. "Why is there more sugar than the world has means to buy?" Atkinson, with his independent income, was freer to take on such a monumental problem than was Nordhoff, the family breadwinner. "I have tried to look into this curious problem of suffering in the midst of abundance, & apparently because of too great plenty," he wrote; "but I don't get ahead. I haven't time; but it is worth some one's care." He continued to puzzle and to question his old notions of natural harmony:

> Does machinery last too long? You used to teach me that it is
> short lived. *I* used to preach that tariff & other interferences
> had drawn too many men away from agriculture & that the
> equilibrium needed to be reestablished between manufactures
> & agriculture. But here comes an evident overproduction of
> wheat! And so great a glut of whiskey ... that the corn market
> is affected.[43]

But if classical economics failed to provide an obvious solution, still it was the very basis of Nordhoff's thinking. Faced with a particularly threatening situation, such as a communications monopoly and a particularly nefarious

---

[43]   CN to Edward Atkinson, 12/28/84. Atkinson Papers, MHS.

individual, such as Jay Gould, he could sanction the idea of governmental intervention, but it was not an idea he espoused with any degree of consistency.

Perhaps, unsure of himself, Nordhoff allowed his attitudes to be swayed by the predispositions of his friends. Particularly with Atkinson, who regarded deviations from classical economics as evidence of foolishness if not of malice, Nordhoff could not discard the old beliefs any more than he could imagine a world without the force of gravity. No, it still must be a question of imperfect conformance to natural law. "One thing I clearly see," he added. As the world grew more complicated, "there *must* be less interference by the governments, by laws, with the natural course of industry." Having grasped this certainty as if he were a drowning man clutching the remains of a torpedoed ship, Nordhoff nevertheless was troubled with forebodings. Until the ultimate perfection of the laissez-faire state, he wondered, "is it possible that the present condition fostered a general & permanent increase of misery? …& that we are taking a ship downward on the Malthusian road?" Disturbed by the dissonance between what he perceived and what he believed and doubtful that Atkinson would take him seriously, he added an uncharacteristically tentative disclaimer, "Excuse all this nonsense?" and closed the letter.[44]

Atkinson's reply was swift and decided. The answers were simple, really. Were businesses failing? "No one has failed here who ought not to have failed," he wrote. He ticked down the list of Nordhoff's questions. Business failures were simply "the clearing away of rubbish." As for overproduction? "There is no overproduction," he wrote dismissively. "…If there is an overproduction of wheat? What of it? It constitutes only 10% of our agricultural product and is the product of machinery rather than of muscle."[45] Atkinson acknowledged Nordhoff's point that "the benefit of the railway, the steamship and the telegraph have been enjoyed mainly by the rich," but he insisted that that benefit was, even as he wrote, being distributed: trickling down to the masses, as it were.

> In the process, …a small part of the population is thrown out of work,—but even at the reduced wages which effect only a small part of the working people of this country, they are still much better off than they were ever before because they can buy more for their money.

And if slowed railroad construction had cut down the need for iron,

---

44.   CN to Edward Atkinson, 12/28/1884. Atkinson Papers, MHS.

45.   Edward Atkinson to CN, January 2, 1885. Atkinson Papers, MHS.

> What of it? There are less than a hundred thousand men engaged in making pig iron in the United States. Adjust them somewhere else. ...Excess of ships. Why? Because every ship carries more cargo ... and the voyages are shorter. ...There is a glut of whiskey. What of it? Better burn the corn than make whiskey of it.

On Atkinson went. Every troubling phenomenon Nordhoff had cited was either insignificant in quantitative (and therefore qualitative) terms, or was really an indirect reflection of progress. And as to the poor? He would waste no compassion on them.

> Suffering in the midst of abundance. Why? Because those who suffer have not the *natural gumption* which would enable them to take advantage of the better conditions placed at their disposal.[46]

But as to Nordhoff's call for "less interference by the government," Atkinson could only say, "Amen. They really do mischief." Atkinson's diagnosis of the conditions that called for less government could not have differed more from Nordhoff's, and perhaps this should have hinted that for at least one of them, the prescribed cure did not follow from the symptoms. But Atkinson was untroubled by doubts. "Increasing misery and Malthusianism. Not a bit of it," he pronounced. Despite temporary dislocations, "we never were making greater progress than we are today."[47]

If the Democrats took no clear stands on the issues, more and more the Republicans possessed for Nordhoff a clear and terrible identity as the party of "protection and monopoly."[48] As the 1880s progressed, and he began to regard large corporations as the enemy of "the people," Nordhoff viewed the continuance of protective tariffs and the constant scuttling of bills favoring regulation or investigation of corporate entities, as well as those prohibiting certain ethically dubious relationships between legislators and corporations, as evidence of the depravity of the Republican-controlled legislature.[49] (Twenty

---

[46.]   Edward Atkinson to CN, January 2, 1885. Atkinson Papers, MHS.

[47.]   Edward Atkinson to CN, 1/2/1885. Atkinson Papers, MHS.

[48.]   CN to Edward Atkinson, March 4, 1880. Atkinson Papers, MHS.

[49.]   For instance [CN,] "Senate Pitfalls," New York *Herald*, December 16, 1886; [CN,] "Senatorial Attorneys," New York *Herald*, January 31, 1887; [CN,] "Republican Tricks," New York *Herald*, February 11, 1888. On the actions of Congress regarding land reform measures, which would have stripped railroad corporations of land

years later, the muckrakers' critique of the Senate as a "millionaires' club" would reach the same conclusion.) "It is not extravagant to say," he had written early in 1883, "that the republicans in Congress are in league with these capitalist monopolists who fatten on bad and unjust laws."[50]

"Capitalist," which had always been a term of approbation to Nordhoff ("every laborer ought to seek to become a capitalist," he had often written in the '60s), had taken on sinister connotations by the early 1880s. "Capitalists" were not producers; they were parasites, accruing wealth through speculation, financial manipulations, and the ruthless exercise of power. And small businessmen were *not* "capitalists" in this formulation. Furthermore, the idea that capital and labor shared a harmony of interests had crumbled for Nordhoff like eggshells beneath the wheels of a train. He harangued the Republicans of one subcommittee for calling on numerous "capitalists" for testimony on the tariff while they did not ask for a single workingman's opinion, which, by implication, would have differed significantly from that of the "capitalists."[51] In Nordhoff's mind, "capitalist" and "monopolist" became interchangeable terms, and the defining difference between them and the enterprises of "the people" was in scale. If centralized government was an evil to be avoided, how much more so was centralized private economic power?

The Democratic Party, by Nordhoff's reckoning, in its opposition to the bought-and-paid-for Republicans, represented Labor. Its "programme," he wrote, of lower tariffs, land reform, and regulation alarmed "monopolists and capitalists, who have grown rich as the favorites of the republican party"; but it would benefit those workers who had "seen their masters grown wealthier while they themselves were half the time out of work." Of course, the Democratic Party's platform was not so clear as Nordhoff hoped on tariffs and regulation, but with the Republicans so obviously beyond redemption, he tried to ignore the rifts within Democratic Party ranks on questions he saw as clear-cut moral

---

grants for which the terms had not been fulfilled, see [CN,] "Land Grabbing. How the Public Domain Has Been Seized by Railroads," New York *Herald*, April 20, 1886; [CN,] "Washington: Manufacturers Must Speak If They Wish a New Tariff," New York *Herald*, April 30, 1886; [CN,] "Washington: Alarm of Congressmen Over the Land Question," New York *Herald*, May 3, 1886; [CN,] "Land Grabbing," New York *Herald*, June 1, 1886; and [CN,] "What They Say On Their Platforms and Do in Congress," New York *Herald*, June 14, 1886.

50. [CN,] "Washington: President Arthur on the Reduction of Taxation," NY *Herald*, January 22, 1883.

51. [CN,] "Republicans and the Tariff," New York *Herald*, July 16, 1888.

issues. The Democratic Party was the only place for reformers to go, even if it was "only not quite so bad as the Repub[lican]s."[52]

Nevertheless, Nordhoff's threnody on the political ineptitude of the Democratic Party continued unabated. The stakes were so much higher now, with the Republicans bought by monopolists, that the bumbling of the only viable opposition frustrated him, and his laments were not calculated to win him friends among the party leaders. The Southern Democrats "have no tact, they have no self-restraint, they have no sense of the fitness of things, and the Northern democrats in the House ... have no sense at all of any kind," he proclaimed one day in the *Herald*. Their efforts on behalf of a "rebel claim," for instance, when worthy Union widows' claims went unaddressed "is not politics. It is mere stupidity." "They have acted like a parcel of innocents," he complained after a session during which the Democrats had carried out an almost entirely negative strategy, leaving them looking obstructionist and the Republicans at least energetic. By this point, Nordhoff was no longer content to see a Congress accomplish little but debate.[53]

Nordhoff welcomed Grover Cleveland's 1884 nomination as the Democratic presidential candidate. Cleveland was, he judged, "undoubtedly a good man—honest & with courage to do right."[54] With Blaine as his Republican opponent, Cleveland was undoubtedly the superior candidate to Nordhoff and to an entire covey of Republican Mugwumps, who found Blaine, with his history of questionable relationships with various corporations, the very definition of corruption. With the ascendance of Grover Cleveland to the Presidency, as the first Democrat to hold that office since before the Civil War, Nordhoff grew briefly hopeful that his cherished reforms might at last be effectively pursued. But Cleveland was not off to an auspicious start, refusing to make any policy statements or provide any guidance to the rudderless Democratic Congress. "The party needs a head, a ruler, a commander," Nordhoff wrote, surveying the divided Democracy:

> Prominent Democrats are found for and against a bankrupt
> law, for and against the national banks, for and against the
> dollar of our fathers, for and against internal taxation, for

---

52. [CN,] "Washington: Futile Efforts of Protectionists to Excite Alarm." New York *Herald*, December 8, 1883; CN to Edward Atkinson, December 26, 1881. Atkinson Papers, MHS.

53. [CN,] "Washington: Flights of Oratory in the House of Representatives." NY *Herald*, January 29, 1881; [CN,] "Washington: Prospects for Tariff Legislation in Congress," NY *Herald*, February 17, 1883.

54. CN to Edward Atkinson, June 16, [1884]. Atkinson Papers, MHS.

and against the Cuban Treaty, for and against the Nicaragua
Canal, and each one urges his policy as positively as though
it were to be the policy of the next administration.

Unless Cleveland made his positions clear, Nordhoff warned, he might find
his party in fragments, "and such fragments as will require much patience and
a very good quality of glue to stick together again." But Cleveland continued
in his passive course.[55]

"What is the use of leaders who don't lead?" he complained after a year of
the Cleveland administration, in which Democratic Congresses squandered
their power and the President "distinctly and positively refused to influence
Congress." All Cleveland seemed to do was dispense offices and veto bills. The
Democratic Party had become, as he quoted one authority, a "'combination
for the benefit of the few to the injury of the many.'"[56] Cleveland, "while an
entirely honest man, ... has developed an amazing incapacity," he wrote; it was
becoming painfully clear of Cleveland "that he seems to be intellectually unable
to comprehend the duties and responsibilities of his place."

Furthermore, myriad issues remained unaddressed by the Congress and the
President: the constitution of the Supreme Court, the "Indian question," electoral
vote-counting procedures to avoid another fiasco like the election of 1876, land
reform, reorganization of the Navy, administration of tariff laws, a reciprocity
treaty with Mexico. None of these matters had been adequately dealt with, and
Cabinet officers could do nothing while the President refused to shape policy.
Perhaps, some critics suggested, Cleveland was simply hastening the much-called-
for disorganization of parties, but on this Nordhoff was adamant. A "president's
task," he wrote, "is not destructive, but creative." Cleveland's very election,
brought about by the defection of sizeable numbers of disaffected Republicans,
had demonstrated the "final result" of such a disorganization. And what had
been the result? "[W]ith a fatal blindness," Nordhoff wrote, Cleveland "has
entirely missed this great opportunity." "It has very seldom happened before,"
he noted bitterly, "that a party which had forty-two majority in the House was led
by the nose during a whole long session by the minority." Once again, politics
as usual, coupled with Democratic incompetence, had triumphed over vision.[57]

---

55. [CN,] "Washington: Democrats All Astray for Want of a Leader," New York *Herald*,
     January 28, 1885. CN to David Ames Wells, February 21, 1885. Wells Papers, LC.
56. [CN,] "Washington: A Muddled Tariff and a Divided Party in the House," New York
     Herald, March 19, 1886.
57. [CN,] "Mr. Cleveland's Mistakes: How the President is Not Leading His Party," New
     York *Herald*, April 8, 1886; [CN,] "Washington: First Caucus of House Democrats
     Held This Session," New York *Herald*, June 25, 1886.

Throughout its pages, during the 1880s, the *Herald* printed detailed, vivid exposés of various social and political problems and almost always called for some ameliorative government role: direct action, regulation, and strict oversight. Its articles bore a distinct resemblance to the work of the Progressive era "muckrakers" of some twenty years later, such as Lincoln Steffens and Upton Sinclair. A *Herald* article exposing graft titled "New Jersey's Shame" foreshadowed Steffens's work, *The Shame of the Cities*. The audience of the *Herald* was a large one, and its message would have travelled far. "It was not yet the day of enormous circulations," recalled one editor, "but the *Herald* went everywhere."[58]

But the *Herald* articles were anonymously written, and no individuals became identified with these articles, their lengthy headlines summarizing their content: "Rear Tenements," one might be headed, "Specimen Blocks Crowded with Dwellings and Teeming with Inhabitants/ Ineffectual Fire Escapes/ Where the Health Board and Building Department Should Intercede/ Life and Health Jeopardized/ Dangerous Man Traps and Sanitary Plague Spots." Or another: "New York's Foulness/ The Perfunctory Work of an Incompetent Street Cleaning Department/ ...Large Expenditures for Which the Citizens Get No Satisfactory Return/ ...Long But Interesting Exhibit of Damnatory Statistics." Others began with attention-grabbing phrases such as "Legislative Robbery," "Lynchers Let Loose," "Perish Patronage," "Horrors of the Steerage," "Wretched Abodes," "'L' Road Perils," "Resetting the Death Trap," "Starvation Wages," and "Little Factory Slaves." The adulteration of food, urban planning, housing codes, municipal corruption, child labor, public safety and health—all characteristic Progressive-era concerns—received full, even lurid coverage in the *Herald* throughout the 1880s. When Joseph Pulitzer bought the NY *World* in 1883 and transformed it into an enormously popular and highly reformist newspaper, he was only amplifying the methods Bennett had been using at the *Herald*.[59]

The struggles of organized labor also received sympathetic treatment in the pages of the *Herald*. The Knights of Labor were frequently the topic of favorable articles, their meetings and movements given prominent coverage, while the activities of Pinkertons and violent strikebreakers were deplored. Even an article with a hostile headline, "Labor Vs. Capital/...Communistic Counsels"[60] turns out, upon reading, to be fully sympathetic to the strikers in question while a March 1882 article was positively celebratory in its treatment of

---

[58.]   Joseph I.C. Clarke, op. cit., 137.

[59.]   For the cited articles, see the New York *Herald*, 1/23/81; 2/14/81; 2/20/81; 3/10/81; 4/12/81; 4/13/81; 5/8/81; 1/22/82; 3/28/82; 3/28/82; 3/30/82; 1/11/87. For more examples, see the Appendix.

[60.]   New York *Herald*, May 7, 1878.

early unionization: "The Knights of Labor," its headline proclaimed, "American Workingmen United for Self-Protection/ Politicians, Stand From Under!/ Equal Rights and Just Rewards for all Men and Women/ A Giant Power that Will Be Felt."[61] During the furor over the Haymarket anarchists in 1886, the newspaper tried to keep organized labor from being tarred with the same brush as the anarchists with articles proclaiming "Knights of Labor All Denounce the Chicago Anarchists," while it also printed "Anarchists' Defense/ ...The Police Alone to Blame for Attacking Harmless Citizens," during the trial, recounting testimony that undermined the charges against the anarchists and showing no signs of trying to downplay or refute it.[62]

The *Herald*'s proto-Progressivism fluctuated in its intensity, and it is likely that certain reporters and editors felt more strongly about social issues than others. The *Herald*, after all, prided itself on its independence of political party and was also read by many of the middle-class and professionals for its comprehensive and accurate coverage of commerce and financial affairs, sports (particularly yachting, of which "The Commodore" was a true master), and entertaining tidbits of gossip and scandal. The newspaper was compulsively readable, even if, as Parton had earlier written, respectable people would rather not be seen reading it.

Its propensity to give full airing to news of scandals and crimes, however, coupled with Bennett's alcoholic sprees, kept the *Herald* in slightly bad odor; and these airings, and such self-promoting stunts as the Stanley-Livingstone expedition, earned the *Herald* a place among the "sensationalistic" or "yellow" journals. Even Nordhoff would admit to a friend, early in the eighties, that the *Herald* "is not always what I would prefer," although it had significant merits, for "it is always honest, freespoken & earnest."[63] By the end of his career, however, he believed that the *Herald*'s reputation for sensationalism was undeserved. "If [Bennett] has often created a 'sensation' in the public mind," Nordhoff judged, "it has been in some such way as sending Mr. Stanley to look for and find Dr. Livingston ...; or in the courageous exposure of some huge swindle; or in the earliest news of some vitally important or interesting event. Or, by taking up independently, and forcing the public attention to an important question or policy."[64]

[61.]   New York *Herald*, 3/23/82. See also "Starvation Wages," 12/15/84; "Shirtmakers' Wrongs," 12/25/84; "Labor and Law," 4/1/86; "Strikers Overawed," 4/11/86; "Coal War and War Prices," 1/14/87; "Bullets in the Strike," 1/21/87.

[62.]   New York *Herald*, 3/3/86.

[63.]   CN to Gordon L. Ford, February 27, 1881. Ford Papers, NYPL.

[64.]   CN, *Reminiscences*, 28.

Frank Luther Mott, in his path-breaking and still-respected *American Journalism*, defined "yellow journalism" as more than simply flashy presentation of lurid trivia. Yellow journalism, in Mott's definition, was characterized by certain methods of presentation and content, but also by "more or less ostentatious sympathy with the 'underdog,' with campaigns against abuses suffered by the common people."[65] The more "respectable" newspapers were seldom guilty of such an ostentatious faux pas as sympathy with labor. The *Evening Post*'s version of the Pullman strike included a heroic George Pullman, valiantly trying to keep in business and his employees at work by lowering wages, and a sinister Eugene Debs, demanding unreasonable concessions such as arbitration. (The *Evening Post* did not mention the record profits that the corporation had enjoyed just months before the strike.)[66]

Mott's definition of yellow journalism echoes the disdain of nineteenth-century moralists for the *Herald*'s "pandering" to the "mob," which, one might cynically conclude, meant pointing out the injustice of shooting down unarmed strikers; and later journalism histories continue to regard mass circulation papers of the late nineteenth century with disdain, even as they grant the utility of the graphic innovations of the period.[67]

---

[65]   Frank Luther Mott, *American Journalism* (New York: Macmillan, 1941), 539.

[66]   *The Evening Post Hundredth Anniversary, November 16, 1801-1901* (NY: Evening Post Co., 1902), 78–80. Nordhoff is as absent from this volume—which discusses the *Evening Post*'s history at length, including lengthy discussions of all its editors except for Nordhoff, who isn't even mentioned as having been an editor—as Trotsky is from Stalinist history. For a more complete view of the Pullman uprising, see Stanley Buder, *Pullman: An Experiment in Industrial Order and Community Planning, 1880-1930* (New York: Oxford, 1967, rep. 1979), 148.

[67]   See James Parton, "The New York Herald," *North American Review* 102 (April 1866), 380, 390: Parton asks whether the *Herald* is popular because of its "excellence as a newspaper, or its crimes as a public teacher," and refers to its "scurrility and indecency." The *Herald*'s course during the draft riots of 1863, in which it reminded the public that the rioters were reacting to a law that seemed, on the face of it at least, patently unfair to the poor, and that they were human beings and not a "mob" to be struck down by force, is a representative one. For a modern version of journalism history, see Michael Emery and Edwin Emery, *The Press and America: An Interpretive History of the Mass Media*, 6th edition (Englewood Cliffs: Prentice-Hall, 1988), 227. The first edition of this book came out in 1954, and most of the revisions seem to have taken the form of adding chapters concerning latter-day developments (broadcasting, etc.), while the earlier chapters remain virtually untouched. This leads to such anachronisms as a chapter on Civil War journalism, which is based on Civil War history dating from the 1930s and '40s, a history now

Leaving aside outright falsehoods, which did not characterize the *Herald* or Pulitzer's *World*, it is hard to escape the conclusion that the focus of nineteenth-century mass-circulation newspapers on graphic depictions of social ills and the uglier sides of city life—which were certainly real enough—was a significant element of what the arbiters of good taste found offensive. Progressive-era muckrakers, who published in more costly monthlies directed at a more affluent audience, were at first charged with displaying the same bad taste, but, unlike the *Herald* and other mass-circulation newspapers, were soon applauded as "crusaders" for justice.

The *Herald*'s reformism was so pronounced by the mid-1880s, echoed many of Nordhoff's opinions so closely, and reflected such a distinct change from the *Herald* of earlier years that people doubted that Bennett, with his image as a dissipated wastrel, could have been responsible for it. But with Bennett viewing all challenges to his authority as just cause for dismissal, Nordhoff took care to make it clear that he answered to Bennett, and that his own role on the *Herald* was a subordinate one. Bennett was "a man of sound and just ideas and policies," he wrote, and "he, *he alone*, and not any other man or men, controlled the *Herald*." There had been, Nordhoff admitted in his retirement, "foolish gossip about men who were said to manage or control the *Herald*," but such rumors were patently false.[68]

The "foolish gossip" Nordhoff alluded to included a report published in a Boston newspaper claiming that Nordhoff was the real power and controlling mind behind the *Herald*, with the absent Bennett a mere figurehead. Realizing, perhaps, that Bennett would not regard such a report favorably, and in any case anxious to refute the story, Nordhoff wrote an indignant letter of denial, methodically ticking off the purported falsehoods. The *Boston Gazette* had reported, in October of 1885, that "Mr. Nordhoff is at present dominant in Mr. Bennett's paper. His word is law," that his "nominees fill almost all the responsible positions." Nordhoff adamantly denied it all. It was not true that he and his "henchmen" ran the newspaper, he insisted. "It is time that this often repeated and contemptible falsehood that Mr. Bennett takes but little part in the management of the *Herald* should cease to be uttered," Nordhoff wrote with some indignation. He added his fulsome praise of the publisher. In his eleven years at the *Herald*, he declared,

---

fully discredited. See also Sidney Kobre, *The Yellow Press and Gilded Age Journalism* (Florida State University Press, 1964), which is highly descriptive if not particularly insightful.

68. CN, *Reminiscences*, 13.

every journalistic success the *Herald* has made in that time, every great policy it has struck out, every important blow it has dealt for the country and for good government, and they have been many, all have been inspired and dictated by Mr. Bennett, and very often to the minutest details.[69]

A condensed version of Nordhoff's letter of refutation appeared on the *World*'s editorial page, under the sarcastic heading "A Tribute to Genius: Mr. Chas. Nordhoff's Impartial Estimate of His Able Employer."[70] Another newspaper editorialized that the initial *Boston Gazette* article was simply "a very delightful piece of persiflage, which every newspaperman in New York understood and laughed over," and it added that Nordhoff's "density" kept him from getting the joke. "No one in his senses," the newspaper continued, would have credited Nordhoff and his compatriots with "sufficient brains to take Mr. Bennett's place in the guidance of the *Herald*." The writer concluded by repeating rumors that Nordhoff had been cozying up to one of Bennett's business partners, under the belief that the partner was about to start a new newspaper.[71]

Meanwhile, the original *Boston Gazette* reporter who had begun the whole contretemps responded to Nordhoff's denials. "Mr. Nordhoff's letter about the New York *Herald* has excited much interest," noted his response in the Boston *Gazette*, picked up and reprinted in the NY *Daily Telegraph*. It was clear to everyone, the writer avowed, that there had been "recent changes" in the *Herald*, which "have provoked abundant curiosity"—possibly referring to the heavily reformist tenor of the paper in the mid-1880s—which implied that there had been some "transfer of the control" away from the flighty Bennett. The author was not surprised that Nordhoff denied responsibility for the new direction of the *Herald*.[72] "I yield to nobody in my admiration of Mr. Nordhoff's courage, ability, and talent for diplomacy," the *Gazette* writer went on. "He was bound, by the nature of his position, to deny my assertions," and he compared Nordhoff and Bennett to the Viceroy of China and the child who was nominally the emperor. Would the viceroy admit to being the real ruler? "I think he would have replied, as a man of tact, that the infant Emperor was the real ruler, the initiator of reforms, the fountain of justice, and one of the most humane,

---

69. CN, letter to the editor, *Boston Gazette*, October 25, 1885.

70. "A Tribute to Genius," New York *World*, October 30, 1885.

71. "Journalistic Oleomargarine," newspaper clipping in the Charles Nordhoff Papers, NYPL (a collection culled from the Gordon L. Ford Papers).

72. "Charles Nordhoff and the New York Herald Again," NY *Daily Telegraph*, November 6, 1885.

enlightened, and far-seeing princes in the world," the reporter explained. "So I sincerely appreciate Mr. Nordhoff's estimate of Mr. Bennett."

Since Bennett's jealousy of his absolute authority over the *Herald* was well-known, it is difficult to see how the author of this article could have truly meant well toward Nordhoff. Bennett had been known to fire men for simply taking credit for an editorial, let alone the entire paper. There was no mistaking this writer's opinion, however:

> Mr. Nordhoff stands to Mr. Bennett much as Socrates stood to
> Alcibiades, or Mentor to Telemachus. It was for Mr. Bennett's
> benefit that he wrote his "Politics for Young Americans".... I
> think it only natural that so able an instructor should take
> pride in the growth of so apt a pupil.

As for Nordhoff's denial of his dominance, "I might appeal to every editor and reporter on the paper. They do not ask, What does Mr. Bennett say? They ask, What does Mr. Nordhoff want?" Everyone on the *Herald* believed he held his position "by favor of Mr. Nordhoff." Furthermore, to incur Nordhoff's displeasure was, he maintained, fatal to one's career at the *Herald*. "Five editors at the beginning of the year declared their hostility or dislike for Mr. Nordhoff," he noted. "All have since been discharged. Each of them attributes his overthrow to Mr. Nordhoff." Finally, did Bennett really control the *Herald*? "Nominally, yes," the reporter admitted, but the publisher had "little communication with the office"; and before his last departure for Paris, he had told another top editor, "'I wish you to regard Mr. Nordhoff as representing me in everything.'" Nordhoff's demurrals were "literally true," the *Gazette* reporter acknowledged, but "he and friends are … as much the masters of the paper as though they owned it. There is not a responsible journalist in New York who does not know this to be true." He could not see why Nordhoff "should any longer conceal a state of things which furnishes him with the crown of a long and honorable career."[73]

With an employer like Bennett, of course, there was every reason for Nordhoff to deny a "dominant" role on the paper.[74] The intentions of the

---

[73.] "Charles Nordhoff and the New York Herald Again: Correspondence of the Boston Gazette," New York *Daily Telegraph*, November 6, 1885.

[74.] Joseph Clarke notes what happened in one analogous case: the Managing Editor, Thomas Connery, "had been undermined in Bennett's eyes by leters from one of the news editors and the cheerfully diabolic tactics of one … who had been retired from the paper for cause. …His was a process of praising Connery as the great man of the paper. The result was inevitable. Faced with a proposal to take a long vacation

Gazette writer cannot be known; there may well have been a hint of sarcasm in the references to Nordhoff's "honorable career" for his career was always controversial; on the other hand, the writer may have been one of those reporters who cared little for the consequences of reporting what he believed to be the truth. Another editor on the *Herald* wrote of Nordhoff with pointed dislike as "a pretty skillful journalist" who, "under a deliberately bluff exterior (he had been a sailor in his youth) ...cultivated the amenities and loaded Mr. Bennett with flattery."[75]

The degree of Nordhoff's influence on Bennett may never be known, but Nordhoff, while he could maintain a judicious silence when expedient, never seems to have knowingly told an out-and-out falsehood. To the end of his life, he insisted on the primacy of Bennett's word in making the *Herald* what it was—and it was, during the '80s, a paper strikingly consonant with Nordhoff's own long-standing reformist ideas.

---

that would surely be a prelude to a pension, Connery ... recognized his fate ..., and flatly resigned," *My Life and Memories*, 143.

[75.]   Clarke, 138.

CHAPTER 10

The Valley of Cross-Purposes

"The sense of duty done is the brave man's solace in failure or misfortune," Charles Nordhoff wrote in 1883. Already, his work in Washington seemed increasingly futile. "He has done what he could," he continued. "The rest he leaves with God."

> The cause he believed in has broken down; the plans he had formed have failed; the good he intended has been brought to naught before his eyes; he sees injustice prevail, and wrong triumphant; but he has done his duty; and, oppressed, in poverty, in disgrace, in sorrow, not for himself but for others, or for the cause he believes right and sacred, he is still serene, for he says, "The end I leave with God."[1]

At first a willing participant in the behind-the-scenes maneuvering that underlay the give-and-take of national politics and policy-making in Washington, Nordhoff grew increasingly alienated from what he perceived as the venality of one side and the incompetence of the other. And unable to hide his disgust in his newspaper writings, he found that the easy confidence that journalists and politicoes cultivated in one another had become for him more and more untenable. Instead, he exerted himself in the exposure of the men and the activities they engaged in, which he saw betraying the promise of American democracy. What else was he to do? But his hope that he might, through journalism, make a difference and that positive social change was possible if only the public were well-informed, had so faded by the end of the decade that he could only dream of escape from Washington, the city he called "this Valley of Cross-Purposes."

---

[1] CN, *Future Life*, 50.

In 1886, President Cleveland refused to turn over some Executive branch papers to a Senate committee; and the resulting dispute went on for some weeks, to Nordhoff's delight. The Senate, arguing against executive privilege in withholding documents, repeatedly referred to "the people's right to know." Their argument was a sound one, Nordhoff pointed out, and it was a pity they would not apply it to their own proceedings, for they continued to hold secret "executive sessions," shielded from public scrutiny as they bargained and deliberated. These Senators dealt with the contradiction, he commented, "with that Senatorial muddle-headedness which regards the people with contempt and looks back longingly to the early days when the high and mighty Senate used to transact all business behind closed doors." But "leaks" from Senators in collusion with journalists rendered their secrecy a farce. Nordhoff noted that one such "leak" reported the Senators "furiously denouncing the press because the press does its duty to the people and exposes the Senatorial shams and pretensions of the secret session." Ominously, he added, "these men forget that most of them are the creatures of the press."[2]

The whole contretemps arose over Cleveland's refusal to release information on his nominations to various offices of the government. Nordhoff, who had already lost faith in Cleveland's leadership, saw in this further proof of the President's abdication of responsibility. "Thorough publicity is the only thing," he declared, but the President refused to be open. "He thinks it is none of the people's business whom he appoints or on whose petition or urgency."[3] The Senate seemed no better. Nordhoff reported with incredulity the speechifying of one Senator bent on preserving the executive session: "A Senator of some note said the other day," Nordhoff wrote, "that he was surprised that any one should want to intrude on the privacy of the executive sessions," comparing this intrusiveness to outsiders trying to gain entrance to private clubs. "How could respectable people wish to force open the doors of the Senate, where they had no business?" Nordhoff paraphrased the Senator's question. "He could not understand it," he continued in wonderment.

> This Senator, and others like him, regard the Senate as their
> club, into which the people ought not to desire to intrude; and

---

2. [CN,] "Senate and President," New York *Herald*, March 10, 1886; [CN,] "Washington: Indications that Senators Are Becoming Tired of Secret Sessions," New York *Herald*, March 12, 1886. [CN,] "Debating About Removals," New York *Herald*, March 13, 1886. [CN,] "Washington: Almost a Disclosure of Star Chamber Secrets in Open House," New York *Herald*, March 20, 1886.

3. [CN,] "Washington: Star Chamber Senators, Fearing Defeat, Propose a Compromise," New York *Herald*, April 2, 1886.

they regard the universal demand for open doors as a piece
of bad business—a deplorable sign that this country is getting
altogether too democratic. The people—the American
people—ought to be ashamed of themselves to wish to know
what their masters, the Senators, are doing.[4]

His populist rhetoric did not soften as the decade grew old, and whenever
the question of secret sessions arose, Nordhoff's column fairly bristled
with indignation at the practice. One treaty "ought to be debated openly,"
he declared, "if for no other reason in order that the public might see how
ridiculously ignorant of the subject and of the questions involved the Senators
are." Without publicity, there was no accountability and no democracy.[5]

"I am weary of dealing with people who can't see beyond the end of their
nose," Nordhoff complained to Atkinson late in 1886. From Cleveland, "no
reform could hope anything," he declared. "He always stops short halfway; & the
blood of life does not course through his veins." And so it went, the Democratic
leadership continually letting Nordhoff down. He had barbed comments for
key party leaders as well as the President: William Morrison was "a leader who
has never led his party anywhere except into a bog"; John Carlisle was barely
serviceable as Speaker, no more. The wonder is that Nordhoff continued to
expect anything from them at all. Ultimately, it always came down to the people,
and it was journalism that might galvanize public opinion and force reform.
Once real issues were discussed publicly, he wrote in 1888, "the country will
be awakened to a condition of things which, when they once know of it, the
people will not tolerate." Monopolists would not benefit from having "their
combines or their huge profits made at the expense of the people published
and discussed," he added.[6]

The nascent Populist movement shared many positions with Nordhoff:
antimonopolism; a rhetoric of "the people" versus "plutocracy"; the labor
theory of value; opposition to the protective tariff; the primacy of class
solidarity over racial divisions; demands for improved election mechanisms,

---

4.   [CN,] "Washington: President Cleveland's Mistakes and How He May Retrieve
      Them." New York *Herald*, April 13, 1886.

5.   See, for example, [CN,] "Riddleberger's War," New York *Herald*, February 7, 1888;
      "Senators' Secrets," New York *Herald*, May 10, 1888; "Extradition Treaty With
      England," New York *Herald*, May 15, 1888.

6.   CN to Edward Atkinson, November 7, [1886]. Atkinson Papers, MHS. [CN,]
      "Wanted—A Policy." New York *Herald*, December 9, 1886. [CN,] "The Tariff Ghost,"
      New York *Herald*, December 8, 1886. [CN,] "Randall Flocks Alone," New York
      Herald, March 16, 1888.

including the secret ballot; and calls for land reform. Nordhoff could not swallow the Populists' various economic positions, such as those calling for an income tax or for the issuance of more greenbacks and increased silver coinage and a more active government role in general. Nordhoff was unwilling to discard his distrust of government, and he believed that only a return to the gold standard would put the country on a sound monetary basis. As the silver and currency issues more and more overwhelmed the Populists' other concerns—culminating in the 1896 campaign of William Jennings Bryan and his "cross of gold" speech—Nordhoff's disapproval of the Populists deepened into inveterate opposition.[7]

Any use of governmental power had to be approached warily. An 1886 Interstate Commerce bill, doomed to failure, drew Nordhoff's criticism for including an amendment that would allow the federal government to take on "the common police duty of arresting and punishing the obstructors of railway trains," a clause clearly aimed at putting down strikers. Appalled that the amendment had been proposed by Democrats (for he had by then come to regard the Republicans as the "corporation party"), Nordhoff struck a note of warning. The "members of labor unions," who had pushed federal arbitration laws and other means for the government to "interfere between them and their employers," could "learn a useful lesson" from the latest bill. "If they encourage Congress to interpose its authority they should see that Congress may use that power in ways very disagreeable to the laborers"; and it "not only may do this, it is very certain to do it," for corporations, with their wealth and power, practically controlled the operations of the government. (In fact, this is exactly what did happen—if not with the ineffectual Interstate Commerce Act of 1897, then certainly with the Sherman Antitrust Act of 1890, under which labor unions were prosecuted as unfair combinations.)

If Nordhoff continued to believe in laissez-faire government as an abstract principle, he could ignore that principle when considering the nonabstract deliberations of Congress. In 1886, the issue of land reform occupied his attention. The railroad corporations that had, fifteen and twenty years earlier, been provided enormous federal subsidies for their construction through grants of land, were under attack as having violated their agreements. Western farmers, in particular, objected to the "grabbing" of thousands of acres of land by the railroads, which they perceived as governmental stacking of the deck against the common people.

---

7.   On the Populists, see Boller, op. cit., chapter 4; Lawrence Goodwyn, *The Populist Moment* (NY: Oxford, 1978); and Norman Pollack, *The Populist Response to Industrial America* (NY: Norton, 1962). Richard Hofstadter gives an unsympathetic account of the Populists in *The Age of Reform.*

In applauding the passage of one land-grant adjustment bill ("it is high time," he wrote), he scored the Department of the Interior's conduct, including its operations under Carl Schurz. Interior had been so run, he wrote, that "the people had no rights which these corporations were bound to respect. ...If the land grant corporations had owned the Interior Department they could not have had a freer or fuller use of it." Nordhoff, the old foe of big government, recommended that Congress appropriate additional funds so that more federal employees might be hired to investigate and adjust the corporations' old claims and thereby strip them of ill-gotten gains.[8]

He also recommended that the Knights of Labor make its force felt by lobbying for land reform rather than diffusing its considerable strength on the dozens of petitions, often conflicting, which their members constantly sent to Congress. Noting that bills then under consideration could "reclaim to the public domain more than a hundred million acres of land, to be added to the small remnant ... which remain after years of rampant and unchecked land grabbing," he cautioned that "hundreds of millions of organized capital" were "arrayed" against the passage of the bills. "If it is true that 'organized labor' wants a tussle with organized capital," he exhorted,

> here is the place, and the time is ripe, for this struggle. Let the Knights of Labor all over the country fix their eyes on Congress. Let them demand, as a body, with one voice, and that a voice as menacing as they choose to make it, that congress shall not trifle with this land question.

In this way, labor might at last gain the respect of Congress, which had long been too much influenced by "organized capital."[9]

In 1886, Nordhoff also suggested that Congress broaden its investigation of railroad and telegraph corporations and applauded a judicial ruling that allowed an injunction to restrain one railroad company's attempts to obstruct the construction of a competing telegraph line. When the controversial Interstate Commerce bill was finally passed in 1887, Nordhoff approved of it, declaring his belief that it was undoubtedly constitutional.[10]

[8.] [CN,] "Washington: Passage of Bill to Adjust Railroad Land Grants," NY *Herald*, May 4, 1886.

[9.] [CN,] "The Knights and the Land. A Chance for Organized Labor to Grapple with Capital." NY *Herald*, May 10, 1886.

[10.] [CN,] "Telegraph Monopoly," NY *Herald*, December 18, 1886; [CN,] "Land Grant Railroads: An Important Commission of Inquiry in Prospect," NY *Herald*, January 17, 1887. [CN,] "No Veto," NY *Herald*, January 30, 1887.

In contrast to his earlier endorsement of a Congress that had done nothing very significant, by the late 1880s, Nordhoff was impatient with political wrangling over needed reforms, and he applauded the Forty-Ninth Congress for having tackled a number of pressing issues with positive action. He enumerated its praiseworthy deeds: it had "vindicated the power of Congress to deal with corporations" in its Land Grant Forfeiture acts; relegated a great deal of business to the Court of Claims and the Pension Bureau, thus freeing itself from the time-consuming consideration of private legislation; passed the Interstate Commerce Act; begun an inquiry into the affairs of the Pacific railroads; prohibited the use of convict labor in federal building projects; appropriated money for a Congressional library building; and finally resolved (he thought) the Indian problem by passage of the Dawes act. The actions of the House, in particular, concerning land and the railroads made, he wrote, "a new departure in a direction long required by the public interest."[11]

By 1887, the corps of Washington "Special Correspondents" was of sufficient popular interest to elicit a syndicated article about them, complete with portraits of each. Nordhoff's representation, among the portraits of other Washington journalists, was brief and somewhat vague; he doubtless refused to be interviewed, and he was known to dislike personal publicity. The image he projected, to the writer of this article at least, was that of thoroughgoing seriousness: he was the author of "excellent … standard books," a "student, philosopher, and author." "[I]n appearance," the article noted, he was "retired and [of] somewhat exclusive ways, bordering on shyness," "the true picture of the earnest German student and thinker," implicitly a ponderous, humorless Teuton. Not surprisingly, Nordhoff regarded the article with distaste.[12]

The sketch was accurate, however, in referring to him as a "student," for his devotion to lifelong learning was manifest in his work. Even Yale cleric Theodore Dwight Woolsey, in his 1879 *Communism and Socialism*, had referred to "Dr." Nordhoff's *Communistic Societies*, eliciting an embarrassed letter from the journalist, who continued to read any new works on alternative social systems that he could find. He was "flattered" that Woolsey had cited his work, but he noted "with alarm" the laurel that Woolsey had bestowed upon him. "I am not a Doctor of any kind," he explained, "and I have (besides a dislike of

---

11.   [CN,] "General Results: Reforms Accomplished by the Forty-Ninth Congress." NY *Herald*, March 5, 1887.

12.   "National News Spinners," Brooklyn *Times*, January 22, 1887. That the article was syndicated can be inferred from CN's letter to Gordon L. Ford of February 1, [1887], thanking him for a clipping of the article: "Be thankful you are not so notorious as to be carted abt. the country in 'patent articles.'"

titles in general) an especial horror of titles wh. have not the warrant of proper authority," and he asked that future editions of the book be corrected.[13]

Nordhoff was a man of broad-ranging interests and kept up on the latest advances in science not only through reading, but also through his personal friendships with scientists. As a deeply religious man, he found the much-discussed "war between religion and science" absurd, brought about by blind fear and ignorance rather than by any thoughtful consideration of the issues involved. By 1880, he had familiarized himself so well with Asa Gray's defense of Darwinism that he gave a talk on the subject to the Literary Society of Washington, apparently hoping to translate Gray's views to the lay audience, as he did in his journalistic attempts to educate *Herald* readers on politics. In his writing, Nordhoff was always playing the role of tutor, explaining the arcana of professionals; his didacticism could be heavy-handed or not, but his work was always accessible.[14]

Evolution had been accepted by much of the educated public by the early 1880s, and Nordhoff followed the trend of accepting Darwin while denying that it conflicted with religion. "The Darwinian hypothesis is sometimes declaimed against as though it were anti-scriptural, which, nevertheless, it is not," his paper read. If there was an omnipotent God, he explained, why should he not have carried on the work of creation through evolution? "Certainly, the thought that the Creator was able to set in motion, in the very beginning, laws which without his further interference produced the infinitely varied results we know," Nordhoff believed, ought only to strengthen faith in the infinite wisdom of God. But the questions of God's continued activity in the universe, and the existence of the human soul, were not affected by the new understanding of the process of creation. "What science has done in this most wonderful of all the centuries," he concluded, "fills all intelligent men with wonder and delight. But after all it remains true that she has penetrated scarcely skin deep into the infinite."[15] Darwin had explained the "what," not the "why," Nordhoff noted, and the "why" was properly in the province of religion.

He elaborated on these premises in his 1883 credo, *God and the Future Life: The Reasonableness of Christianity*. The growing climate of secularization weighed heavily upon Nordhoff's mind, and he used the book to explain his own beliefs

13. CN to Theodore Dwight Woolsey, February 13, 1880, Woolsey Family Papers, Yale; see also Theodore Dwight Woolsey, *Communism and Socialism: Their History and Theory* (London: Sampson, Low, Marston, Searle and Rivington, 1879), esp. pp. 50–84, for Woolsey's paraphrasing of CN's work.

14. The talk was published in pamphlet form: CN, *The Darwinian Theory of Evolution* (Washington: Literary Society, 1880).

15. CN, *Darwinian Theory*, 1.

in a way creditable to the modern age. Work on *God and the Future Life* consumed much of his energy for two years. "Books, like babies, are best untalked about until they are fairly born," he wrote to Atkinson in June of 1883. "I have 2/3 finished ... the little book which has engaged my thoughts (spare thoughts) for some years." Emotionally invested in "the little book," he admitted, "I can't tell whether it is very good, or great trash.... With me, as a book comes toward the last chapter I have always a desperate desire to stick the manuscript into the fire." In fact, the little volume repeated many of the themes of his previous political writings, with tolerance toward differing religions, the necessity of brotherly love for the survival of democracy, the compatibility of reason with religion, and the immorality of power-mongering by monopolies as central tenets. "Few men can attain great wealth, or keep it," he admonished the reader, "without oppressing, or, at the least, lessening the opportunities and narrowing the lives of some others."[16]

Upon its publication, he anxiously awaited the verdict of friends. As he wrote to Gordon Ford, "you & [David] Wells, & all I love, were much in my mind in the years I was thinking it over & writing it." It was an intensely personal work, reflecting the deepening sense of futility of his sixth decade. "Few men," he wrote, "...arrive at middle life without feeling profoundly that, if this life is all that belongs to us, if for us there is no future beyond the grave, we are only the helpless creatures of a monstrous act of injustice." His friend Daniel Coit Gilman wrote to him immediately after the book's November publication with high praise, eliciting Nordhoff's heartfelt reply. "When I have written a book & read the proofs I am so heartsick & full of doubt abt. it that I am ready to rush it into the fire," he confessed, "& you can imagine perhaps what delight & *relief* your kind & generous letter gave me." Gilman's reaction was the first he had heard, he added, "& I was baby enough to read it over & over, & say to myself—'now I don't care—let the world go hang.'" Atkinson similarly praised his friend's effort, and, Nordhoff wrote in reply, "[s]o many persons speak & write to me abt. it—often with gratitude!—that I think I am content to have written it." He was happy to relate, some months later, that "I have a number of letters from eminent clergymen which surprise & please me by the earnestness of their praise."[17]

Raised by a German Methodist bishop in Ohio after his father had died, Nordhoff retained all his life an essentially religious outlook; and by the early

16. CN, *Future Life*, 181; CN to Edward Atkinson, June 15, [1883]. Atkinson Papers, MHS.
17. CN to Gordon L. Ford, n.d. [1883], Ford Papers, NYPL. CN, *Future Life*, 46. CN to Daniel Coit Gilman, November 15, 1883. Gilman Papers, Johns Hopkins University Library. CN to Edward Atkinson, December 31, 1883. Atkinson Papers, MHS. CN to Edward Atkinson, June 6, [1884]. Atkinson Papers, MHS.

1880s, with almost all his cherished beliefs in the secular realms of politics and economics shaken by the challenges of the day, Christianity remained his moral bedrock, his emotional center. If the "natural law" governing economics was growing more and more questionable, and if partisan politics and democracy seemed in their operation flawed at the very least, nevertheless one could always take refuge in religious certainty.

Nordhoff continued to consider unorthodox approaches to political economy while listening to conservative views as well. "I wonder if you have actually solved the great riddle why the world is so poor?" he wrote to David Ames Wells upon reading one of Wells's diagnoses (which centered, as usual, on free trade). Meanwhile, Henry George had moved to New York from California; they had been friends since Nordhoff had first read *Progress and Poverty* in 1879, and the two men occasionally met to talk. Nordhoff, uncertain but intrigued by George's proposals, stopped referring friends to Atkinson's articles and began to send them copies of Henry George's pamphlets.[18]

During George's 1886 campaign for the New York mayoralty as the candidate of the Union Labor Party, Nordhoff began to question George's realism—or perhaps he just pretended to with certain old friends. "Poor George has lost his head completely," he regretfully wrote to Atkinson, "& when he also loses his election will be in a pitiable plight. I'm very sorry for him." Although it is unclear precisely what George had done that Nordhoff so disapproved of, the campaign, which featured gatherings of tens of thousands of cheering workers, augured to some the advent of a potentially dangerous mass politics based, his opponents claimed, upon class warfare; and while Nordhoff sympathized with George, the crowds gathered before the Union Labor candidate may have roused his fear of demagoguery. Nevertheless, he did his best to persuade Bennett to throw the support of the New York *Herald*

---

18. CN to David Ames Wells, June 5, 1887. Wells Papers, LC. Nordhoff was probably referring to Wells's article, "The Economic Disturbance Since 1870," published in *Popular Science Monthly* in its July 1887 issue. Nordhoff could easily have read the article in June, either because Wells sent him a copy of the manuscript, or because *Popular Science*, like many magazines, published numbers before their ostensible date of issue. "[Y]ou'll be sure of lots of readers," Nordhoff added. Wells shared his belief in the necessity of educating the public through journalism. On CN's relationship with George, see, for example, Henry George to CN, May 22, 1888, in which George alludes to their meeting casually. Henry George Papers, NYPL. See also CN to George Bancroft, December 12, 1885, conveying George's pamphlet on the Irish Land question. The Nordhoffs had become acquainted with the Bancrofts in Washington and exchanged pleasantries. It is not surprising that Bancroft, the epitome of Jacksonian democratic idealism, should find a respectful adherent in Nordhoff.

behind George's candidacy, in preference to Democrat Abram Hewitt and Republican Teddy Roosevelt. Henry George, he seems to have concluded, was a leader, not a demagogue.[19]

George seems to have represented, if nothing else, fresh thinking to Nordhoff, who saw excessive rigidity in Atkinson's refusal to even consider new ideas concerning political economy. Too many American "so-called economists" were "secondhanded fellows," he once wrote to Atkinson. "They don't think for themselves, but catch up slavishly" to old ideas, particularly those of the pessimistic Ricardo and Malthus. New problems required a willingness to consider new solutions. "You yourself have a curious intellectual intolerance toward Henry George," he chided his friend. "He may be wrong, but he is worth more wrong, than half the professional economists we have right." Atkinson protested. "No, I am *not* intellectually intolerant of Henry George," he insisted. "I am intolerant with respect to his misrepresentation and perversion of his own ideas," for he saw George as pretending to a radical position against private property, "when in fact all that he has ever suggested is a change in the conditions under which the private possession of land shall be granted."[20] But Atkinson was, apparently, taking George's more hysterical critics' views of his position for those of George himself, for the economist had always insisted that he was not opposed to capitalism per se. "For my part," he had written, "I would put no limit on acquisition. No matter how many millions any man can get by methods which do not involve robbery of others—they are his: let him have them."[21] Even the limited challenge to economic orthodoxy represented by the Single Tax, however, produced such a strong revulsion in Atkinson that any precision of thought that he had possessed was fatally blunted.

Atkinson was still a respected authority throughout the 1880s and '90s, and on occasion, Nordhoff would provide him with publicity in his *Herald* columns. In one instance, Nordhoff's column gave lengthy verbatim quotations from one of Atkinson's reports, which insisted that the economic outlook was bright. Earning power of laborers was steadily improving, unemployment was not as high as people tended to think, and all "intelligent" farmers were prospering. "Thus by Mr. Atkinson's figures," Nordhoff summarized noncommittally, "it would seem that the workingmen of the country were never so well off as they

---

19. CN to Edward Atkinson, n.d. [1886], Atkinson Papers, MHS; CN to Edward Atkinson, 11/7/[86]. Atkinson Papers, MHS. On the mayoral campaign, see John L. Thomas, *Alternative America* (Cambridge: Harvard University Press, 1983), 221–231.

20. CN to Edward Atkinson, [July 1888], Atkinson Papers, MHS; Edward Atkinson to CN, August 1, 1888. Atkinson Papers, MHS.

21. Henry George, quoted in Thomas, op. cit., 188.

are at this time" and that "we shall hear but little for the next few years of any want of occupation on the part of those who are willing to work."[22]

Privately, however, Nordhoff expressed doubts as to Atkinson's judgments, which seemed to him to bear little resemblance to reality. "I have pondered your screed," he wrote Atkinson a few weeks later, concerning another article produced by the prolific economist. "You are right, I think—only legal tender will not be abolished. The tariff will be tinkered. The silver question will be left unsettled. The surplus will be squandered. How does that affect your calculations?" By early 1887, Nordhoff humored Atkinson without paying him much heed. "In regard to Atkinson, I somewhat agree with you," he wrote to David Ames Wells. "He has ceased to be profitable to my mind. But don't let us let the old friendships get cold, old man." It was clear that, however personable he found Atkinson, Nordhoff had lost interest in his views. "I don't write him as much as formerly. He proves too much," Nordhoff added. "His figures, as I told him when he was last here, prove that everybody is comfortable & happy here, and I *know* differently."[23]

The new conditions of life in industrial America, Nordhoff was coming to believe, required a radical rethinking of old concepts of the functioning of the economy. The search for a new economics exposed him to a variety of interpretations, including that of a Columbia University economist, E. R. A. Seligman. One of the new breed of more pragmatic economists, Seligman would go on to publish *The Economic Interpretation of History* (1902), an early Marxist work and an important influence on Charles Beard. "I was particularly struck with what you said about the probable spread of trusts," Nordhoff wrote to Seligman after reading one of the professor's articles, and he hoped that "someone with leisure" would "take up that question broadly. The spread of trusts means controlled, in place of an uncontrolled production.... It must work a complete change in practical political economy."[24] Appreciating the need for new ideas, Nordhoff was abandoning the old classical economics without having found a satisfactory substitute.[25]

The very definition of a liberal thinker, if not always a liberal economist, Nordhoff continued to correspond with all his friends, at loggerheads though

22. [CN,] "Distribution of Wealth. Some Statistics From Mr. Atkinson in Reply to Senator George." New York *Herald*, 12/22/1886.

23. CN to Edward Atkinson, January 8 [87?]. Atkinson Papers, MHS. CN to David Ames Wells, April 20, 1887.

24. CN to E. R. Seligman, November 14, 1888, Seligman Papers, Columbia University.

25. Morton White, *Social Thought in America: The Revolt Against Formalism* (Boston: Beacon Press, 1957 [rev. ed.]), 120, 122. Charles Beard cited Seligman as an important influence upon his own ideas.

they might be. "Whether you will smash the Single Tax movement, I don't know," he wrote to Atkinson in 1889. "But discussion at any rate is valuable." The problem with Atkinson's "discussion" of Henry George and the Single Tax was his refusal to acknowledge even a germ of truth in the latter's theorizing. "I wish it might occur to you, when you write ab[ou]t it, to say that it would be a good way to lay taxes if it were practicable," he gently reproved his friend. "That much is fair I think to concede. Nor ought we to forget that Wells … proposed to tax only land & improvements, & we all I think thought that wise."[26]

"Practicability," which had always been Nordhoff's yardstick of the value of any plan, he deemed almost irrelevant in the case of Henry George. George acknowledged that there were problems in American society, and that acknowledgement was all too rare in Nordhoff's eyes, even if his vaunted solution might be a bit fuzzy. Though George hadn't yet "for this country & our political system shown a practical way to apply his theory," Nordhoff wrote, "if ever he does it will have a very great support."

But Nordhoff kept a foot in both camps. Atkinson's conservative vision might not agree with George's, but it too deserved a fair hearing, and he approved of Atkinson's plans to collect his own articles into a book. "I don't entirely go with you in your persistently optimistic view," he wrote, "but it is eminently worth putting forth; and discussion is the vitally necessary thing."[27] David Wells, too, was writing a book, he told Atkinson, which he looked forward to reading. "I fancy it troubles him," he added a bit sardonically,

> to formulate his conclusions from his facts & illustrations. Neither of you, it seems to me, boldly faces the tendency of our present social system, which is in this country certainly, (as it seems to me) towards the establishment of a plutocracy, and the more & greater difficulty for the average man, to make an independent self developing career, such as would make him a *man* instead of a tool.[28]

Nordhoff was a living embodiment of the self-made man, and he found it hard to discard his faith in the American dream. But he could not ignore the evidence he saw all around him: the doors of opportunity were clanging shut, and the cost of this to America was not just material, but moral. He had no answers, but he believed, as firmly as he believed in anything, that remedies would not be found unless influential people acknowledged the existence

---

26. CN to Edward Atkinson, 4/7/1889. Atkinson Papers, MHS.
27. CN to Edward Atkinson, April 7, 1889.
28. CN to Edward Atkinson, April 7, 1889. Atkinson Papers, MHS.

of undeserved poverty, faced up to altered conditions, and undertook, as he had written to Professor Seligman, "a complete change in practical political economy."[29]

"I have been very busy, in this Valley of Cross purposes," Nordhoff wrote from Washington one year to an old friend. His job could not have been made easier for having incurred the enmity of Blaine by publishing the incriminating Peru-Chile letters, and pillorying the Democratic leadership would have made him no friends on the other side of the aisle. While his connections to some important Senators and Congressmen remained intact, gradually Nordhoff, with his impolitic habit of firing outraged salvoes in his *Herald* column at whatever perfidy or incompetence he discovered (by whichever politician, friendly or not), found his circle of willing sources contracted. His aggressive journalistic work was, he thought, just what was needed, and more of it would do the republic good. One Senator Teller, he noted in an 1887 column, spoke "of 'newspaper clamor,'" but "he ought to know better. He ought to know that the newspapers ... have not made nearly as much 'clamor' about the Senate as they ought to in the public interest," he continued. "Mr. Teller is wrong. The press is not half 'clamorous' enough." But there were reasons for the press's quiescence, and Nordhoff was an object lesson in the fate of the journalist who published unattractive facts about his sources. In the game of cultivating contacts, he was only half competent; he had succeeded in establishing a certain degree of cooperation with politicians, but the second half of the equation—keeping those sources cooperative by discreetly preventing unfavorable publicity about them—was one at which he failed abysmally. And so he was cut off by many of the prime movers in Washington. Possibly as a result of a less comfortable atmosphere, his wife and children came with him to the Capital for the winter less regularly.[30]

But his *Herald* articles continued to be regarded by allies as "the best guides" to political situations and Nordhoff himself as "true as steel." His dispatches were, he told Atkinson, "*very* much read." He had a reputation for influence; a hostile report circulated in 1885, for instance, that he had engineered a

---

29. CN to E. R. A. Seligman, November 14, 1888. Seligman Papers, Columbia University Library.

30. On the relationships between journalists and Congressmen and the necessity for both to maintain good relationships with the other, see Donald Ritchie, *Press Gallery: Congress and the Washington Correspondents* (Cambridge: Harvard University Press, 1991). CN to Gordon L. Ford, March 3, [no year, 1880s]. Ford Papers, NYPL.; CN to Edward Atkinson, December 23, 1883; CN to Edward Atkinson, January 8, 1888; CN to Atkinson, December 1, [1887]. The "clamor" quote is from [CN,] "Senatorial Attorneys," New York *Herald*, January 31, 1887.

particular legislative compromise on the silver issue—a report that he strongly denied. Moreover, writers outside the claustrophobic Washington atmosphere apparently valued Nordhoff's perspective. James Bryce, for one, was well acquainted with him, and certain interpretations of *The American Commonwealth* bear a close resemblance to Nordhoff's own views. (Not surprisingly, Nordhoff thought highly of Bryce's work. "It is a very great book," he wrote to Atkinson upon first reading it. "…It ought to be made part of every college course in the country."[31])

Much depended upon whose ox was being gored. Nordhoff himself seems to have maintained a relative indifference to the more personal aspects of political life. As he had asked Atkinson: what had personal like or dislike to do with important public issues? He simply continued to pillory malefactors and "stir up" opponents into clarifying their positions; he was an enemy of venality and obfuscation, as he saw it, not of any mere individual. These politicians were adroit and slippery creatures. "Morrison would not talk," Nordhoff would write to another *Herald* journalist. "Hewitt I'll try if I can catch him." His own effectiveness with certain politicians was at an end, however: "Randall I've set a stranger at, who may get something. Randall will not speak to me."[32]

In another context, Nordhoff once remarked upon "the strong opposition and hatred which a thoroughly and courageously independent and honest journalist is certain to incur, because he stands in the way of all schemers in all parties, and resolutely defends the general good." After several years in the nation's capital, he had become enough of an irritant to powerful people, or even a potential danger to their political futures, to arouse efforts to discredit him. Blaine was now an implacable enemy and doubtless could throw up obstructions in Nordhoff's path through his influence over rank-and-file Republicans. At the end of one session, Nordhoff wrote with relief to a friend of the impending adjournment. "Between Blaine, Robeson, the star-route thieves and other rascals," he explained wearily, "I have had a disagreeable session of it; have had dirt flung at me by notorious scoundrels, and have seen rogues triumphant, which is always irritating to me."[33]

[31.]   David Ames Wells to R. R. Bowker, January 13, 1884. Quoted in Fred Bunyan Joyner, *David Ames Wells: Champion of Free Trade* (Cedar Rapids: Torch Press, 1939), 141; CN to Edward Atkinson, February 28, 1883; CN to The Editor, *Boston Gazette*, October 25, 1885; CN to Edward Atkinson, August 14, 1890; CN to Edward Atkinson, April 7, 1889. Atkinson Papers, MHS.

[32.]   CN to Worthington Ford, January 25, [1884]; CN to Worthington Ford, January 30, [1884]. Ford Papers, NYPL.

[33.]   CN, *Reminiscences*, 14. In this passage he is referring to Bennett. CN to Gordon L. Ford, July 30, [1884?], Ford Papers, NYPL.

Even erstwhile allies sometimes distanced themselves from the *Herald*'s Special Correspondent. Thomas F. Bayard, whom Nordhoff had favored for the 1880 Democratic presidential nomination, by 1888 would not even speak to Nordhoff, who had spent most of the Cleveland Administration attacking the poor leadership of the Democratic Party—of which Bayard was a conspicuous member. Nordhoff didn't really understand such reactions. "I have always been ready to be on good terms with [Bayard]," he wrote to Atkinson, "but he will not."[34]

For his part, in these chillier later years, Nordhoff tried as a matter of policy (possibly not of his own making) to make no more use of his contacts to benefit friends. By the late 1880s, Nordhoff thought it was "curious" that the President (Grover Cleveland, a political ally of sorts) had come to him about possibly appointing Atkinson to office. But he would freely ask Cleveland's secretary to let him see official correspondence in an effort to nail some would-be "monopolists." And Cabinet Officers would continue to seek him out and ask his advice.[35]

Still, by the late 1880s, there was no question that Nordhoff had grown jaded in Washington: tired, disgusted, and alienated. "The politics are too too crazy," he wrote to Carl Schurz in 1890. "I feel as though I was living in Bedlam." Months would go by without his writing an article for the *Herald*, and those he did write seldom referred to conversations with informed sources; more often, he would cite historical precedent. His faith in party politics was, for all intents and purposes, destroyed; and the American people, in whom he had always vested his greatest hopes, had to be held responsible, if only in an indirect way. He often printed long lists of the names of Senators and Representatives and their votes on measures he considered important and once gave the names of ten Senators who, by abstaining from one vote, cost the Democrats an important victory. But the public kept electing these charlatans, allowing them to make a mockery of representative government without apparent concern. "The great trouble with our people," he glumly wrote Atkinson in 1888, "is that they have so little politics in them."[36]

34.   CN to Edward Atkinson, January 8, 1888. Atkinson Papers, MHS.
35.   CN to Gordon L. Ford, May 27, 1885. CN to Edward Atkinson, April 8, 1887, Atkinson Papers, MHS; CN to Daniel Lamont, April 8, 1887, Grover Cleveland Papers, LC.CN to Mr. Fairchild, April 3, 1888, Fairchild Papers, NYPL.
36.   CN to Carl Schurz, June 6, 1890. Schurz Papers, LC. There are no articles "from our Special Correspondent" in the New York *Herald* for the months of September 1888; January, March, and December of 1889; and February, March, April, and May of 1890. It is important to remember that to make this determination, only the months during which Congress was in session were checked for Nordhoff columns, and

"Yes," Nordhoff answered a query from Atkinson in early 1888, "I have bought a piece of tolerably worthless land ... in *lower* [Baja] California, near the shores of Todos Santos Bay."[37] He had just completed a new book, *Peninsular California*, about the glories and potentials of the Baja region and in his research had fixed upon the tract near Ensenada. Introducing *Peninsular California*, he noted that when he had published *California: For Health, Pleasure, and Residence* sixteen years previously, "I was generally believed to have over-estimated the resources of that State. The event has shown that I really underestimated them greatly," and he was hopeful that the same might be found true of lower California. But *Peninsular California*, researched and written during his infrequent breaks away from the *Herald*, was a shadow of the earlier work: scantily researched, repetitive, and breathing exhaustion on every page.[38] Not surprisingly, the book failed to sell well, and Americans remained reluctant to purchase land over the border in Mexico. For Nordhoff's purposes, however— as a rural, semitropical retreat—Baja California was well-suited.

The following summer, 1889, he took his family out to Ensenada for a few months' vacation, reveling in long walks and "slowly becoming a human being again." The family was next going to visit the town of Nordhoff, a health resort recently established in the Ojai Valley of Ventura County, "a town named for me," Nordhoff noted proudly, "in a most lovely valley full of grand oaks." (His first California book had touted the healthful aspects of the region, spurring on such development, and this trip was meant in part to restore Lida's

---

these lapses encompass the greater part of those sessions' time periods. Nordhoff's non-Washington writing for the *Herald* is impossible to identify with any degree of certainty. For an example of Nordhoff's lack of reliance upon politicoes as sources, see his "Republican Cobdenites," New York *Herald*, May 7, 1888. For naming names, see [CN,] "Washington: How the Demand for Tax Reduction is Answered," New York *Herald*, January 19, 1883. CN to Edward Atkinson, Friday evg. [1888]. Atkinson Papers, MHS.

37. CN to Edward Atkinson, January 8, 1888. Atkinson Papers, MHS. He had been contemplating such a purchase for some time, writing to his friend surveyor/geologist George Davidson that "If I could find a pleasant *seacoast* ranch ..., *very* cheap—I would not mind buying. But it would have to be *very* cheap." CN to Davidson, Sept. [1886], Davidson Papers, Bancroft Library.

38. CN, *Peninsular California* (NY: Harper & Brothers, 1888), 4. Nordhoff probably realized this was not one of his better efforts; he sent a copy to the Ford family, saying only that he hoped they would not "too much dislike" it. CN to Gordon L. Ford, November 5, 1888.

health—which he believed it had.) "You'll see me in October," he added, "very tanned but I fancy *renewed*."[39]

Within a year of the purchase, Nordhoff wrote to Edward Atkinson of his hopes of "transferring myself there as soon as possible." He meant to sell his Washington home on K Street, and Overlook too if he could get a buyer, and shake off the drudgeries of the East permanently. "I am intellectually weary of journalism," he told Atkinson. The profession had trivialized itself. "It seems to me all the newspapers get down on a continually lower plane," he thought. "They do not see that their influence on public affairs is lessened by this; or perhaps they don't care." He no longer expected great things of the government, which seemed to have degenerated into an insular game of posturing and mutual back-scratching, leaving major social problems unaddressed. Politics of the most meaningless sort predominated, the egos and interests of the players scuttling every useful measure to emerge from committee. One such measure was sure to fail, he judged, because of the lack of courage of its sponsor and then "ever so many private influences, spites, ambitions, turn up"; and he cited a case in which "the talk of an 'Allison bill' made Morrill & Sherman mad!" Furthermore, the American people had "no politics in them" to respond to the need for change. "Politics are *very* barren, & likely to remain so," he went on, "and the spirit has gone out of me for the work, wh. seems useless." He no longer even found any pleasure in his association with the *Herald*, for "my dear Mr. Bennett persists in living abroad, and that takes the heart out of the Herald for me. I long for fresh air, sunshine, and a change of occupation."[40]

As his plans crystallized and his actual departure neared, Atkinson remarked to Nordhoff that he had "sometimes worried about you for fear you would make a mistake" in moving so far from the settled East, but, Atkinson allowed, "you know your own business better than I do" and the Nordhoffs would all do well in California. "You are accustomed to be untied," he observed

---

39.   CN to Edward Atkinson, February 2, 1889. Atkinson Papers, MHS. CN to Edward Atkinson, July 25, 1889. Atkinson Papers, MHS.

40.   CN to Carl Schurz, June 6, 1890, Schurz Papers, LC, mentions his asking $50,000 for Overlook; CN to Edward Atkinson, February 2, 1889, mentions his efforts to sell the K Street house, as does CN to Gordon Ford, May 16, 1887, at which time he thought it could fetch $50,000. Overlook, and the Alpine, NJ land which he had bought along with it, proved to be disappointing as a speculative venture; he never did succeed in selling the house on the Hudson River. See CN to Gordon L. Ford, April 11, 1881; CN to Whitman C. Whitney, September 8, 1890, Whitney Papers, LC; CN to Edward Atkinson, May 15, 1890. CN to Edward Atkinson, June 5, 1890; CN to Edward Atkinson, April 7, 1889. Atkinson Papers, MHS.

to his roving friend, "and to go hither and thither with your belongings."[41] Nordhoff, who regarded a continent's distance as no impediment to keeping old friendships alive—not in the age of the transcontinental railroad—was certain that they would remain friends. "No—we shall not lose touch...," he reassured Atkinson as his plans grew nearer to completion. "Presently ... you'll drift out to see me; & meantime ... you'll write me, as I shall you. The world is not very big now. ...The *main* thing is that we shall continue to love each other."[42]

Reportedly, Bennett, in a characteristically mixed mood of imperiousness and generosity, cabled to Nordhoff an offer that he either abandon Washington for the post of "editor-in-charge" of the *Herald* in the New York office "or ... I will give you the alternative to retire on pension on condition that you will live in California."[43] This would have been a laughably easy decision for Nordhoff to make, and he of course accepted the California pension. (As to why Bennett offered the pension only on condition of Nordhoff's relocation to the West Coast, the record is blank, but as Nordhoff's love of California was no secret, his intentions were probably benign enough. Lida had always been reluctant to abandon the East for a permanent home in California, and perhaps Bennett, knowing this, decided to arrange things so that she could not reasonably refuse to go. Perhaps, also, Nordhoff's usefulness in Washington was at an end.) Provisions for one's employees' retirements were by no means standard at the time, and the pension Bennett provided for Nordhoff was reported variously as "generous," "liberal," and "substantial." The Washington *Evening Star* later named the sum of $5,000, half of his active pay and still an enormous amount.[44]

By August of 1890, it was definite. Nordhoff was leaving for California in September, family in tow,[45] leaving behind him Washington and his life's work, which had taken on a bitter tinge in recent years. "The stupidity of our good men has disgusted me with politics," he wrote to Atkinson; "I don't see anything decently interesting in the game; & I guess this country can get along without my help. I've done my share. I am not as dependent as many on

41. Edward Atkinson to CN, April 2, 1890, Atkinson Papers, MHS.

42. CN to Edward Atkinson, July 26, 1890. Atkinson Papers, MHS.

43. Bennett quoted in Richard O'Connor, *The Scandalous Mr. Bennett* (Garden City: Doubleday, 1962), 220. Unfortunately, O'Connor's book has no footnotes, but is largely based on newspaper reports.

44. Obituary, "Charles Nordhoff," *Harper's Weekly,* July 27, 1901; Obituary, "News Notes," *Bergen County [N.J.] Democrat,* July 19, 1901; Charles F. Lummis, "In Western Letters," *Land of Sunshine* 15 (October 1901), 235; "Charles Nordhoff's Death," Washington *Evening Star,* July 16, 1901.

45. CN to Edward Atkinson, August 1, 1890. Atkinson Papers, MHS.

the excitement of the game—for I'd rather not play whist than play with the Bumplepuppy kind." He cited one case in which all the would-be reformers had ignored his advice about political strategy. "Behold the result," he went on with scorn, mentioning the counterproductive actions of "the good Bayard," "the good Cleveland," and their political ineptitude. What point was there in his trying to promote reform when the politicians seemed venal on the one side and incompetent on the other? "Why should a reasonably fair intelligence like mine bother itself any longer with such sterile stuff?" he asked Atkinson. It was too frustrating, too unproductive, too painful to see the futility of one's work borne home again and again. "I am sure I shall be happier out of the muck of the fight," he assured his friend.[46]

By late Autumn, the Nordhoffs were happily ensconced in Coronado, near San Diego, while the Ensenada land was being prepared for habitation.[47] The fall election came and went while Nordhoff looked on with relieved detachment. "The politics interest me as an observer," he wrote to Atkinson, "but I'm devoutly thankful I have no part in them at this time."[48] "I've done my share," he would repeatedly write to his Eastern friends. He was content, he said, to leave "the rest of this fight" to be "fought by those who have a stomach for it." But retirement was to prove less idyllic than he hoped. Almost against his will, he was still not permanently out of "the fight."[49]

46. CN to Edward Atkinson, July 26, 1890. Atkinson Papers, MHS.
47. E. Babcock to CN, November 20, 1890; Hotel del Coronado Collection, San Diego State University, EB letterbook, 15:278. CN to Edward Atkinson, November 30, 1890.
48. CN to Edward Atkinson, November 30, 1890. Atkinson Papers, MHS.
49. CN to Edward Atkinson, December 24, 1890. Atkinson Papers, MHS.

CHAPTER 11

What the Hawaiians Need and Must Have ...Is Self-Government

"The sunshine & fresh breezes here fill my soul with delight," Charles Nordhoff wrote from California to a friend in late 1890. The freedom from "bread & butter cares" that had long been Nordhoff's keenest desire initially proved an exhilarating experience. Arriving in San Diego in October, the Nordhoffs made their home in the Hotel del Coronado, near the small out-of-the-way settlement of San Diego, with a "little rough shantie nearby" for Nordhoff's study.[1]

Coronado was to be Nordhoff's home for the rest of his days, but its isolation could not shield him from political controversy or the glare of national attention. In 1893, he made his final foray into public affairs by writing a series of critical reports on the complicity of an American minister in overthrowing the native Hawaiian government and in opposition to the annexation of the islands by the United States. Facing a well-organized, well-financed, and ruthless opposition in this fight, he was to find his reputation, his freedom, and his life threatened. Still, he stood his ground, backed by Bennett and his New York *Herald*. A hundred years later, the U.S. Congress declared, in essence, that he had been right.

Their first autumn in California, Charles and Lida occasionally travelled to visit son Walter, his wife, Sarah (or Saidee), and grandson Charlie on their ranch in Ensenada, Baja California, a sun-drenched, if drought-prone, expanse

---

1. CN to Edward Atkinson, October 20, 1890. He wrote that he planned to "assay a quarter of a century's accumulations of papers, letters &c." But if the "papers, letters &c." still exist, they haven't been located. With his acute sense of privacy, it seems likely Nordhoff destroyed them, as he hinted in an 1898 letter to Charles Francis Adams.

on the Pacific coast. Nordhoff believed his son was living the American dream. The family seemed "as busy & happy as young people can be," and Nordhoff declared his first visit to the fledgling farmers—planning, tromping around, helping Saidee try Atkinson's new cooker—to be "one of the happiest times of my life." He looked forward to establishing his own home nearby.[2]

His escape from the East finally effected, Nordhoff still could not help turning his thoughts toward politics. Commenting that Atkinson, in one of his crusades, was "so far as Congress is concerned, a voice crying out in the wilderness," Nordhoff reflected bitterly upon his own career. "It is that experience for years in Washington, wh[ich] made me so tired—& forced me to realize that I'd rather have to do with knaves than with fools," he remarked. Atkinson kept writing hopefully of Nordhoff's eventual return to the east; but this, Nordhoff wrote, "makes me smile," and he assured his friend that he would return only if Bennett summoned him, adding, "I don't think he will be so unkind to me." "Happy as a bird" though he described himself, Nordhoff regarded Atkinson, furiously writing and speaking out, predictably, against the free coinage of silver, with sympathy. "Is it not a humiliating thought to you," he queried,"... that we have been preaching sound doctrines, & in good English too, for so many years & only see the most absurd nonsense prevail at the end." Stubbornly, he would not rethink his own economic "doctrine"; his anguished quest for fresh answers to the problem of poverty, in which he sought out such unorthodox thinkers as Henry George and Columbia's E. R. A. Seligman, seems to have been cut short by his move West. He predicted that Atkinson would soon "get as tired of human stupidity as I did in Washington."[3]

The happiness and sheer relief he found in retirement were soon alloyed. According to Walter's daughter, the ranch went through a period of drought, during which the cattle began to die, and Charles placed some of the blame on his son. According to the daughter, her mother believed Walter "never should have left the newspaper business & ... his father's plans for him were wrong, & ... his heart was nearly broken by it." Strong-willed as he was, Nordhoff once

---

2.   CN to Edward Atkinson, November 30, 1890. Atkinson Papers, MHS. See also Walter Nordhoff, *Rancho del Gabo de Todos Santos: Log Books From Maneadero, Alisitos and Ramajal, 2890-1916,* transcribed by and in the possession of Franklin W. Nordhoff, Jr., Torrance, California. Unfortunately, the logbooks are just that: brief memoranda, with almost no commentary. See also CN to Atkinson, December 1 and 24, 1890, and June 29, 1891.

3.   CN to Edward Atkinson, January 5, [1891] and February 14, 1891. Atkinson Papers, MHS. See Thomas Bender's "E.R.A. Seligman and the Vocation of Social Science," in *Intellect and Public Life: Essays on the Social History of Academic Intellectuals in the United States* (Baltimore: Johns Hopkins University Press ÖÖÖ.

admitted to Worthington Ford that it would not "be for either of our happiness" for he and Walter to work together, "for I am impatient, & ruthless of other people's comfort or feelings when work is in question...; though I hope never unjust...." His own dream of an independent homesteaders' existence was not practicable in his son's eyes. Charles never again visited Walter or mentioned him in his letters to Eastern friends.[4]

Then Nordhoff's health broke down, less than fifteen months after his arrival in Coronado. After February 1892, he was "more or less miserable," weak, and lethargic. If "we could peak off & at once die when we are done, it would be a good arrangement," he remarked. "But to live on, feeble & ailing is a bad thing."[5]

Atkinson, unperturbed, assured Nordhoff that he would soon "renew [his] youth." "Are you not coming back?" he added, his mind on the menace of silver. Nordhoff, the go-between, was sorely missed. "You will be needed to help guide the discordant elements." He had no plans, Nordhoff replied, except to continue his restful life on Coronado beach. "I am done with public affairs," he declared. Atkinson protested at Nordhoff's "tormented gloomy letter," and he relented. "I sh[oul]d hate to discourage anyone," Nordhoff wrote back. He and Atkinson shared a belief in the future; it was the "interregnum" that made him weary. With no real vision of what that future might be, Nordhoff preferred to let events take care of themselves.

"The New York Herald has gone to pieces," Atkinson then advised his friend, taking a different tack in his hopes of luring him back. Nordhoff refused to take the bait. "I don't agree with you ab[ou]t the *Herald*," he answered mildly, adding that it was "a great *in*dependent journal." He was glad to let "more energetic men" carry forward "the fight," and he repeated what had become a constant, defensive refrain. "I did my full share & have the utmost confidence that I am not needed," he insisted, "& may rest & be thankful without desolation of conscience." "I ... watch public affairs from a distance," he similarly remarked to Charles Eliot Norton in January of 1893, "& with that tranquil satisfaction with which an exempt fireman ... observes what the reporters call a 'conflagration.'" But events were soon to end Nordhoff's

---

4. CN to Worthington Ford, April 18, 1884, Ford Family Papers, NYPL. Margaret Nordhoff Morrison, undated note in Walter N. Morrison collection, Danbury, New Hampshire. Sarah Nordhoff, Walter's wife who left a memoir for her children, mentions "troubles" with CN, but does not explain what she means.

5. CN to Edward Atkinson, February 3, 1894, March 2, 1893 and April 24, 1892. Atkinson Papers, MHS; CN to Carl Schurz, October 10, 1893. Schurz Papers, LC.

"exemption" and would throw him into the center of the most violent public controversy of his life.[6]

"Mr. Bennett has asked me to run down to the Sandwich Isl[an]ds, & look into things there," Nordhoff wrote to Atkinson in late March of 1893. That January, a group of wealthy Americans, and Hawaiian-born sons of Americans, had, with the cooperation of the American minister there, overthrown the Hawaiian monarchy of Queen Liliuokalani and established a "Provisional Government." The revolution had been successful only because the American minister, John Stevens, called in American marines to assist in the overthrow, thereby intimidating the queen into surrendering her government; Stevens had then raised the American flag raised over the government buildings, declaring the islands—and the Provisional Government—under American protection. The Provisionals had speedily sent a delegation to Washington, its members described by Stevens in a missive to the State Department as representing "the property holders and commercial interests" of Hawaii, in contrast to their opponents, "the lower class of natives." "The Hawaiian pear is now fully ripe," Stevens concluded, "and this is the golden hour for the United States to pluck it." The delegation negotiated an annexation treaty with the Harrison administration by late February; it was readily approved by the Senate Foreign Relations Committee and sent on to the full Senate for ratification. Although Harrison had asked that a plebiscite demonstrating the natives' willingness to be annexed be included as a condition, the commissioners soon convinced the State Department that native support could not be had and had best be ignored.[7]

Alarmingly to Nordhoff, the news that Hawaii was being offered for annexation was welcomed by many newspapers as representing the first step in a far-flung program of expansion upon which the United States was bound to embark. If Hawaii were annexed, the Philadelphia *Press* editorialized, it would "familiarize the public mind with the acquisition of other territory," including

---

6. Edward Atkinson to Charles Nordhoff, November 28, 1892. Letterbook 47, 89; CN to Edward Atkinson, December 8, 1892. Atkinson Papers, MHS. CN to Charles Eliot Norton, January 26, 1893. Norton Papers, Houghton Library.

7. Stevens quoted in Julius W. Pratt, *Expansionists of 1898: The Acquisition of Hawaii and the Spanish Islands* (Chicago: Quadrangle Books, 1936, rep. 1964), 112–113; see Lorrin A. Thurston on the plebiscite, in Pratt, 128. Other good accounts of the 1893 revolution and bid for annexation may be found in Thomas J. Osborne, *"Empire Can Wait:" American Opposition to Hawaiian Annexation, 1893-1898* (Kent: Kent State University Press, 1981); Ralph S. Kuykendall, *The Hawaiian Kingdom, 1874-1893* (Honolulu: University of Hawaii Press, 1967); and Merze Tate, *The United States and the Hawaiian Kingdom* (New Haven: Yale University Press, 1965).

Santo Domingo, Cuba, and other Caribbean islands. Others looked forward to the absorption of Haiti, Canada, Samoa, and Mexico. Naval historian Alfred Mahan believed that Hawaiian annexation would be "no mere sporadic effort, ... but a first-fruit and a token" that the United States was ready to expand beyond its continental borders.[8]

But Grover Cleveland, whose second inauguration as President was only weeks away, was not about to allow such a momentous step to be taken in the last weeks of his predecessor's administration. Believing the situation needed further investigation, he had the treaty blocked by Congressional allies. Once inaugurated, he withdrew the treaty for further study. Washington officials generally only knew of the Hawaiian situation according to the pro-annexation Hawaiian delegation, but President Cleveland had also received an appeal from Liliuokalani that threw a sinister light on the January coup and the United States' role in it, and he decided to send a Commissioner, James Blount, to look into the situation. It was generally believed that Cleveland and his Secretary of State, Walter Gresham, were open-minded on the question of annexation when the inquiry began, though Blount was a known antiexpansionist and had earlier told the white Hawaiian lobbyist, Lorrin Thurston, that he opposed U.S. involvement in any annexation scheme.[9]

Blount was a Georgian, fifty-six years old in 1893, who had only just retired from the House of Representatives, in which he had served since 1873; he had chaired the House Foreign Relations Committee during his last session there. A veteran of the Confederate army—he was generally referred to as "Colonel" Blount—he had opposed the Civil Rights Acts of the early 1870s and worked with other leaders of the so-called "New South" to preserve the antebellum racial order of white supremacy. His Southern background made him an easy target when soon after his arrival in Hawaii, he ordered the American flag, which Stevens had had hoisted above the government buildings, hauled down. One outraged newspaper reminded its readers that Blount was "a Bourbon ex-Confederate, who had fought to tear down the American flag and trample it under foot." Among Washington insiders, untroubled by the New South's racial order, Blount had a reputation for adherence to his principles and a cool rationality: a "deep thinker" interested in preserving the dignity and honor of the U.S. government. Among his confidants, he made it clear that he had retired from the House only to broaden his experience in preparation for a run for the Senate, and the Hawaiian mission would provide just that kind of

8. See Pratt, op. cit., 150–153.
9. Osborne, 5–14.

experience. He was doubtless well-acquainted with Nordhoff, whose tenure in Washington almost exactly coincided with his own.[10]

James Gordon Bennett Jr. opposed annexation from the start, and the New York *Herald* early became one of the strongest critics of the Provisional Government and annexation in general. Nordhoff had strong anti-imperialist beliefs himself, as Bennett no doubt knew; as early as 1869, he had opposed Grant's attempt to annex San Domingo, and in his 1874 book on Hawaii and the Pacific Northwest, he had made it clear that he believed the islands should be left independent. When asked by Bennett to investigate the Hawaiian situation, Nordhoff readily complied, anxious to stave off what he saw as impending catastrophe. "I'm busy preparing to go off—it is not pleasant—but duty, & it must be done," he wrote to Atkinson, "& I hope to put a small spoke in the annexation business."[11]

Nordhoff's motives in opposing Hawaiian annexation were badly mixed. On political and moral principles, above all, he could not stomach the manner in which the Hawaiian Queen had been overthrown using American troops or the way that annexation was being forced upon an unwilling population. Secondary to his core belief that the whole business was undemocratic, though still important in his opposition, were racism of a type common to the time— the reluctance to see a population largely composed of Asians and Pacific Islanders join the American polity—and his distrust of big government and militarism. He detected "jobbery" in the whole scheme and in the way it was being welcomed by the military establishment and its spokesmen, like Alfred Mahan.[12]

The *Herald* was not the only newspaper to oppose annexation; the New York *Evening Post* and *Harper's Weekly* were among the most prominent journals to voice strong opposition. But neither had sent a correspondent to Hawaii, and

---

[10.]   Tennant S. McWilliams, "James H. Blount, the South, and Hawaiian Annexation," *Pacific Historical Review* 57 (1988): 25–46. Interestingly, Tennant attributes much of Blount's anti-expansionist principles to his experience as a Georgian during Reconstruction: feeling white Southerners to have been subjugated and oppressed by a "foreign" invasive force (i.e., the Union army), he would resist subsequent attempts by the United States to treat other countries as it had (he felt) treated the South. On the other hand, he had also been part of the white society in the South bent on subjugating blacks—but he seems to have had reservations about holding the native Hawaiians to be inferior by virtue of their color. The "Bourbon ex-Confederate" remark is from the *New York Press*, April 17, 1893, quoted in *Public Opinion*, April 22, 1893, 69–70.

[11.]   CN to Edward Atkinson, March 21, 1893. Atkinson Papers, MHS.

[12.]   CN, "Hawaii Needs a New Minister," NY *Herald*, May 1, 1893.

they were to largely depend on Nordhoff's reports to make their arguments. Meanwhile, such powerful newspapers as the New York *Tribune* and *New York Sun* were highly vocal proponents of the Provisional Government and annexation, and Nordhoff was a favored target.

Commissioner Blount's first official act in Honolulu was to lower the American flag on April 1, ending the "protectorate," raising the Hawaiian flag in its stead, and receiving considerable abuse as a result. Nordhoff noted in his initial article that the Commissioner was close-mouthed as to his plans of action. "He is accessible to everybody of all parties," Nordhoff noted with approval. "He listens to all who come to him; but ... he never says a word."[13]

Arriving in Hawaii in early April, only days after Commissioner Blount, Nordhoff set to work—he had, in fact, already been at work, in San Francisco and during the voyage, interviewing anyone who was familiar with Hawaiian politics—and immediately sent off a long article, to be published in the *Herald* on April 17 under the headline "Getting at Facts About Hawaii." It was the first of many such dispatches and introduced Nordhoff's impressions of the Hawaiian situation. Briefly stated, they were that Minister Stevens had colluded with the revolutionists without authorization; that the U.S. Marines had been misused to protect the white revolutionaries, not American interests; that the revolutionaries were a tiny group of wealthy businessmen who did not have the support of the vast majority of the public; that the few natives who expressed support for the revolution were, for the most part, coerced by their employers to do so; that the natives were literate, well-educated, Christian, and capable of self-government. He also maintained that the men behind the revolution were interested in annexation for their own selfish purposes, which were to allow the non-natives to run the islands and to let the planters rake in as much profit as possible.[14]

He was largely correct about the planters' economic motives. The new McKinley Tariff had deprived them of the advantage over other sugar-exporting countries that they had enjoyed under the old reciprocity treaty, and they could regain that advantage only by becoming eligible for the "bounty" the federal government extended to domestic sugar producers in lieu of the old protective tariff.

For the first time since his Southern letters of 1875, Nordhoff signed his *Herald* articles rather than leaving them with his impersonal byline, "From Our Special Correspondent," of the Washington years. The reaction was swift and personal. Belying its own claims that Nordhoff lacked credibility and

---

13.   Ralph S. Kuykendall, *The Hawaiian Kingdom, 1874-1893* (Honolulu: University of Hawaii Press, 1967), 623–4.

14.   CN, "Getting at Facts About Hawaii," NY *Herald*, April 17, 1893.

influence, annexationist newspapers, including the Washington *Post*, launched a vindictive campaign against him. In a lead editorial in late April, the *Post* accused Nordhoff of being a mouthpiece for Bennett, twisting the facts to buttress the *Herald*'s preordained position. The *Post* saw nothing wrong with wresting the Hawaiian government away from the natives or, as it put it, replacing "a burlesque monarchy" with "a civilized and wholesome republic." The New York *Tribune*, about a week later, dismissed all criticism of the Provisional Government, referring to it as "extremely wise, prudent and successful," worthy of praise rather than censure for its successful opposition of a tyrannical "semi-civilized royalty."[15]

Because there was no cable connection between Hawaii and North America, it took over a week for Nordhoff's columns from Honolulu to reach San Francisco, where they would be cabled to New York for publication in the next day's *Herald* whereupon the *Herald*, and the numerous other papers across the nation that reprinted Nordhoff's *Herald* articles, would be sent off to Honolulu on the next steamer, where the people anxiously awaited the letters and news of the previous several days. The Hawaiian response to Nordhoff's April 17 article did not appear until May 5—by which time he had already written and sent off more articles to the *Herald*. But the delay did not soften the blow felt by the annexationists when they read Nordhoff's blistering criticisms, reprinted across the entire United States—and to know that their replies would not be heard for weeks afterward.

There were three important English-language newspapers in Honolulu in 1893, and two of them—the *Pacific Commercial Advertiser* and the *Hawaiian Star*—were pro-annexationist, enjoying the patronage and support of the provisional government. The third, the *Honolulu Evening Bulletin*, was anti-annexationist (or "royalist," as all opposition—even nativist Republicans—to the Dole cohort came to be called) and engaged in daily skirmishes with the *Advertiser* and the *Star*. Hawaiian-language newspapers, every one of them royalist, would soon be forced to close by the government for seditious libel.[16] Predictably enough, the English-language papers joined the editorial battle begun by the *Washington Post* over Nordhoff's reports.

The *Advertiser* responded to Nordhoff's initial article about Hawaii with an editorial titled "The Misrepresentations of Mr. Nordhoff"—the first of many hostile rejoinders. In the coming weeks, the *Advertiser* tried to destroy

15.   "The Hawaiian Bugaboo," editorial leader, The Washington *Post*, April 28, 1893; New York *Tribune*, May 8, 1893, quoted in "The United States and Hawaii," *Public Opinion*, May 13, 1893, 145–6.

16.   On the actions against the Hawaiian papers, see "The Libel Cases," *Pacific Commercial Advertiser*, May 17, 1893.

Nordhoff's credibility by taking a variety of inconsistent courses. Nordhoff was a good journalist gone bad, it would state indignantly, or a bad journalist staying true to form; or an alien, a German, working against the best interests of his adopted country;[17] or a hireling mindlessly obeying the dastardly orders of James Gordon Bennett Jr.; or some combination thereof. Perhaps most tellingly, it often buttressed its objections with references to Nordhoff's lack of what would come to be called "objectivity," his unfairness, his prejudice, maintaining that he had found only what he wanted to find and was not to be trusted on that account; it seldom directly answered the charges he leveled against the revolutionaries and the provisional government.

In its reply to Nordhoff's "Facts About Hawaii" article, the *Advertiser* called Nordhoff "a grossly prejudiced, unfair and incompetent observer. ...Every blockhead in Honolulu knows that the revolution was not a planter's revolution." But the editorial was written with American audiences in mind, people who would not be able to judge the situation for themselves, but who might know of Nordhoff's reputation for accuracy; so the paper hastened to comment that Nordhoff was "not a blockhead," mentioned his "supposed character and imputed talents," and then attributed Nordhoff's conclusions to malice, to gullibility, and even to seasickness (a laughable supposition, given Nordhoff's background). "The cause of annexation is the cause of progress, prosperity and civilization," the editorial concluded, "and it will probably triumph without the aid of the New York Herald, or any of its correspondents." Ah, but what about its opposition?[18]

Already, the anti-annexationist press was using Nordhoff's reports to buttress their arguments: the New York *Evening Post*, then edited by E. L. Godkin (who could use sarcasm the way Bach used musical notes), ran an editorial on the very day that "Facts About Hawaii" appeared in the *Herald*, responding to a pro-annexation New York *Sun* editorial that derided any proposal "to put a humbug queen upon a humbug throne." "Humbug for humbug," Godkin

---

17. Nordhoff's patriotism is constantly impugned in the attacks on him, but anti-Germanism is also occasionally explicit: see, for instance, "Another Critic," *Pacific Commercial Advertiser*, May 15, 1893; and the reference to Nordhoff's "suggestive and un-American name" in "A Campaign of Lies," *Pacific Commercial Advertiser*, May 22, 1893. Such anti-German feeling is curious, in light of the fact that the German Ambassador to the United States had told Secretary of State Foster that the German government had always regarded Hawaii as a de facto protectorate of the United States and would not oppose annexation. See Michael J. Devine, "John W. Foster and the Struggle for the Annexation of Hawaii," *Pacific Historical Review* 46 (1977), 36.

18. "The Misrepresentations of Mr. Nordhoff," *Pacific Commercial Advertiser*, May 5, 1893.

retorted, "there are people who would as soon see a humbug queen as a humbug republic," and quoted Nordhoff's report of the unpopularity of the revolution, with 40,000 natives opposed to 1,900 Americans. Adding Nordhoff's facts to a *Tribune* report quoting Dole as saying that a Hawaiian republic would "'necessarily be a government by force' which it would take 'resolute men to manage,'" Godkin concluded, "To lend these resolute men the aid of United States troops for the purpose of coercing the vast majority of the people would be a glorious triumph for 'self-government.'" With such enemies as Godkin, with his acid-tipped pen lying in wait for facts to use against them, facts that Nordhoff's *Herald* reports supplied in abundance, the annexationists would regard Nordhoff as the greatest obstacle in their path, belying their public assertions that his work was of no consequence.[19]

On May 5, the same day that the *Advertiser* was railing against Nordhoff in Honolulu, another long Nordhoff article appeared in the New York *Herald* under the headline, "Natives Opposed to Annexation," in which he elaborated on the coercion leveled against natives and other anti-annexationists by the Provisionals and their supporters. A "savage" environment, in which dissent was scarcely tolerated, was being fostered by the Provisionals. "They make it ugly," Nordhoff noted, "for even well to do people who are opposed to them." If they could abuse the poor by threatening their livelihoods, they could also ostracize and boycott the nonconforming well-to-do. Nordhoff would soon know, however, that their methods extended considerably beyond ostracization.[20]

To Nordhoff, the undemocratic nature of the planter class was clearly seen in their labor laws, which he likened to slavery, with ten-year unbreakable contracts and various laws that gave the planters almost unlimited power over workers. If the islands were annexed, how could the United States sanction such laws? "They might suit some arbitrary and heartless employers of labor in the United States," Nordhoff added caustically, probably thinking of the violent clashes of labor and proprietors so common at the time, "but they would hardly please American workingmen and women."[21]

Nordhoff was not just describing Hawaiian labor; he was criticizing corporate capitalism as a whole, expressing his uneasiness with the modern industrial order. The planters were not "in general inhuman," Nordhoff added, but they had little direct contact with laborers. That was left to managers intent on reaping large profits for stockholders, inviting the abuse of power on isolated

19.   [E. L. Godkin], untitled editorial, New York *Evening Post*, April 17, 1893, 6. See also Godkin's use of Nordhoff's work in an untitled editorial attack on John Stevens, in the New York *Evening Post*, June 3, 1893.
20.   CN, "Natives Opposed to Annexation," NY *Herald*, May 5, 1893.
21.   Ibid.

plantations. In the old days, Nordhoff maintained, the planters "lived among their people on their plantations and looked after the happiness of all about them." This was the sort of paternalistic capitalism of which Nordhoff approved, semifeudal though it might be. But when the plantations were enlarged and turned into corporations, the ties of mutual obligation were broken. Like the absentee landlords of the New York slums, who knew their Irish tenants not as people but as entries on a credit/debit sheet, the "simple living planters" of 1873 had become "nabobs," "no longer planters but stockholders."[22]

By the time this article had reached Honolulu, Nordhoff had begun to get into arguments with the pro-annexation locals, as well as to attract the gratitude of the opposition. The *Advertiser* headlined one account of a relatively innocuous incident "Nasty Nordhoff" and claimed that he had "gone to the length of trying to make converts to the ex-queen's cause from the annexation ranks," which is probably true: Nordhoff would argue a point with anyone. Two days later, the *Advertiser* ran another leading editorial titled "The Herald's Correspondent," calling Nordhoff "untruthful and unscrupulous" and claiming that Nordhoff had privately admitted that he was only following Bennett's orders; it then contradicted itself in the same piece. "Mr. Nordhoff has a perfect right to be a royalist," it went on, but he had no right to "[pervert] the facts of history and [deride] men and principles worthy of at least honest and gentlemanly consideration." The justice of annexation was not a matter of politics in this view: it was a matter of objective truth, which Nordhoff had violated. The "reputation for equitable statement so necessary in the newspaper business at all times," later noted the Washington *Evening Star*, was one that Nordhoff had irrevocably lost.[23]

Meanwhile, the most powerful sugar producer and refiner in the islands, Claus Spreckels, agreed to an interview with Nordhoff, which was published in the *Herald* on May 13. The interview stunned the annexationists: Spreckels was against them. He opposed the annexation treaty, he said, because the contract labor system, so necessary (in his mind) to the profitability of sugar production, would be outlawed under the United States flag. Nordhoff, recognizing an important recruit to the anti-annexationist cause, recorded without comment Spreckels's bland pronouncements on the necessity of maintaining cheap foreign labor in the islands and toned down his critiques of the labor system.[24]

The *Advertiser* at first refused to believe that the "notoriously unreliable" Nordhoff had reported Spreckels's words accurately; when the interview first

---

22. CN, "Natives," 5/5/93; CN, "Chinese Take Root in Hawaii," NY *Herald*, May 6, 1893.
23. "Nasty Nordhoff," *Pacific Commercial Advertiser*, May 17, 1893; untitled editorial, Washington *Evening Star*, June 2, 1893.
24. CN, "Spreckels Opposes Annexation," NY *Herald*, May 13, 1893.

appeared in Hawaii, it editorialized that he had "put up some sort of journalistic job on Mr. Claus Spreckels, and has included some statements ... which Mr. Spreckels will hesitate to endorse." That evening, however, Spreckels wrote a one-sentence note to the local newspapers doing precisely that

> In my interview with Mr. Charles Nordhoff, recently published
> in the local papers, I said just what I wanted to say and what
> I believe to be true.

The *Advertiser* was reduced to feebly arguing that Spreckels represented no one but himself. It didn't retract its branding of Nordhoff as a liar, however.[25]

In the same issue that the *Advertiser* had questioned the accuracy of the Spreckels interview, it hysterically accused Nordhoff ("with a machiavellian turn of mind and a Bourbon cast of conscience") of being the instigator and ringleader of royalist opposition:

> [T]he entire rank and file of the old palace crowd, newspapers
> and all, have fallen in behind Mr. Nordhoff, whom they
> publicly announce they will both imitate and defend. ...The
> absurd defense offered Mr. Nordhoff's conduct that he
> has hitherto possessed a good reputation, 'as an able and
> honorable journalist throughout the United States,' will not
> suffice: the question is, has Mr. Nordhoff borne false witness
> in this specific case of Hawaiian affairs.

In other words, as Nordhoff would later complain, "character" was almost worthless. The opposition would not engage him on the facts of the case for they couldn't (or wouldn't) agree that the facts he reported were true.[26]

Soon, he was faced with charges of libel. Three annexationists whom Nordhoff had named as having been petitioners for the very lottery that annexationists later pointed to as evidence of the depravity of Liliuokalani's government threatened to sue him. At this, Nordhoff later explained, he looked for the petitions from which he had drawn their names. The petitions were gone—lost or, he suspected, stolen—and he obtained a statement from the clerk confirming that fact. Having no longer any proof of the allegations, he

---

[25]   "That Interview," *Pacific Commercial Advertiser*, May 22, 1893; "Mr. Spreckels' Position," *Pacific Commercial Advertiser*, May 23, 1893; CN, "Tried to Silence the Herald," New York *Herald*, June 1, 1893.

[26]   "A Campaign of Lies," *Pacific Commercial Advertiser*, May 22, 1893.

sent an apology and a retraction to the local newspapers that was published May 22.[27]

But he kept writing his dangerous letters to the *Herald*. Since the planter class, which apparently *was* largely in agreement with Spreckels (despite the *Advertiser*'s protestations to the contrary), was now an ally that he did not want to offend, Nordhoff stressed even more the lack of popular support enjoyed by the Provisional Government. He described the annexation movement as "engineered" by non-Hawaiians, aided by the American Minister who called in U.S. troops without which the revolution would have failed. If such assistance were sanctioned, then the United States could "play that trick" on any number of Latin American countries where Americans had settled. "But such a filibustering policy would be a disgrace to us, and put us out of the category of honorable nations," he declared. "...The policy of justice and kindness for us is to keep our hands off."[28]

With his polemics being published, not only in the still-enormously popular *Herald* (which had recently been overtaken by Pulitzer's New York *World* in circulation), but also reprinted by other newspapers across the country, Nordhoff presented an imposing obstacle to the annexationists, who depended on Congress to approve their treaty. There were rumors circulating, he reported, that "troublesome" foreigners would soon be expelled, and he admitted that a government had a right to expel any foreigner "who does not conduct himself in an orderly way." But he did not place words under the same strictures as behavior—particularly words written for publication in another country, even if they did get reprinted in Honolulu. Antagonistic speech and writing were not equivalent to antagonistic acts although he would have been the first to assert that they could be more powerful than any action. His career had been predicated on the assumption that his writings could make a difference and, indeed, were the true and necessary means of fostering change in a democracy. Hawaii in 1893, however, was not a democracy.[29]

The annexationists did not see the distinction; Nordhoff had always worried them. Almost from the day of his arrival in Honolulu, one of their delegates to Washington suggested that Nordhoff might be bought off with proper treatment. Immediately after the Spreckels interview was published in

---

27. CN, "Tried to Silence the Herald," New York *Herald*, June 1, 1893; "Mr. Nordhoff's Experiences in Honolulu," New York *Herald*, July 9, 1893; "Charles Nordhoff: A Condensed Statement of His Doings Here," *Pacific Commercial Advertiser*, May 24, 1893, 5

28. CN, "Hawaiian Pear Not Yet Ripe," NY *Herald*, May 18, 1893.

29. CN, "Spreckels Opposes Annexation," NY *Herald*, May 13, 1893.

Honolulu on May 21, with his limited retraction concerning the lottery petition on the twenty-second, hostility toward him reached new heights.[30]

That day, the editor of the annexationist *Hawaiian Star*, a Dr. McGrew, went to the American naval officer then stationed on the *Boston* in Honolulu harbor. McGrew told Skerrett that many annexationists "were offended by Mr. Nordhoff's letters, and that he had scarcely been able to restrain them from insulting Mr. Nordhoff by applying to him a coat of tar and feathers," as James Blount later recounted to Secretary of State Gresham. Skerrett repeated McGrew's statement to Blount (who had by then unwillingly replaced Stevens as the American Minister), and Blount immediately wrote to Dole of the reported threats. Nordhoff was "an eminent citizen of the United States," he reminded Dole: an implicit warning to which Dole did not reply and apparently paid little heed. If he hoped that Dole would speak out against violence, he was to be disappointed. Dole made no reply.[31]

The well-connected McGrew—who was also president of the Annexation Club, which the San Francisco *Examiner* called "the tail that wags the head of the Government"—later informed Skerrett that there would be no tar-and-feathering, but that Nordhoff would be taken to court. The following day, the Attorney General of Hawaii, William O. Smith, issued a subpoena to Nordhoff, enclosing an extract from one of his *Herald* articles, which had been reprinted in the Honolulu *Daily Bulletin*:

> Minister Stevens has been engaged ... in an intrigue having for its object to alarm the Queen and cause her to abdicate. Mr. Dole ...has been, it is understood, working with the American Minister at this enterprise and reports have been set afloat that President Cleveland wishes her to make a cession of the islands to the United States; that Commissioner Blount would be pleased if she did; that Mr. Blount is going away soon; that he intends to land troops again and hoist the American flag....

30. Opposition papers cited in William Adam Russ, Jr., *The Hawaiian Revolution (1893-94)* (Selinsgrove, PA: Susquehanna University Press, 1959), 206; W. R. Castle to Lorrin Thurston, April 8, 1893; cited in Russ, 205.

31. James H. Blount to S. B. Dole, May 21, 1893. F.O. & Ex., 1893, U.S. Commissioner in Hawaii, Hawaii State Archives; Blount to William Q. Gresham, May 24, 1893, reprinted in U.S. House of Representatives, 53rd Congress, 3rd Session, Executive Document #1, *Foreign Relations of the United States, 1894, Appendix II: Affairs in Hawaii.* Washington: GPO, 1895, hereinafter cited as *FRUS, 1894.*

This statement, Smith informed Nordhoff, was "regarded as malicious and libelous" by the government and demanded a retraction, lest "proceedings will be instituted against you."[32]

Upon receiving this threat, Nordhoff wrote what he later called a "civil," though obviously irritated, letter to the attorney general. "[J]ust what *is* false," he asked, in the disputed report? Blandly ignoring what he knew to be the real heart of Smith's complaint, he wrote that these reports, "while they were certainly false reports, were actually commonly circulated. You don't of course want me to say now that such reports were not floating ab[ou]t?" By the time he read these words, so deliberately beside the point, Smith must have been seething. Nordhoff coolly went on to infer that Smith wanted him to deny the passage about Stevens's collusion with Dole in spreading the rumors to frighten the Queen, and he asked that he be given a day to double-check the allegation with his source. If the source didn't satisfy Nordhoff with the justice of the allegation, "then I'll retract, but if he does [justify the accusation], & I so tell you, I don't suppose you'll want me to retract." He closed by reminding the Attorney General that he hadn't published this article in Honolulu, but only in New York and couldn't be held responsible for the Honolulu newspaper's decision to reprint. "But as an honest journalist," he concluded, "desirous to state only the truth, I am very ready to apologize whenever I have been misled."[33]

Smith immediately sent back an outraged rejoinder (a "peremptory and ridiculous reply," Nordhoff called it). "No man is justified in repeating by publication, false, malicious, defamitory [*sic*], libelous and seditious statements by saying that someone told him so," and he insisted that "the letter and spirit" of his earlier letter would stand. Then he sent Smith's summons and letter to Blount.[34]

---

32.   "Don't You Touch Nordhoff!," San Francisco *Examiner*, June 1, 1893, 4; the CN article extract is in a letter from William O. Smith to Charles Nordhoff, May 22, 1893, which is in turn copied into James H. Blount to Sanford B. Dole, 5/2/93, F.O. & Ex., 1893, U.S. Commissioner in Hawaii, Hawaii State Archives. Smith's letter, *without* the article excerpt, is also in the Attorney General's Files, Misc. Cases, 1893, Hawaii State Archives. See Julius W. Pratt, *Expansionists of 1898* (Baltimore: Johns Hopkins University Press, 1936, rep. 1964), 166–67.

33.   CN to William O. Smith, 5/22/93, Attorney General's Files, Hawaii State Archives; CN, "Tried to Silence the Herald," New York *Herald* (dateline May 23), June 1, 1893.

34.   Attorney General to CN, 5/22/93, Attorney General's files, Hawaii State Archives; CN, "Tried to Silence the Herald," New York *Herald*, June 1, 1893. Nordhoff's account for the *Herald* and Blount's letter to Gresham concerning these events disagree on minor details, including whether Nordhoff sent one or both summonses to Blount

Meanwhile, the Executive and Advisory Councils of the Provisional Government met, angered by his reply to Smith and intent on stopping Nordhoff's reports and resolved that a different Nordhoff report, "Shrewd Lottery Men" (the article for which Nordhoff had already issued a very limited retraction) was "wholly false" and again formally summoned Nordhoff to appear before them the following morning. Apparently, the Council didn't want to publicly challenge Nordhoff on the Dole-Stevens rumors, for fear he would actually prove them to be true, and they decided to harass Nordhoff with one of his less-defensible—or significant—reports although one which he still maintained to be true in all important respects.[35]

Unaware of the second summons, Blount went to Dole about the first summons and told him the U.S. government would not "submit" to having Nordhoff questioned by the Hawaiian government. Dole made some bland conversation and then told Blount that Nordhoff had been "requested" to come before the government's Advisory Council, asking Blount if he thought Nordhoff would come,

> as it was only a request. To this I answered, "I presume not. Whatever information Mr. Nordhoff may have obtained carried with it an obligation of privacy, which I do not believe he would violate."

He was going to see Nordhoff, Blount added; could he assure him that all had been settled? Dole replied, "'I have taken precautions against any violence being done to him, although I do not think he is in any danger.'"[36]

Earlier that day, a policeman came to see Nordhoff and told him that two policemen would be stationed in front of his cottage "and that if they should telephone to headquarters a larger force would come," Nordhoff recounted in the *Herald* column he was writing that day. "So I am living here under the rule of a set of people who call themselves 'missionary children' and having to be guarded against the violence of ...gentlemen of the Annexation Club."

Blount went to Nordhoff's house, where he was stopped, at first, by the policemen guarding the door; when he gained entry, Nordhoff showed him the second summons he had received. "It had very little the appearance to my

---

at this point. I've tried to put the two together to decide the chronology that is best reconciled with the significant elements of both, which consistently agree in the essentials.

35.   Nordhoff gave the summons to Blount, who copied it into his letter to Dole on May 22, 1893. F.O.& Ex., Hawaiian Legation in Washington, Hawaii State Archives.

36.   Blount to Gresham, 5/24/93, in *FRUS, 1894.*

mind of a request," Blount drily recalled. Blount "directed me positively to pay no attention whatever" to either summons, Nordhoff reported. "He said that I was an American citizen, writing for an American paper, and could not and should not be questioned or threatened by any one here for what I had written." He "ordered" Nordhoff not to obey the summons. By that evening, people in Honolulu, unaware of Blount's intervention, were buzzing with speculation about whether Nordhoff would respond to the summons or not. Claus Spreckels reportedly bet $100—about $1,500 in 1990s currency—that Nordhoff would not. The following morning, Blount went to Nordhoff's house and asked him to come to the legation "and remain there," Nordhoff wrote, "until all danger of an attempt to interfere with me by arrest was past."[37]

The twenty-third, the day Nordhoff had been ordered to appear before the Council, happened to be the day Blount was to formally present his credentials as the new American minister to the Hawaiian government, and he "was in no pleasant frame of mind" when he did so, according to the correspondent of the San Francisco *Chronicle*. The Nordhoff matter "still rankled." It was a brief and chilly ceremony. Afterwards, Dole asked to speak with him about the proceedings against Nordhoff, which were scheduled to begin at eleven o'clock. Blount said he hoped the matter would be dropped; he didn't want to have to put his objections in writing. In reply, Dole asked him if Nordhoff would apologize to the Council. Blount answered

> that I did not think he would; that I could not advise him to such a course; that after denunciation by the "Star," the Annexation Club organ, threats of insult by tarring and feathering, proceedings instituted by the attorney-general in the local courts, and the action of the advisory council, such an apology would have the appearance of compulsion, to which I was not willing to see an American citizen subjected.

He reminded Dole of the case of an American reporter named Cutting, who had been imprisoned in Mexico a few years before, but released upon the demand of the United States government, and then he left Dole. Upon returning to the legation, he instructed Nordhoff to stay put.[38]

[37.]   Blount to Gresham, May 24, 1893, *FRUS, 1894*; "Don't You Touch Nordhoff!" San Francisco *Examiner*, June 1, 1893.

[38.]   Blount to Gresham, 5/24/1893, *FRUS, 1894*; "In the Councils: Nordhoff Refuses to Appear," *Pacific Commercial Advertiser*, May 24, 1893; "Disquiet in Hawaii," *San Francisco Chronicle*, June 1, 1893, 4.

The full Council convened soon thereafter, as planned, with Dole and sixteen others present. Dole ordered the secretary to call Nordhoff's name three times, but when Nordhoff did not appear, Dole said that Nordhoff had probably acted according to Blount's advice and mentioned Blount's citing of the Cutting case. Dole called Nordhoff's case "a small thing by itself," according to the *Advertiser*, and judged that "it would be well for the councils to investigate the legal phases thoroughly before proceeding to action." Vice President Damon asked if anything official had been received from Blount, to which Dole replied that that hadn't been necessary. The Council, possibly emboldened by this, decided to have a subcommittee meet privately to discuss the matter.[39]

That afternoon, Blount received a note from Dole, which stated that Nordhoff would be protected from violence—but making no mention of the government's action against him. Blount told Nordhoff he could go home after having him write a statement that he hadn't known the Honolulu *Bulletin* would reprint his letters, which was crucial to the jurisdictional issues. He later asked his secretary to see if Dole intended to come talk with him at the legation, which he believed Dole had said he would do. But Dole refused and added that the Council had referred the Nordhoff case to the attorney general, "to inquire whether any civil or criminal proceedings should be taken against" their antagonist.[40]

The previous day, Blount had written a warning to Dole to leave Nordhoff alone, but had not sent it, hoping the matter could be resolved without official written communications; he now decided the letter would have to be sent. "The New York 'Herald' is a paper not published in the Hawaiian islands," he began, and therefore jurisdiction by the Hawaiian government over any of its authors was "wholly inadmissable." Blount elaborated: the United States would not "permit a citizen of the United States to be called to account by the Hawaiian Government for acts done within the boundaries of the United States," and he insisted the proceedings against Nordhoff be dropped, once again citing the Cutting case.[41]

John Stevens, the former minister who had assisted the revolutionaries, then called on Blount. He was scheduled to depart the islands the following day, and this was his leave-taking. "He was exceedingly bitter against Mr. Nordhoff," Blount later noted, "charging him with treasonable conduct and displaying the most eager interest in the ...action of the Hawaiian Government against

39. "In the Councils: Nordhoff Refuses to Appear," *Pacific Commercial Advertiser*, May 24, 1893.

40. Ibid.

41. Blount to Dole, 5/22/93. F.O. & Ex., 1893, U.S. Commissioner in Hawaii, Hawaii State Archives.

him." Stevens told Blount that Nordhoff had been "conspiring" with royalists to overthrow the Provisional Government and said they had evidence to prove it. "I asked him how this came to his knowledge?" Blount recalled, and "[h] e replied, 'Well, I have it, anyhow; and they ought to have it.'" Blount later stated that he believed that Stevens had "contributed to produce an abnormal excitement" against Nordhoff.[42]

The Provisional Government backed down. The following day, Dole wrote a terse note to Blount, stating that the government had decided against criminal proceedings against Nordhoff although he insisted that the Cutting case was not analogous. Dole filed a civil suit against Nordhoff that same day, asking for $10,000 in damages for "public odium, hatred and disgrace and [injury to] his good name, reputation and feelings." The case was to be heard by the Hawaiian court at its next session, in August—by which time, however, Nordhoff had left the islands.[43]

The annexationist newspapers, confronted with Blount's protection of Nordhoff, let loose another wave of invective, most of which tried to picture Nordhoff as an irresponsible, even criminal troublemaker while (no mean trick) simultaneously praising Blount as "an intelligent, fairminded, honorable man, whose eyes cannot be blinded to the truth, and whose judgment will not be warped by prejudice." The *Advertiser* fumbled around in its denunciations, taking different, often contradictory, rhetorical tacks against Nordhoff and everything he stood for. One editorial stated that "the New York Herald is one of the great newspapers of the world" then claimed that its policy was "dictated from Europe," making it "generally un-American, frequently disloyal, and always mercenary," and another averred that "the Herald has no reputation to lose." While noting "Mr. Nordhoff's well-known reputation as a veteran correspondent," or "his reputation for impartiality," or "his former reputation as a fair-minded and circumspect journalist," the *Advertiser* always hastened to say that that reputation had been proven false by Nordhoff's Hawaiian correspondence.[44]

[42.] Blount to Gresham, 5/24/1893, *FRUS, 1894.*

[43.] Sanford B. Dole to James H. Blount, May 24, 1893. F.O. & Ex., Hawaiian Legation in Washington, Hawaii State Archives; Blount to Gresham, May 29, 1893, *FRUS, 1894*; Sanford B. Dole to Lorrin A. Thurston, May 24, 1893. F.O. & Ex., 1893, Hawaiian Legation in Washington, Hawaii State Archives; and "Sanford B. Dole v. Charles Nordhoff, Plaintiff's Declaration," Attorney General's Files, Hawaii State Archives.

[44.] "The Herald and Mr. Nordhoff," *Pacific Commercial Advertiser*, May 24, 1893; "Chas. Nordhoff: A Condensed Statement of His Doings Here," *Pacific Commercial Advertiser*, May 24, 1893; "No connection," *Pacific Commercial Advertiser*, June 5, 1893.

Blount was still considerably worried that some act of violence might yet be committed, as the abuse of Nordhoff in the annexation press grew ever more strident. He was particularly disturbed when articles appeared in the *Star* and the *Advertiser* mocking the very idea that Nordhoff might need police protection and attributing the alarm to his own paranoia and guilty conscience. "In view of the fact that Mr. Nordhoff is as safe in Honolulu as he could be at his sequestered home on Coronado Beach, the whole episode becomes a tax upon the risibles," sneered the *Hawaiian Star*. It went on to claim that Nordhoff had asked for protection of his own accord, no doubt in order to use the tender of police protection as the basis of a column "with a lurid tale of how he escaped death at the hands of an infuriated annexation mob, only to be saved by Minister Blount." The editor of the *Star*, and the undoubted author of this piece, of course, was Dr. McGrew, the very man who had reported the imminence of violence to Admiral Skerrett in the first place. McGrew had probably realized that the necessity of guarding Nordhoff from rabid annexationists was a public relations disaster for the cause of annexation. At any rate, McGrew was playing a game that made Blount uneasy. He enclosed the *Star* article with his next letter to Gresham, adding, "I hope you will not underrate the excitement which prompted all my actions in regard to Mr. Nordhoff."[45]

Blount knew Nordhoff would not soon leave the islands of his own accord despite the threats. He soon suggested to Dole that "if Mr. Nordhoff was so obnoxious," they might deport him, but "this did not seem to impress them favorably." To Gresham, Blount ventured the opinion that the attempt to prosecute Nordhoff was "animated by the spirit of crushing out all opposing opinions by forceful methods," which mere deportation, of course, could not accomplish. As Blount remarked in a letter to Gresham, he thought nothing more would be done by the government until another *Herald* article criticizing the annexationists reached Honolulu, after which, he supposed, the hornet's nest would be stirred up again.[46]

Meanwhile, an Officer Klemme of the Honolulu police force approached a fellow officer, Harry Juen, with a proposition. Klemme wanted Juen to "join him in a plot," Juen later recalled in a sworn document, "the object of which should be to blow up with dynamite the residences and persons of the Queen, Colonel Claus Spreckels and Charles Nordhoff." Klemme said "he belonged to a secret organization" dedicated to the purpose and that whoever assisted in carrying it out would be well-rewarded; he also assured Juen that he shouldn't be afraid to

---

45. Blount to Gresham, May 29, 1893, *FRUS, 1894*; "The Farce of Protection," *Hawaiian Star*, May 23, 1893, reprinted in *FRUS, 1894*, 28; "Unhappy Nordhoff: Whipped by the Nemesis of His Own Evil Deeds," *Pacific Commercial Advertiser*, May 23, 1893, 2.

46. Blount to Gresham, May 29, 1893, *FRUS, 1894*.

take part because "they had a big and influential backing." As the bombs were being built, Juen later stated, he "refused to have anything to do with such a cowardly and dastardly affair," and the conspirators instead decided to use the dynamite to make it look as though the royalists, and not the annexationists, were resorting to violence. "On the night of May 31ˢᵗ we were ready to move."[47]

They enacted the charade with great effect. On June 1, the *Advertiser* ran a story under the prominent headline, "Was It A Plot?" which described the policemen's discovery of three bombs, ostensibly planted by "the royalists and their sympathizers." Klemme and Juen had found the dynamite, the report went on, and concluded by narrating that back at the station house, after examining the explosives, Juen lit a cigar. "There was a loud report and his hand was thrown back violently," the newspaper gravely reported, adding that Juen was not seriously hurt. Such were the dangers of law enforcement in Honolulu in 1893.[48]

Meanwhile, news of Nordhoff's run-in with the Provisional Government had reached San Francisco, and many prominent American newspapers made it a front-page story. The pro-Annexation San Francisco *Examiner*—which had been turned over to the young William Randolph Hearst, still a local publisher, only six years before—demonstrated Hearst's fondness for attention-grabbing headlines (reminiscent of the *Herald*'s), titled the report "Don't You Touch Nordhoff!" The correspondent called Nordhoff one of

> the two principal figures in Hawaii at this time—...Nordhoff because Minister Blount and the American navy at this port are ready to pour grape and canister into any one who says 'boo' to the correspondent. ...The truth is that Blount was so worked up over the matter that he was ready for anything. He told [British] Minister Wodehouse that if Mr. Nordhoff were arrested by the Government he would order the troops ashore and effect his release.

John Stevens told the Washington *Evening Star* that Nordhoff had "been making a great deal of trouble.... His letters have been false and misleading."

---

47.   Affidavit of Harry A. Juen, December 12, 1893, Attorney General's file, Document #941, Hawaii State Archives.

48.   "Was It A Plot?" *Pacific Commercial Advertiser,* June 1, 1893, 3. See also "Plotters in Hawaii," *San Francisco Chronicle,* June 9, 1893. Juen's affidavit was submitted during a subsequent inquiry into the "royalist conspiracy," and apparently no official inquiry into his version of events was ever undertaken—leading credence to his charges of a cover-up sanctioned by high authority.

The rabidly pro-annexation New York *Tribune* reported that there was "an ugly feeling" between Blount and the Provisionals, exacerbated by the dispute over Nordhoff, and "trouble may occur at any time." The usually staid *New York Times* reported that Honolulu was "agog with excitement" over recent developments, including the arrest of two native newspaper editors, the attempted arrest of Nordhoff for his "false charge" about the Lottery petitioners, and Blount's appointment as a replacement for Stevens. The pro-annexation papers stressed the imputed falsity of Nordhoff's reports and claimed he had asked for protection; anti-annexation newspapers remarked on the threatened violence against him and the Hawaiian government's repression of the local press. The *New York Times* noted that the efforts of the Provisional Government to crack down on opposition newspapers was "a sure indication that it has little genuine support among the people" while a *Herald* editorial remarked that their attempt to silence Nordhoff was "in keeping with their policy of gagging the local press" and evidence of their unpopularity. "If the 'sorcerous and reactionary' Queen had undertaken to muzzle the press and arrest an American correspondent in the style of this liberty-loving Provisional Government," Godkin's New York *Evening Post* editorialized, "what a loud call there would have been for ships and troops and blowing somebody out of the water."[49]

"We think the [Provisionals] have magnified him beyond his merits," the *Washington Post* insisted, and had "thus given him a pretext for putting on the martyr's crown and ascending into notoriety." Nordhoff had made himself "particularly obnoxious," and "most men of good sense and good feeling will sympathize with his victims," the annexationists who were "engaged in an effort to put down a ridiculous, ignorant, and futile monarchy, and to establish in its stead a government by intelligent and responsible citizens." A few weeks later, the *Post* scoffed at Nordhoff's report of a rumor that he and Blount were "in danger of assassination." He had not named the source of this rumor, it noted, implying that it was simple self-aggrandizement. "Nordhoff," the *Post* concluded, "is a mischief maker."[50]

49. "Don't You Touch Nordhoff!" San Francisco *Examiner*, June 1, 1893, 4; "Late Hawaiian News," Washington *Evening Star*, June 1, 1893, 1; "Trouble Brewing In Hawaii," New York *Tribune*, June 1, 1893, 1; "May Be Trouble in Hawaii," *New York Times*, June 1, 1893; *Boston Evening Transcript*, June 2, 1893, 4; "The Hawaiian Situation," *New York Times*, June 3, 1893; "Futile Attempt to Silence the Herald Correspondent in Honolulu" [editorial], NY *Herald*, June 1, 1893.

50. "Poor Business in Honolulu," Washington *Post*, June 2, 1893; "Another Escape of Wild Animals," Washington *Post*, June 9, 1893. See also "Two Arcadians From Hawaii," Washington *Post*, July 2, 1893.

Nordhoff scarcely ever mentioned himself in his columns; he shied away from all personal publicity. But the events of the second half of May were so extraordinary that he realized he could not avoid personal references: he *was* the story. The day he had been sheltered in the legation, Nordhoff wrote out a lengthy account of it all: the surprise of finding himself under police protection, the two summonses from the Attorney General of the Provisional Government, Blount's actions, and even one of the scurrilous articles about those events from "the formerly respectable" *Pacific Commercial Advertiser.* "While the organs are thus free to vilify," he continued, "there is a disposition to crush out the independence of the anti-annexation press," and he cited recent arrests of two editors for seditious libel. "It appears as though these 'missionary children,' as they call themselves, will make an end of free speech and a free press on the islands ..., and make life burdensome to their opponents or to any one who even ventures to question their acts." As an example, he cited the case of his "Lottery Men" article.

> I remarked that a considerable number of persons now in or employed by the provisional government had signed these petitions; that the passage of the bill was a professed cause for upsetting the government and the Queen. This is true, but I had the ill luck to name, among a number of others, three—Messrs. Hoogs, Lansing, and McChesney—who now say they did not sign the petitions. As to all the rest there is no doubt. These three complained to me and I at once published an apology in the local papers, and I express my regret for having been misled as to them. ...I have since looked over all the lottery petitions which remain—for some have been lost or stolen—and find ... more than twenty names of men now in the employ of the provisional government.[51]

This was so narrow a retraction that it could not have pleased the complainants, particularly with its implication that incriminating evidence had been deliberately removed or destroyed and Nordhoff's refusal to deny his larger point about the complicity of annexationists in the lottery movement. The article was as far from contrite as a retraction could be.[52]

Nonetheless, admitting this error—if error it was and not a case of evidence destroyed and then denied—exposed Nordhoff to heated criticism from the pro-annexation press. The Washington *Post* had already resumed its

---

51. CN, "Tried to Silence the Herald," New York *Herald,* June 1, 1893.
52. Quoted in "Poor Business at Honolulu," Washington *Post,* June 2, 1893.

attacks on him with renewed vigor. On May 25 in a lead editorial, it admitted that "unfortunately, Mr. Nordhoff has been able to do harm entirely out of proportion to his personal importance." His *Herald* articles had received "rapturous quotations and endorsements in the New York *Evening Post*, the St. Louis *Republic*, and the rest of the cranks, nondescripts, and Mugwumps." (The *Herald* proudly noted that portions of Nordhoff's Hawaii letters had also been reprinted in Georgia, Salt Lake City, and Harlem.) He had thereby succeeded in "vicariously producing an amount of misapprehension that a whole regiment of Nordhoffs, proceeding on their intrinsic merits, could not have produced in forty years." It would be "intolerable," the *Post* concluded, to lose Hawaii "through the efforts of such a transparent fakir [*sic*] as Mr. Nordhoff."[53]

Privately as well as publicly, the Provisionals were frustrated with Nordhoff's continued freedom to write for the *Herald*. "Nordhoff is more detested here than any man," wrote W. D. Alexander, a member of the Provisional Government, remarking upon Nordhoff's single retraction. "Nordhoff has associated chiefly with men of no character," Alexander continued, "...enemies of American interests. His letters are ingenious mosaics of lies, half truths and rumors, while he ignores the main cardinal facts, on which everything turned," and he suggested that the *Herald* had been bought by the "sugar trust." The sugar planters were, under the leadership of Claus Spreckels, firm opponents of annexation.[54]

Similarly, Lorrin A. Thurston, one of the Provisionals' delegates to Washington, wrote on June 13 to Sanford Dole that Nordhoff "is made the constant subject of ridicule and criticism by papers all over the country," and he quoted some representative slurs from the *Post*. As long as there was a chance that they might secure annexation, Thurston advised that the Provisionals continue their "lenient" course toward the Queen and the royalists. "If, however, we have got to hoe our own row," he cautioned, it would be "a clear case of self-preservation" to take a hard line against "the attempts to overthrow the Provisional Government, whether such attempts are made by the Queen, [the Queen's attorney Paul] Neumann, ... the native newspapers or Charles Nordhoff." He approved of the idea of deporting Nordhoff, "and if Blount takes the matter up, immediately make formal complaint to the Government here, that an American citizen is actively stirring up revolution against the Government." If necessary, the Provisional Government could even suspend the writ of Habeas Corpus as a war measure (which it subsequently did).

---

53. Subscript to CN, "Chinese Take Root in Hawaii," NY *Herald*, May 6, 1893; "A Fakir in Hawaii," editorial, Washington *Post*, 5/25/93.

54. W. D. Alexander, quoted in Ralph S. Kuykendall, *The Hawaiian Kingdom, 1874-1893* (Honolulu: University of Hawaii Press, 1967), 626.

Thurston recommended that Dole immediately pursue such a course, the only obstacle to it being the "stirring up of hard feelings," which, he judged, was less dangerous than allowing Nordhoff to continue his reporting, which he called "dynamite."[55]

Dole declined to follow Thurston's advice, however; the only official action taken against Nordhoff was a resolution proposed in late June before the Advisory Council that declared that Nordhoff had earned "the *contempt of these Councils.*" Even this purely rhetorical gesture was not adopted (and was reported to have not had even a second), which could have been the result of inertia, or perhaps of honesty. Nordhoff had no doubt earned the enmity, and possibly even the hatred, of the Council members; but his work, and the effect it was having, were less likely to arouse contempt than fear of, or even a grudging respect for, the reticent journalist who had told all of America about matters that they would have preferred remain hidden from view.[56]

By this time, Nordhoff's friends in Honolulu had begun to complain that they were being spied upon when they went to visit him. One businessman, who wished to keep his anti-annexationist views to himself, saw a government detective riding slowly up and down the in front of Nordhoff's cottage and felt compelled to hide until the detective followed some other of Nordhoff's visitors down the street when they left. Another man, whom Nordhoff was visiting, interrupted their conversation twice when he heard a noise. He'd once found a spy hiding in his shrubbery, listening to his conversations, and since then was wary, looking around for spies whenever he heard unexpected sounds. On another occasion, one of the annexation newspapers reported a social call he made with Elsie—something he was convinced they had learned by tapping their phone or other surreptitious means. It's probable that by this time, Nordhoff and his friends were jumpy and ready to see Provisionals lurking in every shadow; but often enough, their suspicions were confirmed so that it can't be written off as paranoia.[57]

About the second week of June, Nordhoff and his daughter accompanied the Blounts to Spreckelsville, the sugar company's town on Maui so that Blount could talk with the public away from Honolulu. An announcement was made

---

[55]   Lorrin A. Thurston to Sanford B. Dole, June 13, 1893, in Lorrin A. Thurston, *Memoirs of the Revolution in Hawaii* (Honolulu: Advertiser Publishing Co., 1936), 296 ff.

[56]   William Adam Russ, Jr., *The Hawaiian Revolution (1893-94)* (Selinsgrove, PA: Susquehanna University Press, 1959), 208; "Nordhoff on Hawaii," *San Francisco Chronicle*, June 29, 1893, 5; "Mr. Nordhoff's Experiences in Honolulu," New York *Herald*, July 9, 1893; untitled editorial, Honolulu *Daily Bulletin*, August 1, 1893, 2.

[57]   CN, "Near the End of the Big Humbug," New York *Herald*, June 27, 1893.

that the commissioner would receive anyone who wanted to see him, and about four hundred people, almost all native Hawaiians, came to the plaza where he awaited them one evening. The natives gathered on a broad lawn, lit by lanterns, and a choir sang some native songs before the addresses began. Men representing various districts, Nordhoff later wrote, stood and "with dignity and directness" asked that the Queen be restored and the islands be allowed to regain their independence. "We ask only justice," several speakers said. Most remarkable, Nordhoff thought, was the lack of bitterness or anger "toward the authors of the trouble, toward either Minister Stevens, the United States or the revolutionists, who, under the shelter of United States bayonets and gatlings, seized the government," and he reiterated his conclusion that the Queen would have to be restored. Blount, as always, made a noncommittal answer to the crowd, but added that he hoped he intended his report to reflect only "truth and justice."[58]

Nordhoff and Elsie booked passage on the steamer *Australia*, departing from Honolulu for San Francisco on June 21. Two days before their departure, they went to see Liliuokalani to make their farewells; and Nordhoff, assuring her that he saw the injustice of the revolution, told her that "he never was in a place where people had no hesitation to tell lies and stick to it," Liliuokalani recalled. In what may have been the understatement of the year, she added that Nordhoff "hadn't had a very pleasant visit here on that account." But he hoped to return one day, under better circumstances, and the Queen thanked him "for the good he had done for my people by writing such favorable articles for our side and stating the whole truth."[59]

That day, Nordhoff wrote an extended denunciation of the Provisional Government, which seemed "incapable of ruling except by the use of the most tyrannical measures" and seemed bent on suppressing all dissent, by fair means or foul. A plot to assassinate Liliuokalani had recently been foiled, he remarked, and although Dole had assured her that the government had had nothing to do with it, Nordhoff scoffed at such window dressing. No one thought Dole or his cohorts would resort to assassination, he stated, but they had "a rough crowd at their backs and they permit things in their subordinates which would be a disgrace to them." And there was talk of doing away with elections. He reported that one provisional had stated in a speech that "the ballot was not useful in a country like this," a statement reminiscent of the New York Citizens'

---

58.   CN, "Near the End of the Big Humbug," New York *Herald*, June 27, 1893; Liliuokalani's diary, entry for June 11, 1893, Hawaii State Archives.

59.   "Wise and Otherwise," *Pacific Commercial Advertiser*, June 19, 1893; [unreadable] entry for June 19, 1893, Hawaii State Archives.

Association's 1867 petitions against the Irish having "the unrestricted use of the ballot-box" – and no less certain to raise Nordhoff's hackles.

Immediately before departing from Honolulu, Nordhoff was sanguine about the likely outcome. The Provisionals had by now passed sedition laws for Annexation, and other repressive measures, but they could not survive an election; their methods had aroused the "contempt and hatred" of "nine-tenths of the voters, native or foreign born." They were on the way out. ...

[A section of the original text located here is missing]

... Adolph Spreckels. Nothing could keep the native people away, if they chose to bid Nordhoff and Spreckels—whom they regarded as their friend—a fond farewell.[60]

The next morning, the *Pacific Commercial Advertiser* noted that Nordhoff was leaving at last. Good riddance, it editorialized: "With the brand upon his brow of this impudent slander of the whole community, we dismiss this unworthy falsifier." But at the wharf where the *Australia* had docked, "a great crowd, native and foreign, assembled," Nordhoff recalled, what one partisan called "the greatest demonstration ever seen in Honolulu," with two thousand people, the Queen, and various native organizations present. The Nordhoffs were "almost smothered with wreaths of flowers," everyone seemed to want to shake their hands, and several speeches were made thanking Nordhoff for his courage and honesty. One speaker, John E. Bush (an old rabble-rouser who, before the revolution, had been working to democratize the Hawaiian government), spoke in the Hawaiian language:

> On this steamer ... there is a prominent journalist connected
> with one of the leading papers in the United States. He has
> been many days among us and has never written a word about
> Hawaiian afairs which was not the whole truth. Because he
> opposed the trickery of the provisional government, he
> brought down the ill will of that body on his head and it has
> lied about him ever since. You know and I know that what Mr.
> Nordhoff has written ... is true.

The Hawaiian Patriotic League, the chief anti-annexationist organization in the islands (with a membership of 7,500 natives out of a total of 13,000) then

---

[60.] CN, "Annexation Unpopular," NY *Herald*, June 22, 1893; "The Other Side of the Story," NY *Herald*. June 29, 1893 (reprinting a June 28 article from the San Francisco *Evening Report*).

presented Nordhoff with a gold-handled cane and an engraved memorial. In Nordhoff's long career, he had always maintained a public facade of reticence and stoicism—but not this day. "The Memorial to Mr. Nordhoff was very prettily worded," the Queen noted, "and tears filled his eyes while he read it." Nothing he had worked for had turned out as he hoped; the politics to which he had devoted his life seemed corrupt and grievously ineffective, if not downright destructive; he was ill, publicly vilified, estranged from his only son, and in fragile condition altogether. He could barely contain his tears. "The expressions of gratitude to the Herald and to your correspondent," wrote Nordhoff simply, "were very touching."[61]

As the *Australia* pulled away from the wharf, with the Nordhoffs and Spreckels on deck, "the great company assembled gave three cheers for the *Herald* and for your correspondent," Nordhoff wrote, and more cheers for Grover Cleveland (who the anti-annexationists believed, correctly, was on their side), for Spreckels, and for the United States. "The cheers went up again and again," Adolph Spreckels later recalled, and two bands—one made up of the royal musicians who had refused to sign an oath of loyalty to the Dole government, and another, pro-annexation group, trying to counter the effect of the first—played alternately, in musical battle, as the ship receded from view.[62]

Many annexationist newspapers in the United States ignored the whole episode, but when Nordhoff's published account of the demonstration reached Honolulu, the *Advertiser* denied any such thing had happened—despite its earlier reports of "a large number of people" on the wharf as the Australia departed, the bands' "hoodlumism" that ensued, and its elliptical mention of "the whole absurd send-off to Mr. Nordhoff." But the *Advertiser*, well aware of how badly such a demonstration would reflect on the annexationist cause, nastily insisted that Nordhoff had made it all up. He was insane, it declared, or old and "feeble-minded."[63]

---

61.   "Charles Nordhoff," *Pacific Commercial Advertiser*, June 21, 1893; CN, "Annexation Unpopular," New York *Herald*, June 29, 1893; "Local and General," *Pacific Commercial Advertiser*, June 22, 1893, 3; "The Other Side of the Story," NY *Herald*, June 29, 1893; "Nordhoff on Hawaii," San Francisco *Chronicle*, June 29, 1893; Liliuokalani's diary entry for June 20, 1893. Hawaii State Archives. (It seems likely that this entry is dated one day early, for evidence of only one such demonstration—on the twenty-first—has been found.) Pratt, op.cit., 135.

62.   CN, "Annexation Unpopular," NY *Herald*, June 29, 1893; untitled editorial, *Pacific Commercial Advertiser*, August 5, 1893, 2; "The Other Side of the Story, NY *Herald*, June 29, 1893 (reprinting a June 28 article from the San Francisco *Evening Report*).

63.   Untitled editorial, *Pacific Commercial Advertiser*, August 5, 1893; "Local and General," *Pacific Commercial Advertiser*, June 22, 1893; "Under Consideration,"

He and his daughter, Elsie, arrived back home in Coronado on July 3, to find a "mass" of newspaper articles and editorials that his friends had clipped for him about his Hawaii reports. "I had no idea," he wrote, "how much or how bitterly my letters have been discussed" by annexationists in the United States. His departure from Hawaii did not halt the editorial attacks against him, and his declaration that Liliuokalani should be restored to her throne was met with cries of outrage.

The New York *Sun*, avidly annexationist, ran a brief item on its editorial page that began with the words "Mr. CHARLES NORDHOFF, recently in Hawaii ... appears to be crazy." This could be the only explanation for his "behavior and utterances" in advocating the restoration of the Hawaiian monarchy. Nordhoff quickly responded with a column in the *Herald* with a headline that accurately summarized its contents:

> Why We Should Restore the Queen. Mr. Nordhoff Explains the Nation's Responsibility for Affairs in Hawaii. Not the "Counsel of Madness." He Simply Declares that We Should Disavow the Illegal Acts of Our Minister. Against the People's Will. The Revolutionaries Hold Office in Defiance of the Citizens of the Islands.

"I should call it rather the counsel of honor and safety," Nordhoff retorted, suggesting that there was danger of a popular uprising that would be "signalled by the burning of cane fields and sugar mills." Bennett had already placed the editorial policy of the *Herald* firmly behind Nordhoff. The *Washington Post* heartily scoffed at this and seconded the *Sun*'s original idea. "This suggestion [of Nordhoff's insanity] seemed so appropriate," it editorialized, "...that it was accepted with spontaneous enthusiasm from one end of the country to the other." That Nordhoff responded with "bitter resentment" in the *Herald* the *Post* mockingly regarded as simple confirmation of the *Sun*'s hypothesis.[64]

A few days later, the *Herald*'s Washington correspondent claimed that "[t] he President and Secretary Gresham appreciate the fact that the Herald has very clearly outlined the policy of the administration regarding the proposed annexation of Hawaii," and unnamed authorities praised Nordhoff. The

---

Pacific Commercial Advertiser, June 23, 1893, 3; untitled editorial, *Pacific Commercial Advertiser,* June 23, 1893.

64. "A Talk With Nordhoff," San Diego *Union,* July 4, 1893; "Mr. Nordhoff's Experiences in Honolulu," New York *Herald,* July 9, 1893; "The Council of Madness," New York *Sun,* July 3, 1893; CN, "Why We Should Restore the Queen," New York *Herald,* July 5, 1893, 6; "Giving Himself Away," *Washington Post,* July 6, 1893.

writer questioned Gresham about rumors that he had reprimanded Blount for protecting Nordhoff, to which Gresham reportedly denied that he had ever reprimanded Blount for anything whatsoever. "I am sure he has acted with good judgment and restriction," the reporter quotes Gresham as saying. The *Pacific Commercial Advertiser* and the *Hawaiian Star*, still fulminating against Nordhoff six weeks after his departure, indignantly stated that the *Herald* was, no doubt, making inaccurate and unauthorized statements, wholly without truth while the *Washington Post* huffed furiously for some weeks on the presumption and injustice of it all. But no Washington correspondent, however willing to exaggerate, would be likely to misquote an important official like Gresham or impute to him contrary opinions than those he actually held because maintaining sufficient good faith that Gresham (and others) would willingly submit to future interviews would have been crucial to the performance of his job. As it turned out, the *Herald* reporter was right, whether Gresham had told him so or not.[65]

ŏ ŏ ŏ

"Do you know that I sometimes think if I had my life to live over," Nordhoff wrote to his old friend, Edward Atkinson, soon after the appearance of the *Sun*'s attack, "I would eschew trying to keep things right—what idiots people are." He continued to argue against annexation in the pages of the *Herald*, however. Atkinson reassured him that he had done "a big job" and would certainly go on to do more of the same. "Why should you get discouraged and think you won't do any more of the same kind? I differ with you wholly," Atkinson went on and hinted at the work Nordhoff used to do in Washington, adding, "Had you been in Washington since the first of April, about one-half the distrust and disturbance would have been prevented. You would have got at the facts." He blamed the "panic" that had precipitated the nation's disastrous slide into economic depression on "the totally erroneous reports circulated by the various newspaper men, taken up by Bank men who sat at home and took no pains to inform themselves, making their stupid comments on false reports." Nordhoff, he believed, could have prevented it all.[66]

65.   "Trying Hard To Save Themselves," New York *Herald*, July 7, 1893; untitled editorial, *Pacific Commercial Advertiser*, July 31, 1893, 2; untitled editorial, *Hawaiian Star*, August 1, 1893, 2; "Have We Wronged Hawaii?" Washington *Post*, July 9, 1893, and "The *Herald*'s Great Responsibility," Washington *Post*, July 31, 1893.

66.   CN to Edward Atkinson, July 6 & 29, 1893; CN, "Annexationists Attack Mr. Cooley," NY *Herald*, July 22, 1893; Edward Atkinson to CN, July 13, 1893, Atkinson Papers, Letterbook 49: 201.

Nordhoff thanked him. "But think what abuse in the U.S. papers I have got for telling the truth out there! It is ridiculous, & makes *character* almost worthless." But journalism was changing, and Nordhoff's opponents had developed a new club to beat him with. For more than thirty years, he had been accustomed to being criticized for his political opinions, frankly expressed as they were in his columns, and he relished the newspaper debates about the meaning and implications of events and public policy. But now, he was criticized not only for his opinions, but also for the very fact that he *had* opinions. He was not an objective observer, his critics charged, and of course, they were right. Their error lay in claiming that other accounts of the situation in Hawaii—even more colored by politics, more distorted by annexationist fever and racism— *were* objective.

By October, after the worst of the attacks on Nordhoff seemed to be over, he partially recovered his equanimity and told fellow anti-imperialist Carl Schurz that "I am very happy at having gone over to the Islands, for I believe I did a public service there." But this period of calm satisfaction soon came to an end.[67]

"A diplomatic bombshell will burst within the next few days…," began a report from Washington in the November eighth New York *Herald*. What was the nature of this bombshell?

> Briefly stated, the present administration will do all in its power to restore the condition of affairs which existed in Hawaii at the time Minister Stevens …ordered the marines ashore from the *Boston* and brought about the overthrow of Queen Liliuokalani. This is another great HERALD victory.

The article went on to state that a "prominent" Cabinet member had credited Nordhoff for his "very accurate and detailed evidence," without which "not half the situation would ever have been known." Although no official pronouncement had yet been made from the Cleveland administration, the *Herald*'s correspondent proved to be accurate: four days later, an official announcement was made confirming the report.[68]

A final torrent of invective against Blount and Nordhoff erupted. While the *Sun* and the *Cincinnati Commercial Advertiser* led the protests of the annexationist press in the United States, the New York *Herald* reacted with praise, and more

---

67.　CN to Carl Schurz, October 10, 1893. Schurz Papers, LC.

68.　"Will Restore Hawaii's Queen," New York *Herald*, November 8, 1893, 10. The date of the release of Gresham's recommendations is in Osborne, *Empire Can Wait*, 57.

Nordhoff articles appeared. He noted the annexationist outrage that "the United States, a republic, would favor a monarchy" and replied to it:

> Well, the United States, "being a republic," whose principle
> is to let people govern themselves, cannot surely be so idiotic
> as to cram a republic down the throats of people who don't
> want it.

Covering all the "jingo" arguments, Nordhoff went on to insist, "American property interests do not justify the theft of a country." One of the Provisional Government's delegates, W. D. Alexander, wrote to President Dole that the *Herald* was their "greatest enemy." When James Blount's report to Gresham on the Hawaiian situation was released a week later, a striking similarity between his observations and those of Nordhoff's *Herald* dispatches was remarked upon—both by the *Herald* with pride and by annexationists with suspicion and outrage. Alexander wrote a furious article, which he forwarded to Dole, "which exposes Nordhoff's lying and his collusion with Blount." In Congress, Blount was attacked by prominent Republicans, who brought up his past as a Confederate officer and likened his report to the treason that brought on the Civil War.[69]

On December 5, the New York *Sun* attacked Nordhoff and Blount for collusion that verged on the illegal: Nordhoff's articles for the *Herald*, published before the Blount report had been released, included information on testimony that the State Department was supposedly keeping secret—from Congress and the public at large. So what was Nordhoff doing with it? It called for a Congressional inquiry, maintaining that hearings would shed light on the "inwardness of the conspiracy to destroy the Hawaiian Government and to restore Liliuokalani."[70]

Nordhoff wrote to Gresham reassuring him that all of Blount's points were "established on Provisional Government people's testimony"; he had obtained the material that the *Sun* had accused Blount of leaking to him from the witnesses themselves. "In their fury," the annexationists "are making this

69.   William DeWitt Alexander to Sanford B. Dole, November 19, 1893, quoted in Osborne, *Empire Can Wait*, 141, n. 20. CN, "Do Not Want A Republic," New York *Herald*, November 22, 1893, 6; CN, "Examples Stevens Failed to Follow," New York *Herald*, November 30, 1893, p. I-10; CN, "His Own Evidence Convicts Stevens," New York *Herald*. December 8, 1893; William DeWitt Alexander to Sanford B. Dole, December 8, 1893, in Thurston, *Memoirs*, 408. For Congressional abuse of Blount, see McWilliams, 41–42.
70.   "Getting at Spreckels Through Nordhoff," New York *Sun*, December 5, 1893, 6.

mistake of howling abt. the discovery of facts, instead of looking at the bearing of the facts," he added. "That folly I have seen before." Enough credence was given to the rumors, however, that Blount had to answer several questions from a Senate committee on the matter. At least one other witness referred to "Messrs. Blount and Nordhoff" as a unit while one anti-annexationist Congressman, calling Nordhoff an able journalist "whose ability and integrity none will question," used his *Herald* correspondence to verify the accuracy of Blount's report—rather than vice versa.[71]

The Cleveland administration tried to restore Liliuokalani to her throne through diplomacy. But before trying to restore her, the new American minister to Hawaii, Albert Willis, was instructed to obtain her acquiescence in several conditions, one of which was that she would grant a general amnesty to the revolutionaries once she was restored to the throne. No, she replied; the revolutionaries would have to be beheaded, in accordance with Hawaiian law. Flummoxed, Willis could do nothing but continue his insistence while the Provisionals grew more assured that they were safe from the interference of the United States and adamantly refused to step aside. Nordhoff, disturbed by the vengefulness of Liliuokalani and maintaining that the United States could not cause to be executed the very people that Stevens had encouraged to revolution, wrote a weary column that the *Herald* headlined "The Queen's Refusal of Cleveland's Proposal Leaves Us Nothing More to Do." Liliuokalani eventually agreed to the conditions, but by then it was too late; the Provisionals had dug in. The use of force requiring the approval of Congress, Cleveland simply turned the matter over to the legislature.[72]

Congress responded by holding hearings, the intent of which seems to have been to undermine the authority of Blount's report. Representatives of the Provisional Government were given full and sympathetic receptions while Blount was grilled by hostile Congressmen about his methodology—and

---

[71]   CN to Walter Q. Gresham, December 9, 1893. Gresham Papers, LC. U.S. Senate, Committee on Foreign Relations, *Hawaiian Islands. ... Jan. 1, 1893 to March 10, 1894* (Washington: GPO, 1894), 414, 416, 516; James B. McCready, February 2, 1894, speech recorded in *The Congressional Record*, 53rd Congress, 2nd Session, volume 26, part 2, 1821.

[72]   Charles W. Calhoun, "Morality and Spite: Walter Q. Gresham and U.S. Relations with Hawaii," *Pacific Historical Review* 52 (1983): 292–311; Tennant S. McWilliams, "James H. Blount and Hawaiian Annexation," *Pacific Historical Review* 57 (1988): 25–46; Sanford B. Dole, *Memoirs of the Hawaiian Revolution* (Honolulu: Advertiser Publishing Co., 10936), 104–137; W. D. Alexander, *History of Later Years of the Hawaiian Monarchy and the Revolution of 1893* (Honolulu: Hawaiian Gazette Co., 1896), 91 ff; Osborne, *Empire Can Wait*, 53–67.

about his relationship with Nordhoff, for Blount's report had been remarkably close to Nordhoff's articles in its facts, interpretations, and conclusions. "Mr. Nordhoff ... would talk," Blount insisted, "but I did not confide in Mr. Nordhoff." "You listened to what he had to say?" demanded one suspicious senator, to which Blount could only reply, "I let him talk."[73]

In May 1894, Congress voted to take no action: they would not restore the queen, nor would they annex. Blount went home to Macon, Georgia, his hopes for an enlarged career in politics at an end; isolated, he stayed out of the public eye for the rest of his life and died in 1903.[74]

Dole and his compatriots were content to bide their time, putting down Royalist uprisings and waiting for a more auspicious political climate to raise the possibility of annexation once more. Although expansionist newspapers such as the New York *Tribune* continued to fulminate against Cleveland's "conspiracy against civilization and progress," the Islands were to remain at least nominally independent of the United States until 1898. Nordhoff's role in the debate rankled the imperialists for some time. John Hay wrote to Henry Adams from Paris that March; his wife subscribed to the Paris edition of the New York *Herald*, he remarked, which included "occasional references to the deputy omniscience of one C. Nordhoff," which was "almost more than I can stand."[75]

Hay would go on to preside, as Secretary of State in 1898, over the Spanish-American war, the Filipino-American war, and the annexation of Hawaii, Puerto Rico, and the Philippines in the name of uplifting the benighted natives. But in 1893, with Hawaiian annexation seemingly defeated, Nordhoff was hopeful that the principle of self-government expressed in the Declaration of Independence and the United States' long-held policy of isolationism would continue to win out over "general jingoism." There were dangers afoot, he admitted. "Still," he ventured, "I don't believe we have yet been bitten by the spirit of 'National Glory.'" Within five years he would learn, to his despair, just how wrong he had been.

One hundred years later, in November of 1993, Public Law 103-150 was signed by President Clinton. The resolution detailed how Minister Stevens had "conspired with a small group of non-Hawaiian residents of the Kingdom of

---

73. *Testimony Before the Senate Committee on Foreign Relations*, Senate Report 227, 53rd Congress, 2nd Session, 417.

74. Tennant S. McWilliams, "James H. Blount and Hawaiian Annexation," *Pacific Historical Review* 57 (1988): 25–46.

75. *Tribune* quoted in Sylvester K. Stevens, *American Expansion in Hawaii, 1842-1898* (Harrisburg: 1945), 280; *Life and Letters of John Hay* (NY: Houghton-Mifflin, 1929), vol. 2, 109–110.

Hawaii" to overthrow the kingdom and institute a government "without the consent of the Native Hawaiian people …and in violation of treaties between the two nations and of international law." It stated that without the support of the United States, the revolution would have failed "for lack of popular support and insufficient arms" and noted that the Blount report had stated these facts "clearly and accurately." Despite Blount's and Cleveland's efforts, *PL 103-150* continues, Congress ignored them and went on to conduct hearings at which the Provisionals "justified and condoned" Stevens's actions, paving the way for the annexation of Hawaii four years later.

"The Congress," the conclusion states,

> …apologizes to Native Hawaiians on behalf of the people of the United States for the overthrow of the Kingdom of Hawaii … with the participation of agents and citizens of the United States, and the deprivation of the rights of Native Hawaiians to self-determination.

Although Congress has been (and will ever be) capable of enacting less-justified measures, this particular resolution of apology was accurate, just (as far as it went), and long overdue. But Charles Nordhoff, were he alive today, would not have to be included in the apology. Vindication is seldom so clearly awarded as this.

CHAPTER 12

He Did His Damnedest

Nordhoff maintained an ongoing discussion of public affairs with Edward Atkinson, who tried to convince him to return to the East. On one occasion, Atkinson disparaged the ability of the journalistic profession in general. But Nordhoff, who similarly saw a decline in the quality of reporting, saw it as a problem much larger than simply the incapacity of current journalists. Government officials had "more & more severed themselves from the Press," which Nordhoff considered "an unmitigated evil for the country." He recalled the 1879 change in Congressional rules that excluded reporters from the House and Senate floors. With his connections, the change in rules hadn't mattered much to Nordhoff, but he thought it had done "great harm, by preventing even men from talking over matters with Senators & Representatives in the *only place where they are to be found, together*." Democrats, Republicans, Independents—all might be made part of a discussion, interrupting and correcting each other, clarifying the issues, reaching compromises satisfactory to all. Congress's "ability or effectiveness" had deteriorated as a result of this exclusion of newspapermen from the floor.

Nordhoff doubted that the old rules could ever be reinstated. "You could rightly say that it makes necessary bigger men in the Press," he added, "but I don't know how you are going to get them." A new breed of journalists was emerging, looking for dramatic stories rather than serious issues requiring the public's sustained attention. More thoughtful writers, Nordhoff maintained, had no desire to practice this new kind of journalism. "It is all a leveling downwards," he complained, "— & an ignorant reporter, if he is an active & brassy fellow, does better (I mean *worse* of course) than the wisest man of affairs who will not, because he cannot, run after men." "There has not yet been one to take your place," Atkinson replied.[1] As to the *Herald*, which Atkinson probably

---

1. Edward Atkinson to CN, 8/2/95, letterbook 55: 847. Atkinson Papers, MHS.

tolerated only so long as his friend's articles might be found within its pages, Nordhoff's loyalty was absolute.[2]

As the Hawaii brouhaha subsided, Nordhoff settled back into seclusion with relief. Politics, "barren & very foolish" as it seemed, elicited indignant letters from him, but little else. Unwilling to again involve himself in a public controversy, cautioning his friends not to use his name if they repeated his views, he remarked sourly upon the early beginnings of the welfare state, or what he called "premeditated socialism," in England. He feared that "ignorance" would lead the United States down the same primrose path to government control of all facets of life, and that reason would be of no avail. He regarded the Populists, with their demands for free coinage of silver and an inflationary fiscal policy, a progressive income tax, and nationalization of the railroads and communications systems (the last, having once seemed reasonable to him, marking his growing conservatism) with alarm. They seemed to "have in view a new purpose in government...; & ... discussion, information, facts, experiences, are thrown away upon them, because," he observed quite accurately, "they don't mean what we mean." The Populists had discarded the old verities of laissez-faire government and, had they been able to prevent their program from being coopted by the Silverites, might have heralded a shift away from the developing corporate order. In Nordhoff's eyes, all their proposals were "the work of men to whom the old landmarks are hateful; ... & who consciously mean state socialism, imperialism, the precise reverse of what we have for a century gone on."[3]

Nordhoff's old uneasiness with labor unions had hardened into outright distrust by the time of the Pullman strike of 1894. By then, America was once more in a deep depression, and wage cuts had prompted Pullman employees to launch a boycott of Pullman railroad cars, whereupon Grover Cleveland had sent in federal troops. The result was a violent confrontation in which several were killed, and the workers were ultimately forced to return to work without any concessions from the corporation. Nordhoff thought the strikers were mistaken in following Eugene Debs, the charismatic leader of the American Railway Union. With their potential power, labor might achieve great things, he lamented, "if they had sense enough to act under the leadership of trained

2.   CN to Edward Atkinson, July 29, [1893]. Atkinson Papers, MHS. Nordhoff later praised Bennett and the *Herald* for their anti-silver stance during the election of 1896 and their opposition to imperialism throughout the '90s. CN to Edward Atkinson, 11/30/97 and 4/2/98, and to Charles Eliot Norton, 5/20/98, Norton Papers, Houghton Library, Harvard.

3.   CN to Carl Schurz, 10/10/93 and 10/27/93; Schurz Papers, LC. CN to Edward Atkinson, 3/9/94.

economists!" But unscrupulous demagogues like Debs were leading them astray.

If his belief in the harmony of interest between labor and capital had been shaken during the '80s, it reasserted itself during Nordhoff's years of isolation in his retirement from urban America. In pitting workers against managers and capitalists, he thought, the unions were "bound ... to do harm & no good to Christian Civilization—to work towards strife for mean ends & not toward peace for higher ends." Nordhoff simply could not see any sense in the unions' actions. "On the whole," he wrote, "I am glad that I am not 30, with all the fight before me." Liberty, the "main & only thing," was being attacked on all sides, he believed—by the "plutocrats, by the socialists & anarchists, by the ignorant & presumptuous, by the stupid labor & Unionist people ... & often in the very name of liberty." Liberty was a negative: these positive attempts to interject the government, to favor one side over another, or to unnaturally alter the economy were "a queer reaction." The march of "Coxey's army"—hundreds of unemployed men demonstrating in Washington for a public works bill—made him "blush for my country."[4]

He roused himself to write a series of "letters to wage workers" for the New York *Herald* in July of 1895, trying to mitigate the "stupidity" of organized labor. In them, he sounded many familiar themes: that bad times were caused by the tariff, unsound currency, monopolistic practices, and boss politics, as well as a depressed European economy that deprived the United States of healthy markets—none of which might be helped by strikes. And what was the cause of Europe's economic ills? Militarism. War was always a waste. Even a just war, like the Civil War, was a waste, brought about by "aristocratic" Southern planters at the cost of the common man. The money spent on the Civil War, Nordhoff calculated, "would have paid for every slave the highest market price, and saved the lives of nearly half a million of men." He could not concede that the issue then at stake—or any issue—would not yield to sweet reason.

Again and again, Nordhoff returned to the problem of militarism, imperialism, and its consequences. He had long considered Arthur Thayer Mahan, the advocate of a strong navy and a network of colonial outposts, "a jingo of the worst kind," despite, or perhaps because of, his "clever books" on sea power. In his *Herald* letters of 1895, he tried to convince his audience that Mahan and his imperialist ideas had to be stopped. "A peacably disposed man," he pointed out, "is better off with a good strong lock on his front door than keeping a couple of dozen irritable bulldogs barking around the yard all night and attacking quiet people passing along the road." Treaties and other attempts to involve the country abroad while staying out of wars were fruitless. "Sherman

---

4.   CN to Edward Atkinson, 6/28/94 and 6/17/94, Atkinson Papers, MHS.

rightly told the mayor of Atlanta that war is war," Nordhoff reminded Atkinson, "& you can't carry it on without loss. So as to Hawaii, Samoa, & interoceanic canals; you may make all the agreements you like, but when there is war every fellow will help himself.[5]

Predictably, the election of 1896 appalled him. William Jennings Bryan's presidential candidacy portended no good. The Democratic convention, at which Bryan was nominated, "staggered" him, with its platform demanding the free coinage of silver and Bryan declaiming against the "cross of gold" upon which the People were being crucified by the Eastern Money Power. To many people, Bryan and the Populists were "anarchists," "Jacobins," and worse; and Nordhoff substantially agreed. The nearly religious belief that only "sound money"—gold—was a suitable standard for the nation's currency had Nordhoff still in its grip. The only solution was for "friends of sound money" to unite. Nordhoff wrote that Bryan, both a "silver man" and a *"populist,"* was the worst possible choice of the Democrats. "If he & his tribe get in," Nordhoff predicted, "we shall have great wildness in many directions," and he found it "disgusting that, to save ourselves we must have such a poor creature as McKinley." When McKinley defeated Bryan, Nordhoff was only slightly relieved. "But can you reasonably hope or expect *any* real reform, of currency or anything else, from the Republicans?" he asked Atkinson. He feared that McKinley and his party would "go jingo strongly," and it was likely they'd get the United States into a war.[6]

His worst fears were soon confirmed. Cuban revolutionaries, attempting to overthrow Spanish colonial government, were subjected to repressive measures by Spain which elicited the popular sympathy of Americans for the rebels. War between Spain and the United States officially began in April of 1898, and talk of expansionism rose to a fever pitch. It had already became clear, by November of 1897, that the United States would annex Hawaii, and Nordhoff predicted with gloom and anger that "that great & infamous act of unrighteousness we shall have to answer for as [a] nation someday."[7] It was establishing a dangerous precedent. "If we eat that small bit of forbidden fruit, Hawaii," he asked Atkinson, "do you suppose the taste is not going to lead us to further

---

5. CN to Schurz, 10/27/93, Schurz Papers, LC; CN, "Letters To Wage Workers," NY *Herald*, 7/14/95; "Letters to a Wage Earner," NY *Herald*, July 21, 1895; "Wage Earners and the Navy," NY *Herald*, 7/28/95, and "To the American Wage Earner," NY *Herald*, 8/4/95. CN to Edward Atkinson, 1/26/96, Atkinson Papers, MHS.
6. CN to Edward Atkinson, July 14, 1896 and 11/12/96, Atkinson Papers, MHS.
7. That day was to arrive in 1993, when the U.S. government officially apologized to the Native Hawaiian people for assisting in the 1893 overthrow of Liliuokalani.

eating?" Americans—"a wholesale & not a retail people"—would not stop at Hawaii.

Yet the anti-imperialists—men as diverse as Charles Eliot Norton, Carl Schurz, William James, and Andrew Carnegie—did not launch their protests until the spring of 1898, well after the annexation of Hawaii was a foregone conclusion. (A joint resolution of Congress annexed the islands that August, but an annexation treaty had already been signed in July of 1897, although it failed of ratification.) Nordhoff warned Atkinson, editor of *The Anti-Imperialist*, to not mention his views in his own anti-imperialist diatribes. The events of 1893 left him unwilling to become the object of public abuse in the same cause. And he soon grew disgusted with these latecomers, who had done so little to stave off the events of 1898. As E. L. Godkin had written in the New York *Evening Post* following the passage of the annexation resolution, "All that can be said against the policy of annexation has been said, and it would be useless now to repeat it."[8]

"I suppose we are going to have war—& a capitalists' war at that," he wrote to Charles Francis Adams shortly before the declaration of war with Spain. When war finally came—"an unjust & needless war"—he was almost resigned to it. Many of Nordhoff's aging acquaintances and allies took strong public stands against the war, and at first Nordhoff applauded from the sidelines. In an appreciative letter to Charles Eliot Norton, the Harvard professor of Fine Arts at whose elitist political views he had once scoffed, Nordhoff wrote of being "rejoiced" at Norton's "plain talk," telling his Harvard students that the war was a crime and exhorting them to refuse to serve.[9]

As Nordhoff saw it, "we have been carried into a war wh. nobody, barring Jingoes & adventurers—wanted" and the nation was to be "wrenched from an old & natural & safe career as a nation into a new career of conquest & colonies without being consulted as a nation." Jingoism "will make me feel a loss of interest in my country," he added sadly, "-- & that is hard."[10]

In all these discussions, Nordhoff held himself aloof from Atkinson's circle, which seemed to have become aroused only after the Americans attempted to suppress the Filipino drive for independence. "As to myself," he explained

---

8. CN to Edward Atkinson, 11/14/97 and 11/30/97; Godkin quoted in Sylvester K. Stevens, *American Expansion in Hawaii, 1842-1898* (Harrisburg, PA: 1945), 295.

9. CN to Charles Eliot Norton, May 20, 1898. C.E. Norton Papers, Houghton Library, Harvard University. CN to Charles Francis Adams, 4/3/98. Adams Papers, MHS. Box 5, folder 6 (reel 20). CN to EA, 4/22/98. See Robert L. Beisner, *Twelve Against Empire: The Anti-Imperialists, 1898-1900* (NY: McGraw-Hill, 1968), 80.

10. CN to Edward Atkinson, 6/20/98 and 9/14/98. Atkinson Papers, Massachusetts Historical Society.

รร

caustically, he had no sympathy with the "so-called 'Anti-Imperialists.'" He reminded Atkinson:

> You accepted the Hawaiian annexation, & that of Porto Rico, & the Cuban occupation, & have nothing to say agst. these things; but you make a great fuss only abt. the Phillipine business.

He didn't wish Atkinson to mistake him for an imperialist, of course. He found "the whole colonial enterprise unwise & hazardous," but he found the protests against absorbing the Phillipines "unprincipled, not based on principle in any way." Nordhoff believed that his own persistent exhortations had defeated Hawaiian annexation in 1893. Why had nobody taken the same role, early, in 1897 or '98? Was there not something disingenuous about the whole anti-imperialist enterprise, with its tardy entry and half-hearted early efforts?

When Atkinson was quoted as saying, in one of his vigorous anti-imperialistic speeches, that the annexation of Hawaii was relatively unimportant, Nordhoff exploded. He sat down to write his friend a blistering letter about Atkinson's call to "'lock the stable door' *after* the horses have been stolen." Far from being unimportant, the annexation of Hawaii was "a monstrous act of injustice—the most shameful act in our history. It had *no* excuse." If only "this monstrous act & fallacy & injustice," had been opposed, Nordhoff believed that it would have been beaten, and the subsequent follies in Cuba and the Philippines averted. Instead, public opinion was quiescent—Nordhoff doesn't seem to have considered the possibility that the public actually favored expansionism and that publicity wouldn't have altered the feeling—and McKinley was allowed to take "the part of Dictator," dragging America "into a new & very mischievous career." "*Now,*" he added, "-- when it is too late—far too late—you good people begin to protest. The time to protest, & that very loudly, was when McKinley first brought up Hawaiian annexation; but there was an almost universal silence." The only way to salvage the situation was to "keep all these countries *outside* of the union of states" by instituting a system of colonial government akin to that of England. He could not and would not accept the idea of the Hawaiians voting in federal elections. What was done was done, and America was left to stand, Nordhoff thought, as "a pack of heedless idiots."[11]

Atkinson hastened to assure Nordhoff that he thought the annexation of Hawaii only a calamity of lesser magnitude than that of the other new American

---

11. CN to Edward Atkinson, October 27, 1898. Atkinson Papers, Massachusetts Historical Society.

possessions, an iniquity as well as a mistake.[12] Nordhoff, in turn, noted that the idea of the "Baltimore Anti-Jingoes" that the United States had to begin by "restoring Hawaii to its people" was the "only logical & effective ground." His certitude in the American people's opposition to imperialism had flagged, however, for he then noted curtly that such a move "would not be popular."[13]

Anticipating the coming presidential election, Nordhoff considered the likely alternatives of Republican William McKinley (whom Charles Francis Adams called "a political invertebrate") and Democrat/Populist William Jennings Bryan. "With two parties, both wrong, what becomes of us?" he asked Atkinson. The only chance the anti-imperialists had to gain a reasonable outcome was to somehow rouse the country to nominate a more acceptable candidate, and this was to be done only through an appeal to morality and justice. "May I say to you again without offense," Nordhoff put it,

> that unless & until you *begin* by demanding the restoration
> of the Hawaiian flag and nationality, you will not succeed,
> &—I judging—will not deserve to? All your arguments are
> as to expediency; & on that you can't convert the public...[14]

They might be faced with an unwelcome choice come the following year's election. The idea had a perverse fascination for Nordhoff and reignited his old impatience with the political ineptitude of reformers. Given a choice between the imperialistic McKinley and the dreaded Bryan, he asked, would "the 'anti-imperialists' have the courage of their convictions & vote for Bryan & his platform?" The question was which would take precedence: fiscal orthodoxy or anti-imperialism. There was only one true path to take, though Nordhoff doubted they would take it. They would have to favor Bryan despite his hated opposition to the gold standard. "If they flinch they will of course be contemptible to God, & men. There can't, *honorably for them*, be any 'Third party' humbug."[15] Bryan was electable, even if his anti-imperialist credentials had been marred by his support of the Treaty of Paris.

But Nordhoff had seen the "Independents" and mugwumps choose the "third party humbug" too often to be anything but pessimistic. But Nordhoff had given up trying to talk sense to inept and impolitic reformers. "I don't suppose your people will do anything except vote for McKinley," he wrote

---

12. Edward Atkinson to CN, December 15, 1898. Atkinson Papers, MHS.

13. CN to Edward Atkinson, December 21, 1898. Atkinson Papers, MHS.

14. Charles Francis Adams is quoted in Beisner, 123; CN to Edward Atkinson, January 30, 1899.

15. CN to Edward Atkinson, September 7, 1899.

sardonically. For himself, the imperialists' betrayal of America's honor and democratic principles ultimately transcended all other considerations—even the long-cherished "sound currency." "Gold Democrats hereabouts … will generally vote for Bryan," he informed Atkinson. "I think they are right."[16]

In February of 1894, Charles Nordhoff wrote his friend Edward Atkinson a long letter. "You ask me 'How do you regard your own past?' & your question has made me stop a moment to consider," he began. The furor over his Hawaiian letters having just died down, he was thoughtful and measured in his answer. "Well—I am very thankful that I have been able to somewhat (not much) influence men & events—it seems to me an excuse to myself for having lived," he admitted. But the frustrations of that life had been freshly brought home to him during the previous year, and if he had found meaning in the attempt, "yet I have found it a most tedious & ungrateful thing to attempt to inform or lead men," and he reminded Atkinson of their twenty-five years of earnest labor ending with, it seemed, little effect. "Eternal vigilance is the price of liberty—but constant outpost duty becomes tedious—to me," he acknowledged. But he tried to be philosophical. "What, as you know has happened to me in my old age"—the public vilification he experienced in 1893, his broken health, the quarrel with his son—had "darkened" his life, he admitted,

> but it has not changed my beliefs. It brought home to me what I wrote in … my "God & the Future Life:" "Plan yr life as carefully, as prudently as you may, bend all yr. energies to the achievement of yr. purposes, and yet you may discover in the end that your plans were blunders, & that your labors have led only to the disappointment of your hopes."

"And yet," he added, "I would not change the general course of my life if I had it to live over."[17] In fact, he didn't really believe that his life had been pointless, for he insisted that he could not measure success by external factors, such as the number of Congressional votes he had influenced. "I am devoutly thankful that I was so led as to despise wealth & not give myself to moneymaking, & that I have been able to serve my day & generation," he added. "I believe that God is so great that he is able to guide & overrule us for our own eventual good; & I have great expectations of the Future Life, so great that I am sometimes impatient to begin it—with, as I hope—its boundless & easier access to greater knowledge of God's works & will."

---

16. CN to Edward Atkinson, 7/13/1900 and 8/1/1900. Atkinson Papers, MHS.
17. CN to Edward Atkinson, February 3, 1894. Atkinson Letters, MHS.

If the new age was disappointing and baffling, if technological advances did not seem to reduce the burdens of life, if "the great consolidation of little states into …vast wholes was a mistake for the human race," nevertheless he took comfort in his faith, and he settled back to live out his days by the Pacific shore. Although he would not regret death, "meantime," he wrote, "the ability to live near sea & mountains in the open air, in a mild & sunny climate, to be relieved from the turmoil of Washington politics, & yet to have the chance to do a public service when occasion offers, … seems an inestimable blessing for my old age."[18]

The final years of Nordhoff's life brought their share of sorrows, as old friends died and his own health deteriorated.[19] Though estranged from his son, Nordhoff remained close to his daughters. They often lived with him and their mother at Coronado, horseback riding and running greyhounds for the hotel keeper, reading to him as cataracts dimmed his eyesight. His attempts to raise active, independent women had succeeded, perhaps in ways he had not anticipated. He followed with pride Evelyn's career as an arts-and-crafts bookbinder, investigating other possibilities for Amy and Elsie. "Understand that in my mind girls can do nothing so well as to marry," he explained to his friend, "—but my girls … despise marriage. Therefore I am willing they shd. try something else while I am alive & able to support their efforts."[20] It came as a shock when, in late 1898, Evelyn died suddenly of peritonitis at the age of thirty-three—and back east, too, so that he was not at her side at the end. The only consolation, Nordhoff sadly wrote to Atkinson, was that she was free of "all worries troubles, illness loneliness, disappointments, incident to later life."[21]

For one who lived most of his life free from illness, Nordhoff's health deteriorated with surprising rapidity after he retired, so much so that Atkinson suspected it was more a result of boredom and isolation than any physical cause. "I am not strong—& mainly sit in my verandah & read," Nordhoff admitted to Atkinson. He doubted his ability to do any good work. He had managed to write some articles for the *Herald*, he added. "But I broke down once or twice over them—& they may be trash."[22] After a series of such complaints, Atkinson wrote him back rather sharply. "What is the matter?" he asked. "Do you not need the stimulus of our eastern climate once more? You are not as old as I am

---

18. CN to EA, 2/3/1894.

19. Nordhoff's letters are filled with sad comments on the illnesses and passing of friends: CN to EA, 6/17/94, 11/30/97, 9/14/98, and Lida Nordhoff to Phoebe Hearst, 12/15/1900, for example.

20. CN to Edward Atkinson, December 16, 1894.

21. CN to EA, 11/14/98.

22. CN to EA, 8/8/95.

and with the strong constitution which you laid up in your early years you ought to be in better condition."[23] Atkinson similarly wrote a letter to Wells, which the latter passed on, to Nordhoff's great displeasure. "I wish Nordhoff were here again to join in this fight," Atkinson had written. "...He is pining away there, I am afraid, not in good condition, and I suspect partly because he has nothing to do or nothing that he must do."[24]

"On the contrary, I am not 'pining away,'" Nordhoff insisted to Atkinson, "but thank God (and Mr. Bennett) every day of my life that I may live out of the hateful turmoil & see things as they are. I am not well or strong—that is true enough—& to go east would probably kill me very quickly, & I would be of no use there. Nor have I been idle." He had, he reminded Atkinson, written his series of "Letters to Wage-Earners" for the *Herald*, and of course in 1893 there had been the Hawaii business. He was defensive about Atkinson's accusations of idleness, as anyone with his strong work ethic would be. But in writing the "Letters," and in making the Hawaii excursion,

> I so used myself up that I was for long disabled, & have since the last six months had an attack of bleeding at the lungs, & for another trouble the necessity of an operation; so am now ... still weak & easily used up. So leave alone, & bear in mind that I have done my share, & that everybody has not the activity that you have.[25]

He couldn't come east, he insisted, not even to visit a dying friend: "a journey East would kill me; & my life is important to my wife & girls." He did not say it mattered to himself.[26]

He developed cataracts in his seventieth year, so severe that he needed to have the newspapers read to him and, eventually unable to see well enough to put pen to paper, was forced to dictate his letters. "I think, joyfully & very gratefully of the many years, from 14 to 61, in which I had the most untainted health & vigor," he wrote to Daniel C. Gilman.[27] Unwilling to risk the total blindness that might result if an operation to remove the cataracts were to fail, he assured Gilman that the problem with his eyesight had not "disturbed my

23.   Edward Atkinson to CN, 6/24/96.

24.   EA to DAW, enclosed in CN to EA, 7/20/96.

25.   CN to EA, 7/20/96.

26.   CN to EA, 11/30/97.

27.   CN to D. C. Gilman, April 6, 1900. Gilman Papers, Johns Hopkins University, Eisenhower Library.

equanimity; ... and I remain entirely cheerful and serene. ... I don't want you to feel too sorry for me."[28]

Ill once more with influenza, diabetes, and incident troubles, Nordhoff was confined to his bed in early 1901 and dictated a brief letter to Atkinson, with very little "news that I know of," as he remarked wryly, "trained nurses and lying in bed do not help to brighten one's wits."[29] By May, he was in a hospital in San Francisco; there were no effective treatments to keep him going. In late June, the San Diego *Union* reported that his doctors "despair[ed] of his recovery."[30] He died on July 14.

"Did I ever tell you of an old shipmate in my sea days," he once remarked to Edward Atkinson, "-- a stalwart & noblehearted fellow, Captain of the Maintop—who when a lot of us were once discussing what we would like on our tombstones if we should chance to have a shore burial, said 'as for me, I'd like to have them put on mine—"Here lies Jack Haley—he did his damnedest!"' It seems to me," Nordhoff concluded, "rather a grand epitaph."[31]

---

28. CN to D. C. Gilman, 12/5/1900, Gilman Papers, Johns Hopkins University, Eisenhower Library.

29. CN to EA, 2/18/1901.

30. "Charles Nordhoff Ill," San Diego *Union*, June 26, 1901. Prominent obituaries of Nordhoff appeared across the country in periodicals that had been unfriendly as well as friendly to him in life: Washington *Evening Star*, 7/16/01; *Harper's Weekly*, 7/27/01; Washington *Post*, 7/16/01; NY *Tribune*, July 15, 1901; LA *Times* [editorial], 7/16/01; San Diego *Union*, 7/15/01 and 7/17/01; NY *Evening Post* printed an extended, if delayed, memorial, on 12/7/01; Bergen County [NJ.] *Democrat*, 7/19/01; Hackensack [NJ] *Republican*, 7/18/01; San Francisco *Examiner*, 7/15/01; NY *Times*, 7/16/01; NY *Herald*, 7/15/01; San Francisco *Call*, 7/15/01; San Francisco *Chronicle*, 7/15/01.

31. CN to Edward Atkinson, 2/3/1894. Atkinson Papers, MHS.

EPILOGUE

Lida Nordhoff left California within two months of Charles's death, bearing his ashes with her back to their home in Alpine, New Jersey. She died slightly more than a year later while travelling in India, in December 1902, at the age of sixty-three. Their remains are interred with their daughter Evelyn's in the Alpine (NJ) Methodist Church, under a small brass plaque bearing no epitaph. Walter continued to prosper and published respected historical novels, although the Ensenada ranch was never a success and his son Charles Bernard went on to fame as coauthor of the Mutiny on the Bounty Trilogy. Amy married; Elsie also married a few years after her father's death and, as a widow, lived on into the 1950s in a New Hampshire farmhouse in which she refused to install electricity or indoor plumbing. She was an avowed socialist for the rest of her life.[1]

In 1916, Nordhoff, California, officially changed its name to Ojai, for "Nordhoff" was declared too unpatriotic-sounding during the years of World War I. Nordhoff Peak, which looms above the Ojai Valley, retains its original name. Nordhoff Avenues remain in Los Angeles and Riverside, California; Englewood, New Jersey (called "Nordoff Avenue"); and Honolulu, Hawaii.

James Gordon Bennett, Jr., died in France in 1918 at the age of seventy-seven, only a few years after his first and only marriage, fittingly enough to the Baroness von Reuter, whose fortune rose from the Reuter's wire service. The New York *Herald* languished for a few years after Bennett's death, and in 1924, it was absorbed by the New York *Tribune* to form the New York *Herald-Tribune*. When microphotography was developed in the 1930s, the Herald-Tribune Company microfilmed their back issues of the old *Tribune*, but they did not

---

[1.] The second Charles Nordhoff wrote a brief memoir of his grandfather in the introduction to *In Yankee Windjammers*, an abridged version of *Nine Years a Sailor* published by Dodd, Mead in 1940. On Lida's return east, see Walter Nordhoff's logbook, entries for August, 1901, in the possession of Franklin Nordhoff, Torrance, California. On Elsie, see letters from Franklin Nordhoff to the author, August 28, 1989, and Frank Morrison, September 1989.

film the *Herald* files. The *Herald-Tribune* was one of the nation's preeminent newspapers until 1966, when it ceased publication.[2]

The New York *Evening Post* celebrated its centennial in 1901, only a few months after Nordhoff's death, with a volume commemorating its history and an elaborate dinner with speeches by many old *Evening Post* editors and staff members. Charles Nordhoff's name was omitted from the chronology of *Evening Post* editors given at the dinner and in the book published afterward. None of the major speech-makers—Carl Schurz, Horace White, E. L. Godkin, Parke Godwin—mention Nordhoff although one of the less-important speakers, a man who had worked under Nordhoff at the *Post*, spoke of him with great pride and affection. The *Evening Post* changed publishers several times in the ensuing decades, and today is published as the *New York Post*—an ill-regarded tabloid, though still bearing Alexander Hamilton's likeness on its masthead.[3]

Six years after Nordhoff's death, President Theodore Roosevelt decried "muckraking" in a speech, giving a new name to the journalism of exposure that was then spurring on Progressive reforms. Lincoln Steffens, probably the foremost of that generation of muckrakers, later declared that he had written the very first "muckraking" article in 1902, and the idea that factually based journalistic reformism was an innovation of the twentieth century became firmly entrenched. Like many historical truisms, it simply was not true.

[2.]   On Bennett, see Don C. Seitz, *The James Gordon Bennetts, Father and Son* and "James Gordon Bennett, Jr.," in the *Dictionary of Literary Biography*, volume 43. On the *Herald-Tribune*, see Richard Kluger, *The Paper* (NY: 1986). On microfilming, see abstracts of articles on "microphotography" in the *Library Index*.

[3.]   *The New York Evening Post Hundredth Anniversary* (NY: Evening Post Co., 1902) presents the texts of speeches delivered at the commemorative dinner. See also Allan Nevins, *The Evening Post* (NY: 1922). The modern-day New York *Post* is available in libraries.

ACKNOWLEDGMENTS

In piecing together and making sense of Charles Nordhoff's life, I relied on many people for help of various kinds. Librarians and archivists at the Library of Congress, the Massachusetts Historical Society, the New York Public Library, the San Diego State University Library, and the many other repositories noted in the bibliography provided crucial help in person and through the mail, allowing me to gather the badly scattered fragments on Nordhoff's life. The interlibrary loan staff at Brown University deserve special thanks for cheerfully fulfilling my unending requests over several years, allowing me to complete a project that might otherwise have been impossible. Kathleen Fernandez, of the Zoar Historic Site in Zoar, Ohio, provided me with copies of valuable documents relating to the impact of Nordhoff's work on Zoar. Thomas Culbertson, of the Rutherford B. Hayes library, provided me with copies of the wonderful Nordhoff-Hayes correspondence. Anne Shepherd, of the Cincinnati Historical Society, answered questions on Cincinnati local history and located early Nordhoff correspondence in the collections there. Ellen Coxe, of the Alpine Methodist Episcopal Church, and John Spring, Cresskill Borough Historian, provided me with help on the local history of Alpine, New Jersey. Gail Malmgreen pointed me toward some important letters in the Henry George Papers, while Beverly Wilson Palmer directed me to the microfilm edition of the Charles Sumner Papers. Thomas Adema located newspaper articles in the San Diego newspapers that were useful, while Dennis Laurie of the American Antiquarian Society tracked down what may be the only extant issues of *The Workingman*. I would also like to thank the descendants of Charles Nordhoff, Franklin Nordhoff of Torrance, California, and Frank Morrison of Sudbury, Massachusetts, for their willingness to share their grandmother's memoir and other family papers.

Brown University supported me virtually throughout the completion of this project, and Dean Bernard Bruce has been a sympathetic ally. A grant from the New Jersey Historical Commission enabled me to do on-site research in that state, and Mary Murrin was a great help while I was preparing the grant proposal. Many members of the Brown University American Civilization and

History departments were generous with their time and knowledge, often providing valuable bibliographic tips as well as general interpretive insights while the support of both departments during my graduate career, of course, has been crucial. Mari-Jo Buhle's lectures on women's history provided valuable information on nineteenth-century life, Bob Lee and Rich Meckel gave me helpful information on Chinese and German immigrants, and Bruce Rosenberg graciously read through and conscientiously critiqued the entire manuscript. I would also like to thank Donald A. Ritchie of the U.S. Senate Historical Office and Paul M. Buhle of the Rhode Island School of Design for reading and commenting on the manuscript. Joanne Melish, Teresa Bill, Julie Weiss, and Martha Burns all endured numerous lunchtime dissections of the meaning of Charles Nordhoff's life over the past several years and brought their considerable knowledge of various fields to our discussions, to my great profit. Bill McLoughlin was a superb teacher and a model of the conscientious and diligent scholar; his comments have allowed me to sharpen the biography's focus at important points, and his recent death is a terrible loss.

Jack Thomas deserves the greatest thanks for agreeing to direct this dissertation and good-naturedly kicking ideas around with me—often when the ideas needed some good kicking—frequently and with great insight and imagination. He has also been a superb editor, providing frequent commentary on the fragments of the interminable first draft. His suggestions on how to shape it into more manageable form were invaluable. The final product, of course, with its flaws, is my responsibility, but its flaws would have been greater without his help.

My friends outside the academy, including Judy, Teddy, and Louise Throm, Patricia and Von Hardesty, Susan Wiener, Elise Quasebarth, and Naomi Glass and her minions, have provided moral support and needed perspective. Clare Durst provided generous help with computer problems. Sheldon Buzney deserves special thanks. I am most grateful for the moral support provided by my parents, Albert and Rita Frost, and my several siblings throughout the long, long life of this project.

APPENDIX

Sample Titles from the NY Herald
Concerning Progressive Issues

March 5, 1879: "Stifling the Young/ Absence of Ventilation in the Public Schools."

December 9, 1880: "Public Health/ ...Disease in Emigrant Ships/ Sanitary Value of the Florida Ship Canal/ Quarantine Laws Needed."

January 23, 1881: "Rear Tenements/ Specimen Blocks, Crowded With Dwellings and Teeming With Inhabitants/ Ineffectual Fire Escapes/ Where the Health Board and Building Department Should Intercede/ Life and health Jeapardized/ Dangerous Man Traps and Sanitary Plague Spots."

February 14, 1881: "New York's Foulness/ The Perfunctory Work of an Incompetent Street Cleaning Department/ A Bureau Without An Apologist/ Large Expenditures for Which the Citizens Get No Satisfactory Return/ Three Years' Labor Compared/ Long but Interesting Exhibit of Damnatory Statistics."

February 20, 1881: "Lynchers Let Loose/ Five Negroes Taken From A Court Room and Hanged/ The Bloodiest Tragedy On Record/ Details of the Crime Which Led to the Lynching/ A Fearful Butchery and Its Ending/ Ten Lives as an Atonement for One Murder."

March 30, 1881: "Legislative Robbery/ An Extraordinary Water Bill Before the New Jersey Lawmakers/ Giving Away the Passaic/ The Rights of Farmers, Millowners and Cities Disregarded/ ...And All to Increase the Powers of an Arrogant Monopoly."

April 12, 1881: "Clean the Streets/ Arrangements for an Indignation Meeting in this City/ Who Shall Govern Us?/ Physicians of New York Emphasize the Danger of Pestilence/ Voice of the People."

April 13, 1881: "Perish Patronage, Parties and Politics Subservient to the General Weal/ Clean Streets and Public Health/ The Demands of New York's Indignant Citizens Emphatically Renewed/ Last Night's Great Meeting/

Recreant Servants of the People Held Up to Shame and Contumely/ No Compromise/ The Battle for Sanitary Reform to Be Waged Resolutely."

April 18, 1881: "Street Cleaning/ Death Rate for the City of New York for the First Three Months of 1880, 6,802/ Death Rate for the City of New York for the First Three Months of 1881, 9,105!!/ Increase, 2,303!!!" [Article names assemblymen opposing street cleaning bill.]

May 8, 1881: "Horrors of the Steerage/ Description of Emigrant Quarters on an Ocean Steamer/ A Scene Worthy of Dante's Inferno/ Treading on the Writhing Bodies of Men and Women..."

May 13, 1881: "The People's Health/ A Department Charged With Important Functions Running in the Ruts of Routine/ Responsibility Lacking/ Commissioners Whose Private Engagements Interfere With Their Public Duties/ Health Board Circumlocutions."

January 22, 1882: "Wretched Abodes/ The Official Inspection of the Cheap Lodging Houses/ Dangers From Fire and Disease/ Four Sleeping Rooms for One Hundred and Fifty Lodgers." calls for Health Dept. action.

January 23, 1882: "The City's Wrongs/ ...The Public Interest and Republican-Democratic Bargaining/ ...A Relic of the Notorious Tweed Legislation."

March 28, 1882: "Resetting the Death Trap/ Third Avenue 'L' Trains Again to Cross the Second Avenue Track/ ...The Interlocking Switch System to be Used/ Its Insecurity Shown."

March 28, 1882: "'L' Road Perils/ Systematic Violations of the Law by the Servants of the Company/ Trains Starting With Open Gates/ Popular Suggestions for Better Security to the Traveling Public."

March 30, 1882: "New Jersey's Shame/ Unscrupulous Means Employed to Sustain the Railroad Bill/ Bribery Exposed/ ...Five Hundred Given and One Thousand Dollars Offered for a Vote."

March 23, 1882: "The Knights of Labor/ American Workingmen United for Self-Protection/ Politicians, Stand From Under!/ Equal Rights and Just Rewards for All Men and Women/ A Giant Power That Will Be Felt."

December 15, 1884: "Where Poverty Abides/ Professor Adler's Descriptions of the Homes of the Poor/ Squalor in London and New York/ A Plague Spot in the Heart of the City/ Practical Reforms."

December 25, 1884: "Shirtmakers' Wrongs/ Ten Thousand Women Look to the Herald for Relief from Their Sufferings/ An Appeal to Governor Cleveland/ How an American Family Lived for Several Days on Bread, Molasses and Water."

January 2, 1885: "The Poor Shirtmakers/ The Starvation Rates At Which They Toil—Their Cry for Help/ An Appeal to the Women of New York/ The Need of Organized Opposition to Insure Living Wages."

April 1, 1886: "Labor and Law/ Providing for National Intervention in Railroad Strikes/ Mr. O'Neill's Bill Introduced/ 'Arbitration, If Not Voluntarily Accepted, Must Be Enforced'/ Greed of Monopolies Denounced."

April 6, 1886: "Battle for Cheap Gas/ Hundreds of Thousands of Consumers Interested in the Albany Struggle/ Corrupt Tactics of Cosolidationists/ A Telling Exposure of Their Plots and Intrigues..."

April 11, 1886: "Strikers Overawed/ State Troops in Possession of East St. Louis/ A Night of Fire/ ...Much Valuable Railroad Property Totally Destroyed/ The Deputies' Bloody Work/ Witnesses All Agree That the Guards Fired Without Cause."

January 11, 1887: "Little Factory Slaves/ Professor Adler Compliments the *Herald* and Hopes It Will Investigate/ ...None of His Statements Questioned by Children's Society."

January 12, 1887: "A Tale From Texas/ Strange Allegations of Outrage Upon Peaceable Republicans/ Murders By Ku Klux/ Three Citizens Complain That They Were Driven From Home/ A Locality to Avoid."

January 12, 1887: "Education Not Force/ Workingmen Denounce the National Militia Bill/ A Plot to Crush Organization/ Labor an Army of Peace and Not of Violence."

January 14, 1887: "Coal War and War Prices/ The Heavers Attempt No Violence and Joke With the Police/ How the Poor Suffer/ Knights of Labor Show Their Hand and the Companies Protest."

January 21, 1887: "Bullets in the Strike/ A Boy Shot Down in Jersey City by One of Pinkerton's Guards/ Pistols for Slight Cause/ Peace Preservers Who Couldn't Stand the Jeers of Youngsters At Play/ Suppressed Rage Among the Strikers..."

January 21, 1887: "Deadly Electric Wires/ A Man Killed At A Fire While Cutting Lighting Cables/ Slow Ambulance Service/ Twenty Minutes Required for the Ambulance to Go Six Blocks."

January 22, 1887: "Pinkerton's Terrors/ Intense Excitement in Jersey City Over the Killing of Young Hoban/ Trades Unions Protest/ The Sharpshooting Guards Will Have No More Practice on Citizens."

January 27, 1887: "Smallpox/ An Increase Rather Than a Decrease in the Number of Cases/ Will It Become Epidemic?/ Health Officials Charged With Neglect/ Dr. Taylor's Reply."

January 15, 1888: "Greed!/ How Food, Fuel, Clothing and Light are Cornered by Conspiring Monopolists/ An Industrial Crime/ The People At the Mercy of Successful 'Combines' to Depress Production and Exact High Prices/ Alarming Growth of the Trust System/ Standard Oil's Iniquitous Example Followed by Many Branches of Trade--Pools in Every Line." [Advocates' legislative remedies.]

January 22, 1888: "Greed!/ Something More About the Commercial 'Combines' Which Hold Consumers in an Iron Grip/ The Trust System's Evils/ Monopolists Who Successfully Conspire to Restrict Production, Lower Wages, and Raise Prices Exorbitantly/ Food Supplies At Their Mercy."

February 12, 1888: "Saccharine Slavery./ It Brings Our Favorite Luxury, but It Is Not So Sweet to the Slaves./ Oppressions of the Sugar Barons./ Men Who Average $30 a Month and Who Pass One-Half of Their Lives in an Earthly Inferno."

March 7, 1888: "Trusts Condemned/ The Senate Committee Has Dissected Them and Found Them Evil/ All Tarred With One Brush/ Each is a Giant Monopoly That Holds the Public At Its Mercy/ Now Let Them Be Squelched/ Public Policy Demands That These Combinations Should Be Suppressed By the Law."

March 19, 1888: "The Right To Steal/ Dr. De Costa Says the Present Social System Creates Thieves and Anarchists/ A Railroad vs. A Loaf of Bread."

March 26, 1888: "Greasy Frauds/ Methods of Producing Lard From the Fat of Sick Hogs/ Evidence of a Pork Packer/ Carelessness as to the Condition of Animals Slaughtered for Food." [Includes discussion of appropriate public policy.]

April 7, 1888: "Standard Oil Trust/ Paying Men to be Idle in Order to Fleece the Public/ Investigating the Octopus/ No Drilling New Wells Until the Corporation Graciously Permits."

April 20, 1888: "Arbitration/ Delegation of 'Bosses' and Journeymen State Their Grievances to the Commissioners./ To Break Up the Unions./ Rumors of an Employers' Conspiracy—Dictation of Workingmen."

April 29, 1888: "Do Policemen Pony Up?/ A Pertinent Question Asked of the Mayor and the Commissioners./ And Voorhis Says Yes./ While He Gives Some Cogent Reasons For His Answer."

April 29, 1888: "Give the Boys A Chance/ The Girls Should Have One as Well as Anybody/ Where Shall the Children Play?/ How They are Hunted and Driven From Pillar to Post."

April 29, 1888: "Might Not Right./ Threatened Eviction of a Whole Negro Colony Near Newberne, N.C./ Uncle Sam's Blunder./ Emancipated Slaves 'Given' Title to Land Which the United States Did Not Own./ James City Built./ How Mr. Bryan Claims Entire Ownership of All Homes, Stores and Improvements./ An Appeal to Humanity."

July 1, 1888: "Corrupt Union Pacific/ ...A Scheme to Confirm the Title to Colossal Robberies/ Will Congress Submit?"

July 6, 1888: "Officials Who Shirk Work/ Brooklyn Public Officers Close at Two O'Clock and Everybody Goes Home/ The Supervisors Are To Blame."

July 27, 1888: "Congress in the Slums/ A National Committee Sees the Horrors of Mulberry Street/ Escorted By Herald Reporters/ Scenes of Squalor, Filth and Misery in the Tenements/ ...Men, Women and Children Huddled Together Like Beasts/ Babes in Death Gasps/ Young Girls Sharing Rooms with Fathers, Brothers, and Strangers."

October 4, 1888: "Grain Men Must Submit/ Justice Brown of the Supreme Court, Sustains the McEvoy Bill/ The Public Good Paramount/ Elevator Charges are Rightly Limited By Law."

October 8, 1888: "Trusts Must Go/ Organized Labor Declares Against These Monstrosities/ ...Advocating Paternal Government Aid for the Immigrant."

October 8, 1888: "Blind Man's Bluff/ The Nice Little Game the Politicians Are Playing/ Leaders Have All the Fun/ While the Eyes of the Voters are Screened."

October 8, 1888: "Coal Barons and Serfs/ The Beggarly Earnings of Men Who Toil in the Mines/ Very Like Robbery/ Enormous 'Profits' Plucked from the Workers on Supplies Purchased."

January 16, 1889: "Perished in a Death Trap/ Three Young Women Lose Their Lives in a Cigar Box Factory/ Building Laws Violated/ The Fire Escape Was Not in Place—An Illegal Partition Obstructed the Escape of the Unfortunate Inmates..."

March 17, 1889: "Wherein Asylums Fail/ Ex-Judge George M. Curtis on the Needless Hardships of Lunatics/ Nurses That Are Brutal/ The Laws Pronounced All Right in Purpose, But Their Administration Worse Than Slipshod."

December 1, 1889: "Bogus Bankers Must Go/ Public Sentiment Demands the Suppression of Unscrupulous Financiers/ Restricting Legislation Necessary/ Outline of a Bill Designed to Protect Ignorant Immigrants."

December 7, 1889: "Nice Bolognas Made From Old Horses/ ...Discarded Animals Are Chopped Up Into Food/ Delicacies for French Palates/ Aged and Cheap Nags Minced for Export, But New York May Get Some of Them Too." (Calls for pure-food laws.)

December 18, 1889: "Lights on the Race Question/ A Convention of Colored Men to be Held in Washington/ Wrongs to Remedy/ Formation of a National Organization to Protect Constitutional Rights/ List of Promoters." Highly positive publicity.

LIST OF ABBREVIATIONS

CN	Charles Nordhoff
EP	New York *Evening Post*
LC	Library of Congress
MHS	Massachusetts Historical Society
NYPL	New York Public Library
RBH/RBH Library	Rutherford B. Hayes/Rutherford B. Hayes Library, Fremont, Ohio

BIBLIOGRAPHY

Manuscript Collections

John A. Andrews Collection, Massachusetts Historical Society
Adams Family Papers, Massachusetts Historical Society
Alpine Methodist Church files, Alpine, New Jersey
John Andrews Papers, Massachusetts Historical Society
Alfred Anthony Collection, New York Public Library
Chester A. Arthur Papers, Library of Congress
Edward Atkinson Papers, Massachusetts Historical Society
Edward Atkinson Papers, New York Public Library
Autograph collection, Vineland Historical and Antiquarian Society, Vineland, New Jersey
George Bancroft Papers, Massachusetts Historical Society
Bancroft-Bliss Collection, Library of Congress
Belmont Family Papers, Butler Library, Columbia University
Samuel Bowles Papers, Yale University Library
Crosby Boyd Collection, Misc. Mss., Library of Congress
Bryant-Godwin Collection, New York Public Library
Davis W. Clark Collection, Cincinnati Historical Society
Grover Cleveland Papers, Library of Congress
Augustin Daly Papers, Folger Shakespeare Library
George Davidson Papers, Bancroft Library
Fairchild Papers, New York Historical Society
Hamilton Fish Papers, Library of Congress
S.G. Flagg Papers, Yale University Library
Gordon Lester Ford Papers, New York Public Library
Sydney Howard Gay Papers, Butler Library, Columbia University
Henry George Papers, New York Public Library
Daniel Coit Gilman Papers, Eisenhower Library, Johns Hopkins University
Edward L. Godkin Papers, Houghton Library, Harvard University
Parke Godwin Collection, Princeton University

Walter Q. Gresham Papers, Library of Congress
William Grosvenor Collection, Butler Library, Columbia University
Charles Graham Halpine correspondence, Huntington Library
Harper Brothers Papers, Butler Library, Columbia University
Benjamin Harrison Papers, Library of Congress
Friedrich Hassaurek Papers, Ohio Historical Center Library
Rutherford B. Hayes Papers, Hayes Library, Fremont, Ohio
Phoebe A. Hearst Papers, Bancroft Library
Hotel del Coronado Collection, San Diego State University
Laurence Hutton Correspondence Collection, Princeton University
Charlton T. Lewis Papers, Yale University Library
Liliuokalani Diaries, Hawaiian State Archives
Abraham Lincoln Papers, Library of Congress
Benson J. Lossing Papers, Huntington Library
Benson J. Lossing Papers, New York State Library
Manton Marble Collection, Library of Congress
Miscellaneous Manuscripts: Evans, O'Beirne, Library of Congress
Morgan Papers, New York State Library
Ephraim Morse Correspondence, San Diego Historical Society
Allan Nevins Papers, Butler Library, Columbia University
Nixon Family Papers, Ohio Historical Society Library
Charles Nordhoff Papers, New York Public Library
Sarah Cope Whitall Nordhoff memoir, private collection of Franklin Nordhoff,
     Torrance, California
Charles Eliot Norton Papers, Houghton Library, Harvard University
James Parton Letters, Houghton Library, Harvard
James Phelan Papers, California Historical Society
William F. Poole Papers, Newberry Library
William C. Ralston Papers, Bancroft Library
Whitelaw Reid Papers, Library of Congress
Carl Schurz Papers, Library of Congress
Edwin Seligman Papers, Butler Library, Columbia University
Smithsonian Institution Archives, Papers, Office of the Secretary
Charles Sumner Papers, Houghton Library, Harvard University
Charles Sumner Papers, Library of Congress
Samuel Tilden Papers, New York Public Library
J. M. Toner Papers, Library of Congress
William Lee Trenholm Papers, Library of Congress
David Ames Wells Papers, Library of Congress
Whitman C. Whitney Collection, Library of Congress
Woolsey Family Papers, Yale University Library
John Russell Young Papers, Library of Congress

Obituaries

Bergen County [NJ] *Democrat*, July 19, 1901

Hackensack [NJ] *Republican*, July 18, 1901

Lummis, Charles. "In Western Letters," *Land of Sunshine*, 15 (October 1901)

Harpers' Weekly, July 27, 1901

New York *Evening Post*, December 7, 1901

New York *Herald*, July 15, 1901

New York *Tribune*, July 15, 1901

San Diego *Union*, July 17, 1901

San Francisco *Chronicle*, July 15, 1901

San Francisco *Examiner*, July 15, 1901

Washington *Evening Star*, July 16, 1901

Washington *Post*, July 16, 1901.

Government Records

Marriage license, Charles Nordhoff and Eliza Letford, 25 August, 1857, Hamilton County Courthouse, Hamilton County, Ohio.

Foreign Office and Executive Files, U.S. Commission in Hawaii; Hawaiian Legation in Washington. Hawaiian State Archives.

Probate records, Bergen County Courthouse, Hackensack, New Jersey.

Affidavit of Harry A. Juen, December 12, 1893, document 941 in the Attorney General File, Public Archives of Hawaii.

Works by Charles Nordhoff

America for Free Working Men! 39 pp.

--New York: Harper & Brothers, 1865.

--New York: Loyal Publication Society, 1865.

California: For Health, Pleasure, and Residence. A Book for Travellers and Settlers. 255 pp.

--New York: Harper & Brothers, 1872.

--New York: Harper & Brothers, 1873.

--New York: Harper & Brothers, 1874.

--New York: Harper & Brothers, 1875.

--New York: Harper & Brothers, 1876.

--San Francisco: Ten Speed Press, 1973.

--*Revised edition.* 206 pp. New York: Harper & Brothers, 1882.

La California par Charles Nordhoff. 32 pp.
--Londres: Le Chemin de fer du Pacifique du Sud, 1883.

Cape Cod and All Along Shore: Stories. 235 pp.
--New York: Harper & Brothers, 1868.
--New York: Harper & Brothers, 1880.

La ciencia administrativa al alcance de los jovenes. Obra escrita en ingles por Charles Nordhoff, tr. al castellano, y arreglada a las instituciones y al caracter del pueblo mexicano por el Lie. Eduardo Ruiz.
--Mexico City: Oficina tip. de la Secretaria de fomento, 1890.
--Mexico City, 1885.

The Communistic Societies of the United States: From Personal Visit and Observation. 439 pp.
--New York: Harper & Brothers, 1874.
--New York, Harper & Brothers, 1875.
--New York: Hillary House, 1960.
--New York: Schocken Books, 1965.
--New York: Dover, 1966.

The Cotton States in the Spring and Summer of 1875. 112 pp.
--New York: D. Appleton & Co., 1876.
--New York: Burt Franklin, [1971].

Crossing the Line: A Cruise in a Whaler. A Book for Boys. 190 pp.
--Edinburgh: JA. Hislop & Co., [1869].
--Edinburgh: Oliphant, Anderson, & Forrier, [1881].

The Darwinian Theory of Evolution.
--Washington: Literary Society of Washington, D.C., 2/9/1880.

The Freedmen of South Carolina: Some Account of Their Appearance, Character, Condition, and Peculiar Customs. 27 pp.
--New York: C. T. Evans, 1863.

God and the Future Life: The Reasonableness of Christianity. 228 pp.
--New York: Harper & Brothers, 1883.
--New York: Harper & Brothers, 1884.

Guia de California, el estada del oro. 31 pp.
--Londres: La Compania del Ferro-carril del Pacifico dal Sud, 1883.

A Guide to California, the Golden State. 31 pp.
--London: Southern Pacific Railroad, 1883.

I Served in Windjammers. 401 pp.
--London: Chapman & Hall Ltd., [1941].

In Yankee Windjammers. 401 pp.
--New York: Dodd, Mead & Co., 1940.

Man-of-War Life: A Boy's Experiences in the United States Navy, During a Voyage Around the World, in a Ship of the Line. 286 pp.
--New York: Dodd, Mead, [1855].
--Cincinnati: Moore, Wilstach, Keys & Co., [1855].
--Cincinnati: Moore, 1856.
--New York: Miller, Orton & Mulligan, 1856.
--New York: Dodd, Mead, & Co., 1883.
--New York: Dodd, Mead, & Co., 1881.
--New York: Dodd, Mead, & Co., 1885.
--New York: Dodd, Mead, & Co., 1895.

The Merchant Vessel: A Sailor-Boy's Voyages to See the World. 288 pp.
--New York: Dodd, Mead, & Co., 1855.
--Cincinnati: Moore, 1856.
--New York: Dodd, Mead, & Co., 1877.
--New York: Dodd, Mead, & Co., [1884].
--New York: Dodd, Mead, & Co., 1895.

The Misgovernment of New York: Suggestions toward a New Charter. 21 pp.
--New York: American News Company, 1871.

Nine Years a Sailor.
--Cincinnati: Wilstach, Baldwin & Co., 1874.
--Cincinnati: Moore, Wilstach, Keys & Co., 1857.
--Cincinnati: Moore, Wilstach, and Baldwin, 1866.

Northern California, Oregon, and the Sandwich Islands. 256 pp.
--London: S. Low, Marston, Low & Searle, 1874.
--New York: Harper & Brothers, 1874.

--New York: Harper & Brothers, 1875.
--New York: Harper & Brothers, 1877.
--San Francisco: Ten Speed, 1974.

Peninsular California. 130 pp.
--New York: Harper & Brothers, 1888.

Politica para los jovenes americanos. Traducido del ingles por Gabriel Zendegui. 328 pp.
--Buenos Aires: Felix Lajouane, 1891.

Politics for Young Americans. 200 pp.
--New York: Harper & Brothers, 1875.
--New York: Harper & Brothers, 1786.
Revised for schools and colleges:
--New York: Harper & Brothers, 1877.
--New York: Harper & Brothers, 1878.
--New York: Harper & Brothers, 1879.
--New York: Harper & Brothers, 1880.
--New York: Harper & Brothers, 1881.
--New York: Harper & Brothers, 1882.
--New York: Harper & Brothers, 1883.
--New York: Harper & Brothers, 1884.
--New York: Harper & Brothers, 1886.
--New York: Harper & Brothers, 1887.
--New York: Harper & Brothers, 1890.
--Cincinnati: American Book Company, 1899.

Reminiscences of Some Editors I have Known. 32 pp.
--San Diego: Tuesday Club, March 6, 1900.

Sailor Life on Man-of-War and Merchant Vessel.
--New York: Dodd, Mead & Co., [1884].

Secession Is Rebellion! Rebellion Cannot Succeed!! 20 pp.
--New York: Baker & Godwin, 1860.

Stories of the Island World. 315 pp.
--New York: Harper & Brothers, 1857.

Whaling and Fishing. 383 pp.
--New York: Dodd, Mead & Co., [1855].

--Cincinnati: Moore, Wilstach, Keys & Co., 1856.
--London: Addey, [1860?].
--New York: Dodd, Mead & Co., 1895.

The Young Man-of-War's Man: A Boy's Voyage Round the World. 216 pp.
--Edinburgh: W. P. Nimmo, [1866?].
--Edinburgh: W. P. Nimmo, [1874?].
--London and Edinburgh: W. P. Nimmo, 1877.

Charles Nordhoff's Work for Periodicals

The New York Herald

Of greatest significance are the columns Nordhoff wrote from Washington for
the New York *Herald* between 1874 and 1890, under the heading "From Our
Special Correspondent." They appeared only while Congress was in session. A
series of reports from Hawaii appeared during 1893 (specific citations for which
appear in the final chapter), and several "Letters to Wage Workers" appeared
in the *Herald* during July, 1895.

The New York Evening Post

More difficult to determine is Nordhoff's role in the editorializing of the New
York *Evening Post,* of which he was managing editor between 1861 and 1871.
Although William Cullen Bryant and Parke Godwin were the chief editors,
Nordhoff's input was evidently substantial, although none of the editorials are
bylined.

Harper's Monthly Magazine

Nordhoff wrote extensively for *Harper's,* usually travel articles notable for their
lack of romanticism; sometimes they are "guts" of books, one of his duties as
an editor with the magazine prior to his involvement in newspaper journalism.
Although these articles are seldom bylined, *Poole's Index* attributes the following
to Nordhoff:

> "Burton's Lake Regions of Africa," 21:622
> "Reade's travels in Africa," 23:16
> "Vambery's travels in Asia," 31:13
> "Babbage's calculating machine," 30:34

"California," 44:865; 45:65; 45:255
"Northern California," 47:98; 48:35
"Dice and Card-Playing," 26:163
"Columbia River and Puget Sound," 48: 338
"Capture of Elephants," 20:155
"Farallon Islands, California," 48:617
"Follies of Fashion," 18:310
"Cosmopolitan Bill of Fare," 18:653
"Hawaii-Nei," 47:382; 47:544
"Romance of Insurance," 19:661
"Lighthouses of the U.S.," 48:465
"Martyr Church of Madagascar," 18:586
"Cape Cod, Nantucket, and the Vineyard," 51:52
"Octopus and Sea Serpent," 21:178
"Two Weeks at Port Royal, South Carolina," 27:110
"Sailors' Superstitions," 16:183
"The Sea and Shore," 46:704
"Rights and Wrongs of Seamen," 48:556
"Modes and Causes of Suicide," 18:516
"Culture and Commerce of Tea in the U.S.," 19:762
"Tiger Hunting in Central India," 16:751
"History of Tobacco," 20:180
"Legal wit and humor," 19:369
"Wreckings on the Florida Keys," 18:577

Charles Nordhoff's Articles for Magazines other than Harper's

"Chesapeake & Ohio Railroad," *Every Saturday* II: 479
"Elkanah Brewster's Temptation," *Atlantic Monthly* 4:710
"The Misgovernment of New York," *North American Review* 113:321 (10/1871)
"Writings of Theodore Winthrop," *Atlantic Monthly* 12:153
"A Girl's School Wanted," *Nation* 27:55
"School-Hunter Again," *Nation* 27:97–98
"Letter to the editor," *Boston Gazette* 10/14/1885
"Letter to the editor: A visit to the courthouse," New York *Times* 7/26/1871
"The New York *Herald*: Letter from Mr. Charles Nordhoff," Boston *Gazette*, October 25, 1885
"Pictures Without Frames—From the German," *Ladies' Repository*, 15 (1855)
"Harpooning a Hippopotamus," *Ladies' Repository* 15 (1855)
"Concerning Authors," *Ladies' Repository*, 16 (1856)

"Concerning Books," *Ladies' Repository*, 16 (1856)

"Our First Whale," *Ladies' Repository*, 16 (1856)

"Can We Preserve Our Youth," *Ladies' Repository*, 17 (1857)

"Wife of Luther," *Ladies' Repository*, 17 (1857)

"Fortune-Telling," *Ladies' Repository*, 17 (1857)

"That Hundred-Barrel Whale," *Ladies' Repository*, 17 (1857)

Other Primary Published Sources

Alexander, William D. *Later Years of the Hawaiian Monarchy and the Revolution of 1893.* Honolulu: 1896.

Belmont, Perry. *An American Democrat.* New York: 1939.

Boynton, Henry Van Ness. "The Press and Public Men." *Century* 43 (October 1891): 853–62.

Burnett, Frances Hodgson. *Through One Administration.* New York: 1883.

Cleveland, Grover. *Presidential Problems.* New York: 1904.

Crawford, T. C. "Special Correspondents at Washington." *Cosmopolitan* 12 (January 1892): 351–60.

Dana, Charles A. *The Art of Newspaper Making.* New York: Appleton, 1895.

———. "Greeley as a Journalist." *A Library of American Literature.* Edited by Edmund C. Stedman and Ellen M. Hutchinson. New York: W. F. Benjamin, 1889.

Editor & Publisher: The Fourth Estate. New York: Editor & Publisher Company, 1884–[at least 1858]. Weekly trade organ of the daily newspaper industry in the U.S.

"Freedom of the Press." *The American Annual Cyclopedia and Register of Important Events.* New York: Appleton, 1861–1965.

Hawaiian Islands. Report of the Committee on Foreign Relations, U.S. Senate … Jan. 1, 1893 to March 10, 1894. Washington: GPO, 1894.

Hudson, Frederic. *Journalism in the United States, from 1690-1872.* New York: Harper & Brothers, 1873.

James, Henry. *Henry James: Literary Criticism.* New York: Library of America, 1984.

Maverick, Augustus. *Henry J. Raymond and the New York Press for Thirty Years.* Hartford: A. S. Hale, 1870.

Merrill, Samuel. *Newspaper Libel: A Handbook for the Press.* Boston: Ticknor & Co., 1888.

Newmark, Harris. *Sixty Years in Southern California: 1853-1913.* New York: Houghton-Mifflin, 1930.

"National News Spinners." *Brooklyn Times.* January 22, 1887.

North, S. N. D. *History and Present Condition of the Newspaper and Periodical Press of the U.S.* Washington: G.P.O., 1884.

Oldcastle, John. *Journals and Journalism: With a Guide for Literary Beginners.* London: Field & Tuer, 1880.

Parton, James. "Falsehood in the Daily Press." *Harper's Monthly* 49 (July 1874).

———. *The Life of Horace Greeley.* Boston: 1896.

———. "The New York Herald." *North American Review* 102 (April 1866): 373–419.

Philips, Melville, ed. *The Making of a Newspaper.* New York: Putnam's, 1893.

Poore, Benjamin Perley. "Washington News." *Harper's Monthly* 48 (January 1874).

Publishers' Auxiliary. Weekly trade journal. Chicago: Western Newspaper Union, 1866–[at least] 1958.

Ralph, Julian. "The Newspaper Correspondent." *Scribner's Magazine* 14 (August 1893): 150–156.

Reid, Whitelaw. "Journalism." *Careers for the Coming Men.* New York: Tribune Association, 1902; Saalfield Publishing Co., 1904. 201–213.

———. *Some Newspaper Tendencies: An Address Delivered Before the Editorial Associations of New York and Ohio.* New York: Henry Holt, 1879.

Sanborn, F. B. "Journalism and Journalists." *Atlantic Monthly* 34 (July 1874).

Sotheran, Davis. *Horace Greeley and Other Pioneers of American Socialism.* New York: Humboldt, 1892; Mitchell Kennerley, 1915.

Shuman, Edwin L. *Steps Into Journalism: Helps and Hints for Young Writers.* Evanston, IL: Correspondence School of Journalism, 1894. ("...[A]n outgrowth of Shuman's Chautauquan course in journalism..." Price).

Thurston, Lorrin A. *Memoirs of the Revolution in Hawaii.* Honolulu: Advertiser Publishing Company, 1936.

Warner, Charles Dudley. *The American Newspaper: An Essay.* Boston: James R. Osgood & Co., 1881.

Wilmer, Lambert. *Our Press Gang: Or, a Complete Exposition of the Corruptions and Crimes of the American Newspapers.* Philadelphia: J. T. Lloyd, 1859.

Wingate, Charles F., ed. *Views and Interviews on Journalism.* New York: F. B. Patterson, 1875.

Newspaper Directories and Advertisers' Handbooks

Ayer, N. W., and Son. *Directory of Newspapers and Periodicals.* New York: Ayer, 1880-date.

Edwin Alden and Bro.'s American Newspaper Catalogue, etc. Cincinnati and New York: Alden & Brothers, 1883.

Kenny, Daniel J. *The American Newspaper Directory and Record of the Press*. New York: Watson & Co., 1861.

Pettingill's Newspaper Directory and Advertisers' Handbook. New York: Pettigill Co., 1878–1899.

Remington Brothers Newspaper Manuals. New York: Remington Brothers, 1884–1898.

Rowell's American Newspaper Directory. New York: George P. Rowell & Co., 1869–1908. (1869 edition includes concept behind directory).

Memoirs and Autobiographies of Contemporary Journalists

Barry, David S. *Forty Years in Washington*. Boston: Little-Brown, 1924.

Bigelow, John. *Retrospections of an Active Life*. New York: Baker and Taylor, 1910. 5 volumes.

Brockway, Beman. *Fifty Years in Journalism*. Watertown, New York: Daily Times, 1891.

Bryant, William Cullen. *Letters*. New York: Fordham University Press, 1974–84.

Chambers, [James] Julius. *News Hunting on Three Continents*. New York: Mitchell Kennerley, 1921.

Clarke, Joseph I. C. *My Life and Memories*. New York: Dodd-Mead, 1925.

Congdon, Charles Taber. *Reminiscences of a Journalist*. Boston: Osgood, 1880.

Crockett, Albert Stevens. *When James Gordon Bennett Was Caliph of Bagdad*. New York: Funk & Wagnalls, 1926.

Croffutt, William A. *An American Procession, 1855-1914: A Personal Chronicle of Famous Men*. Boston: Little-Brown, 1931.

Dunn, Arthur Wallace. *From Harrison to Harding: A Personal Narrative Covering a Third of a Century, 1888-1921*. New York: Putnam's, 1922. 2 volumes.

———. *Gridiron Nights*. New York: Stokes, 1915.

Eggleston, George Cary. *A Rebel's Recollections*. New York: Hunt & Houghton, 1875.

———. *Recollections of a Varied Life*. New York: Holt, 1910.

The Evening Post Hundredth Anniversary, November 16, 1801-1901. New York: Evening Post Publishing Co., 1902.

Ford, James L. *Forty-Odd Years in the Literary Shop*. New York: Dutton, 1921.

Garrison, Wendell Phillips. *Letters and Memorials of Wendell Phillips Garrison, Literary Editor of the Nation, 1865-1906*. Cambridge: Riverside, 1908.

Gobright, Lawrence A. *Recollections of Men and Things at Washington During a Third of a Century*. Philadelphia: Claxton, Remsen, and Haffelfinger, 1869.

Greeley, Horace. *Recollections of a Busy Life*. New York: J.B. Ford & Co., 1868.

Hill, A. F. *Secrets of the Sanctum: An Inside View of an Editor's Life.* Philadelphia: Claxton, Remsen & Haffelfinger, 1875.

Hudson, William Cadwallader. *Random Recollections of an Old Political Reporter.* New York: Cupples & Leon, 1911.

Jordan, Elizabeth. *Three Rousing Cheers.* New York: Appleton, 1938.

Leach, Frank A. *Recollections of a Newspaperman: A Record of Life and Events in California.* San Francisco: Samuel Levinson, 1917.

Ludlow, Louis. *From Cornfield to Press Gallery: Adventures and Reminiscences of a Veteran Washington Correspondent.* Washington: W. F. Roberts Co., 1924.

Maverick, Augustus. *Henry J. Raymond and the New York Press for Thirty Years.* New York: A. S. Hale & Co.: 1870.

McClure, Alexander Kelly. *Recollections of Half a Century.* Salem, Mass.: Salem Press Co., 1902.

Mitchell, Edward P. *Memories of an Editor.* New York: Scribner's, 1924.

Older, Fremont. *My Own Story.* San Francisco: Call Publishing Co., 1919.

O'Shea, J. A. *Leaves from the Life of a Special Correspondent* (cited in Salmon, *The Newspaper and the Historian*).

Poore, Benjamin Perley. *Perley's Reminiscences of Sixty Years in the National Metropolis.* Philadelphia: Hubbard Brothers, 1886. 2 volumes.

Ralph, Julian. *The Making of a Journalist.* New York: Harper & Bros., 1903.

Reid, Whitelaw. "An Editor's Reflections" *American and English Studies.* New York: Scribner's, 1913. 2 volumes.

Richardson, Abby Sage. *Garnered Sheaves from the Writings of Albert D. Richardson.* Hartford: Columbian Book Co., 1871.

Richardson, Francis A. "Recollections of a Washington Newspaper Correspondent." *Records of the Columbia Historical Society* 6: 24–42. Washington: The Society, 1903.

Riis, Jacob. *The Making of an American.* New York: Macmillan, 1901.

Rowell, George P. *Forty Years an Advertising Agent, 1865-1905.* New York: Printer's Ink, 1906.

Russell, Charles Edward. *Bare Hands and Stone Walls: Some Recollections of a Side-Line Reformer.* New York: Scribner's, 1933.

———. *These Shifting Scenes.* New York: George H. Doran, 1914.

Salisbury, William. *The Career of a Journalist.* New York: B.W. Dodge & Co., 1908.

Schurz, Carl. *The Reminiscences of Carl Schurz.* New York: McClure, 1907. 3 volumes.

Stillman, William James. *The Autobiography of a Journalist.* Boston/New York: Houghton Mifflin, 1901.

Stoddard, Henry Luther. *As I Knew Them.* New York: Harper's, 1927.

Stone, Melville. *Fifty Years a Journalist.* New York: Doubleday, 1921.

Taylor, Bayard. *Unpublished Letters of Bavard Taylor in the Huntington Library.* San Marino: Huntington, 1937.

Townsend, George Alfred. *Washington Outside and Inside: A Picture and Narrative of the Origin, Growth, Excellences, Abuses, Beauties, and Personages of Our Governing City.* Hartford: James Butts & Co., 1873.

Villard, Henry. *Memoirs, 1835-1900.* New York: Houghton Mifflin, 1904. 2 volumes.

Villard, Oswald Garrison. *Some Newspapers and Newspapermen.* New York: Knopf, 1923.

Watterson, Henry. *The Compromises of Life: And Other Lectures and Addresses.* New York: Duffield and Co., 1906.

————. *"Marse Henry": An Autobiography.* New York: George B. Doran & Co., 1919. 2 volumes.

Whitman, Sidney. *Turkish Memories.* cited in Salmon, *The Newspaper and the Historian.*

Wingate, Charles F., ed. *H. G.: 1811-1872. Sketch of the Celebration of the Sixty-First Birthday of the Hon. Horace Greeley...* Privately printed: 1872.

Young, John Russell. *Men and Memories: Personal Reminiscences.* New York: F. Tennyson Neely, 1901. 2 volumes.

Secondary Sources (and Edited Primary Sources)

Adler, Jacob. *Claus Spreckels: The Sugar King of Hawaii.* Honolulu: University of Hawaii Press, 1966.

Allen, Helena G. *The Betrayal of Liliuokalani: Last Queen of Hawaii, 1838-1917.* Glendale, CA: Arthur H. Clark, 1982.

Andrews, J. Cutler. *The North Reports the Civil War.* Pittsburgh: University of Pittsburgh Press, 1955, 1983 rep.

Armstrong, William A. *E. L. Godkin: A Biography.* Albany: SUNY Press, 1978.

————, ed. *The Gilded Age Letters of E. L. Godkin.* Albany: SUNY Press, 1974.

Baldasty, Gerald J. *The Commercialization of News in the Nineteenth Century.* Madison: University of Wisconsin Press, 1992.

————. "The Nineteenth-Century Origins of Modern American Journalism." Edited by John B. Hench. *Three Hundred Years of the American Newspaper.* Worcester: American Antiquarian Society, 1991.

Baur, John E. "Charles Nordhoff: Publicist Par Excellence." *Ventura County Historical Society Quarterly* 19 (Summer 1974).

Beisner, Edward. *Twelve Against Empire: The Anti-Imperialists, 1898-1900.* New York: McGraw-Hill, 1968.

372 Carol J. Frost, PhD

Bender, Bert. *Sea-Brothers: The Tradition of American Sea Fiction From Moby-Dick to the Present.* Philadelphia: University of Pennsylvania Press, 1988.

Bender, Thomas. *New York Intellect: A History of Intellectual Life in New York City From 1750 to the Beginnings of Our Own Time.* Baltimore: Johns Hopkins University Press, 1987.

Benedict, Michael Les. *The Impeachment and Trial of Andrew Johnson.* New York: 1973.

Berkhofer, Robert F. *The White Man's Indian: Images of the American Indian from Columbus to the Present.* New York: Knopf, 1978.

Bernstein, Iver. *The New York City Draft Riots: Their Significance for American Society and Politics in the Age of the Civil War.* New York: Oxford, 1990.

Boller, Paul F., Jr. *American Thought in Transition: The Impact of Evolutionary Naturalism, 1865-1900.* Chicago: Rand-McNally, 1969.

Boris, Eileen. *Art and Labor: Ruskin, Morris, and the Crattsman Ideal in America.* Philadelphia: Temple University Press, 1986.

Briand, Paul. *In Search of Paradise: The Nordhoff-and-Hall Story.* New York: Duell, Sloan, & Pearce, 1966.

Brown, Charles H. *William Cullen Bryant.* New York: Charles Scribner's Sons, 1971.

Brown, Dee. *Bury My Heart At Wounded Knee.* New York: Holt, Rinehart, & Winston, 1970.

Brown, Francis. *Raymond of the Times.* New York: Norton, 1951.

Buder, Stanley. *Pullman: An Experiment in Industrial Order and Community Planning, 1880-1930.* New York: Oxford University Press, 1967.

Buenker, John D. *Urban Liberalism and Progressive Reform.* New York: Charles Scribner's Sons, 1973.

Calhoun, Charles W. *Gilded Age Cato: The Life of Walter Q. Gresham.* Lexington: University Press of Kentucky, 1988.

Carlson, Oliver. *The Man Who Made News: James Gordon Bennett.* New York: Duell, Sloan & Pierce, 1942.

Censer, Jane Turner, ed., *The Papers of Frederick Law Olmsted, Volume IV: Defending the Union.* Baltimore: Johns Hopkins University Press, 1977–.

Clapp, Margaret. *Forgotten First Citizen: John Bigelow.* Boston: Little Brown, 1947.

Cleland, Robert Glass. *The Cattle on the Thousand Hills: Southern California, 1850-80.* San Marino: The Huntington Library, 1941 (1990 rep.).

Clonts, Forrest William. "The Political Campaign of 1875 in Ohio." *Ohio History* 31 (1922): 38–97.

Cross, Robert D. *The Emergence of Liberal Catholicism in America.* Chicago: Quadrangle, 1968.

Crouthamel, James L. *Bennett's "New York Herald" and the Rise of the Popular Press.* Syracuse: Syracuse University Press, 1989.

Crozier, Emmett. *Yankee Reporters, 1861-65.* New York: Oxford University Press, 1956.

Curl, Donald W. *Murat Halstead and the Cincinnati Commercial.* Boca Raton: University Presses of Florida, 1980.

Davison, Kenneth E. *The Presidency of Rutherford B. Hayes.* Westport: Greenwood Press, 1972.

Dawley, Alan. *Struggles for Justice: Social Responsibility and the Liberal State.* Cambridge: Harvard University Press, 1991.

Dicken-Garcia, Hazel. *Journalistic Standards in Nineteenth-Century America.* Madison: University of Wisconsin Press, 1989.

Donald, David. *Charles Sumner and the Rights of Man.* New York: Knopf, 1970.

Downey, Matthew T. "Horace Greeley and the Politicians: The Liberal Republican Convention in 1872." *Journal of American History* 3 (1967): 727–50.

DuBois, Paul Z. *Paul Leicester Ford: An American Man of Letters.* New York: Burt Franklin, 1977.

Easton, Loyd D. "German Philosophy in Nineteenth-Century Cincinnati— Stallo, Conway, Nast, and Willich." *Bulletin of the Cincinnati Historical Society* 20 #1 (January 1962): 15–28.

Emery, Fred A. "Washington Newspaper Correspondents." *Records of the Columbia Historical Society* 35–36 (1935).

Evening Post Company. *The Evening Post Hundredth Anniversary, November 16, 1801-1901.* New York: 1902.

Exman, Eugene. *The Brothers Harper.* New York: Harper & Row, 1965.

———. *The House of Harper.* New York: Harper & Row, 1967.

Fehrenbacher, Don E. *Prelude to Greatness: Lincoln in the 1850s.* Stanford: Stanford University Press, 1962.

Fine, Sidney. *Laissez-Faire and the General Welfare State: A Study of Conflict in American Thought, 1865-1901.* Ann Arbor: University of Michigan Press, 1956.

Fitz, Henry E. *The Movement for Indian Assimilation, 1860-1890.* Philadelphia: University of Pennsylvania Press, 1963.

Flack, J. Kirkpatrick. *Desideratum in Washington: The Intellectual Community in the Capital City, 1870-1900.* Cambridge: Schenkman Publishing Co., 1975.

Fogarty, Robert S. *All Things New: American Communes and Utopian Movements, 1860-1914.* Chicago: University of Chicago Press, 1990.

Foner, Eric. *Free Soil, Free Labor, Free Men: The Ideology of the Repubican Party Before the Civil War.* New York: Oxford, 1970.

———. *Reconstruction: America's Unfinished Revolution.* New York: Harper & Row, 1988.

Foster, Lawrence. *Religion and Sexuality: Three American Communal Experiments of the Nineteenth Century*. New York: Oxford University Press, 1981.

Francke, Warren T. "Investigative Exposure in the Nineteenth Century: The Journalistic Heritage of the Muckrakers." PhD dissertation, University of Minnesota, 1974.

———. "James Gordon Bennett." *Dictionary of Literary Biography: American Newspaper Journalists, 1690-1872*. Vol. 43. New York: Gale, 1985.

Fritz, Henry E. *The Movement for Indian Assimilation, 1860-1890*. Philadelphia: University of Pennsylvania Press, 1963.

Fry, Patricia L. *The Ojai Valley: An Illustrated History*. Ojai: Matilija Press, 1983.

Fuchs, Lawrence H. *The American Kaleidoscope: Race, Ethnicity, and the Civic Culture*. Hanover: University Press of New England, 1990.

Geer, Emily. *First Lady: The Life of Lucy Webb Hayes*. Kent: Kent State University Press, 1984.

Gillette, William. *Retreat from Reconstruction, 1869-1879*. Baton Rouge: Louisiana State University Press, 1979.

Goodwyn, Lawrence. *The Populist Moment*. New York: Oxford University Press, 1978.

Gourvennee, Jean-Christophe P. *Un Journal Americaine a Paris: James Gordon Bennett et le New York Herald, 1887-1918*. Paris: Musee d'Orsay/International Herald Tribune, 1990.

Graham, Thomas. *Charles H. Jones, Journalist and Politician of the Gilded Age*. Tallahassee: Florida A & M University Press, 1990.

Green, Constance M. *Washington: Capital City, 1879-1950*. Princeton: Princeton University Press, 1963.

———. *Washington: Village and Capital, 1800-1878*. Princeton: Princeton University Press, 1962.

Grenier, Judson A. "The Origins and Nature of Progressive Muckraking." PhD dissertation, University of California, Los Angeles, 1965.

Grob, Gerald. *Workers and Utopia: A Study of Ideological Conflict in the American Labor Movement, 1865-1900*. Evanston: Northwestern University Press, 1961.

Harper, J. Henry. *The House of Harper*. New York: Harper & Brothers, 1912.

Hofstadter, Richard. *The Age of Reform*. New York: Vintage, 1955.

Hoogenboom, Ari. *The Presidency of Rutherford B. Hayes*. Lawrence: University of Kansas Press, 1988.

Howard, Vincent. "The Two Congresses: A Study of the Changing Roles and Relationships of the National Legislature and Washington Reporters, As Revealed Particularly in the Press Accounts of Legislative Activity, 1860-1913." PhD dissertation, University of Chicago, 1976.

Hornberger, Theodore, ed. *William Cullen Bryant and Isaac Henderson: New Evidence on a Strange Partnership: Twenty-One Letters Hitherto Unprinted.* New York: Haskell House Publishers, Ltd., 1973.

Hutchison, William R. *The Modernist Impulse in American Protestantism.* New York: Oxford University Press, 1976.

Huttmacher, J. Joseph. "Urban Liberalism and the Age of Reform." *Mississippi Valley Historical Review,* 1962.

Irwin, Will. *The American Newspaper: A Series First Appearing in Colliers, January - July, 1911.* Ames: Iowa State University Press, 1967.

Jacob, Kathryn Allamong. "High Society in Washington During the Gilded Age, 1865-1900: Three Distinct Aristocracies." PhD dissertation, Johns Hopkins University, 1986.

Johnson, Curtis A. *Politics and a Belly-Full: The Journalistic Career of William Cullen Bryant.* New York: Vantage Press, 1962.

Joyner, Fred Bunyan. *David Ames Wells: Champion of Free Trade.* Cedar Rapids: Torch Press, 1939.

Keller, Morton. *Affairs of State: Public Life in Late Nineteenth-Century America.* Cambridge: Harvard University Press, 1977.

Klein, Maury. *The Life and Legend of Jay Gould.* Baltimore: Johns Hopkins University Press, 1986.

Kloppenberg, James T. *Uncertain Victory: Social Democracy and Progressivism in European and American Thought, 1870-1920.* New York: Oxford University Press, 1986.

Kobre, Sidney. *The Yellow Press and Gilded Age Journalism.* Tallahassee: Florida State University Press, 1964.

Kuykendall, Ralph S. *The Hawaiian Kingdom, 1874-1893.* Honolulu: University of Hawaii Press, 1967.

Lancaster, Paul. *Gentleman of the Press: The Life and Times of an Early Reporter, Julian Ralph of the Sun.* Syracuse: Syracuse University Press, 1992.

Lavender, David. *California: Land of New Beginnings.* Lincoln: University of Nebraska Press, 1987.

Littlefield, Roy Everett, III. *William Randolph Hearst: His Role in American Progressivism.* Boston: University Press of America, 1980.

Litwack, Leonard F. *Been in the Storm So Long: The Aftermath of Slavery.* New York: Knopf, 1979.

Luger, Richard. *The Paper: The Life and Death of the New York Herald-Tribune.* New York: Random House, 1986.

Lunde, Eric S. *Horace Greeley.* Boston: Twayne, 1981.

Lydenberg, John. "Pre-Muckraking: A Study of Attitudes Toward Politics as Revealed in American Fiction From 1870 to 1901." PhD dissertation, Harvard University, 1946.

Marbut, F. B. *News from the Capital: The Story of Washington Reporting.* Carbondale: Southern Illinois University Press, 1971.

Mardock, Robert W. *The Reformers and the American Indian.* Columbia: University of Missouri Press, 1971.

Marszalek, John F. *Sherman's Other War: The General and the Civil War Press.* Memphis: Memphis State University Press, 1981.

Martin, Robert K. *Hero, Captain, and Stranger: Male Friendship, Social Critique, and Literary Form in the Novels of Herman Melville.* Chapel Hill: University of North Carolina Press, 1986.

May, Henry F. *The Protestant Churches and Industrial America.* New York: Harper & Row, 1967.

McCormick, Richard. "The Discovery that Business Corrupts Politics." *American Historical Review* 86 (April 1981).

McFeely, William S. *Grant: A Biography.* New York: Norton, 1982.

McGerr, Michael E. *The Decline of Popular Politics: The American North, 1865-1928.* New York: Oxford University Press, 1986.

McKittrick, Eric. *Andrew Johnson and Reconstruction.* Chicago: University of Chicago Press, 1960.

McPherson, James. *Ordeal by Fire.* New York: Alfred A. Knopf, 1982.

Michaelson, Robert. "Common School, Common Religion? A Case Study in Church-State Relations, Cincinnati, 1869-70." *Church History* 38 (1969): 201–217.

Milne, Gordon. *George William Curtis and the Genteel Tradition.* Bloomington: Indiana University Press, 1956.

———. *Ports of Call: A Study of the American Nautical Novel.* Lanham: University Press of America, 1986.

Mohr, James C. *The Radical Republicans and Reform in New York During Reconstruction.* Ithaca: Cornell University Press, 1973.

Mott, Frank Luther. *American Journalism.* New York: Macmillan, 1941.

Neely, Mark E. *The Fate of Liberty: Abraham Lincoln and Civil Liberties.* New York: Oxford University Press, 1991.

Nevins, Allan. *The Evening Post: A Century of Journalism.* New York: Boni & Liveright, 1922.

Nord, David Paul. *Newspapers and New Politics: Midwestern Municipal Reform, 1890-1900.* Ann Arbor: UMI Research Press, 1981.

———. "Working Class Readers: Family, Community, and Reading in Late Nineteenth Century America." *Communications Research* 13, 2 (1986): 156–181.

Norton, Charles Eliot, ed. *Letters of James Russell Lowell.* New York: Harper & Brothers, 1894.

O'Connor, Kaori. "Introduction." *Nordhoff's West Coast.* New York: Kegan Paul International, 1987.

O'Connor, Richard. *The Scandalous Mr. Bennett.* Garden City: Doubleday, 1962.

Osborne, Thomas J. *"Empire Can Wait": American Oposition to Hawaiian Annexation, 1893-1898.* Kent: Kent State University Press, 1981.

Paludin, Phillip Shaw. *A People's Contest: The Union and the Civil War, 1861-1865.* New York: Harper & Row, 1988.

Philbrick, Thomas. *James Fenimore Cooper and the Development of American Sea Fiction.* Cambridge: Harvard University Press, 1961.

Polakoff, Keith Ian. *The Politics of Inertia: The Election of 1876 and the End of Reconstruction.* Baton Rouge: Louisiana State University Press, 1973.

Pollack, Norman. *The Populist Response to Industrial America.* New York: Norton, 1962.

Pruche, Francis Paul. *The Great Father: The U.S. Government and the American Indian.* Lincoln: University of Nebraska Press, 1984.

Rader, Benjamin. *The Academic Mind and Reform: The Influence of Richard T. Ely in American Life.* Lexington: University Press of Kentucky, 1967.

Reeves, Thomas C. *Gentleman Boss: The Life of Chester Alan Arthur.* New York: Alfred A. Knopf, 1975.

Reps, John W. *Washington On View: The Nation's Capital Since 1790.* Chapel Hill: University of North Carolina Press, 1991.

Ritchie, Donald. *Press Gallery: Congress and the Washington Correspondents.* Cambridge: Harvard University Press, 1991.

Roper, Lauren Wood. *FLO: A Biography of Frederick Law Olmsted.* Baltimore: Johns Hopkins University Press, 1973.

Rose, Willie Lee. *Rehearsal for Reconstruction: The Port Royal Experiment.* New York: Oxford University Press, 1964.

Rothman, David. *Politics and Power: The U.S. Senate, 1869-1901.* Cambridge: Harvard University Press, 1966.

Russ, William Adam, Jr. *The Hawaiian Revolution (1893-94).* Selinsgrove, PA: Susquehanna University Press, 1959.

Salmon, Lucy Maynard. *The Newspaper and Authority.* New York: Oxford University Press, 1923.

———. *The Newspaper and the Historian.* New York: Oxford University Press, 1923.

Samuels, Ernest, et al., eds. *The Letters of Henry Adams.* Cambridge: Belknap Press, 1982.

Saxton, Alexander. *The Indispensable Enemy: Labor and the Anti-Chinese Movement in California.* Berkeley: University of California Press, 1971.

Schudson, Michael. *Discovering the News: A Social History of American Newspapers.* New York: Basic Books, 1978.

Seitz, Don. *The James Gordon Bennetts, Father and Son*. Indianapolis: Bobbs-Merrill, 1928.

Sproat, John G. *"The Best Men": Liberal Reformers in the Gilded Age*. New York: Oxford University Press, 1968.

Starr, Kevin. *Americans and the California Dream, 1850-1915*. New York: Oxford University Press, 1973.

————. *Inventing the Dream: California through the Progressive Era*. New York: Oxford, 1985.

Starr, Louis M. *Bohemian Brigade: Civil War Newsmen in Action*. New York: Alfred A. Knopf, 1954.

Still, Bayrd. *Mirror for Gotham: New York as Seen By Contemporaries from Dutch Days to the Present*, New York: New York University Press, 1956.

Stovall, James Glen. "Fletcher Harper." *Dictionary of Literary Biography*, vol. 79, pp. 174–80. Detroit: Gale Research, Inc., 1988.

Sutton, Albert Alton. *Education for Journalism in the United States from Its Beginnings to 1940*. Evanston: Northwestern University Press, 1945.

Swanberg, W. A. *Citizen Hearst*. New York: Macmillan, 1961, rep. 1986.

————. *Pulitzer*. New York: Charles Scribner's Sons, 1967.

Thayer, William Roscoe. *The Life and Letters of John Hay*. New York: Houghton-Mifflin, 1929.

Thelen, David P. *The New Citizenship: Origins of Progressivism in Wisconsin, 1885-1900*. Columbia: University of Missouri Press, 1972.

Thomas, John L. *Alternative America: Henry George. Edward Bellamy, Henry Demarest Lloyd and the Adversary Tradition*. Cambridge: Belknap Press, 1983.

Thompson, Margaret S. *"The Spider Web": Congress and Lobbying in the Age of Grant*. Ithaca: Cornell University Press, 1985.

Tomsich, John. *A Genteel Endeavor: American Culture and Politics in the Gilded Age*. Stanford: Ctanford University Press, 1971.

Trachtenberg, Alan. *The Incorporation of America*. New York: Hill & Wang, 1982.

Trefousse, Hans. *Carl Schurz*. Knoxville: University of Tennessee Press, 1982.

Van Deusen, Glyndon G. *Horace Greeley: Nineteenth-Century Crusader*. Philadelphia: University of Pennsylvania Press, 1953.

Voss, Thomas G., and William Cullen Bryant III. *The Complete Letters of William Cullen Bryant*. Bronx: Fordham University Press, 1975–.

Weisberger, Bernard A. *Reporters for the Union*. Boston: Little, Brown, 1953.

Welch, Richard E., Jr. *The Presidencies of Grover Cleveland*. Lawrence: University Press of Kansas, 1988.

White, Morton. *Social Thought in America: The Revolt Against Formalism*. Boston: Beacon Press, 1957.

White, Ronald C., Jr. *Liberty and Justice for All: Racial Reform and the Social Gospel (1877-1925)*. San Francisco: Harper & Row, 1990.

Whyte, James H. *The Uncivil War: Washington During the Reconstruction.* New York: Twayne Publishers, 1958.

Wiebe, Robert H. *The Search for Order, 1877-1920.* New York: Hill & Wang, 1967.

Williams, T. Harry, ed. *Abraham Lincoln: Selected Speeches, Messages, and Letters.* New York: Rinehart & Company, 1958.

Williamson, Harold F. *Edward Atkinson: The Biography of an American Liberal, 1827-1905.* Boston: Old Corner Book Store, 1934.

Williamson, Joel. *After Slavery: The Negro in South Carolina During Reconstruction, 1861-1877.* Chapel Hill: University of North Carolina Press, 1965.

Wilson, R. Jackson. *In Quest of Community: Social Philosophy in the United States, 1860-1920.* New York: Wiley, 1968.

Woodward, C. Vann. *Origins of the New South, 1877-1913.* Baton Rouge: Louisiana State University Press, 1951, rep. 1970.

Woodward, C. Vann. *Reunion and Reaction: The Compromise of 1877 and the End of Reconstruction.* Garden City: Doubleday, 1956.

ABOUT THE AUTHOR

Carol Jean Frost's early passion for reading and history took her to graduate studies at Brown University where she discovered Charles Nordhoff, an influential journalist and activist of the late 1800s. In spite of myriad debilitating health problems, she conducted extensive research and family interviews, earned PhD in American Civilization, and created the remarkable and important volume you have before you.

INDEX

CPSIA information can be obtained
at www.ICGtesting.com
Printed in the USA
BVOW04s0801290417
482709BV00001B/153/P